LINCOLN
AND HIS
ADMIRALS

Also by Craig L. Symonds

Decision at Sea: Five Naval Battles That Shaped American History

American Heritage History of the Battle of Gettysburg

Confederate Admiral: The Life and Wars of Franklin Buchanan

Stonewall of the West: Patrick Cleburne and the Civil War

Joseph E. Johnston: A Civil War Biography

The Naval Institute Historical Atlas of the U.S. Navy

Navalists and Antinavalists: The Naval Policy Debate in the United States, 1775–1827

Gettysburg: A Battlefield Atlas

A Battlefield Atlas of the American Revolution

A Battlefield Atlas of the Civil War

Edited by Craig L. Symonds

The Civil War Reader, 1862

New Interpretations of Naval History

New Aspects of Naval History

The Civil War Recollections of General Ellis Spear (co-editor)

A Year on a Monitor and the Destruction of Fort Sumter

Recollections of a Naval Officer

Charleston Blockade: The Journals of John B. Marchand, U.S. Navy 1861–1862

LINCOLN
AND HIS
ADMIRALS

ABRAHAM LINCOLN,
THE U.S. NAVY,
AND THE CIVIL WAR

CRAIG L. SYMONDS

OXFORD
UNIVERSITY PRESS

OXFORD
UNIVERSITY PRESS

Oxford University Press, Inc., publishes works that further
Oxford University's objective of excellence
in research, scholarship, and education.

Oxford   New York
Auckland   Cape Town   Dar es Salaam   Hong Kong   Karachi
Kuala Lumpur   Madrid   Melbourne   Mexico City   Nairobi
New Delhi   Shanghai   Taipei   Toronto

With offices in
Argentina   Austria   Brazil   Chile   Czech Republic   France   Greece
Guatemala   Hungary   Italy   Japan   Poland   Portugal   Singapore
South Korea   Switzerland   Thailand   Turkey   Ukraine   Vietnam

Copyright © 2008 by Craig L. Symonds

Published by Oxford University Press, Inc.
198 Madison Avenue, New York, NY 10016

www.oup.com

First issued as an Oxford University Press paperback, 2010

Oxford is a registered trademark of Oxford University Press

Library of Congress Cataloging-in-Publication Data
Symonds, Craig L.
Lincoln and his admirals / Craig L. Symonds.
p. cm.
Includes bibliographical references and index.
ISBN 978-0-19-975157-0 (pbk.)
1. Lincoln, Abraham, 1809–1865—Military leadership.
2. United States—History—Civil War, 1861–1865—Naval operations.
3. Presidents—United States—Biography.
4. United States. Navy—History—19th century.
5. Welles, Gideon, 1802–1878.
6. Fox, Gustavus Vasa, 1821–1883.   I. Title.
E457.2.S94 2008 973.7092—dc22   2008004251

CONTENTS

ACKNOWLEDGMENTS

AS ALWAYS, I am indebted to a number of friends, colleagues, and fellow scholars who aided me with this book. At Oxford University Press, Peter Ginna first signed me up for the project, and Timothy Bent encouraged it through to completion. Dayne Pohusta guided me through the design process, and Joellyn Ausanka through production. Sue Warga, the diligent copy editor, saved me from a number of embarrassing errors.

Many friends, colleagues, and fellow scholars read all or part of the manuscript, offered helpful suggestions, or assisted me in finding materials. These include William W. Freehling, Singletary Professor of History at the University of Kentucky; Jeff Flannery at the Library of Congress; Eric Foner, the DeWitt Clinton Professor of History at Columbia University; William Gladstone, an expert in African American Civil War soldiers; Charles E. Greene, Keeper of the Rare Book Reading Room in the Firestone Library at Princeton; John W. Hinds at the College of Marin; Harold Holzer at the Metropolitan Museum of Art, a noted Lincoln scholar with whom I shared numberless rich conversations and almost as many glasses of wine; Gary Joiner at LSU, Shreveport, who read chapter 10; Jim McPherson, the dean of Civil War scholars, who read the entire manuscript and offered many excellent suggestions; Edward "Ted" O'Reilly at the New-York Historical Society; John C. Rhodehammel at the Huntington Library; William Lee Miller at the University of Virginia; John Sellars at the Library of Congress; Richard W. Peuser at the National Archives; Florence "Flo" Todd of the Nimitz Library at the U.S. Naval Academy, who handled all my interlibrary loan requests; Budge and Russ Weidman, who offered their hospitality, support, and friendship; Frank Williams, Chief Justice of the Rhode Island Supreme Court and Lincoln expert; and John F. Witt, professor of law and history at Columbia University, who helped me with legal aspects of the blockade. I also want to thank Laura Waayers and Ed Finney at the Naval Historical Center, who helped with the illustrations.

Also, as ever, my greatest debt is to my wife, Marylou, best friend, travel companion, and peerless editor. This is her book, too.

INTRODUCTION

THIS IS A BOOK ABOUT THE EMERGENCE AND GROWTH of Abraham Lincoln as a wartime commander in chief. To illustrate that evolution, it focuses on Lincoln's relationship with, and management of, the United States Navy. In the middle of the last century, the historian T. Harry Williams published a book entitled *Lincoln and His Generals*. In it, he posited that Lincoln was "a great natural strategist, a better one than any of his generals." Most of those generals do not fare well at Williams' hand. Though he had some good things to say about Grant and Sherman, his scorn for the likes of Ambrose Burnside, Joseph Hooker, William S. Rosecrans, and Don Carlos Buell is palpable, and he reserved his most vitriolic condemnations for the erstwhile young Napoleon, George B. McClellan. In part, no doubt, this was because McClellan was (and is) an easy target, but in addition Williams was offended by McClellan's dismissive treatment of the president, including Little Mac's private references to Lincoln as "the original gorilla." Williams began his work by declaring that "I have written in this book the story of Abraham Lincoln the commander in chief." But that is only partly true, for he did not include any discussion of Lincoln's relationship with the navy. Indeed, there is only one entry for the navy in his index, and it is "Navy, United States, and McClellan," for which there is but a single page reference. Other scholars since then have tried their hand at assessing Lincoln's role as commander in chief, but none of them paid any serious attention to the naval war.[1]

When he took office in March 1861, navies and naval matters were utterly foreign to Lincoln. Yet as president he would preside over the development and deployment of the largest naval force in American history to date, a force that would not be eclipsed in size or number until the emergence of the gray steel armadas of the world wars. From virtually the first day of his presidency when he had to consider dispatching a naval expedition to rescue the garrison of Fort Sumter, Lincoln was compelled to become a student of naval warfare. At least some of his education took place at the Washington Navy Yard. Barely a week after the fall of Sumter, Abraham and Mary Lincoln visited the Navy Yard to view the body of Lincoln's young friend Elmer Ellsworth, shot dead after hauling down a Confederate flag from the roof of a hotel in Alexandria. Two weeks later, Lincoln was at the Navy Yard again, this time to enjoy a concert of martial tunes by the band of the 71st Pennsylvania regiment. From that day until virtually his last day as president—which was also his last day on earth—the Navy Yard was one of the places, along with the War Department telegraph office, that he visited regularly. He became a close friend of the yard's commandant, Commander (later Rear Admiral) John A. Dahlgren, and he often arrived there unannounced, sometimes with a friend or cabinet member, sometimes with his wife, sometimes alone, to witness the test firing of one or another new weapon or simply to get away from the White House for a few hours.

Besides Dahlgren, Lincoln was also tutored in his naval education by his earnest, candid, and often cranky secretary of the navy, Gideon Welles, and by Welles' efficient and ambitious assistant secretary, Gustavus Vasa Fox. Though he had a steep learning curve, Lincoln was a quick student. His early missteps during the Fort Sumter crisis and in managing the blockade were soon eclipsed by his active and efficient intervention in the war on the oceans, along the coast, and on the western rivers. As in his dealings with his generals, he sometimes found that his early trust in the navy's top leaders was misplaced and he had to make changes. Moreover, the lack of an established protocol for army-navy cooperation compelled him to insert himself in the planning and execution of combined operations.

From the beginning, Lincoln's management of the serial crises of his administration was characterized by remarkable patience. He was often willing to let events determine not only the timing of his decisions but also the decisions themselves. This is what he meant when he famously remarked late in the war, "I claim not to have controlled events, but confess plainly that events have controlled me."[2] Though Lincoln had several fixed stars in his ideology—opposition to slavery in every form being among the brightest—he did not embark on his presidency with a list of predetermined objectives or goals other than the preservation of the Union. He had no hundred-day program of reform in mind, and given the speed of events as he encountered them, he was from the very outset thrown into a reactive mode rather than a proactive one. From his consideration of what to do about Fort Sumter to his program for Reconstruction, Lincoln regularly adopted a wait-and-see attitude in responding to the multiple and various crises of his unprecedented administration. His genius derived more from what might be labeled inspired patience than from insistent direction.

When he did act, Lincoln demonstrated that he was unwilling to be hamstrung by established doctrine. He believed in a government strong enough to maintain itself and far reaching enough to serve the people as a whole, not merely some privileged segment of it. Because the Civil War created an unprecedented number of problems for government to solve, it provided Lincoln with an equally unprecedented number of opportunities to exercise his pragmatic approach to problem solving. In nearly every crisis he sought solutions unfettered by concerns about how it had always been done before, or even by conventional limitations on government authority. Lincoln was no scofflaw; as both a lawyer and a statesman, he revered the law, and especially the Constitution. But he did not believe that a reverence for the law should justify inaction or tolerate injustice. Laws were created to serve the needs of the whole country, and when they ceased to do that, Lincoln believed that those laws should be replaced by new ones. Intelligent and responsible men of goodwill could—and should—find ways to do the things that would benefit society. In short, Lincoln's fundamental pragmatism led him to seek new and creative ways to fulfill what he conceived of as his sacred responsibility.

A third factor in Lincoln's makeup that proved critical to his success as a wartime president was his willingness to embrace not just new ideas but new technologies. Soon after he took office, Lincoln confessed to Welles: "I know but little about ships."[3] But his was a naturally creative mind that could bend itself to the solution of all sorts of issues. He may not have been a naval expert, but he was fascinated by gadgets. During the Civil War, he became interested in the gadgetry of warfare, and not incidentally naval warfare, as demonstrated by his frequent escapes to the Navy Yard to witness, and occasionally participate in, the testing of new weapons. Eventually he would become an advocate—and a knowledgeable one—of heavy-caliber naval guns, armored warships, floating mortar platforms, and other elements of the revolution in naval ordnance that took place simultaneously with the Civil War. Indeed, given the innate conservatism of many senior naval officers, it sometimes took Lincoln's gentle prodding to get them to accept and employ the new technology.

As he grew comfortable in holding the reins of power, Lincoln became more assertive as commander in chief. In 1861 he hoped that Winfield Scott would manage the armed forces with as little oversight as possible; by 1862 he was beginning to exercise hands-on management, even issuing operational orders to division commanders; and by 1863 he was hitting his full stride as an activist commander in chief. As tentative as he was early on, he eventually became one of the most audacious of all American chief executives, authorizing a blockade and approving a conscription law, paper money, an income tax, and—most revolutionary of all—emancipation. Then, once he found military leaders whom he trusted to fulfill his strategic vision, he retreated once again from his activist role and delegated military questions to his uniformed commanders while he focused on the larger question of how to reconstruct a postwar America once the bloodshed ended.

While Lincoln has been admired and extolled for these accomplishments by later generations, his early missteps are often ignored or overlooked. It is curious that conventional explanations of Abraham Lincoln emphasize his astonishing trajectory from humble roots to the presidency without acknowledging that this progress continued into and during his term in office. Lincoln's first-term vice president, Hannibal Hamlin, believed that Lincoln's "eulogists make the mistake of constructing a Lincoln who was as great the day he left Springfield as when he made his earthly exit four years later."[4] Such a deification of Lincoln does him a disservice since it assumes that Lincoln's mastery of the great national trauma of civil war came to him easily and naturally. It did not. In 1861 Lincoln was not a great commander in chief, a fact he freely acknowledged; by 1865 he had become the greatest in American history. Hamlin concluded that "no man ever grew in the executive chair in his lifetime as Lincoln did." One of the themes of this book is to demonstrate not only how Lincoln managed the navy, and particularly its admirals, during its great national trauma, but also how—and how much—he grew in the job during his metamorphosis into greatness.[5]

This is also, and necessarily, a book about Lincoln's admirals. Though Lincoln did not have to deal with "political admirals" in the same way he did "political generals," there was nevertheless a political dimension to managing their activities. The Civil War was the first conflict in which American naval leaders bore the rank of admiral, and they were a mixed lot: from the stolid and reliable David Glasgow Farragut to his boisterous and self-confident foster brother David Dixon Porter; from the touchy and aristocratic Samuel Francis Du Pont to the flamboyant and confrontational Charles Wilkes; and from the meticulous and careful Samuel Phillips Lee to the ambitious ordnance expert John A. Dahlgren, the presidential friend who desperately wanted command at sea despite a debilitating tendency to seasickness, a predilection that Lincoln shared. Collectively, but not always harmoniously, these men commanded the largest navy ever assembled by the United States. This is not, however, a history of the Civil War navy. Operational history is included only when it helps explain the context for the problems and issues that made their way to Lincoln's desk.

Finally, two of the key characters in the story are Lincoln's navy secretary, Gideon Welles, and the assistant secretary, Gustavus Fox. Welles was open and honest with Lincoln, politically adept and yet disarmingly straightforward. He was by turns blunt, challenging, cantankerous, and tiresomely earnest. He was protective of his commander in chief and jealous of the influence exercised on him by others, especially Secretary of State William Henry Seward. For his part, Fox was a former naval officer turned businessman whom Lincoln adopted during the Fort Sumter crisis and for whom he created the post of assistant secretary. During the war, Fox was often the intermediary between Lincoln and his admirals and operated as a kind of chief of naval operations.

On many issues, Lincoln left the management of the navy to Welles, Fox, and the admirals. But just as he was forced to do in the land war, he found that it was necessary to intervene when naval operations touched upon legal, political, diplomatic, financial, or other issues of national moment. In doing so, Lincoln demonstrated not only his native intelligence and his remarkable patience but also his keen political sensitivity, his deft touch as a manager, his willingness to make a hard call and assume full responsibility for the consequences, and throughout it all, despite personal and national tragedy that could easily have broken him, his humor and his humanity.

1861

GETTING UNDER WAY

I

"What Have I Done Wrong?"

Lincoln and the Fort Sumter Crisis

IN THE TENSION-FILLED WEEKS leading up to his inauguration, Abraham Lincoln probably spent little time thinking about the U.S. Navy. After all, the handful of vessels showing the flag on widely scattered overseas stations was an unlikely instrument in the secession crisis, which was grounded in a sectional dispute about the expansion of slavery into the western territories. Lincoln had been president for barely twenty-four hours, however, when he read a report from Major Robert Anderson, commander of beleaguered Fort Sumter in the middle of Charleston Harbor. For more than two months, Anderson had written near-daily reports to Washington, describing his garrison's increasing isolation and vulnerability. In reply he had received little from the lame duck Buchanan administration beyond orders to do nothing "to disturb the public peace." Meanwhile, South Carolina, and later Confederate authorities, had constructed artillery batteries all around the harbor, literally surrounding his small command. Now, in a letter dated February 28 (and carefully marked as number 58), Anderson reported not only that he was running out of supplies but also—far worse—that it would require an army of at least twenty thousand well-trained soldiers to deliver the supplies he needed. The news was a bombshell for, as Anderson surely understood, in asking for twenty thousand men, he might as well have asked for twenty million. The entire U.S. Army, scattered in seventy-nine forts and outposts across half a continent, numbered barely seventeen thousand. In effect, what Anderson was telling the new president was that the men in Fort Sumter could not stay where they were without immediate support, and that the support they needed was beyond the power of the government.[1]

It was a devastating challenge to Lincoln's policy. Just the day before in his inaugural address, the new president had pledged himself to "hold, occupy, and possess" government property in the seceded states. His plan was to cling to the federal posts in the South to preserve the principle of national unity while avoiding any provocative act that might drive the wavering border states out of the Union. He hoped that this combination of resolve and restraint might create an opportunity for the latent Unionism that he still believed to exist in the South to assert itself. Anderson's gloomy report, however, suggested that Lincoln must now choose—and soon—between two equally undesirable options: he must either evacuate Anderson's garrison from Fort Sumter and begin his administration with a craven act of surrender or commit a provocative act that not only was sure to alienate the border states but also was likely to fail.[2]

Alarmed, Lincoln consulted the country's most senior general, Winfield Scott, who confirmed Anderson's estimate. Indeed, Scott suggested that if anything, Anderson had understated the case. Sending supplies to Fort Sumter meant sending ships into Charleston Harbor—the fort, after all, sat on an island. But, Scott declared, no ship could enter the harbor until the hostile shore batteries had been captured or suppressed. To do that, it would be necessary to conduct large-scale amphibious landings on both Morris Island and Sullivan's Island, and those landings must then be followed by lengthy sieges. Not only would such a campaign require more men than the U.S. Army possessed, it would take more time than Anderson had. Still, in the end, Scott acknowledged that "the question was . . . one for naval authorities to decide."[3]

Scott's deference to the navy was not merely a courtesy. In the nineteenth century, the Department of War and the Department of the Navy were separate and independent branches of government. Though Scott had been a general for nearly half a century—almost as long as Lincoln had been alive—he could not give orders concerning the navy, nor could any naval officer, no matter how senior, give orders to the army. Consequently, as valuable as Scott's advice might be, at some point Lincoln would have to seek the navy's views, and that meant talking with his new secretary of the navy, Gideon Welles.

Welles was one of only two cabinet members (Secretary of State William H. Seward being the other) to hold his job throughout Lincoln's administration. Eventually Lincoln would come to rely on Welles' loyalty and honesty, as well as his passion, but Welles had obtained his position in the first place mainly because of political geography. The Republican Party was a patchwork quilt of Free-Soilers, anti-Nebraska Democrats, Conscience Whigs, and Know-Nothings, and Lincoln sought to include representatives from each faction in his cabinet. In addition, it was traditional for the cabinet to include at least one individual from each section of the country. There was no shortage of former Whigs from New York and the Midwest, but what Lincoln needed, as he wrote to Vice President–elect Hannibal Hamlin, was "a man of democratic antecedents from New England." Welles was both a former Democrat and a politician of proven skill in his home state of Connecticut, where he had been an influential publisher and the postmaster of Hartford, an important position in terms of local patronage, and he had the support of the vice president, who, as a Maine man, was expected to have some influence in the naming of the New England member of the cabinet.* Welles fit the political requirements, but it was not clear which job in the cabinet he would be asked to fill. Until the very day that Lincoln sent his name to the Senate, Welles thought he was likely to be named postmaster general. Instead that job went to Montgomery Blair in acknowledgment of his family's considerable influence in both Maryland and Missouri, and Welles ended up as secretary of the navy.[4]

Although Welles had legitimate expertise in naval matters, including a term as chief of the Bureau of Provisions and Clothing under President Polk (the only civilian ever to hold such a post), the appointment was not popular in all quarters. Seward, the new secretary of state, whom many insiders expected to dominate the administration, was disappointed— even annoyed—by it. The gaunt Seward and the comfortably plump

---

*Hamlin later came to regret his support for Welles and decided that the appointment had been a mistake.

Welles not only were different physically but had vastly different personal styles. Seward had been the titular head of the Republican Party almost since its founding and carried himself with a restrained gravitas that befitted a great statesman. Welles was more excitable, tended to speak his mind, and generally allowed his expressive face to mirror his strongly held opinions. Moreover, the urbane Seward found Welles not only annoyingly voluble but also unsophisticated, even comical. The fifty-nine-year-old Welles wore a wig that he had purchased years before when his hair was still light brown and only tinged with gray. He continued to wear that same wig as a cabinet secretary even though his beard was now snowy white, and the contrast was jarring. Moreover, Welles tended to wear his wig like a hat, plunking it on his head in the morning without paying serious attention to how it rested on his balding dome, and pushing it back on his head absentmindedly as he worked at his desk. If he sneezed or shook his head violently, the wig skittered about independently. Seward's political adviser, Thurlow Weed, shared his chief's disdain for Welles. Though he had supported the appointment—mainly for reasons of political balance—he subsequently suggested to Lincoln that if the president really wanted "an attractive figure-head, to be adorned with an elaborate wig and luxuriant whiskers," he could easily "transfer it from the prow of a ship to the entrance of the Navy Department" and it would be "quite as serviceable" as the incumbent. The president fended off this indecorous jibe with his typical goodwill and humor. "Oh," he replied, "wooden midshipmen answer very well in novels, but we must have a live secretary of the navy."[5]

 If Seward and his supporters dismissed Welles as a bit ludicrous, Welles thought Seward too cunning and manipulative. In his journal he routinely called him "the trickster." While he admired Seward's talents, he suspected his motives. Welles acknowledged that the secretary of state was a man of "restless activity, [and] unceasing labors," but he distrusted Seward's "showy manifestations, and sometimes incautious exercise of questionable authority." Welles believed that Seward was a political animal whose talents were "more versatile than profound" and who had "no great [or] original conceptions of right, nor systematic ideas of administration." The tension between the two men would affect how Lincoln managed the Fort Sumter crisis and, indeed, the war that followed.[6]

Both men were present at the first full cabinet meeting of the Lincoln administration on March 9, when the president shared Anderson's alarming report.* After the assembled cabinet ministers expressed their shock and surprise, most of them instinctively declared that Anderson must be resupplied. If the secessionists were successful in driving the American flag from the national forts, the government might as well acquiesce in a divided country. Lincoln had asked General Scott to attend as well, and after the cabinet members had expressed their determination and resolve, Scott patiently instructed them about the military realities that made a successful relief expedition to Fort Sumter impossible.

The seventy-four-year-old Scott had brought along reinforcements in the form of the army's seventy-three-year-old chief engineer, General Joseph Totten. Between them, Scott and Totten had more than a century of military experience, and their opinions were not to be taken lightly. Their testimony did not impress Montgomery Blair, however, who was adamant that Fort Sumter must not be surrendered "at any cost or any sacrifice." A West Point graduate himself, Blair was an old-fashioned Jacksonian nationalist who believed that the current crisis was the result of insufficient firmness on the part of the national government. His muttonchop sideburns framed a face dominated by close-set dark eyes and a sharp nose that gave him a belligerent look to match his mood. "The time had come," he insisted, "when the government should assert its power and authority."[7]

In the midst of Blair's blustering, Seward stepped forward to establish his leadership in the cabinet—and in the administration—by offering a solution. Seward's unstated objective was to do whatever was necessary to ward off a confrontation for a few crucial months, at the end of which, he was convinced, cooler heads would prevail in the South and "a counter-revolution would take place." To accomplish this, he had to prevent Lincoln from taking any precipitate action in

---

*Some scholars cite March 6 as the date of Lincoln's first meeting with his cabinet, but according to Edward Bates' diary, the meeting on that date was "formal and introductory," and Welles noted that only "two or three" of the cabinet members attended. The meeting on March 9 was the first where substantive issues were discussed and all the members were present.

Charleston. The evacuation of Sumter, he now declared, was apparently inevitable. The unimpeachable testimony of the military experts made that clear. But the political cost of such a move could be mitigated by shifting public attention away from Fort Sumter to Fort Pickens, off the Gulf coast of Florida near Pensacola. It, too, was a federal fort built by the Army Corps of Engineers; it, too, was being held by a small federal garrison threatened by noisy militia forces who insisted that it be turned over to them. The difference was that Pickens was not completely surrounded by hostile batteries. The government could therefore make a public show of reinforcing Fort Pickens, where the local geography made such an effort relatively simple, while quietly evacuating Fort Sumter, where geography and circumstance made it impossible. As Lincoln himself put it later, the reinforcement of Pickens "would be a clear indication of *policy*, and would better enable the country to accept the evacuation of Fort Sumter as a military *necessity*." It was not a perfect solution, but it was better than simple capitulation.[8]

Not everyone in the room believed that the rescue of Fort Sumter was so hopeless as to require looking elsewhere for a political fig leaf. Blair continued to hammer away at the symbolic importance of Sumter, and Welles disputed the conclusion that a naval relief expedition there was impossible. Welles had brought along an expert of his own in the form of sixty-three-year old Commodore Silas Stringham, who could point to fifty-two years of naval service thanks to the fact that he had accepted a midshipman's warrant at the age of eleven. Stringham testified that a relief expedition to Sumter was not at all impracticable. In fact, he had championed two separate plans to resupply the fort back in January, one proposed by Commander James H. Ward and another by a former navy lieutenant named Gustavus Vasa Fox.

Each man had a friend at court: Ward had been a boyhood friend of Gideon Welles, and Fox was Montgomery Blair's brother-in-law. Their plans were similar in several important ways. Ward suggested using small Treasury Department steamers—revenue cutters—to run supplies into Fort Sumter at night, and Fox argued for doing much the same thing using New York City tugboats. To Lincoln's question whether such a plan could work, Scott acknowledged that either plan would almost certainly have worked if executed back in January, when they had first been proposed, or perhaps even in February, but he insisted that it was now too late. The harbor defenses were just too strong.[9]

Though Scott and Stringham were carefully deferential to each other, a vast gulf divided them. Conventional wisdom held that, as the *New York Tribune* had recently declared, "ships are no match for land batteries." That assumption governed Scott's and Totten's advice. As the army's chief engineer, who had supervised the construction of many of the nation's coastal forts, including Sumter, Totten was a champion of their effectiveness, and he insisted that even modest land batteries could easily dispatch any naval expedition. Stringham did not respond directly to Totten's lengthy dissertation, but his silence was eloquent. As Attorney General Edward Bates noted in his diary, "The *army* officers and *navy* officers differ widely about the degree of danger to rapid[ly] moving vessels passing under the fire of land batteries. The *army* officers think destruction almost inevitable, where the *navy* officers think the danger slight."[10]

Without choosing between the army and the navy, Lincoln saw that the Ward-Fox plan offered at least the possibility that Anderson could be sustained at Fort Sumter without risking either a direct provocation or a humiliating repulse. If so, it would not only buy time but also might shift the burden of decision making from Washington back onto the secessionists. Seward dismissed the idea. He noted that the previous administration had erred by sending the unarmed steamer *Star of the West* into Charleston in January only to see it driven off after being struck twice by shots from shore. If the government now tried to support Anderson by sending New York City tugboats to Charleston and the effort failed—which was almost certain—the new administration would appear ridiculous. Better not to try at all, he maintained, than to try with insufficient force and fail. Besides, even if the effort succeeded, it would infuriate the border states, a primary concern of both Lincoln and Seward. Until shots were fired, there was always a chance that the sectional schism could be resolved short of open conflict.

Nevertheless, Lincoln was interested enough to ask Welles to flesh out the Ward-Fox plan, and he told Scott to invite both men to Washington to present their plans in person. In the meantime, the government could ensure the safety of Fort Pickens in Florida by landing the hundred or so men that had been sent there more than a month before on board the USS *Brooklyn*, and who had been bobbing uselessly off Pensacola ever since. This fell far short of the grand public gesture that Seward wanted in order to redirect the nation's attention away from Sumter, but it would, quite literally, hold the fort. In spite of the ticking clock, Lincoln refused to be rushed. As Welles expressed it, Lincoln "was disinclined to hasty action and wished time for the administration to get in working order" before committing to a particular policy.[11]

Not everyone agreed that a decision could be postponed. Montgomery Blair remained adamant in his support for immediate action. Two days later, on March 11, Blair's father, Francis Blair Sr., all but forced his way into Lincoln's office to lecture the president on the symbolic importance of holding Fort Sumter. A former member of Andrew Jackson's "Kitchen Cabinet" and publisher of the influential *Globe*, the elder Blair had been one of the founders of the Republican Party. He was also prone to fits of temper. On this occasion he became so exercised that he subsequently felt obliged to apologize for being "impertinent." But Blair's passion had its impact. If Frank Blair saw Fort Sumter as a metaphor of national unity, so would others. Welles believed that Blair's visit "aroused and electrified the President."[12]

If so, Lincoln still kept his options open. He was willing to listen to the naval experts, but he leaned toward evacuation. Certainly, the visit of Commander Ward did little to change his mind. Whatever enthusiasm Ward had once had for a relief mission to Charleston evaporated under the pointed questioning of Scott and Totten. Alerted to the nature of the new fortifications in Charleston Harbor, Ward now agreed that a nighttime relief mission was no longer practical.

The next day Montgomery Blair escorted Gustavus Vasa Fox into Lincoln's office. Fox was not particularly martial in appearance: he was of medium stature with a broad face, a high forehead, and dark, piercing eyes above a pear-shaped body. (Montgomery Blair's sharp-tongued sister routinely referred to him in her private correspondence as "Fatty.") He combed his dark, thinning hair straight back, and though his cheeks were clean-shaven, he sported a drooping walrus mustache that blended into a luxuriant curling beard cascading from his chin to his chest, giving him the appearance of a Chinese mandarin in a business suit. Though Fox had served as a naval officer for fifteen years, including a circumnavigation of the globe in the early 1850s, he had left the navy in 1853 to pursue more lucrative employment and was now a private citizen. Of course, he was also Blair's brother-in-law. Fox and Blair had each married a daughter of Andrew Jackson's secretary of the navy, Levi Woodbury, and that connection, as much as his naval expertise, gained Fox entry into Lincoln's office.[13]

Unlike Ward, Fox was convinced that his resupply scheme was still viable. Urged on by the younger Blair, he outlined it for the president. New York City tugboats, Fox explained, could be escorted to Charleston by the USS *Pawnee* and the revenue cutter *Harriet Lane*, practically the only ships readily available in America's tiny marine arsenal. The *Pawnee* could ascertain the strength of the secessionist batteries by approaching the harbor in daylight. If those batteries opened fire, the *Pawnee* would not challenge them; instead it would clear the channel of any secessionist gunboats, the only threat that Fox considered important. Meanwhile, the shallow-draft tugs, loaded with both supplies and reinforcements, and with their machinery protected by two rows of cotton bales, would wait for the dark of night to run into the harbor at fourteen knots to deposit their cargo on Fort Sumter's small wharf. It would be virtually impossible, Fox insisted, for secessionist batteries on Cumming's Point or Sullivan's Island, each of them some three-quarters of a mile away, to hit such small, fast-moving targets at night.[14]

Lincoln saw some drawbacks to the scheme. First of all, it meant sending a warship to Charleston, and that would almost certainly be perceived as aggressive by the secessionists. Lincoln had promised in his inaugural that "the government will not assail you. You can have no conflict without being yourselves the aggressors." If he ordered the *Pawnee* to Charleston Harbor and it used its guns to clear the channel of hostile vessels, just who was the aggressor? Perhaps sensing the president's wariness, Blair suggested that Lincoln could at least send Fox to Charleston to talk with Major Anderson and assess the situation there. Always willing to obtain more information, Lincoln agreed, though he made no commitment and was still leaning toward evacuation when he bade Fox farewell.[15]

Lincoln also wanted to know more about the political mood in South Carolina. Seward's argument for restraint was based on the assumption—which Lincoln shared—that a large percentage of the southern population still bore an affection for the old Union and was simply being carried along by the emotion of the moment. Seward argued repeatedly that this latent Unionism might still assert itself if the administration refused to provoke the secessionists. Welles was skeptical. A friend from Tennessee had recently written him that enthusiasm for secession in the cotton states was near universal, and that it was wishful thinking to assume that "the majority are trampled down by the seceding minority." Just how much latent Unionism was there in South Carolina? To find out, Lincoln decided to send his friend and unofficial bodyguard Ward Hill Lamon to find out. On his own, Stephen A. Hurlbut, who had been born in Charleston before moving to Illinois in the 1840s, decided to go with him.[16]

As Fox, Lamon, and Hurlbut each traveled south on different missions, Lincoln met with his cabinet again, this time asking each man to commit his views regarding Fort Sumter to paper. This was an exercise he used regularly to clarify his own thoughts, and he hoped it would do the same for his advisers. Seward replied with a lengthy essay arguing that any attempt to relieve Sumter would be perceived as both aggressive and hostile by the loyal slave states at a time when they hovered precariously in the balance, and that even if the attempt were successful—an unlikely prospect—Sumter itself would be "practically useless to the government." The result, Seward concluded, would be that "we will have inaugurated a civil war by our own act, without an adequate object." His argument carried the day. Only Secretary of the Treasury Salmon P. Chase and the pugnacious Blair voted in favor of a resupply effort. Even Welles voted against it.[17]

Buoyed by the vote in the cabinet, Seward privately assured a trio of Confederate commissioners, through an intermediary, that the administration had decided to evacuate the fort. That intermediary, Supreme Court justice John A. Campbell of Alabama, promised the rebel commissioners that Fort Sumter would be evacuated within the next five days, and even signed an affidavit to that effect. Later, when Seward sensed that administration policy was shifting, he backtracked a bit, telling Campbell that if for any reason the government *did* try to resupply Sumter, it would at least send formal notification first.[18]

FOX LEFT WASHINGTON on March 19 and traveled south by train through Virginia and the Carolinas, arriving in Charleston on March

21. Part of the way he sat with former South Carolina congressman Robert Holmes, who told everyone he saw that he had it on the highest authority that Fort Sumter was soon to be evacuated. At the time, Fox kept silent, though he later wondered if that information had not come from Seward via Justice Campbell. In Charleston, Fox met with South Carolina's governor, Francis Pickens, who agreed to let him go out to Fort Sumter and talk with Anderson if Fox would assure him that his visit was for peaceful purposes. With perhaps a qualm or two, Fox agreed.*

Rowed out to Sumter after nightfall, Fox found Anderson despondent. Even the news that the government had granted him two brevet promotions in recognition of his stalwart resistance could not dispel his gloom. Like his fellow army professionals, Anderson believed that any naval expedition that attempted to force its way into the harbor was doomed; eager to avoid open hostilities, he strongly opposed any effort to reinforce or supply him. To support his case, Anderson pointed out the silhouettes of the new fortifications on every side as he and Fox stood on the ramparts of Fort Sumter in the darkness. The navy man, however, looked at the harbor defenses with different eyes and continued to believe that those batteries posed little threat to a small, fast-moving target at night. For him, the clincher came when the boat that had brought him out to Fort Sumter returned two hours later to ferry him back. Fox could hear the creak of oars in the oarlocks, but the boat remained virtually invisible from the fort's small pier "until she almost touched the landing." If a small boat could not be seen from Fort Sumter at twenty feet, how could it be seen from Fort Moultrie at three-quarters of a mile? Fox returned to Washington on March 24 more convinced than ever that "he could reinforce the garrison with men, and supply it with provisions."[19]

A few days later, Lamon returned with his report. Neither he nor Hurlbut had been able to discover any evidence of Unionism, latent or

---

*Just over two weeks later, South Carolina authorities intercepted and opened a report from Anderson to the government that referred to "the proposed scheme of Captain Fox." Based on that report, Pickens decided that he had been deceived by Fox's "treachery" and suspended all communication and commerce between the fort and the outside world.

otherwise, in South Carolina. Only elderly Judge James Petigru, who had famously declared that South Carolina was too small to be a nation and too large to be an insane asylum, and who was tolerated in Charleston as a local crank, was exempt from the popular enthusiasm for the new secessionist government. This news suggested that restraint and forbearance were unlikely to cool the secessionist ardor or to encourage Unionism.* Lamon also reported that although Anderson was "deeply despondent," he acknowledged that he could probably hold out until April 15 if necessary.[20]

These reports led Lincoln to consider a rescue mission to Fort Sumter more seriously, but what finally changed his mind was a disturbing memorandum from Scott who offered an unsolicited assessment that the evacuation of Sumter would not be enough to ensure the allegiance of the upper South. He now insisted that the government should evacuate both Sumter *and* Fort Pickens. "The evacuation of both the forts," Scott declared, "would instantly soothe and give confidence to the eight remaining slave-holding states." Government firmness, Scott suggested, could still be demonstrated by clinging to Fort Taylor at Key West and Fort Jefferson in the isolated Dry Tortugas, which, he said, should "never be abandoned."[21]

This gratuitous advice was well outside Scott's authority as commanding general, for it was based not on military circumstances but his political judgment.† Still, its contents gave Lincoln "a cold shock." Indeed, Scott's recommendation was nearly as distressing as the letter Lincoln had received from Anderson more than three weeks before that first informed him of a problem. The public might eventually come to understand the imperative of military necessity as an explanation for the

---

*Lincoln was reluctant to abandon the idea that most Southerners remained loyal to the old Union. In his July 4 message to Congress he declared, "It may well be questioned whether there is, to-day, a majority of the legally qualified voters of any State, except perhaps South Carolina, in favor of disunion. There is much reason to believe that the Union men are the majority in many, if not in every other one, of the so-called seceded States" (*Collected Works of Abraham Lincoln*, ed. Roy P. Basler [New Brunswick, NJ: Rutgers University Press, 1953], 4:437).

†Though Scott's argument was based on political factors, Totten believed that military factors also dictated the abandonment of Pickens. "If we do not vacate this fort," he wrote to Cameron on April 3, "the result predicted as to Fort Sumter will certainly be realized here also."

abandonment of Sumter, but Pickens was different. It was not under any immediate threat. To surrender both forts would signal a deliberate policy of accommodation, the same policy that had been pursued by Lincoln's discredited predecessor. Moreover, the absence of any latent Unionism in South Carolina reported by Hurlbuts and Scott's estimate that the evacuation of Sumter would do little to rekindle that Unionism suggested that a policy of restraint was unlikely to yield any tangible benefit. Here Lincoln's hope for a national reconciliation gave way before his determination to uphold his oath. After a sleepless night, he decided sometime on the morning of March 28 that he would hold both forts, and that meant he would have to authorize an expedition to provision Fort Sumter. The cumulative impact of Frank Blair's diatribe, Fox's confident enthusiasm, the reports from Hurlbut and Lamon, and Scott's unsolicited political advice each played a role, but the decision was Lincoln's alone. That evening at a state dinner, the president quietly asked each of his cabinet members to stay behind for a brief word. With a serious expression and in solemn tones, he shared with them the contents of Scott's memorandum and told them he wanted them to meet with him the next day to make a final decision about Fort Sumter.[22]

At that meeting, Lincoln informed his advisers that he was now inclined to send an expedition to Sumter to reprovision Anderson's garrison and, as he often did, he asked each of them to write a short response. Bates managed to sound both determined and undecided at the same time. "The time is come," he wrote, "either to evacuate or relieve it." Chase was more direct. He wanted to provision Sumter and to hold Pickens. Welles concurred in Lincoln's proposal "to send an armed force off Charleston with supplies & provisions." He recognized that this might well lead to war, but noted that "armed resistance to a peaceable attempt to send provisions to one of our own forts will justify the government in using all the powers at its command." Seward remained opposed to the end. Even if war eventually became necessary, he did not want a war to begin "at Charleston." "I advise against the expedition in every view," he wrote. It was too late; Lincoln had made up his mind. Twenty-five days after reading Anderson's alarming letter, he had determined to order a naval expedition to Charleston to resupply him.[23]

Seward had one more card to play. In his written response, the secretary of state had urged the president to "call in Capt M. C. Meigs forthwith." Whether Lincoln agreed to do so, or Seward simply acted on his own suggestion, that same afternoon Seward brought Meigs to the White House. Seward declared that besides listening to senior generals such as Scott and Totten, they should also hear from an officer (in Seward's uncharitable words) "who could get on a horse in the field." Meigs, at forty-four, was certainly capable of mounting a horse, and was in Washington at that time because he was supervising the construction of the new Capitol dome. Seward had brought him to the White House to convince Lincoln that the expedition should be sent not to Sumter but to Fort Pickens. Lincoln welcomed Meigs in his convivial way and asked him if Pickens could be saved.

"Certainly," Meigs replied, "if the Navy . . . has not lost it already."

When asked by Lincoln if he could "go down there" and secure it, Meigs protested that he was only a captain and it would be inappropriate for him to have such a command.

Seward thought that problem was easy to fix: "Captain Meigs, you have got to be promoted," he declared.

Only with difficulty did Meigs convince the two civilians what a breach of military protocol that would be. As Lincoln mulled over the idea of sending a captain to command such a crucial expedition, Seward offered the president a parallel from history. When the British needed to reclaim Quebec, he noted, they did not send an aged and infirm senior commander, but the thirty-two-year-old James Wolfe, whose victory had secured a continent. "Would the president do this now?" Seward asked.[24]

Lincoln agreed to consider it, but even if he did decide to send an expedition to Pickens, he was determined to send one to Sumter as well, and time was running out. Anderson had told Lamon that he could hold out only until April 15, and it was already March 29. Lincoln wanted the expedition to move by April 6. The test of the government now was not its willingness to make a decision, but its ability to pull together a combined operation quickly and efficiently.

THE WHEELS WERE TURNING AT LAST, but the gears did not mesh. Instead, the last-minute effort to rescue Anderson's garrison was marked by confusion and inefficiency so profound that it led some to suspect treachery. For all his clarity of purpose, Lincoln's management of the

Fort Sumter expedition demonstrated three things: that he had not yet taken the reins of authority firmly into his own hands; that his talented cabinet members had not yet melded into an efficient or even a competent team; and that the machinery of America's peacetime military establishment could not shift smoothly or easily into crisis mode.

First, there was the question of who would command. Presumably, this would have to be a navy man. Commodore Stringham was the logical choice, but he declined to assert his claim, and because Fox had devised the plan and scouted the objective, Lincoln decided that Fox should command. Fox, however, was a private citizen with no military standing or rank. As Scott put it in his orders, he was simply "a gentleman of high standing." So while Fox might command the tugs and the supply vessel, he could not exercise command authority over the escorting navy warships, which would necessarily be under the authority of navy officers. Consequently, Fox's orders directed that if he encountered resistance at Charleston, he was to notify "the senior officer of the harbor," who would "use his entire force to open a passage." The orders did not name the "senior officer" largely because no one yet knew who it was going to be.[25]

Second, the ships had to be found and prepared. While Fox arranged to lease or charter the supply ships, Welles fired off telegrams to various navy base commanders ordering them to prepare the warships that would accompany the expedition. These included the steam frigate *Pocahontas* at Norfolk, the *Pawnee* at Washington, and the revenue cutter *Harriet Lane* at New York. Fox had named these three in his plan simply because they were "all that was available." Fox himself would ride the *Baltic*, a chartered civilian steamer that would carry Sumter's supplies and the reinforcement of two hundred soldiers. A day later, Welles added the USS *Powhatan* to the expedition. It had just returned from a long deployment off Veracruz, and Welles included it because it possessed the firepower to force the issue if that became necessary. Moreover, it could carry an additional number of small boats that might be used to help carry supplies to the fort. All these various ships, plus three New York City tugboats, were to put to sea independently and rendezvous ten miles outside Charleston eleven days hence. Altogether, the United States was committing most of its available naval force to the expedition.[26]

In the administration's first important policy decision, Seward's arguments had failed to carry the day. His disappointment led him to dictate a remarkable document to his thirty-one-year-old son Frederick, who served as his secretary. Entitled "Some Thoughts for the President's Consideration," it was delivered to Lincoln's hand on the morning of April 1, the same day that the orders to mobilize the expedition to Sumter went out from Welles' office. Whether he intended it as such, Seward's memorandum was a direct criticism, even a rebuke, of Lincoln's first month in office. Seward declared challengingly, "We are at the end of a month's administration and yet without a policy, either domestic or foreign." Uncharitable as this was, it was also mostly correct; Lincoln's preference to wait and see had cost the government precious time. There was nothing new in Seward's assertion that the government ought to divert public attention from the issue of slavery to one of national union. What was new was his suggestion that the United States should achieve this by questioning European intentions in the Western Hemisphere. He would demand that Spain, France, Great Britain, and Russia explain themselves, and he suggested that if those nations did not respond satisfactorily, it would be appropriate to "declare war on them." Even if it did not lead to actual war, the crisis would, as Seward had explained to the British ambassador, "divert the Public excitement." Moreover, Seward declared in his note that "it must be somebody's business to pursue and direct" this policy. "Either the President must do it himself . . . , or devolve it on some member of his Cabinet."[27]

Lincoln deftly turned aside this clumsy challenge to his authority. He recognized at once that Seward's pique derived from the decision to reinforce Sumter, and he composed a reply in which he wrote, "I do not perceive how the re-inforcement of Fort Sumpter [sic] would be done on a slavery or party issue, while that of Fort Pickens would be on a national or a patriotic one." As for devolving authority on some member of the cabinet, Lincoln wrote that whatever "must be done, *I* must do it," adding deliberate emphasis to the personal pronoun. He did not, however, deliver the letter to Seward. As he often did during his presidency, Lincoln "answered" his critic on paper, then quietly put the answer in a drawer. Very likely, Lincoln replied to Seward in person, perhaps, as his biographer Benjamin Thomas has suggested, in a quiet "heart-to-heart talk."[28]

If so, Seward was not chastened. Later that same day, he returned to the White House with Meigs in tow, hoping to revive his plan to reinforce Pickens. This time he also brought along a dark-bearded navy officer named David Dixon Porter. Porter was destined to become one of the naval heroes of the Civil War, but at this point he was merely a forty-eight-year old lieutenant frustrated by the slow rate of promotion in the peacetime service. The son of David Porter, a hero of the War of 1812, he was also the brother of William Porter, another navy officer, and the foster brother of David Glasgow Farragut. Porter was something of a free spirit in the navy, a confident, even brash individual who was not averse to self-promotion. Lincoln's secretary John Hay described him as "a ready offhand talker [with] a slight dash of the rowdy." For his part, Welles acknowledged that Porter had "dash and energy," but he was concerned that, like Seward, he was "given to intrigues."[29]

Meigs had been busy promoting Seward's plan to secure Fort Pickens. He even got General Scott to write to the president insisting that it was "of prime importance" to send a war steamer to Pensacola immediately. Lincoln listened respectfully as Meigs and Porter outlined an impromptu plan in which the steamer *Powhatan* would act as a screen to prevent interference while four to six companies of infantry landed at the fort. Lincoln was not averse to the idea. He had not chosen to hold Sumter *instead* of Pickens—he wanted to hold them both, and he was aware that the one company of soldiers from the *Brooklyn* that he had ordered into Fort Pickens did not guarantee its security. Lincoln was certainly aware that Seward was running his own game here. Especially in the wake of the astonishing memo Seward had handed him that morning, Lincoln must have wondered if this visit was not merely an attempt by Seward to reactivate his plan to reinforce Pickens while sacrificing Sumter. But if both forts could be secured, wasn't that a better outcome? Lincoln quickly consulted the list of ships that Welles had put together indicating which vessels were to be sent on the Fort Sumter expedition. The *Pocahontas*, *Pawnee*, and *Harriet Lane*, as well as the *Baltic*, were all listed there, but not the *Powhatan*. Still, he wanted to make sure that the various elements of his administration were working in unison. "What will Uncle Gideon say?" the president asked. Seward waved off that detail: "I will make it right with Mr. Welles."[30]

Lincoln thereupon gave his consent to organize a second expedition, this one to Fort Pickens, and since time was short, Meigs and Porter went into the next room to write the pertinent orders on the spot. Porter wrote one order giving himself command of the *Powhatan* and another authorizing the acting commandant of the Brooklyn Navy Yard, Andrew Hull Foote, to prepare that ship for an undisclosed sea duty. Largely because Porter insisted that the fewer people who knew about the mission, the less likely it was that news of it would leak out, that second order also directed that "under no circumstances" was Foote "to communicate to the Navy Department the fact that she is fitting out." Similarly, Meigs' order to the commander of the embarked soldiers declared that "the object and destination of this expedition will be communicated to no one to whom it is not already known."[31]

There was more. Meigs wrote out another order transferring Commodore Stringham from Washington to command the squadron off Pensacola. Welles had previously appointed Stringham to head a new Office of Detail, where his principal job was to vouch for the loyalty of officers being considered for key assignments. Meigs' order now elevated Commodore Samuel Barron to head this new bureau. Porter added a postscript to these orders authorizing Barron to assign officers "for special purposes as the exigencies of the service may require," a responsibility that nominally belonged to the secretary of the navy. Lincoln signed this order along with the others—six altogether—as they were brought to him, saying as he did so, "Seward, see that I don't burn my fingers." Lincoln was right to express concern. Under the direction of the secretary of state, an army captain and a navy lieutenant were reorganizing the armed forces of the United States.[32]

Lincoln told one of his private secretaries, John Nicolay, to ensure that Welles got copies of the papers—but not all the papers. Seward supported Porter's desire to keep the mission to Pensacola a close secret, and he convinced Lincoln to withhold information about it even from the Navy Department. As a result, Nicolay took to Welles only those papers concerning Stringham's reassignment and Barron's new appointment. That was enough, however, to provoke an instant response from the prickly navy secretary. Welles was eating his dinner at Willard's Hotel when Nicolay found him in the dining room and handed him the papers. Welles glanced at them quickly; greatly alarmed, he threw down his napkin and left at once for the White House. Lincoln was working at his desk when Welles burst in on him. The president looked up to see the bewhiskered navy secretary bearing down on him under a full head of steam, clutching a sheaf of papers in his hand and bearing an expression so confrontational that Lincoln impulsively blurted out: "What have I done wrong?"[33]

Welles showed him. What Welles found "singular and remarkable" was not so much Stringham's reassignment to Pensacola but the elevation of Barron to head a Bureau of Detail endowed with duties that rivaled those of the navy secretary. Welles' alarm was not merely a product of his pique at this challenge to his authority. In these early days of the administration, Welles was paying a lot of attention to the issue of officer loyalty—precisely why he had wanted Stringham by his side—and Barron was one of those officers whom Welles eyed suspiciously. Not only was Barron southern-born and a vocal champion of the secessionist cause, but he was also a close friend of Jefferson Davis. In Welles' mind, to make such a man responsible for officer assignments was foolish at best, and indeed, Welles' instinct about Barron proved to be correct, for within weeks Barron would be in Richmond wearing Confederate gray.*

Lincoln claimed to be surprised that he had signed such an order. The president explained that Seward and two young officers had been there all day writing orders and that he had merely signed the papers as they were presented to him. He had, he told Welles, "left the details to Seward and signed the papers without reading them." Welles wanted to know who the two officers were, and Lincoln told him: one was Captain Meigs and the other was "a naval officer named Porter." Welles suspected at once that Porter had become involved in a palace intrigue for the purpose of elevating his friends within the navy.[34]

Lincoln readily and immediately countermanded the order regarding Barron's assignment, and Welles was momentarily mollified. He thought he had averted a catastrophe by nipping the Seward-Porter plot in the bud. In his journal he referred to the episode as Seward's

---

*Barron's official appointment as a captain in the Confederate Navy was dated March 26, 1861, five days *before* the Meigs-Porter order that would have made him chief of the Bureau of Detail in the U.S. Navy.

"Barron conspiracy." But he remained unaware of the Fort Pickens expedition. When Welles asked Lincoln about the broader purpose of Seward's visit, Lincoln told him only that it was a special project of the secretary of state and that Seward preferred it to be kept secret. Welles let it go. He should have pressed harder, for elevating Barron was only one element, and not the most consequential, of Seward's intrigue.[35]

BY THE EVENING OF APRIL 1, two naval expeditions were being assembled, one for Fort Sumter and one for Fort Pickens, but in the entire country only four men—the president, the secretary of state, and two junior officers—were aware of it. Consequently, the flurry of orders sent out that day created as much confusion as direction. The greatest confusion concerned the USS *Powhatan*, a decade-old side-wheel steamer armed with ten 9-inch Dahlgren guns and one 11-inch pivot. Though the *Powhatan* was worn down by recent service, it was one of the more powerful vessels in the navy's small arsenal of steam warships. On the very evening that Porter sat in the White House writing himself orders to command it, Foote at the Brooklyn Navy Yard received a telegram from Welles ordering him to "fit out the *Powhatan* to go to sea at the earliest possible moment." Foote explained by return telegram that the *Powhatan* had just returned from Veracruz and had been put temporarily out of commission—just that day, as it happened—but that he would immediately recall the officers and crew and try to have it back and ready for service as soon as possible. Then, later that afternoon, Foote received a second telegram with nearly identical wording from the president himself: "Fit out the *Powhatan* to go to sea at the earliest possible moment under sealed orders." Foote logically assumed that this was a confirmation of Welles' order. In fact, of course, it referred to a completely different expedition.[36]

Meanwhile, Fox headed for New York to line up the supplies he would carry to Anderson's garrison in Fort Sumter. At the last minute, the supplier of the "desiccated" (dehydrated) foods backed out, fearful of contributing to the outbreak of war, and Fox had to scramble to obtain substitutes. William Aspinwall, the owner of the *Baltic*, was similarly concerned, and Fox had to stay up until late into the night on March 30 before Aspinwall finally agreed to let the government charter his ship. Disgusted with such timidity, Fox confided to Blair that the "delays, obstacles, and brief time allowed" made him "heart sick but not discouraged."[37]

As the preparations went forward, Lincoln continued with the routine political and social obligations of his office. On April 3 he attended a wedding at the Washington Navy Yard, where the daughter of the yard's commandant, Captain Franklin Buchanan, was marrying a marine lieutenant, Julius Meiere. Buchanan himself was a Marylander with strong ties to the slaveholding aristocracy on Maryland's eastern shore, and he and his family were less than thrilled that the tall, gangly president honored them by his appearance. The bride's younger sister, fifteen-year-old Elizabeth Buchanan, at first refused to shake hands with the new president, but Lincoln cheerfully teased her about being a "little rebel" and she eventually relented. In the end, Lincoln escorted the bride into the reception dinner. It was a measure of both the precarious political environment and Lincoln's strategic isolation that although Buchanan was one of the most senior naval officers in the capital, the president could not mention to him either of the two naval expeditions that were being prepared.[38]

That night, Fox returned to the White House to report that he had completed the preliminary arrangements for the expedition to Sumter, and Lincoln gave him his official orders. Fox expressed his concern that the delays he had encountered meant that he might not arrive at Charleston in time. Lincoln shared his concern. Just that day he had read the latest missive from Anderson, who now reported that instead of holding out until April 15, his supplies would be gone by April 10. Even if everything went on schedule, the expedition could not arrive at Charleston until late on the eleventh. But the bit was in his teeth now. He ordered Secretary of War Simon Cameron to tell Anderson to "hold out, if possible," though it was unlikely the order would reach him in time, and he "calmly assured" Fox that whatever happened, "he should best fulfill his duty by making the attempt."[39]

Seward's earlier assurances to southern representatives that the government would make no attempt to reinforce Sumter without notice put him in an awkward position, and he insisted now that the administration must live up to that pledge. Welles opposed it. After all, he argued, a key element of Fox's expedition was stealth. To notify the secessionists that an expedition was en route jeopardized its potential for success and put Fox and all those who sailed with him in increased peril. Lincoln decided that he would send a notification of the impending mission to South Carolina, but only after the expedition had sailed. The note he sent stated that if local authorities permitted the resupply of Anderson's garrison, the U.S. government would not land any reinforcements, but if they resisted, then both supplies and reinforcements would be landed. It is impossible to know what Lincoln expected such a message to accomplish. He may have genuinely hoped that South Carolina authorities would allow the supplies to be delivered to Anderson. More likely, he calculated that his message might provoke the secessionists to act, and in acting, assume the burden of the consequences.[40]

The next day (April 4), Porter showed up at the Brooklyn Navy Yard with orders signed by Lincoln giving him command of the *Powhatan*. Foote was perplexed and even suspicious. He wanted to confirm the orders with Welles, but the order signed by Lincoln specified that "under no circumstances" was he "to communicate to the Navy Department the fact that she is fitting out." This was absurd. Of course Welles knew the ship was fitting out—Welles had personally ordered it to be done four days earlier and had sent several telegrams since urging Foote to hurry. Briefly, Foote even wondered if Porter were not a southern sympathizer trying to gain possession of a warship for the Confederacy. Foote did all that he thought he could do under such curious circumstances. He sent Welles a cryptically worded telegram reporting that he had received orders "to have certain preparations made and things placed on board of vessels soon to go to sea . . . but as the orders do not come direct, I make this report." Welles, of course, assumed this was a reference to the Sumter expedition and that everything was proceeding on schedule.[41]

Not until late on April 5 did all of the parties involved in this comedy of errors begin to read off the same script, and it was Seward who exposed the confusion. That day Welles sent final orders to the captains of all four ships assigned to the Sumter mission, including the *Powhatan*, to rendezvous off Charleston on April 11. From New York, Meigs wired Seward to complain that Welles was interfering with the expedition to Pensacola by sending orders to the *Powhatan*. Seward suspected that "Uncle Gideon" was trying to sabotage the expedition, and, determined to get this straightened out, he and his son Fred dashed across Lafayette Park to Welles' home, which was only a few hundred yards away, woke the navy secretary from a sound sleep, and demanded to know why he was meddling in Porter's command of the *Powhatan*.[42]

Surely there was some mistake, Welles told him. Porter had no such command—Samuel Mercer commanded the *Powhatan*, which was the flagship of the expedition to Fort Sumter. Not so, Seward declared. The *Powhatan* was ordered to Fort Pickens under Porter's command. Welles very nearly lost his temper (he admitted in his diary that his conversation included "some excitement on my part"). Only one person could resolve the dispute, and together the two cabinet secretaries and young Fred recrossed Lafayette Square to the White House to wake up Lincoln, even though it was nearly midnight.[43]

Lincoln wasn't asleep. He heard both men, and at first he sided with Seward, declaring that the *Powhatan* was not part of the Sumter expedition. The sputtering Welles was sure that it was. He charged off to his office to get copies of the orders and soon returned with the evidence. Once he read them to the president, Lincoln recalled having approved them, and he declared that since Sumter was the more important objective, the *Powhatan* must be reassigned to that duty. He told both men that he had approved of sending the ship to Fort Pickens in the first place only because it was not on the original list of vessels destined for Charleston. Now that he knew better, he told Seward to relieve Porter from command of the *Powhatan* and return it to Captain Mercer. Welles later recalled that "Mr. Seward remarked to me that, old as he was, he had learned a lesson from this experience, which was that he had better attend to his own business, not interfere with others, and confine his labors to his proper Department." Savoring his rare triumph over the secretary of state, Welles dryly added: "To this I cordially assented."[44]

But the comedy of errors had one more act. It was past midnight by the time the fate of the *Powhatan* was resolved, too late to send a telegram that night. Earlier that evening, Welles had taken the precaution of wiring Foote to "delay the *Powhatan* for further instructions." Now that order seemed providential, for it would keep the disputed vessel in port until Seward's clarifying orders could arrive the next day. Such an assumption overlooked Porter's "dash and energy." When he received Welles' delay order, Porter's first reaction was anger. He told Meigs that he would "do nothing more for this government." He would go to California and spend his time surveying. Meigs tried to calm him down, suggesting that the order was probably "bogus." It seemed unlikely to him that Welles "would dare to countermand an order (written order) of the President." In a kind of compromise, Meigs sailed that night on the steamer *Atlantic* with his four infantry companies, and Porter agreed to wait until morning. If he did not receive new orders from the president by then, he would carry out his mission.[45]

When Porter awoke at six o'clock the next morning, no new orders had arrived. If he had an opportunity to glance at the morning's *New York Times* as he headed for the Navy Yard, he might have read a headline that proved that Seward's concerns about secrecy were well founded: "THE IMPENDING CRISIS, Threat to Bombard Sumpter [*sic*] in Forty-Eight Hours . . . The Powhatan to Sail Immediately." Porter rowed out to the *Powhatan*, ordered the crew to get up steam, and at two-thirty that afternoon, the *Powhatan* left New York Harbor bound for Pensacola. A half hour later, at three o'clock, Seward's telegram arrived at the Navy Yard ordering Porter to "give up the *Powhatan* to Captain Mercer." Foote sent a fast tug in pursuit of the *Powhatan*, and it caught up with the steamer in the New York Narrows, where it had paused to drop off Captain Mercer. Foote's messenger climbed aboard and handed Seward's telegram to Porter.[46]

Porter now had to do some swift thinking. He noted that the telegram was signed "Seward." But Porter had orders in his pocket—orders of whose provenance he was certain since he had written them himself—that were signed by the president. Seward's order was more recent, to be sure, but could the secretary of state countermand orders from the chief executive? Another consideration was that if he complied with this order and returned to port, Meigs' four companies of infantry, already en route, would arrive at Fort Pickens without their naval support and without their artillery, which was stowed in the hold of the *Powhatan*. Porter knew that his mission had been planned in the White House, and despite the orders from both Welles and Seward, he still had not heard from Lincoln. Porter acknowledged his predicament to Foote:

"This is an unpleasant position to be in," he wrote. "The President says nothing and I must obey his orders; they are too explicit to be misunderstood. I got them from his own hand. He has not recalled them." Porter was certainly aware that his decision here would affect not only his career but also his honor. In the end, however, he characteristically determined that it was better to err on the side of action than that of caution. "Am sustained by my sense of duty," he wrote to Foote, "and will leave the rest to that kind Providence which has never deserted me in very trying circumstances." He delivered the note to Foote's emissary along with a brusque telegram to Seward reading: "I received my orders from the President and shall proceed and execute them." Then, after the tug cast off, he ordered the engine room to go ahead full.[47]

AT ALMOST THE SAME MOMENT that Porter and the *Powhatan* steamed out of New York, Welles received "a secret confidential communication" from Captain Henry Adams, the officer commanding the U.S. Navy squadron off Pensacola. It had been hand-carried to Washington by Lieutenant Washington Gwathmey, a southern sympathizer who would spend the war in a Confederate uniform but who dutifully delivered Adams' communication before resigning. In this message, Adams declared his "painful embarrassment" in reporting that despite the orders sent to him in March to land the troops on the *Brooklyn* at Fort Pickens, he had not done so.* His justification was that back in January the government and the secessionists at Pensacola had agreed to a truce. The secessionists had promised not to attack Fort Pickens if the U.S. government pledged itself not to land any reinforcements, and the Buchanan administration had ordered Adams "not to land the company on board the Brooklyn unless said fort shall be attacked." Lincoln's March 11 order to land the troops had arrived, but it bore the signature of the army's adjutant general, Edward Townsend. Once again, the strict separation of departments allowed a navy officer to question the validity of an order from Washington. Adams decided that absent a confirming order from the Navy Department, orders from the army's adjutant general were not enough to compel him to an act that might provoke civil

---

*By late March, the soldiers originally consigned to the *Brooklyn* had been transferred to the sailing frigate *Sabine* so that the *Brooklyn* could return to Key West to re-coal.

war. "Such a step is too important to be taken without the clearest orders from proper authority," he wrote. Like Anderson, Adams did not want the responsibility of starting a civil war.[48]

Welles at once took the news to Lincoln. Here was another complication to an already complicated situation, and the implications of Adams' timorousness became dire once Lincoln learned that Porter and the *Powhatan* were bound for Fort Pickens after all. To be sure, there was little doubt that Porter would do what Adams would not—reinforce Pickens—but the *Powhatan* could not arrive there for at least ten days (in fact, it took eleven), and in the meantime Fort Pickens was bereft of infantry support. Once the secessionists in Pensacola learned of the expedition to Sumter, they might decide to assault Fort Pickens, and without the additional reinforcements, their assault might well succeed. If the Sumter expedition failed because the *Powhatan* was dispatched elsewhere and Pickens fell because a punctilious navy captain would not obey orders, both forts would be lost and the government's policy would be in shambles.

Lincoln and Welles agreed that they would have to send a special messenger by train with peremptory orders for Adams to land the troops at once. Who was available for such a mission? Whoever it was would have to be found and instructed quickly, for it was already late in the afternoon, and the evening steamer across the Potomac left at seven o'clock. The man Welles chose was Lieutenant John L. Worden, a forty-three-year old scientific officer who had spent most of his career at the Naval Observatory. The suspicious Welles was satisfied that Worden was "untainted by treason," and after writing out orders in his own hand for Adams to land the troops at Fort Pickens "immediately," he required Worden to memorize them so that if he was searched and had to destroy them, he might recite them from memory.[49]

That night, as the *Powhatan* steamed southward along the Jersey coast and Worden's train rumbled through Virginia en route to Pensacola, Fox was having trouble getting out of New York Harbor. The officers on one of the tugs refused to leave, fearing that they were being sent into harm's way. Then the deep-draft chartered steamer *Baltic* failed to get over the bar outside New York Harbor on April 8, and Fox had to anchor overnight, hoping to get out with the morning tide. He fumed at the delay, writing his wife: "I am afraid we are too late."

When the *Baltic* finally did get to sea on the morning of April 9, it encountered a gale that buffeted the ship throughout its passage. For most of four excruciating days, the two hundred soldiers below deck suffered horrible seasickness before the *Baltic* finally arrived at the rendezvous coordinates ten miles off Charleston at three o'clock in the morning on April 12. The only other vessel in sight was the *Harriet Lane*, though the *Pawnee* arrived a few hours later. There was no sign of the tugs, the *Pocahontas*, or, of course, the *Powhatan*.[50]

Fox went on board the *Pawnee* and asked its captain, Stephen C. Rowan, what support he could provide. Rowan offered him the *Pawnee*'s launch and cutter—hardly satisfactory replacements for three steam tugs, but apparently all that was immediately available. Fox returned to the *Baltic* to conduct a reconnaissance of the harbor entrance. As the *Baltic* approached the shoreline, Fox heard the rumbling growl of artillery fire and soon saw "with horror" that shells were exploding above the ramparts of Fort Sumter. As he had feared, he was too late. As Fox headed back out, he met the *Pawnee* coming in. Rowan, too, had heard the firing, and he announced his determination "of sharing the fate of his brethren of the Army," though he lacked a pilot who could take him in. Fox took it upon himself to speak for the administration in saying that the government wanted no unnecessary loss of life such as would certainly result from such a noble but hopeless gesture.[51]

The Confederate decision to open fire on Fort Sumter that morning had been triggered not by the arrival of the *Baltic* but by the note that Lincoln had sent to South Carolina's governor, Francis Pickens. It had arrived on April 8, and Pickens passed it on to Brigadier General Pierre G. T. Beauregard, who in turn passed it to the Confederate government in Montgomery. In the end, it was Jefferson Davis who made the decision not to allow Sumter to be reinforced or resupplied. He ordered Beauregard to demand the immediate surrender of the fort, and if Anderson refused, the general was to reduce it by gunfire. The first shot was fired just minutes after the *Baltic* reached the rendezvous point, ten miles offshore.

In spite of the bombardment, Fox still hoped to send supplies and reinforcements into the harbor once it was dark enough. The problem was that none of the tugs had arrived for they had been thwarted by the same storm that had buffeted the *Baltic*. Fox was "sure that the *Powhatan*

would arrive during the night," and so he took the *Baltic* out "to the appointed rendezvous and made signals all night." There was no answer, of
course, and the next morning, desperate to do something, Fox prepared
to load the sixteen boats he carried on the *Baltic* with the embarked soldiers and accompany them on the long pull into the fort, though the
continuing "severe weather" made that a daunting prospect.[52]

Rowan had a better idea. On his own authority he seized a privately
owned schooner that was bringing a cargo of ice to Charleston and offered that vessel to Fox. While the ice boat was being prepared, a cloud
of heavy black smoke roiled up from Sumter, and it was evident that
something in the fort, most likely the barracks, was on fire. Soon afterward, the USS *Pocahontas* arrived off Charleston, and Commander
John Gillis assumed responsibility as senior officer present. While Fox
and Rowan briefed Gillis on the situation, the firing in the harbor suddenly stopped and lookouts reported that the American flag was no
longer flying over the fort. Gillis sent in a party with a flag of truce,
which returned with the news that Anderson had surrendered.[53]

On April 15 Robert Anderson and his garrison evacuated Fort
Sumter and joined their would-be rescuers aboard the *Baltic*. They
had occupied the most famous fort in America for 108 days, commanding the attention of the entire nation, including its new president. Though they had endured a lengthy siege and a two-day
bombardment before capitulating, not a single member of the garrison, astonishingly, had been killed in all that furious cannonade. Anderson had made it a condition of his surrender that he be allowed to
fire a salute to the flag before he departed. He intended to fire a hundred guns, but around the fiftieth shot one of the fort's guns went off
prematurely, killing a simple-minded thirty-five-year-old private
named Daniel Hough, the first of some 620,000 mortal casualties of
the American Civil War.[54]

ON THE SAME DAY that the *Baltic* appeared off Charleston, Lieutenant
Worden arrived at the train station in Pensacola. En route from Atlanta, the cars were "filled with Confederate soldiers," who taunted
him with the promise that he would be arrested as soon as they arrived
in Pensacola. Worden "went into the water closet, opened, read, and
destroyed the dispatch" he was carrying. Once in Pensacola, he ob-

tained permission from local authorities to go out to see Adams, to whom he delivered Lincoln's order to land the soldiers, now on board the USS *Sabine*, who had come out some five months before on the *Brooklyn*. This time Adams obeyed, landing 86 soldiers and 115 marines to reinforce the garrison of 83 men already in the fort. The secessionists in Pensacola were furious, and insisted that the move was not only a violation of their agreement but also an act of treachery. It might have started a war if war had not already begun that morning at Fort Sumter. Having completed his mission, Worden rather foolishly went ashore and boarded a train for the return trip to Washington. He made it as far as Montgomery before he was arrested by Confederate authorities and confined as a prisoner of war.[55]

Five days later, the *Powhatan* steamed into sight off Pensacola. En route south, Porter had ordered the crew to paint over the gunports and make other changes to disguise the *Powhatan* as a mail steamer. He planned to steam past the rebel forts directly into the harbor and dare the locals to try to stop him. Unlike either Anderson or Adams, Porter was perfectly willing to start a war. As he wrote later, "I thought it was time to be firing bullets." As he steamed toward the harbor, however, he found himself cut off by the USS *Wyandotte* with Meigs on board signaling furiously. Meigs had arrived the day before on the *Atlantic*, and after a conversation with the local army commander, he became convinced that the 284 men now in the fort were more than adequate to defend it, and that a further hostile act now would be counterproductive. He urged Porter to "put off the day of collision as long as possible." Porter was annoyed. He asked Meigs to put his request in writing, and Meigs did so. "My connection with the expedition," Meigs wrote, "justify me in making the request with almost the force of an order from the President." Porter grudgingly acquiesced, but he declared his readiness to enter the port and challenge the rebel batteries "at a moment's notice." In a prosaic anticlimax, the *Powhatan* took up duty as a guard ship assigned to stop and search inbound vessels, a task that Porter found "humiliating."[56]

ALMOST EVERYTHING HAD GONE WRONG. Lincoln's goal had been to pursue a policy of quiet firmness in the hope of preserving the loyalty of the border states and buy time for the rebellious states to appreciate their foolishness. Porter later recalled with barely suppressed scorn that

"when I left Washington it had seemed to be the leading idea that nobody should get hurt, and that the sensitive feelings of our Southern
brethren should not be ruffled." Even Lincoln's close friend and admirer Ward Lamon thought that Lincoln had been "slow to realize or
to acknowledge, even to himself, the awful gravity of the situation."
The result of Lincoln's reluctance to force the issue was that his long
delay gave the secessionists more time to prepare for the confrontation.
Then, when he did act, the result was a hasty and ad hoc mission sent
at the last moment in order to beat the deadline dictated by Anderson's
dwindling supplies. Finally, in executing that mission, Lincoln's government had demonstrated a level of confusion and clumsiness so pro-
nounced it led some to conclude that its failure must have been the
product of deliberate sabotage.[57]

Certainly Fox thought so. He learned of the detachment of the
Powhatan on April 13 while he watched from the deck of the *Baltic* as
ordnance rained down on Fort Sumter. It should have been evident to
him that the Confederates would have opened fire whether the
Powhatan had been there or not. Nor could the *Powhatan* have fought
its way into the harbor, for it could not have passed over the bar. True,
its boats might have been useful in a nighttime relief effort, but even if
Fox had somehow managed to throw some men and supplies into the
fort on the night of the twelfth, it would not have halted the bombardment, and unless the government planned to make such resupply missions a regular event, the government would have had to evacuate Fort
Sumter sooner or later anyway. Nevertheless, the frustrated Fox convinced himself that the absence of the *Powhatan* had ruined his expedition, and in time his frustration turned to anger. With barely suppressed
fury, he complained to Secretary of War Cameron that he had been permitted to sail "without intimation that the main portion—the fighting
portion—of our expedition was taken away." Both at the time and later,
he thought that "some one determined to utterly extinguish the expedition," and he was pretty sure who it was. The blame, he wrote his wife,
belonged "on the head of that timid traitor W. H. Seward." Then, reading it over, he carefully erased the word *traitor*. Angry as he was, he
knew there were some things he should not commit to paper.[58]

Welles, too, believed that whatever his motives, the secretary of
state had played fast and loose with the various branches of govern-

ment. Seward had sent Meigs off to Pensacola without notifying the Department of War, and he had arranged for Porter to take command of the *Powhatan* without informing the Department of the Navy.* But while the suspicion of Fox and Welles is understandable, Seward's role in sponsoring the expedition to Fort Pickens reflected clumsy earnestness rather than subversive treachery. If Seward's goal had been to sabotage the Fort Sumter expedition, he never would have dashed across Lafayette Square to Welles' house on the night of April 5 to wake up the navy secretary and ask why Welles was sending orders to the *Powhatan*. To be sure, it had been inappropriate for him to insist that the Fort Pickens mission be kept a secret from the Navy Department, but that was very likely motivated by his concern for security. Two weeks earlier Seward had written to Lincoln that "in this season of excitement, with a daily press, daily mails, and an incessant operating telegraph," keeping any expedition secret was likely to be extremely difficult. And, as the *New York Times* headline announcing the imminent departure of the *Powhatan* proved, he was right. In a final irony, Seward eventually convinced himself that he had been a full and supportive partner in the decision to relieve Fort Sumter. In 1864 he told John Hay that "the Cabinet meeting in the Navy Department when it was resolved to relieve Fort Sumter was the significant act of the administration: the Act which determined the fact that Republican institutions were worth fighting for." He did not mention, and probably did not remember, that he had voted against that resolution.[59]

Welles was nearly as furious about the role that had been played by David Dixon Porter. Welles believed that the dark-bearded officer with "a dash of the rowdy" had allowed his head to be turned. Porter had been "flattered and gratified" to be invited to help the president of the United States make national policy. He found the hurried trip to the White House and the clandestine planning session exhilarating. In the

---

*Secretary of War Cameron wanted to arrest Meigs for desertion and have him court-martialed. Two months later, when Lincoln sought to appoint Meigs (by then a colonel) to the post of quartermaster general of the army, Cameron opposed the nomination. Lincoln wrote to Scott to ask him to use his influence "to remove Gen. Cameron's objection." Scott's efforts were successful, and Meigs became quartermaster general in June.

end, Porter was so giddy to be at the center of things, he did not use sound professional judgment. He withheld critical information from the Navy Department, ignored orders to give up the *Powhatan*, and at Pensacola he was fully prepared to start a war on his own recognizance. Even Porter's friends thought he had stepped over the line. Foote later told him: "You ought to have been tried and shot." Welles felt he had good reason to keep a wary eye on this mercurial and unpredictable officer. Indeed, Welles harbored some doubts about Porter's basic loyalty. He suspected that if Confederate authorities had offered Porter the same kind of adventurous command that Seward had done, he might just as easily have ended up in rebel gray.[60]

Porter was untroubled by Welles' disapproval. Years later, he boasted of having pulled a fast one on the prissy navy secretary and insisted that both Lincoln and Seward fully supported his decision to circumvent Welles by steaming off to Pensacola with the *Powhatan*. He believed that his bold action "made a warm friend" of both Lincoln and Seward, who thereafter stood by him "whenever Mr. Welles—who was not partial to me—was disposed to be annoying."[61] He was wrong on both counts. Welles subsequently supported Porter's advance in the navy, whereas Lincoln, though officially supportive, remained concerned about Porter's volatility. It is a measure of Lincoln's deft handling of these two men that each believed that the president was a special ally. Whatever Lincoln's actual views, he made sure that Porter was not punished for his behavior. "Lieutenant D. D. Porter," Lincoln wrote to Welles, "was placed in command of the steamer Powhatan . . . by my special order" and should not be held "responsible for any apparent or real irregularity . . . in connection with that vessel." Porter remained on active duty and in time became a key figure in the eventual Union victory.[62]

Of all the characters in this drama, Lincoln expressed the greatest appreciation for the role that Fox had played. Indeed, Fox's efforts in those crowded April days proved the making of him. Even before he left for his reconnaissance of Charleston Harbor, Fox wrote exuberantly to his wife that "Uncle Abe has taken a high esteem for me." After the mission's failure, Lincoln wrote directly to Fox to absolve him of any responsibility. "I most cheerfully and truly declare," Lincoln wrote, "that the failure of the undertaking has not lowered you a particle, while the qualities you developed in the effort have greatly heightened you in my estimation."

Indeed, Lincoln told Fox that "for a daring and dangerous enterprise . . . you would to-day be the man, of all my acquaintances, whom I would select." Lincoln at first wanted Fox to have the command of one of the navy's new warships, but Blair suggested that his brother-in-law might be more useful as a permanent fixture in the Navy Department, and Lincoln consequently appointed Fox chief clerk of the navy. When Congress authorized the new post of assistant secretary of the navy, Fox moved into that position, an office that became a permanent part of the government and a springboard for two future presidents—both of them named Roosevelt. When Lincoln heard some grumbling about Fox's swift elevation, he put a quick stop to it. "I understand there is some opposition to the appointment of Capt. G. V. Fox to the clerkship we talked of," he wrote to Welles in early May. "My wish, and advice is, that you do not allow any ordinary obstacle prevent his appointment. He is a live man, whose services we cannot well dispense with."[63]

Despite his twenty-five-day delay in choosing a policy and his contributions to the confusion surrounding the expedition to Fort Sumter, Lincoln had the clearest view of both the causes and the consequences of the bungled mission. The president knew that it was his own mistakes, not those of Seward, Porter, or anyone else, that had contributed most to its failure. His long delay before choosing a course of action had narrowed the window of opportunity in which any relief mission had to operate. He had then authorized a second expedition to Fort Pickens and kept it secret from his own Navy Department. He had allowed two junior officers to write orders in support of that second expedition—orders he did not read carefully before signing—without making those orders available to anyone else in the government.

In the end, however, the crucial step was Lincoln's decision to send formal notice to South Carolina's governor that the expedition was en route, for it threw the burden of decision making onto Jefferson Davis. In receipt of that notice, Davis had to either acquiesce in Anderson's resupply or assume the responsibility of the first blow. His order to Beauregard to open fire on Fort Sumter allowed Anderson to emerge from the crisis as a martyr and galvanized the North for the war to come. As Welles wrote to his son a few days afterward: "Our seeming misfortune proved to be [a] blessing. The firing on Sumter electrified the heart of the nation." Quite possibly, Lincoln had this outcome in mind all along, but he also knew that he had been lucky rather than skillful in managing it, and aware of that, he was unwilling that Seward, Welles, Fox, Porter, or anyone else should shoulder any blame for the confusion.[64]

Despite the clarity of his vision, Lincoln's first experience as commander in chief of the U.S. Navy showed that he had not yet mastered the skills that would later define him as a wartime president. Hannibal Hamlin later insisted that this first challenge of Lincoln's presidency was a learning experience. Hamlin argued that there were two Lincolns: "the one who came from Illinois, inexperienced in wielding great power," and the one who emerged later as "the conqueror of a gigantic civil war, the emancipator of slaves, master of the political situation, and savior of the nation." The first Lincoln had erred in following Seward's argument "that the secessionists would listen to a conciliatory policy," but "the second Lincoln, armed with his experience, . . . would have approached the crisis" differently.[65]

Nevertheless, some of the elements of Lincoln's future greatness were evident in his first exercise of presidential authority over the U.S. Navy. First, he had sought expert advice wherever he could find it, not only from the aged and authoritative Scott and Totten but also from more unlikely sources such as Fox, Meigs, and Porter. Second, he allowed, even demanded, free discussion among the advocates of different policy options, asking his advisers to put their ideas in writing to clarify their thoughts. Third, he was willing to consider unconventional solutions and independent thinking. And finally, when a decision had to be made, he made it himself, saw it through, and accepted both the responsibility and the consequences. Lincoln took all the blame on himself even when there was plenty to go around. In one respect, however, the outcome of the botched rescue mission proved salutary, for the Confederate attack on April 12 galvanized the nation to fight the war that would save the Union.

2

"A Competent Force"

Lincoln and the Blockade

AN HOUR BEFORE MIDNIGHT on May 10, two days short of a month after Fox first appeared off Charleston in the *Baltic*, the screw steamer USS *Niagara* arrived off that city to inaugurate a naval blockade. The *Niagara* was an imposing vessel. Newer, larger, and more heavily armed than the *Powhatan*, whose absence had so infuriated Fox a month earlier, it displaced more than 5,500 tons and boasted a dozen giant eleven-inch smoothbore Dahlgren guns, each weighing eight tons and capable of hurling either a 165-pound iron bolt or an eleven-inch explosive shell more than a mile. Powerful as it was, however, no single vessel could close down the port of Charleston which could be entered by at least three different ship channels. Its presence was a gesture, a symbol of Lincoln's determination to assert continued national authority over the seceded states.

On her first day of blockading duty, the *Niagara* warned off a large merchant ship flying English colors. Early the next morning, the *Niagara* warned off several more vessels bound for Charleston, but one of them, instead of departing, edged in toward the shore and began making signals. His suspicions aroused, the *Niagara*'s captain, William W. McKean, fired a shot across its bow and sent a boat alongside. Finding evidence on board the *General Parkhill* that convinced him it was attempting to run through the blockade, McKean "took possession of her," placing on board a prize crew of ten men commanded by a twenty-one-year-old midshipman named Winfield Scott Schley with orders to take the prize into Philadelphia for adjudication.* It was the first of many that would be seized by American warships on the Charleston blockading station.[1]

Eventually the Union blockade spread to all the Atlantic and Gulf ports, and before the war ended it would employ more than five hundred ships manned by a hundred thousand sailors. In its sheer size and ambition, it was the greatest naval operation ever undertaken by the United States. Its effectiveness was controversial at the time and has been debated by historians ever since. But whether the blockade was a key element of Union victory, as many insist, or "a naval sieve," as one authority has claimed, establishing and maintaining the blockade was a central component of Lincoln's strategy for the war that began at Fort Sumter.[2]

It proved to be a gargantuan task that brought with it a number of difficulties, both expected and unexpected. From the first there were legal problems that strained relations with the powers of Europe and provoked a number of domestic court cases with the potential to undercut administration policy. There were also unprecedented matériel and manpower problems as the navy expanded from a handful of vessels to several hundred. And there were logistical problems as the government tried to maintain this steam-powered armada off the southern coast. Some of these problems Lincoln had anticipated; most of them he had not. To resolve them, the new president found that he frequently had to adjust both his expectations and his policies. As in his management of the Fort Sumter crisis, Lincoln's experience with the blockade taught him several things: that his advisers were fallible, that every decision had unexpected and unintended consequences, and that patience and flexibility were at least as important as firmness and determination in resolving difficulties. In the end, Lincoln's willingness and ability to adjust, his pragmatic approach to problems of every kind, and his keen political instinct helped him overcome the various crises

---

*This was Midshipman Schley's first command, but hardly his last. Thirty-seven years later, as Rear Admiral Schley, he would participate in a much-celebrated, but also controversial, victory over a Spanish naval squadron off Santiago, Cuba.

that emerged from the unprecedented national effort to blockade half a continent.[3]

LINCOLN'S FIRST PROBLEMS with the blockade were legal. Though he was a lawyer, and a good one, his legal work in Illinois had never included an international dimension. A possibly apocryphal story told after the war by Pennsylvania congressman Thaddeus Stevens portrayed Lincoln as completely adrift in the legal ramifications of his own policy. Stevens claimed that he had pointed out to Lincoln that a blockade could be executed only by nations at war, and that by announcing a blockade of the Confederacy Lincoln had effectively recognized the rebel government. Lincoln's reply, according to Stevens, was self-deprecatory: "Well, that is a fact; I see the point now. But I don't know anything about the law of nations and I thought it was all right." When Stevens protested that Lincoln was himself a lawyer, Lincoln replied, "Oh, well, I'm a good enough lawyer in a western law court, but we don't practice the law of nations up there, and I supposed Seward knew all about it, and I left it up to him."[4] If, in fact, Lincoln ever made this statement, he was being not only self-deprecating but also disingenuous, for certainly he had considered the legal ramifications of a blockade before declaring it. That did not save him from the many legal and diplomatic difficulties that ensued, some of them so severe that they threatened the survival of his war policy.

It was a central tenet in all of Lincoln's policy decisions that the Union remained undissolved. The Confederacy, he insisted, was a legal fiction—a rebellious part of the United States, not a separate nation. In order to demonstrate that, he and Seward discussed how they might maintain the appearance of continued national sovereignty over the southern coastline without declaring a blockade, which was, after all, an act of war. One way was to post U.S. warships off the principal southern ports in order to collect the import duties (tariffs) at sea, as Andrew Jackson had sought to do during the Nullification Crisis in 1833. Seward tried this idea out on a group of foreign diplomats at a dinner party in late March even before the Fort Sumter crisis had reached its denouement. The British minister in Washington, Richard B. Pemell, known as Lord Lyons because of the earldom he had inherited from his admiral father, hosted the party, which included the representatives of most of the European powers. Seward took advantage of their presence to test the policy he and Lincoln had discussed. When Baron Edward de Stoeckel, the Russian minister, suggested that what Seward described sounded very much like a blockade, Seward insisted that "it was not a Blockade," because "the U.S. Cruisers would be stationed off the South Coast to collect duties and enforce penalties for the infraction of the United States Custom laws." The ministers were not buying it. To Lyons, the policy seemed "to amount to a paper blockade," and he noted archly that "it placed foreign Powers in the dilemma of recognizing the Southern Confederation or of submitting to the interruption of their Commerce." Indeed, Lyons was not particularly impressed by the new administration, reporting privately to London that "Mr. Lincoln has not hitherto given proof of his possessing any natural talents to compensate for his ignorance of everything but Illinois village politics."[5]

In the end, Lincoln's April 19 declaration employed the word *block-ade* despite what it implied about the legitimacy of the Confederate government. Lincoln tried to have it both ways by claiming that while the operation was "in the nature of a blockade," it was not an actual blockade. Indeed, Lincoln very nearly tied himself into syntactical knots while preparing his special message to Congress in July, writing that it hardly mattered "whether the proceedings in the nature of a blockade be technically a blockade" because both the United States and Europe had agreed to treat it as such. Reading over Lincoln's draft, Seward thought it best not to try that gambit, and Lincoln cut the awkward passage. Under whatever name it paraded, the closure of the southern coast—if it could be accomplished at all—would carry the baggage, and the legal requirements, of a blockade.[6]

A second legal problem addressed in Lincoln's declaration concerned the threat of Confederate privateers. In fact, that issue very likely played a major role in the timing of Lincoln's blockade announcement. Lord Lyons, who was greatly disappointed that he had been unable to convince Seward not to establish a blockade in the first place, was convinced that Lincoln had done it because "the great North Eastern Cities insisted upon it."[7] He was partly right. Initially, at least, Lincoln's blockade declaration was not part of a grand strategy for Union victory—the so-called Anaconda Plan would not emerge for another two weeks. His April 19 declaration was instead an independent and largely ad hoc decision, the timing of which was determined by an announcement made two days before by Jefferson Davis. On April 17, the same day that Virginia seceded from the Union, Davis announced that he would begin issuing letters of marque to private armed vessels to prey on U.S. commerce. Letters of marque were quite literally licenses to steal. They authorized shipowners to arm their vessels (at their own expense) in order to capture, burn, or destroy merchant vessels of the enemy—a practice known as privateering.*

For a hundred years and more, privateering had been the weapon of choice (or of necessity) used by weaker nations against more powerful maritime foes. It had been America's principal maritime instrument against the British during both the American Revolution and the War of 1812. As the name implied, the ships were privately owned, privately armed, and privately manned—they cost the government nothing. The incentive for the privateers (the term refers to both the ships themselves as well as the men who engaged in the practice) was economic: the ship's owner and crew got to keep whatever they captured. The incentive for the sponsoring government was strategic: with enough privateers, a nation with virtually no navy could nevertheless strike a heavy blow at its opponent's shipping industry. Naturally, the major maritime powers of Europe viewed privateering as little better than state-sponsored piracy, and in 1856 they had signed the Declaration of Paris, which decreed that "privateering is and remains abolished." The United States, however, remembering its previous (and perhaps future) dependence on privateering, had refused to sign the protocol, and since the Declaration of Paris was binding only on the signatory powers, the United States was exempt. By implication, at least, so was the Confederacy.[8]

The news that the Confederacy was authorizing privateers sent a wave of near-panic through the American shipping industry. The day

---

*Ironically, when the Confederate Congress followed up on Davis' declaration by authorizing privateers on May 6, 1861, the justification cited in the legislation was that Lincoln had "set on foot a blockade of the ports of the Confederate States." In effect, the threat of Confederate privateers provoked Lincoln's blockade declaration, and the South used Lincoln's declaration to justify the authorization of privateers.

after Davis' declaration, Lincoln received a number of petitions from alarmed northern businessmen who entreated the president to protect American commerce "by vigorous and energetic measures." Lincoln asked his advisers what could be done about it, and it was Seward who suggested that a blockade—a real blockade—might be an appropriate countermeasure. After all, if rebel privateers could not get to sea, they would be unable to attack American shipping. In his proclamation, therefore, Lincoln justified the blockade because of the threat by "pretended letters of marque" to prey upon "the good citizens of the country lawfully engaged in commerce on the high seas." The concern for privateers was also evident in the orders Welles subsequently gave to the captain of the *Niagara* "to seize and capture all privateers or armed vessels acting under authority or pretended authority of the insurrectionary States."[9]

In an effort to forestall Confederate privateering, Seward asked Britain and France if the United States could now belatedly adhere to the Declaration of Paris. The British found his request "rather amusing" given the circumstances, but they were perfectly willing. On the other hand, they also insisted that even if the United States joined the protocol, its strictures would not apply to the conflict already under way. Seward insisted that this made no sense. The southern states, he declared, were still part of the Union, and an adherence to the treaty by the United States should be binding on all parts of the nation. Not necessarily, the British responded. Whether the Confederacy existed as a separate nation was an issue that would be decided by war, but whatever its final outcome, there was no doubt that war existed, and it was impossible to apply new treaty restrictions on a war already in progress. Moreover, if the South was still part of the Union, as Seward insisted, the blockade itself was illegal since blockades applied "only to two nations at war." Seward saw that there was nothing to be gained by U.S. adherence to the declaration, and he offered a number of excuses to fend off further enquiries. With that, both sides let the matter drop.[10]

Though the community of nations declined to declare Confederate privateers illegal, Lincoln took the public position that because the Confederacy was not a legitimate government, it lacked the authority to issue letters of marque. Consequently, his blockade declaration held that any persons acting under "the pretended authority" of such a government "will be held amenable to the laws of the United States for the prevention and punishment of piracy."[11] Lincoln no doubt hoped his hard line would be a deterrent as well as a statement of principle. Perhaps he hoped that he would never have to make good on the threat. Almost at once events proved otherwise.

On June 3 the USS *Perry* was cruising some sixty miles east of Charleston when it encountered two vessels apparently in company: a brig with a schooner following. The movements of the schooner incited the suspicion of the *Perry*'s captain, Enoch Parrott, who closed to investigate. When the schooner bore away, the *Perry* gave chase. A shot across the schooner's bow caused it to raise a flag that in the growing darkness could not be seen clearly, and the schooner continued its attempt to escape. Finally the *Perry* opened fire, which the schooner returned briefly before dropping its sails in a gesture of capitulation. It turned out to be the Confederate privateer *Savannah*, which had just put a prize crew on board the brig when the *Perry* came into view. In his report of the capture, Parrott noted that the *Savannah* had been "commissioned by Jefferson Davis, President of the Confederate States of America," but of course Lincoln recognized no such authority, and Commodore Stringham, who was more politically astute, referred to the vessel in his cover letter as "a piratical schooner."[12]

The men on the *Savannah*—its captain, lieutenant, sailing master, purser, and ten crewmen, fourteen altogether—were taken aboard the *Perry*, locked in irons, and delivered eventually to New York to be tried as pirates. The *Savannah*'s prize, the brig *Joseph*, managed to escape under the command of its prize crew, but a second group of privateers fell into Union hands a few weeks later when the USS *Albatross* recaptured the Boston schooner *Enchantress*, a prize of the Confederate privateer *Jeff Davis*. Thus by midsummer, there were two groups of rebel privateers being held in Union prisons in New York and Philadelphia, not as prisoners of war, but, in accordance with Lincoln's announced policy, as pirates, for whom the only prescribed penalty was death by hanging.

In early July, Winfield Scott arrived at the White House bringing a letter addressed to Lincoln that had been carried through the lines in Virginia under a flag of truce. The letter was signed by none other than Jefferson Davis himself. Officially, of course, Lincoln could not acknowledge a letter from the president of the Confederacy, but neither could he ignore it. Davis wrote that he had read in the New York papers that the captured crew of the *Savannah* had been incarcerated in that city and that the men were being treated "not as prisoners of war, but as criminals." He concluded that it was the apparent intention of the government that these men be "brought before the courts of justice on charges of piracy and treason." Davis then delivered a threat: "A just regard to humanity and to the honor of this government now requires me to state explicitly, that painful as will be the necessity, this government will deal out to the prisoners held by it, the same treatment and the same fate as shall be experienced by those captured on the Savannah."[13]

Lincoln could not respond to Davis' letter, of course, nor, perhaps, did Davis expect him to do so. But the message was delivered. If the privateers were found guilty and executed, an equal number of Union prisoners would die as well. This placed Lincoln in the position of having to choose between maintaining his public position that rebel privateers were pirates and saving the lives of Union prisoners of war. Lincoln was not a man who clung stubbornly to an announced policy if it led to an unhappy end; he did not see any benefit to calling Davis' bluff—if bluff it was. The best he could hope for now was that events would somehow allow him to back away from his original declaration without seeming to do so. It was Lincoln's good fortune that the courts, the passage of time, and his patience allowed him to do just that.

In the trials of the privateers, held separately but simultaneously in New York and Philadelphia, the accused benefited from skilled counsel who argued that even if Jefferson Davis lacked the legal authority to issue letters of marque (as Lincoln insisted), the men who served on the privateers *believed* that he possessed such authority, and their belief absolved them of any personal guilt or legal liability for their actions. They were, the attorneys argued, victims of Davis' pretended authority. This was a line of argument that would allow Lincoln to maintain his central tenet that the Confederacy was a fiction without having to execute its sailors. Alas, not all of the defense attorneys were willing to cleave to this line of reasoning. One of them, Algernon Sullivan, declared that his clients were innocent because the Confederacy was a legitimate government and had full authority to issue letters of marque. For that assertion, Seward ordered Sullivan arrested. Only after he recanted and took an oath of loyalty was he eventually released.[14]

Though the New York jury failed to reach a verdict concerning the crew of the *Savannah*, the Philadelphia jury found the prize crew of the *Enchantress* guilty of piracy and sentenced them all to hang. In response, the Confederate Congress authorized Davis to select an equal number of men from among the population of Union prisoners and place them in holding cells. Davis promised to execute them man for man if the Union carried out the sentences on those the courts had found guilty. In this impasse, Lincoln blinked first. The threat of retaliation, more than the legal arguments presented in court, determined the fate of the privateers. The executions were postponed indefinitely, and after a salutary passage of time, the privateers from both vessels were quietly transferred from the judiciary to the War Department. Eventually they were exchanged as prisoners of war.[15]

A third legal issue proved the most serious, for it touched on the ability of the administration to conduct a blockade at all. The owners of several of the vessels that were captured while attempting to run the blockade sought to recover their losses by claiming that the seizures were unlawful. Blockades, they insisted, could exist only in time of war, and because Congress had never declared war, the blockade itself was illegal and all seizures made in support of it were also illegal. Welles tried to convince Lincoln that he should rescind the blockade declaration entirely and replace it with one that simply closed southern ports to trade. The navy secretary argued that the initial blockade declaration had been made "on the impulse of the occasion," and had endowed the rebels with "the rights of a belligerent government." Because there was "a difference of opinion among legal gentlemen as to the validity of a blockade," every capture was likely to be challenged in the courts.[16]

Lincoln's attorney general, Edward Bates, assured the president that all of his acts—including the blockade declaration—had been retroactively approved by Congress when it met in July. But the wording of that legislation was vague, since it simply declared that "all of the extraordinary acts, proclamations, and orders" of the president "are hereby approved." Congress never formally declared war, mainly because Lincoln would not acknowledge that the Confederacy was a nation, and the litigants used that as grounds for their lawsuits. Lincoln saw that he would have to clarify this murky legal situation, and a week later he issued another proclamation that he hoped would resolve it. On August 16, he declared the seceded states were "in a state of insurrection" in consequence of which, "all goods and chattels, wares and merchandise," coming from or going into any of the said states "shall be forfeited," including "all ships and vessels." Lincoln explained his policy in a letter of instruction to his minister in England: "This government has a clear right to suppress insurrection" and "a blockade is a proper means to that end." The new public statement did not halt the lawsuits, however, and the court cases worked their way through the appeals process and headed for the Supreme Court.[17]

That was a problem, too. There were only six members on the high court in 1861. Both Peter Daniel and John McLean had died (the latter just a month after Lincoln took office), and they had not yet been replaced. A third justice, the Kentuckian John A. Campbell, who had acted as an intermediary with the Confederate commissioners during the Fort Sumter crisis, had resigned.* Of the six justices who remained, four were Democrats from slaveholding states, including Chief Justice Taney, who had already clashed with Lincoln over the reach of his war policies. If the Supreme Court declared that Lincoln was fighting an illegal war, it would be disastrous.

Fortuitously, the case did not reach the high court until 1863, but even then, the outcome was uncertain. The day before the court handed down its ruling, the administration's chief lawyer, Richard Henry Dana (whose seagoing experience was chronicled in *Two Years Before the Mast*), wrote to a friend asking him to "contemplate, my dear sir, the possibility of a Supreme Court deciding that this blockade is illegal! What a position it would put us in before the world. . . . It would end the war!" Aware of the stakes, Republicans in Congress rushed through a law expanding the size of the court from nine to ten. It was a clearly implied threat and, as one modern authority has written, "a direct challenge to the Supreme Court." Lincoln signed the law a week before the Court handed down its decision, and it is at least possible

---

*Before resigning, Campbell relieved himself of a lengthy and self-righteous letter dated the day after the first shot was fired at Fort Sumter. In it, he argued that he had been deliberately deceived by Seward, whom he accused of "systematic duplicity."

that the votes of two of the justices—Robert Grier and James Wayne—were influenced by this implied threat to pack the court if the decision went the wrong way.[18]

It didn't. In a 5–4 vote, both Grier and Wayne voted with Lincoln's three newly appointed justices, agreeing that when the rebellion began it created "a war" and that it was the president's duty to respond to that reality "without waiting for Congress to baptize it with a name." As for the blockade, it was "official and conclusive evidence to the court that a state of war existed." This was a tautological argument: the blockade was legal because war existed, and war existed because a blockade had been declared. But Lincoln was not about to criticize the logic of the court, for it allowed the government to continue with its blockade policy. Writing for the majority, Justice Grier declared, "The ports of the respective countries may be blockaded, and letters of marque and reprisal granted as rights of war." Of course, by implication the decision also gave legal status to Confederate privateers, but by 1863 this had become a moot issue: privateering had all but died out because most would-be privateers had turned to blockade running as both more profitable and less dangerous. Lincoln had won his central point: The United States was legally engaged in a war against an enemy that did not legally exist.[19]

In this, as in most things, Lincoln's commonsense pragmatism served him well. Having won the legal point, he did not insist on it in all circumstances. When foreign powers complained about seizures of their vessels by overzealous blockaders, Lincoln gave way without complaint, asking Congress to spend the small sums demanded as compensation to the Spanish, Danish, and Norwegian governments who protested. There was no need to insist on punctilio as long as the government could maintain its central policy.[20]

Lincoln not only survived these legal challenges to the blockade but may have learned from them as well. By the time the Prize Cases had been decided, the Union had begun to field a number of African American regiments. Outraged, Jefferson Davis responded with the same kind of draconian threat that Lincoln had promulgated back in 1861. Just as Lincoln had pledged to treat rebel privateers as pirates, Davis threatened to treat black Union soldiers as slaves in revolt and their white officers as men inciting servile insurrection. To forestall this,

Lincoln responded with the same counterthreat Davis had employed in 1861: he pledged to put a Confederate prisoner into hard labor for every black Union soldier returned to slavery, and to execute a Confederate officer for every Union officer executed. Lincoln's threat was only partially effective. Though in 1864 the U.S. assistant commissioner of exchange reported that there had not been "a single case of a black prisoner of war being treated as a slave," African American POWs were routinely put to work constructing rebel fortifications, and their names were sometimes published in local papers so that their white "owners" could claim them.*

The legal problems that emerged from the blockade compelled Lincoln to retreat from several of his initial policy positions, but they did not derail his strategy. Whatever it was called, the blockade grew in strength and expanded in purpose. From a deterrent to privateers it grew into an increasingly efficient cordon that weakened an already strained southern economy. Its mission expanded along with the size and number of the blockading squadrons. By the end of 1861, Welles was informing the squadron commanders that the purpose of the blockade was not to interdict privateers but "to distress and cripple the states in insurrection."[21]

Just how much the blockade crippled the Confederacy remains uncertain. For every vessel that was captured trying to run the blockade, three others made the run successfully. On the other hand, the blockade acted as a powerful deterrent that discouraged merchants from trying to run it at all. The total number of ships trading in or out of Confederate ports declined to roughly a third of prewar levels, and this reduction in trade contributed to matériel shortages, personal hardship, and monetary inflation in the Confederacy. If it was not decisive in the outcome of the war, it was a contributing element in the overall Union victory. Though the European powers occasionally questioned

---

*The Confederate Congress codified Davis' threat into law in May 1863. The question of black prisoners became a recurring political issue for Lincoln because while the Confederacy agreed to exchange black soldiers who had been free when they enlisted, they refused to include escaped slaves in prisoner exchanges. That contributed to a breakdown in the whole prisoner-of-war exchange, and Lincoln's political opponents argued that his administration's insistence on including black soldiers in the protocol meant that thousands of white soldiers languished in southern prisoner-of-war camps.

its efficiency, none openly challenged its legality. Having declared the blockade, Lincoln made it a reality by patience, flexibility, compromise, and some hard-nosed politics.

IN ADDITION TO LEGAL PROBLEMS, Lincoln's blockade policy also bred serious matériel and logistical difficulties. It was probably Seward who provided the words in Lincoln's proclamation that "a competent force will be posted so as to prevent entrance and exit of vessels from the ports aforesaid." Such a statement was necessary because, according to the Declaration of Paris, a government could not merely *assert* that a port or an entire coastline was closed to trade—such an assertion was known as a "paper blockade" and was nonbinding on neutrals. Nations were obligated to respect a blockade only if "a force sufficient . . . to prevent access to the coast of the enemy" was posted offshore.[22]

In 1861, however, Lincoln's reference to "a competent force" invited skepticism if not outright scorn, for as the Fort Sumter crisis had demonstrated, the navy that Lincoln inherited was feeble even by the prewar standards of a peacetime republic. Fearing to aggravate the sectional crisis during the several months prior to Lincoln's inauguration, James Buchanan's navy secretary, Isaac Toucey, had declined to activate any vessels that were laid up, to alter the rotation cycle of ships overseas, or do anything else that might look like preparation for a conflict. Similarly, during the first six weeks of his own administration, as long as he hoped that a pacific solution still might be found, Lincoln, too, had avoided taking any action—including a naval augmentation—that might be construed as aggressive. Consequently, the U.S. Navy was dramatically unprepared for war in April 1861.[23]

Officially the U.S. Navy in 1861 consisted of some seventy-six ships, but that figure was hugely misleading because half of them were laid up in ordinary, and most of the rest were assigned to distant station patrol in the Mediterranean, the Far East, and elsewhere. When, in March, Lincoln asked Welles what naval force he could make available to control the coast, Welles responded by listing twelve vessels that could "at once be put under orders." A handful of others could be made ready in two to five weeks, but it would take longer to bring home the vessels from overseas and prepare those laid up in ordinary. It was obvious, therefore, that the first order of business for the Navy Department was somehow to obtain the "competent force" that might prove capable of enforcing the ambitious presidential declaration. Alas, the prospect of conjuring such a force was dimmed almost at once by terrible news that arrived four days later from Norfolk.[24]

During those four days, Lincoln's greatest concern was for the security of Washington itself. His call for volunteers had passed through the North like an electric shock, and in response Lincoln received enthusiastic—even bombastic—telegrams from northern governors pledging rivers of soldiers, but few of them flowed into the capital for what seemed an interminable ten days. On the very day that Lincoln announced the blockade, a street mob attacked the 6th Massachusetts regiment as it passed through Baltimore en route to Washington. The soldiers fought back, and before it was over four soldiers and twelve civilians were dead. Within hours, railroad and telegraph lines running through Maryland to Washington had been cut, and the nation's capital was effectively isolated. There was widespread fear in the city that unless the promised troops arrived soon, the capital might fall to the insurgents. Rumors raced through Washington that thousands of armed rebels were gathering on the south bank of the Potomac preparing to seize the city and put everyone to the knife. Welles wrote to his wife in Hartford about "the villainous conduct of the mob at Baltimore" and worried that since "the mails are interrupted . . . I know not how soon this may reach you."[25]

Outwardly, Lincoln manifested little concern. Thurlow Weed remembered that "his nature was so elastic, and his temperament so cheerful, that he always seemed at ease and undisturbed." It may have been an act. In the rare moments when he could escape the "audible and unending tramp of applicants" for government jobs outside his office, Lincoln frequently moved over to the window that gave him a clear view of the Potomac to peer downriver in the hope of seeing troopships bringing Union forces to defend the capital.* He was standing there four days after the riot in Baltimore, unaware that he was being watched, when John Nicolay heard him mutter, "Why don't they

---

*Lincoln did not use the now-famous Oval Office during his years in the White House. That space was then the White House library, and Lincoln set up his office in the space now commonly called the Lincoln Bedroom.

come? Why don't they come?" Later that same afternoon, Lincoln's vigilance was rewarded by the sight of two warships coming upriver to the Navy Yard—a steamer under its own power and a sailing warship being towed by a tug. He strode back to his desk and dashed off a quick note to Welles: "I think I saw three vessels go up to the Navy Yard just now. Will you please send down and learn what they are."[26]

It was not good news. The lead ship was the *Pawnee*, which had been part of the Sumter expedition and which was now under the command of Hiram Paulding. Behind it the tug *Yankee* towed the sailing frigate *Cumberland*. They were returning from Norfolk, home of the largest concentration of U.S. warships on the East Coast. In addition to the warships based there, the Navy Yard itself was of inestimable value. Its machine shops, naval stores, and hundreds of pieces of artillery made it the single most important naval asset in the Republic. Yet as long as the loyalty of Virginia teetered in the balance, Lincoln had declined to send reinforcements there lest it provoke the antagonism of Virginians. The most Welles could do was to order that the steam frigate *Merrimack*, which was in Norfolk undergoing repairs, be made ready to go to sea. Alas, the aging and nervous commandant of the Navy Yard, Commodore Charles McCauley, refused to let the ship depart. The rumor that McCauley was "stupefied, bewildered, and wholly unable to act" had prompted Welles to dispatch Paulding in the *Pawnee* with orders to do all in his power "to protect and place beyond danger the vessels and property belonging to the United States." Now the *Pawnee* was back followed only by the *Cumberland*. Welles might have surmised that this was probably not good news, but he hardly could have imagined how bad it was.[27]

McCauley, who had returned to Washington on the *Cumberland*, reported that raucous crowds outside the Navy Yard had convinced him that "the yard was no longer tenable"; believing that obstructions had been placed in the Elizabeth River downstream from the Navy Yard, he ordered that all the ships under his authority should be immediately scuttled lest they be seized by the rioters. When Paulding arrived at Norfolk, having passed the nonexistent obstructions, the destructive work had already begun. Paulding decided that it was too late to adopt an alternative to McCauley's plan and sent his men to complete the destruction already under way. They set fire to the machine shops and other public buildings, as well as the ships that McCauley had scuttled in the shallow water, then they reboarded the *Pawnee* to return to Washington. Only the sailing frigate *Cumberland* had escaped, towed to safety by the little tug *Yankee*.[28]

It was a disaster of the first order. In a single day the navy lost no fewer than ten warships, including the big steam frigate *Merrimack*. Worse, the machine shops and dry dock had not been seriously damaged in the last minute flurry of destruction, thus bequeathing to the secessionists naval assets that existed nowhere else in the Confederacy. The hasty evacuation left behind nearly twelve hundred cannon that the Confederacy subsequently used to defend itself from the Potomac to the Gulf and from Charleston to Vicksburg. Though Lincoln sought to maintain a stoic's demeanor, this blow began to look, in Nicolay's words, "like an irresistible current of fate." The enemy flag flew across the Potomac River within sight of the White House; the city was cut off from the North with no means of secure communication; now virtually half the navy had been lost. Whatever the president's outward appearance, Nicolay believed that Lincoln was "in a state of nervous tension."[29]

Two days later, on April 25, the gloom in the nation's capital was partially lifted by the arrival of the New York 7th regiment, and it provoked a holiday atmosphere. As the *New York Times* reported, "The windows of the private houses, the doorways of the stores, and even the roofs of many houses were crowded with men, women, and children, shouting and waving handkerchiefs and flags." Lincoln himself went out to the sidewalk with Seward and Simon Cameron and stood hatless under what the *Times* reporter called a "broiling sun" to receive the salute of the regiment as it marched past. In the ensuing days two more New York regiments and two Massachusetts regiments arrived, and by the end of April the city hosted more than ten thousand soldiers. The sense of isolation eased. Welles wrote home that "we shall soon have the roads open through Baltimore and travel uninterrupted." Whatever sense of relief he felt, Lincoln's outward demeanor never changed, and he continued to perch at his office window when he could, sometimes leaning back in his chair with his heels on the windowsill and a long navy telescope balanced on his toes as he watched the river traffic. On April 27, following the secession of North Carolina and Virginia, he issued a second proclamation extending the blockade to the coasts of those states as well.[30]

Lincoln understood that with the loss of Norfolk and its ships, it was problematical that the tiny U.S. Navy would be able to establish a real blockade any time soon, if at all. The *Niagara*, posted off Charleston in its solitary vigil, was unlikely to be considered a "competent force" by any of the European powers. After ensuring the security of the capital, therefore, the first priority of the government was somehow to conjure not only an army but also a navy that was capable of blockading thirty-five hundred miles of hostile coastline. As Lincoln told a visiting friend, the best way to convince the Europeans that the blockade was legitimate was to "increase the navy as fast as we could." To accomplish that, the United States embarked on the greatest naval mobilization in its history, one that would not be matched until the months following the Japanese attack on Pearl Harbor eighty years later.[31]

WELLES AND FOX MANAGED THE MOBILIZATION personally from Washington, assuming not only administrative duties but operational command as well. In effect they filled the roles of both navy secretary and chief of naval operations, the latter a post that did not even exist until the twentieth century. Welles dealt with "large mountains of letters" as he presided over the acquisition of ships, their repair and armament, the appointment and detailing of officers, the deployment of individual vessels, even the purchase, shipment, and distribution of coal for the steamers. At first there was little order in all this activity, as, much like their commander in chief, Welles and Fox were compelled to make ad hoc decisions about almost everything. Their personal relationship was amicable enough, though Fox was a bit taken with his new authority and soon began to issue orders on his own. Welles and others noticed it, and some officers complained to Welles that Fox was "officious," but Welles tolerated it, concluding, "Most men like to be, or to appear to be, men of authority, he as well as others."[32]

Lincoln interfered little. He gave Welles and Fox a long leash, and as long as they produced results, he did not try to micromanage their activities. This contrasted dramatically with his relatively close oversight of the army's mobilization effort. Lincoln's correspondence in the

spring and summer of 1861 is filled with notes about accepting regiments and appointing officers for the army, often several of them a day.
On at least one occasion, he even requested the appointment of a particular second lieutenant. There is nothing comparable in his correspondence about authorizing ships or appointing naval officers. In
large part this was due to the fact that while mayors, congressmen, and
other political leaders clamored for commissions as colonels or even
generals as the nation prepared for war, none sought similar rank in the
navy. For one thing, naval service, especially on the blockade, seemed
to promise less opportunity for martial glory. For another, while most
office seekers assumed that the leadership characteristics that had made
them successful businessmen or politicians would transfer easily to the
command of a regiment or a brigade, they were less confident that it
qualified them to command a steam warship at sea. Consequently,
there was no maritime counterpart to the contingent of so-called political generals that caused Lincoln so many difficulties during the war.

As a result, Lincoln's personal involvement with the naval mobilization was far less evident than his involvement with the army. When a
letter concerning a naval issue reached his desk, Lincoln usually just
endorsed it to Welles' consideration without comment. On those few
occasions when he did ask a particular favor of Welles, often to pay a
political debt, he did so deferentially. "I know but little about ships,"
he wrote Welles in May, "but I feel a good deal of interest for George
W. Lawrence of Maine." Lawrence had been a delegate at the 1860 Republican convention and was now seeking a contract for the manufacture of barges (which Lincoln spelled "barches"). Welles made sure that
Lawrence got his share of contracts for new construction.[33]

But Welles was not merely a yes-man, even when the request came
from Lincoln. He occasionally declined to appoint individuals whose
names Lincoln forwarded to him, and in particular he took a much
harder line than Lincoln did about naval officers who had trouble deciding where their loyalties lay. Of the 571 officers listed in the Navy
Register in 1861, 253 of them (44.3 percent) were southern-born, and
many of them faced a conflict of conscience about their loyalty. Some
resigned at once when their states seceded; others pledged themselves
to the federal Union; a few sought to have it both ways by requesting
service overseas so that they would not have to fight against their

friends. Border state officers faced a special quandary and sought consideration for their dilemma. Welles would have none of it. He expected every officer to do his full duty. He was disgusted by "the host of pampered officers who deserted their flag . . . when their loyalty should have upheld it." He prescribed a new loyalty oath for all officers and dismissed those who refused to take it. When Captain Buchanan, the Marylander whose daughter's wedding Lincoln had attended just weeks before, tendered his resignation following the street riot in Baltimore, Welles refused to accept it and instead ordered that Buchanan's name be struck from the rolls of the navy despite his forty-five-year career. Later, when it became evident that Maryland was not going to secede, Buchanan and several others sought reinstatement. Welles refused them all. "Ungracious and painful as it was," Welles explained to his son, "I had no alternative," for they had been "faithless to their country in the time of peril."[34]

One of those officers was Lieutenant Augustus McLaughlin, who bypassed Welles and appealed directly to Lincoln for reinstatement. Lincoln was inclined to welcome any individual who wanted to serve the country, but he did not want to interfere with Welles' management of the department, nor did he want to set a precedent that might bind him in handling others who recanted. "If you think fit to allow him to withdraw the resignation," Lincoln wrote, "I make no objection; but I can not take the lead." Welles was happy to take the lead. He refused McLaughlin as he refused all the others, and the disappointed lieutenant eventually joined the Confederate Navy, as did Buchanan, who became the Confederacy's first admiral. In the end, almost exactly half of all southern-born U.S. Navy officers (126 of 253) resigned to go south and fight for the Confederacy. An equal number stayed by the old flag.[35]

Lincoln's empathy clashed with Welles' rigidity on other issues as well. A few days later, Lincoln asked Welles if he would look into the case of Commander Edward Boutwell, who had been suspended from the service for "neglect of duty and scandalous conduct." Lincoln asked if, given the national emergency, Commander Boutwell might be restored to duty. When Welles did not reply, Lincoln prodded him: "I am now informed that his case is not yet acted upon. I make no complaint of this, knowing you are overwhelmed with business; but I will be obliged if you will attend to it as soon as possible." Welles replied bluntly that he knew of no fact which would justify a mitigation of Boutwell's sentence. And that was that. Lincoln offered no objection to Welles' hard line, or to most of Welles' other decisions. Busy as he was with eager and demanding office seekers while overseeing the mobilization of an army for the defense of the capital, he was perhaps relieved not to have to peer over Welles' shoulder.[36]

Even more than personnel issues, Welles' highest priority was the acquisition of more ships. Welles and Fox did the obvious things first: they called home the ships serving overseas, and they activated those that had been laid up in ordinary. The next step was a bit more problematic. Lincoln had called for Congress to meet on July 4, but Welles was unwilling to wait two months before beginning the construction of new ships. He therefore let contracts for the construction of two dozen new gunboats in the expectation that the funding would subsequently be approved by Congress, as, in fact, it was. Because he specified that the new vessels were to be built in three months' time, they came to be known as ninety-day gunboats, and eventually the Union built twenty-three of them. Though there is no public record to substantiate it, Welles could hardly have taken such a step without the approval of the president. It was another measure of Lincoln's unwillingness to be hamstrung by peacetime conventions. As he wrote to New York governor Edwin Morgan on another matter, "We are in no condition to waste time on technicalities."[37]

One innovative notion explored at this time was the idea that southern ports could be closed down entirely by sinking old vessels laden with ballast in their ship channels. The navy acquired a few dozen old whaling ships and loaded them with granite from Massachusetts with the idea of sinking them in the Charleston ship channels. At best, however, this gambit kept the port closed for only a short time. The tidal currents and the pressure of the Gulf Stream soon swept away the sunken ships, and it was clear that an effective blockade could only be maintained the old-fashioned way: by placing warships manned by vigilant officers and men off the harbors.

Slowly the number of available warships increased. The return of vessels from overseas and the activation of vessels laid up in ordinary gave the nation some four score warships, about half of them steamers.

The ninety-day gunboats, all of them steamers, boosted the total to over a hundred. That was certainly a good start, but still a long way from the kind of force that would be needed to blockade a thirty-five-hundred-mile coastline. The shortfall was filled by purchasing existing merchant vessels and converting them to wartime use. Often such a conversion required little more than strengthening the ship's deck so that it could bear the weight of a few naval guns. These vessels might not be able to stand hull to hull with European warships, but they were more than adequate to enforce a blockade where their opponents would consist mainly of lightly armed privateers and unarmed merchantmen.

At first Lincoln hoped that the acquisition of appropriate vessels for this duty could be delegated to the various Navy Yard commandants. Two days after he declared the blockade, he asked Welles to order each of the commandants to "procure five staunch steamers" capable of carrying a single nine-inch pivot gun. They were to lease or "charter" these vessels for a period of three months. But shipowners were understandably reluctant to lease their ships to the government for war service, especially for only three months. Moreover, Navy Yard commandants, who were generally senior captains holding their positions as comfortable sinecures after a lifetime of sea service, were not necessarily good businessmen. Two things became clear almost at once: the government would have to buy ships rather than lease them, and this could best be accomplished by designating "a special & confidential agent" for the navy.[38]

The man Welles chose as the navy's purchasing agent was George D. Morgan. In one respect it was an inspired appointment, for Morgan was both honest and a savvy businessman. He was also Welles' brother-in-law. Though he proved to be active and efficient in procuring scores of ships at reasonable prices, especially considering the inflated wartime market, the appointment caused the administration one more political headache. As one suspicious constituent wrote to Lincoln: "It strikes me there is a mighty big cat in that meal tub." John P. Hale, the influential chairman of the Senate Naval Affairs Committee, seized on the disgraceful abandonment of the Norfolk Navy Yard and the fact that Welles' own brother-in-law was collecting a 2½ percent commission off each ship purchased to launch a public investigation of Welles' management of the department. Hale's motive was as much pecuniary as political: he was angered that Welles did not see fit to extend sufficient patronage to several of Hale's own clients, and he hoped to generate enough of a public outcry to compel Welles' resignation.[39]

There was little Welles could say in defense of the disaster at Norfolk, though he thought Hale's report about it was "factious, partisan, untruthful, unjust, and iniquitous." The charge of nepotism was harder to dismiss. Morgan had carte blanche to buy any vessel he deemed suitable, to do so without oversight, and to take a commission for himself in the process.* Clearly, such a broad mandate was subject to abuse, and even though Morgan served honestly and energetically, it provided administration enemies with a blunt instrument to assail the Navy Department. Overall, Morgan bought a total of eighty-nine vessels for the navy at a cost to the government of $3.5 million—a bargain at less than $40,000 per ship. Nevertheless, Morgan also pocketed commission fees of $70,000, and Hale made that the focus of his enquiry. Morgan was devastated that he caused the department embarrassment. "I cannot always buy as cheap as I could wish," he wrote apologetically to Welles from New York. "I only say I have done all in my power to buy cheap, [and] always have bought honestly."[40]

It worked to Morgan's advantage that affairs in Simon Cameron's Department of War during this same period were considerably worse. Cameron was simply overwhelmed by his new duties, and if affairs in the Navy Department sometimes seemed chaotic, they were a model of efficiency compared to Cameron's War Department, where government agents spent millions buying outdated muskets and thin cotton blankets at absurd prices, occasionally buying back supplies that the department had sold only weeks before. Nevertheless, Hale's enquiry put Morgan and Welles on the defensive. Morgan offered to step down and return all the commissions he had received. Characteristically, Welles would not hear of it, and he defended "the integrity, im-

---

*Morgan's commission of 2½ percent was in line with industry standards but was more than the 1½ percent that George Trenholm, the Confederate purchasing agent in England, accepted for his work.

partiality, fidelity, and capacity" of his kinsman before Congress. But it was Lincoln's response to the crisis that mattered. Morgan himself feared that "if Jack Hale should get a doubtful answer from the President he might get a vote of censure in the Senate." Instead Lincoln stood behind his secretary, and Hale's motion of censure failed by a vote of 31–5.[41]

The Navy Department survived Hale's investigation in part because Hale was unable to find any examples of actual abuse, but also because Lincoln stood staunchly behind his navy secretary, declaring publicly, "I am not aware that a dollar of the public funds, thus confided without authority of law to unofficial persons, was either lost or wasted." Of course, the president also defended Cameron's administration of the War Department, insisting that whatever errors had occurred belonged to the administration as a whole rather than to any one individual. The judgmental Welles believed Lincoln was absorbing the blame for Cameron's ineptitude. "President Lincoln never shunned any responsibility," Welles wrote, "and often declared that he, and not his cabinet, was in fault for errors imputed to them."[42]

Nevertheless, Lincoln saw that Cameron had become a liability. Even if the secretary of war was not crooked, as his detractors insisted, he was clearly overwhelmed by his job, and aware of that, Cameron sought to bolster his position by ingratiating himself with the radical wing of the Republican Party. In his December 1861 report, Cameron announced a new policy of enlisting and arming black soldiers without having discussed the issue with Lincoln or even notifying him. This Lincoln could not ignore, and almost at once he began planning Cameron's departure. For his part, Welles was gratified that Lincoln had supported him during the public quarrel with Hale. Indeed, Welles was becoming one of the stalwarts of the cabinet, and he confided to his diary that "the President . . . approved of my course, and was fully satisfied with it."[43]

By the end of the year, the navy boasted a total of 264 warships in commission, half of them converted merchantmen. From a single ship, the squadron off Charleston had grown to nine vessels, six of them steamers. Blockades had also been initiated at most of the South's other harbors, from Galveston, Texas, to Hampton Roads, Virginia. The blockade, if not yet thoroughly effective, was at least more than a fatuous assertion, and the offshore squadrons were on the road to becoming the "competent force" Lincoln had pledged in April.

WHILE WELLES BUILT A NAVY, General Scott assembled an army. As the number of ships rose dramatically through the spring and into the summer, so too did the number of regiments arriving in Washington and assigned to the force (not yet an army) that was gathering in northern Virginia. By July, as many as fifty thousand men were encamped in and about the capital. Their commander was thirty-three-year-old Major General Irvin McDowell, a six-foot-tall professional soldier who had spent a year at the leading French military schools and was Scott's choice as the best young field officer available. Like virtually every officer in the Civil War—on both sides—McDowell had been elevated to his new responsibilities with breathtaking speed. In April he had been a major; in July he was a brigadier general who commanded a force three times larger than any previous American army, albeit one composed almost entirely of green volunteers. He would have preferred to wait until he had a chance to drill and train his command before beginning an advance, but Lincoln felt the pressure of public expectations. The national flag had been insulted, the country's honor impugned. The public expected action, and Lincoln did not feel politically strong enough to resist it. Against Scott's advice, Lincoln ordered McDowell to begin an offensive in July.[44]

It was a disaster. McDowell's army marched out of its camps on July 16 and the battle opened two days later with some preliminary skirmishing along the banks of Bull Run north of Manassas. McDowell began his main effort in the predawn darkness of July 21, and by dinnertime that evening the news in Washington was that the battle was going well; the enemy had been forced back from Bull Run to Manassas Junction, though losses were said to be heavy. In a hopeful mood, Lincoln went for a carriage drive. When he returned, he went to Scott's headquarters, where he was handed a telegram from McDowell reporting a defeat. The army had panicked and fled when Confederate reinforcements had arrived. Even as he read the news, refugees from the broken army were straggling back toward Washington.

The defeat marked a turning point in Lincoln's administration. Though the president maintained his composure and told both Scott and McDowell that the defeat was not their fault ("my faith is unshaken," he told Scott), the news was a severe blow. Lincoln relied heavily on the advice of his experts: Seward in statecraft, Scott in military affairs, and Welles and Fox in naval matters. He had deferred to these experts even when he had doubts about their advice. Though he trusted his own instincts, he knew that he lacked expertise and for that reason was inclined to defer to expert authority. Now he began to question his faith in those experts. To be sure, Scott had advised against the advance to Manassas as premature, but the general's pre-battle bravado, and especially his lethargy and apparent confusion afterward, undermined Lincoln's confidence in Scott despite the reassuring words. Perhaps it was time for new leadership. The next day, Lincoln sent for Major General George McClellan, who had won a number of small victories in western Virginia.[45]

While McClellan made his way toward Washington, Lincoln sat down to write a memorandum, mostly to himself, about national strategy. In it, he listed the nine actions "suggested by the Bull Run defeat." At the top of the list was "1. Let the plan for making the Blockade effective be pushed forward with all possible dispatch." Most of the other items listed had to do with the security of specific sites, from Harpers Ferry to Fort Monroe. Lincoln put the memorandum in a drawer while he continued to think about it. He pulled it out again four days later and added two more items: seize Manassas Junction and mount "a joint movement from Cairo [Illinois] on Memphis, and from Cincinnati on East Tennessee." These three offensives, conducted simultaneously, would force the rebels to spread their forces across a broad front and allow the Union to take advantage of its numerical superiority. At the same time, the navy would tighten the blockade. The anaconda would begin to constrict.[46]

That July, however, the blockade seemed nearly as unorganized as the volunteer army that was fleeing back from Manassas. As ships were added to the blockading force, they steamed south to take up positions off southern ports, but there was little system or order to the deployment. To his friend Orville Browning, who had been appointed to replace the recently deceased Stephen A. Douglas as senator from Illinois, Lincoln expressed his fear that "we could not make the blockade of all the Ports effectual." In late June, Lincoln had asked Nicolay to collect data about "the number of men enlisted as soldiers or seamen" as well as "the number and description of War vessels and transports at present owned or chartered by the government." But it was clear that this was a project that should not be managed from the White House.[47]

In fact, a group of officers known as the Blockade Board or the Strategy Board had been meeting at the Smithsonian Institution for some weeks, and four days after Bull Run, Welles brought Fox to a cabinet meeting to report on their findings. In addition to advocating a reorganization of the blockade force, the principal thrust of their report was the absolute necessity of acquiring a few secure coaling stations on the enemy's coastline. It had been evident from the very first, Fox reported, that sailing vessels, despite their seakeeping capability, were ineffective on the blockade. Only steamships could perform the duties required of blockading vessels. But steamers had to be refueled regularly. Most steamships of the mid-nineteenth century burned a ton of coal for every five to seven miles of steaming. Moreover, when on station they had to keep steam up round the clock, burning precious coal even as they sat idle, for no one knew when a blockade runner might attempt to dash out of the harbor or appear over the horizon. With no coaling stations between Hampton Roads, Virginia, and Key West, Florida, some vessels used up their entire fuel supply merely getting to and from their blockading stations. The only solution to this unacceptable circumstance was to establish coaling stations somewhere on the enemy coastline. Fox told the president that the navy wanted to seize Bull's Bay in South Carolina and Fernandina in Florida with a combined army-navy force. It would be the nation's largest amphibious operation since the landing at Veracruz in the Mexican War, and Welles and Fox already had a man in mind for the command, the man who had become the dominant voice on the Strategy Board: Captain Samuel Francis Du Pont.[48]

Du Pont came with a peerless pedigree. The first to be born in the United States of this family of French émigrés, he was the son of Victor-Marie du Pont, who had founded a woolen mill in Delaware, and the nephew of Eleuthère Irénée du Pont, who founded a gunpowder factory (which later became the du Pont chemical company) across the Brandywine River from his brother's mill. Both his father and his uncle had been friends of Thomas Jefferson, the Francophile third

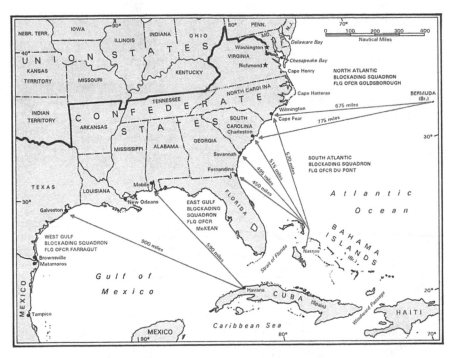

UNION BLOCKADING SQUADRONS. Map by Bill Clipson, reprinted with permission from *The Naval Institute Historical Atlas of the U.S. Navy* by Craig L. Symonds, © 1995.

president. That connection had secured young Frank Du Pont a midshipman's appointment at the age of eleven. By 1861 he had spent forty-six years in uniform. Moreover, Du Pont had long been the leader of a group of so-called progressive officers who worked hard to replace the navy's traditional system of promotion by seniority with a new system that allowed "efficient" officers to be promoted on the basis of merit. He seemed to have triumphed in 1855 when a so-called Efficiency Board reported the names of 201 officers who were to be eased out—placed on a reserved list, furloughed, or dismissed entirely—to make room for younger and more promising officers. The subsequent outcry from the congressional advocates of many of those who were on the list forced a reconsideration, and the reform proved in the end to be less than revolutionary.[49]

Du Pont was therefore thrilled when the frantic mobilization effort after Fort Sumter swept away most of the impediments to progress and brought reform almost overnight. For most of his professional life, he had butted his head against a bureaucracy headed by sexagenarian captains who seldom went to sea but who nevertheless knew exactly how things should be done. Now there was "much less stickling with forms and red tape." To a friend he wrote that the Navy Department, "hitherto the most rickety and stupid of all of them, . . . has a vitality and energy never seen there before." But energy without system is directionless. Within a week he was complaining that "the want of system is disheartening."[50]

It was precisely to instill system to the mobilization effort that Fox had called Du Pont to Washington. In a series of meetings in July and August, at about the same time that McClellan was emerging as the nation's new hope in the land war, Du Pont emerged as the dominant voice not only on the Strategy Board but in the navy itself. At age fifty-eight, Du Pont was more than two decades older than McClellan, but his work on the Strategy Board convinced Welles and Fox that just as McClellan had the youthful drive and enthusiasm to replace the superannuated Scott, Du Pont was the man needed to replace Commodore Stringham, who had begun to disappoint Welles as too hidebound for the emergency. Like McClellan, Du Pont was surprised to find himself soaring so quickly to heights of responsibility that previously he had only dreamed of. The same week that McClellan wrote to his wife that "by some strange operation of magic I seem to have become the power of the land," Du Pont was writing his own wife that due to "a curious and natural sequence of things . . . I find myself suddenly thrown up in connection with the most important armament ever made in this country."[51]

Nor was the timing of their elevation the only connection between these two men. Du Pont greatly admired McClellan, and like him, he was less than overwhelmed by Lincoln. His first impression of the new president was that he was "the ugliest man I had ever seen," though he later decided that Lincoln was "younger and finer looking than his portraits." He thought the president's inaugural address had been a good one but was disappointed that Lincoln had not followed it up immediately with more vigorous action. He wrote a friend that Lincoln was "evidently more of a thinker than an actor." He even wondered if Lincoln was in control of the government, and like many others, he suspected that Seward was actually pulling the strings. He was unimpressed with the bungled expedition to Fort Sumter, concluding (correctly) that it "was gotten up in too much hurry." Nor was the judgmental Du Pont impressed by Lincoln's cabinet. "The Cabinet is not much," he wrote to a fellow officer, "Seward being the ablest man and the most moderate." As for Welles, Du Pont declared that "we have the worst of the pack." With unbecoming sarcasm, he wrote another friend that the best thing he could say about the new navy secretary was that when he had been in charge of the Bureau of Clothing and Supply, he "once made a remarkable contract for *cheese.*"[52]

Lincoln cared little what Du Pont may have thought of him or his cabinet; he was concerned more with his efficiency as an officer. Since Welles, and especially Fox, assured him that Du Pont was the right man to lead the Union's first great amphibious expedition, Lincoln was satisfied. He was pleased, too, by the clarity and detail of Du Pont's plan to seize coaling stations on the southern coast, and he readily accepted the recommendation that Du Pont have the naval command, with Brigadier General Thomas W. Sherman acting as his army counterpart.* The co-commanders would gather their force in New York, stop at Hampton Roads to consolidate, then proceed down the coast to South Carolina to begin paying that state what Lincoln called "the little debt we are owing her." The expedition would depart New York sometime in early August.[53]

Alas, both services had trouble gathering the necessary force. Du Pont was frustrated that every time he had a ship ready for service, Welles whisked it away for some other duty. With some of those ships, Stringham in August captured two small forts at Hatteras Inlet guarding the entrance to Pamlico Sound, but while that was a bracing little victory, it necessarily postponed the departure of Du Pont's expedition. Similarly, it seemed to Sherman that whenever he had a regiment ready, it was sent to Washington to enlarge McClellan's ever-growing army. Fox was distressed that the fine summer weather was slipping away, and he urged Du Pont to "give things an impetus." Du Pont paid a visit to McClellan to see if he could move things along. It was a meeting of

---

*He is often called "the other Sherman," to distinguish him from the more famous William T. Sherman. Many contemporaries, and some historians, occasionally made the error of referring to the men as brothers, though in fact they were not related.

mutual admirers. "I was captivated," Du Pont wrote afterward to his friend and political mentor Henry Winter Davis, "there is no other word for it." McClellan was equally smitten, telling Du Pont that if he had known who was waiting to see him, he would have rid himself of his "other company," which happened to be Lincoln and Seward. Du Pont basked in his close association with the "Young Napoleon," though in the long run it was an association that would not work to his benefit.[54]

Prodded by Fox, Welles made a bit of a stink in the cabinet about all the delays, and it prompted Lincoln to write Scott a peremptory order that Du Pont's expedition "is in no wise to be abandoned, but must be ready to move by the first of, or very early in October. Let all preparations go forward accordingly."[55] Of course, Lincoln was already experienced enough to know that simply insisting that things happen was no guarantee of action. The principal difficulty was that there was no guiding hand controlling both the army and navy elements of the operation. As the expedition to Fort Sumter had demonstrated, there was no protocol in the American military for the command of a combined force. Army officers could not give orders to the navy, and navy officers could not command the army; there was no individual below the president himself who had joint command of both services. When September passed and the expedition had still not departed, Lincoln saw the need to bring all the parties together. He ordered a meeting for October 1 at Seward's home, across from the White House, where Lincoln often went to discuss war issues. Alas, that meeting provided a case study of the problems inherent in joint, or combined, operations in 1861.*

Lincoln was already settled in Seward's parlor when Fox arrived with Du Pont. Substantive discussion could not begin, however, until Du Pont's army counterparts could be found, so Fox and Du Pont sat down with the president and the secretary of state to wait. Du Pont was fascinated by the dynamic in the room. Seward, acting as host, offered

---

*In modern parlance, joint operations are those involving more than one branch of the U.S. military (as in the Joint Chiefs of Staff), while combined operations are those involving one or more foreign allies. But in the nineteenth century, combined operations generally referred to army-navy expeditions.

Fox a cigar, and the two men puffed away happily. Du Pont noted that although the smoke seemed to go directly into Lincoln's face, the president did not object or even move his chair. It was some time before anyone else could be rounded up, and in exasperation Seward blurted out, "There's nobody nowhere tonight!" Finally Cameron appeared, followed not long afterward by Thomas W. Sherman. Sherman, as it happened, had gone to bed, and when a messenger had arrived, he had at first refused to get up until he was told that the president wanted to see him.[56]

Even after everyone was on hand, confusion dominated as the command team discussed which troops were supposed to go where. Some regiments that had been intended for the Du Pont–Sherman expedition had been sent instead to Ambrose Burnside, who had been charged with clearing the Potomac of rebel batteries. Cameron mentioned that he understood this was a special project of the president's, but Lincoln declared that he had never heard of it. Cameron then suggested that perhaps Seward had initiated it, adding the barb that this seemed likely since Seward "regulated all the business of all the departments." At this, the normally patient Lincoln "got his dander up a little" and demanded to know what was going on. Both Cameron and Seward claimed to be ignorant of the Burnside expedition. Finally someone found a memo "from someone on McClellan's staff" that explained it. One of Burnside's Rhode Island regiments intended for Washington had been ordered back to New York on the assumption that it was to be part of the Du Pont–Sherman expedition, when in fact it was intended for the Chesapeake—a circumstance eerily reminiscent of the confusion that had surrounded the *Powhatan* during the Fort Sumter crisis. Lincoln shook his head and muttered that if his memory was as treacherous as that, perhaps he should simply go back to Illinois.

The discussion of Burnside's operation lasted for some time, and finally, at Du Pont's suggestion, Cameron declared that perhaps they should deal with one issue at a time and the conversation returned to the project at hand. "Just then," Du Pont recalled, "McClellan walks in with a lighted cigar, bows respectfully, and takes a seat." McClellan affected the air of being bemused by the evident lack of direction in this council of war, almost as if this was what one should expect when amateurs got together to plan a campaign. Only now, at the last minute, was the target of the expedition changed from Bull's Bay to Port Royal, a more commodious anchorage halfway between Charleston and Savannah. Lincoln began to wonder if the expedition was even feasible, since there was so much evident confusion, and he remarked, too, that "it would cost so much money." Du Pont thought briefly that after all the effort he had put into the expedition, it might now be called off altogether. In the end, however, McClellan agreed to supply the manpower as long as Lincoln and Cameron promised him new regiments to make up the loss. After all, he reminded the group, he had only 114,000 men to defend the capital. Nevertheless, he pledged to commit 9,000 men from the Washington garrison along with another 5,000 men still in New York. They would embark in twenty troop transports escorted by twenty men-of-war. The two groups would rendezvous in Hampton Roads for the push southward. With all that finally decided, the civilian authorities declared that the expedition for Port Royal would leave in four days. Four days! A moment before, Du Pont had feared that there would be no expedition at all; now he feared there would not be enough time to put all the pieces together.

One final problem that had to be solved was rank. Once the expedition departed, Du Pont would command the ships and Sherman the soldiers, but who would be in overall command of the expedition? As a navy captain, Du Pont bore the highest rank then available in the sea service, but officially a navy captain was the equivalent of an army colonel, and Sherman was a brigadier general. It was Fox who suggested the solution, and four days later, Lincoln issued an order creating the rank of navy "flag officer," declaring that "Flag Officers of the United States Navy . . . will rank with Major Generals of the United States Army." This made Du Pont senior to Sherman, though Welles pointedly reminded him that "no officer of the Army or Navy, whatsoever may be his rank, can assume any direct command, independent of consent, over an officer of the other service." Welles declared that the president expected Du Pont and Sherman to display "the most cordial and effectual cooperation." Scott sent nearly identical orders to Sherman.[57]

When Sherman came on board Du Pont's flagship, the *Wabash*, Du Pont did his best to get in the spirit of things by saluting him, a gesture the general appreciated. In reality, however, Du Pont did not think much of Sherman or his troops. "Soldiers and marines are the most helpless people I ever saw," he confided to his wife. He noted that Sherman was positively agog at the fine order and discipline on board the navy ships, lamenting that he had "whole regiments who do not know how to shoulder a musket let alone firing one."[58]

Du Pont's warships left New York on October 16 and arrived in Hampton Roads two days later. During the ensuing week, other vessels dropped anchor in the roadstead until there were more than seventy ships of all types: steam warships, sailing vessels, troop transports, and coal ships—seventy-eight in all—looking, Du Pont thought, like "a city on the waters." A week later, the entire armada made its way out of the roadstead and into the Atlantic. For almost two weeks, Lincoln heard no more about it, and he continued with his routine duties, visiting McClellan at his headquarters, driving out to the Washington Navy Yard to inspect a battery of repeating guns, and spending several evenings at Seward's house. On November 1, he accepted the resignation of General Scott as the army's commander in chief and immediately bestowed that title on McClellan. The president reminded the young general that exercising the overall command of all Union armies in addition to his command of the Army of the Potomac would "entail a vast labor," but McClellan reassured him, saying, "I can do it all."[59]

The next day the steamer *Belvedere* limped back into Hampton Roads with her upper works badly damaged and with twelve dead horses on board. Its captain reported that the fleet had been off Cape Fear, North Carolina, when a terrible storm "burst upon it." The papers reported that a storm "had fallen with great fury upon the great naval expedition . . . scattering the vessels in every direction." There was nothing Lincoln could do except wait and hope for the best. Would it be a naval Bull Run? Could the country stand another such disappointment after having its hopes raised? Finally, on November 9, word arrived by telegraph from Hampton Roads that Du Pont had achieved a stunning success.[60]

The fleet had, in fact, been scattered by the Atlantic gale, but it had slowly reassembled at Port Royal, and on November 7, Du Pont's steam warships had entered the roadstead and pounded the Confederate forts there so badly that the Confederates evacuated them and gave up the roadstead even without an army landing. It was spectacular news. This was the first major victory of the war by either the army or the navy, and it did much to raise the gloom that had settled on the capital since Bull Run. Du Pont's victory not only established a secure base and coaling station for the South Atlantic Blockading Squadron but also suggested that steam warships firing explosive shells were more than a match for hastily erected shore fortifications. Ships, it seemed, could defeat forts after all. Welles issued a general order instructing every navy command to fire a national salute, and he sent Du Pont his "heartfelt congratulations and thanks of the government" for his "brilliant success." Lincoln, too, was thrilled by the victory in Port Royal. The navy had not let him down, and he recommended that Congress offer Du Pont a vote of thanks, the highest military honor available. Then, almost in the same moment, he learned of another naval triumph, unplanned and unlooked for, with far-reaching consequences.[61]

3

"No Affront to the British Flag"

Lincoln and the *Trent* Affair

ON NOVEMBER 9, 1861, while Du Pont was writing Fox that his success at Port Royal was "more complete and more brilliant than I ever could have believed," the twelve-gun sloop-of-war *San Jacinto* was cruising slowly in the Old Bahama Channel, off the north coast of Cuba, where the deep water south of the Great Bahama Bank narrowed to a width of less than fifteen miles.[1] Named for the battle that had secured the independence of Texas in 1836, the *San Jacinto* was a fifteen-year-old screw steamer that had been ordered to take part in Du Pont's attack on Port Royal. Instead, thanks to its capricious captain, on the day of that battle it was more than six hundred miles south of Port Royal lying in wait for quite another prize. The captain of the *San Jacinto* was Charles Wilkes, whose clean-shaven face and close-cropped hair were distinctly unfashionable in that hirsute era. He had dark, piercing eyes above a long nose and a firm mouth, and his face routinely wore a confident, even challenging expression that bespoke his complete comfort with the exercise of authority. Wilkes had guided his vessel to this precise location for a particular purpose. He knew that any vessel bound from Havana to St. Thomas would have to pass this way, and he was anticipating the arrival of the British packet steamer *Trent*, making its regular run from Mexico to St. Thomas via Havana.[2]

Wilkes was something of a maverick in the U.S. Navy. If Du Pont was the navy's rising star, Wilkes was its Peck's Bad Boy. He had achieved notoriety twenty years earlier as a relatively young lieutenant while in command of what became known as the Great United States Exploring Expedition. The command of a five-ship squadron bound on a global circumnavigation ordinarily would have gone to a more senior officer, but none found it attractive. The expedition was scientific rather than military in its objective, the cruise would be burdened by a gaggle of scientists and their equipment, and it was certain to keep its commander away from home and hearth for several years. After five navy captains declined it, the department had finally offered the command to Wilkes.

Ordered to chart the islands of the Great South Sea (the Pacific) and to explore the edge of the southern ice pack to determine if the glaciers and ice floes hid solid land, perhaps even another continent, Wilkes led his squadron on a four-year, round-the-world cruise that achieved a number of scientific and geographic successes, including confirmation of the existence of Antarctica (where Wilkes Land is named for him). At the same time, however, the cruise exposed Wilkes' domineering, even tyrannical style of command. Though the ostensible purpose of the voyage was to cover as much area as possible in the hope of making new discoveries, Wilkes insisted that the vessels sail in a compact line ahead so that he could maintain strict control over them. He bullied his subordinate officers mercilessly (and unnecessarily), earning their sullen hatred. When he became aware that the enlistment terms of some of his sailors and marines were near expiration, he badgered them to reenlist. When they declined, he took more vigorous action: he had the marines flogged, and he threatened to abandon the sailors on a deserted island.[3]

The fallout from all this was a series of lengthy courts-martial after the return of the expedition in 1842, and a legacy of bitterness and resentment that generated years of unprofessional bickering within the navy. Throughout it all, Wilkes was unapologetic, even arrogant. He believed that he had been singularly virtuous in all his actions and that his enemies were driven solely by bitterness and jealousy. When the court failed to find him guilty, he gloated: "I had thus been set upon by all the branches of the Navy Department from the Secretary down and had triumphed over each and every one of them."[4]

Wilkes' uncooperative belligerence kept him from obtaining another command. After spending several years overseeing the publication of a five-volume narrative of the expedition (during which he feuded with everyone from the typesetters to the lithographers), Wilkes spent most of the 1850s traveling independently or filling undemanding shore duties; in April 1861 when the war began, he was chairman of the Lighthouse Board. The war revived his career. The unprecedented expansion of the navy and the consequent need for experienced officers encouraged Wilkes to expect a squadron or fleet command. Instead, Welles ordered him to bring the steamer *San Jacinto*, then on the African station, to Philadelphia to join the concentration of forces for Du Pont's expedition to Port Royal. Though such an assignment appeared straightforward, it did not take into consideration Wilkes' tendency to interpret orders as he saw fit.

Wilkes dutifully reported on board the *San Jacinto* at Fernando Po, off Equatorial Guinea, and took command, but rather than leave at once for the American East Coast, he cruised the eastern Atlantic for nearly a month, hoping to find and capture some rebel privateers. When that proved fruitless, he headed west across the Atlantic, but not for Philadelphia to join Du Pont. Instead, he sailed for the Caribbean, where he presumed the pickings would be better. At the British Cayman Islands, south of Cuba, he learned that a Confederate raider, the CSS *Sumter*, had been in that same harbor only a few days before.* The residents, many of them sympathetic with the Confederate cause, boasted of the recent exploits of the rebel cruiser, which for Wilkes was like waving a red flag before a bull. Determined to find the *Sumter*, he headed north for the coast of Cuba.[5]

Wilkes did not find the *Sumter*, but at Cienfuegos, on the south coast of Cuba, he encountered another piece of information pregnant with opportunity. He learned that the designated Confederate emissaries to England and France, James Murray Mason of Virginia and John Slidell of Louisiana, had successfully run through the blockade off

---

*In his *Autobiography*, Wilkes skips over his month-long cruise in the eastern Atlantic as well as his decision to head for the Caribbean instead of Philadelphia. He claimed that he stopped at the Caymans because his crew needed fresh fruit. Only then, he insists, did he decide to violate orders by searching for the *Sumter*.

Charleston several weeks before and had arrived in Havana en route to their diplomatic posts in London and Paris. Here was a prospect even more promising than the capture of the *Sumter*. He decided at once to find them and take them prisoner. Wilkes filled the *San Jacinto* up with coal and put to sea, steaming around Cape San Antonio at Cuba's western tip to arrive in Havana on the last day of October, where the news about Mason and Slidell was confirmed by the U.S. minister, Robert W. Shufeldt. Shufeldt told Wilkes that the rebel diplomats were indeed in Havana and that they had booked passage on the British steamer *Trent*, due to depart in a few days on its regular run to St. Thomas. From there, presumably, the rebel commissioners would book passage for England. Wilkes made a quick trip to Key West, where he took on board some additional furniture and bedding suitable for his anticipated prisoners, whom he intended to treat as distinguished guests, then he headed for the Old Bahama Channel.[6]

Wilkes shared his intentions only with his executive officer, Donald Fairfax, who was more than a little alarmed. The *Trent*, after all, was a British-flag vessel that had committed no transgression; it could not be accused of trying to run the blockade, since it had come nowhere close to American waters. Moreover, it was not just a British registered vessel; it was a mail packet on a regularly scheduled transit in international waters from one neutral port to another, which gave it a quasi-official character. Since international law held that ships at sea carried their nationality with them, stopping the *Trent* on the high seas and removing some of its passengers was tantamount to a violation of British sovereignty. The United States had gone to war with England in 1812, in part at least, in protest of exactly this kind of behavior. But Fairfax's arguments made no impression on his commander, and once Wilkes made it clear that he intended to proceed nonetheless, Fairfax capitulated.[7]

A few minutes before noon on November 9, the lookout at the masthead of the *San Jacinto* hailed the deck to report a thin column of smoke on the western horizon, the unmistakable sign of an approaching steamer, and Wilkes called his officers to his cabin to tell them of his plans. Anticipating that some of them might object more strongly than Fairfax had done, he placed several of them under arrest as a precaution and a warning. As the unarmed *Trent* approached, its side paddlewheels churning the blue water of the Caribbean, Wilkes ordered the crew to quarters. Once the *Trent* was within easy range, he ordered a shot fired across her bow. The *Trent* responded by hoisting English colors and continued on her way. Wilkes then ordered the gun crew to fire a shell across her bow. The explosion of the shell brought the *Trent* to a stop, and its astonished captain angrily shouted through a speaking trumpet: "What do you mean by heaving my vessel to in this manner?" Wilkes called back that he was sending a boat.[8]

Fairfax led the boarding party, and to ensure there was no bungling, Wilkes gave him written orders. He was to demand papers from the *Trent*'s captain, including a list of her passengers, and if Mason and Slidell were on board, Fairfax was to arrest them, along with their secretaries, and bring them to the *San Jacinto*. He was then to "take possession of her [the *Trent*] as a prize." Within a few minutes, Fairfax was alongside the *Trent* in the *San Jacinto*'s first cutter. He had two other officers with him, plus the boat's crew of eight, though to minimize the confrontational character of his visit, he told the crew to wait in the cutter while he talked to the captain of the *Trent*. Despite Wilkes' orders, Fairfax had privately resolved "not to do anything . . . which would necessitate my taking her as a prize."[9] It turned out to be a crucial decision.

Upon reaching the deck of the *Trent*, Fairfax introduced himself and asked the captain, James Moir, to produce the ship's passenger list. Moir politely but firmly refused. Fairfax then declared that he believed that James Mason and John Slidell were on board along with their secretaries, George Eustis and James McFarland. Moir was in the process of repeating his refusal to provide a passenger list when Slidell, overhearing Fairfax's demand, came forward and introduced himself. John Slidell was an experienced and savvy politician. Among his contemporaries, he was considered a master of political maneuver. As one put it, he "would conspire with the mice against the cat." It may well be that Slidell saw at once that he could do more for his cause by provoking a confrontation on the high seas between the United States and Britain than he could as Confederate minister to Paris. Mrs. Slidell subsequently remarked to Fairfax that this confrontation was "the very thing" that the Confederates had been hoping for: "something to arouse England." Or it may simply have been that Slidell believed his presence on a British-flag vessel protected him. In either case, his appearance obviated the need for a passenger list or a search of the vessel, and it took Moir out of the conversation.[10]

Soon Mason and the two secretaries joined Slidell, and Fairfax told them that he was under orders to arrest all four men and take them on board the *San Jacinto*. At that, there were loud comments and protests—not from the four men concerned but from the other passengers on deck who were within hearing distance. "Did you ever hear of such an outrage?" one expostulated. "These Yankees will have to pay well for this," another declared. The British mail agent on board, a retired Royal Navy officer named Richard Williams, was particularly outraged, and declared that this highhandedness would cause the British fleet to "raise the blockade in twenty days." The sound of this dispute reached the ears of the men Fairfax had left behind in the cutter, and they clambered on board the *Trent* to back up their lieutenant. For a dangerous moment or two, things threatened to get out of hand, but Fairfax squelched it by ordering the men back into the cutter.[11]

When Mason and Slidell refused to come along quietly, and insisted that they would "yield only to force," Fairfax called for the second cutter from the *San Jacinto*. It brought another dozen armed men, including six marines whom Fairfax stationed on the deck of the *Trent*, provoking more angry murmurs from the passengers. ("Marines on board!" one sputtered. "Why this looks devilish like mutiny!") Fairfax asked one more time if Mason and Slidell would accompany him voluntarily, but they insisted that Fairfax must use force—or at least symbolic force. Fairfax then took hold of Mason's shoulder and told Third Assistant Engineer George Hall to "lay hands on him." Hall seized Mason by the collar and the two American officers walked the sixty-three-year-old Virginian over to the ship's side, where he stepped down into the cutter.[12]

While this was going on, the sixty-eight-year-old Slidell, intent on dramatizing the confrontation as much as possible, retreated to the ship's main cabin. When Fairfax followed him, he was greeted by a storm of "disagreeable and contemptuous noises" from the other passengers in the cabin. Worried that Fairfax might have his hands full, the Marine commander, Lieutenant James Greer, ordered his half dozen men into the cabin as well. As they rushed in with bayonets fixed, the alarmed passengers shrank back. This led to subsequent claims in the British press that armed U.S. marines had threatened "defenseless women and children." Another assertion was that Fairfax made inappropriate advances toward Slidell's seventeen-year-old daughter. Fairfax denied it. What had happened, he explained, was that the young woman had stood defiantly in the cabin's doorway to shield her father. When the *Trent* rocked unexpectedly, she fell against him and he caught her to keep her from falling.* Fairfax ordered the marines out of the cabin, but he and two other officers took hold of Slidell as they had Mason and walked him out to the main deck and over to the cutter, which he entered grudgingly but without violence. The two secretaries went more quietly. Fairfax invited the men's wives to accompany their husbands, but they declined.[13]

Once all four captives were on board the *San Jacinto*, Fairfax reported to Wilkes that he had not taken the *Trent* as a prize, despite the instructions to do so. His excuse was that it was still possible that the *San Jacinto* could join Du Pont's expedition, and putting a prize crew on the *Trent* would deplete the ship's manpower just before a battle. Moreover, the seizure of the ship would seriously inconvenience the innocent passengers on board and delay delivery of the mails. Thus there were both practical and humanitarian reasons not to take the *Trent* as a prize. It was risky of Fairfax thus to defy his commander's direct order—especially such a commander as Charles Wilkes—but Wilkes received the news calmly. "Inasmuch as you have not taken her, you will let her go." Perhaps breathing a sigh of relief, Fairfax returned to the *Trent* to tell Muir that "he might proceed on his voyage." The two ships then separated, the *Trent* continuing eastward toward St. Thomas and the *San Jacinto* heading westward and northward for the American coast.[14]

WILKES' SEIZURE OF MASON AND SLIDELL from the *Trent* presented Lincoln with the most serious foreign policy crisis of his administration, and in his management of that crisis, his unwillingness to disappoint

---

*It is revealing to consider Wilkes' reaction to this story. In a passage that would certainly be considered politically incorrect today, he wrote in his *Autobiography* that "Fairfax was a very good looking fellow, and the girl being pretty, it was a fair reward for his trouble of making the search to have taken a kiss."

the public enthusiasm very nearly led him to a critical misstep. Eager for good news, sensitive to the pulse of public opinion, and reassured by several legal experts that Wilkes had behaved properly, the president initially succumbed to the popular celebration of what looked to almost everyone like another great success by the navy. Consequently, instead of moving proactively in anticipation of difficulties, Lincoln adopted a wait-and-see policy. Politically sensitive as he was, he may have surmised that the initial effusion of support for Wilkes would moderate over time and allow him to resolve the crisis amicably without directly opposing the public will. If so, he played his cards close to his chest and maintained the bluff until the very last moment.

Lincoln certainly knew that it was essential to keep the South isolated—that, after all, was one of the primary goals of his blockade strategy. From the very outset of the war, it was evident that the self-styled Confederacy would seek to gain foreign recognition and support from Britain, France, or both. Southerners conceived of their war as a second American Revolution, and they were aware that the original thirteen colonies had won their independence in no small part because of aid from the French. Moreover, southerners believed as a matter of faith that their agricultural products, especially cotton, made them indispensable to Britain. The southern decision to embargo cotton exports had been motivated by the belief that an England starving for cotton would send its fleet across the Atlantic to raise the blockade in order to have continued access to southern "white gold." From the first days of its existence, therefore, the Confederate government sought to induce Britain into concluding an alliance.

Concerned about that possibility, Seward urged taking a firm line with the British. It was a popular position in a nation that had fought two wars with Britain, one of them within the living memory of many citizens. Seward had hand-picked Charles Francis Adams as the American ambassador to the Court of St. James, and he had drafted the instructions to guide him in his dealings with the British government. Seward told Adams that he was to emphasize that the United States had "a clear right to suppress insurrection," and because a blockade was "a natural means to that end," the United States expected that the blockade would "be respected by Great Britain." Even more pointedly, Seward wanted Adams to warn the British that if they acknowledged the existence of the Confederacy in any way, either by referring to it publicly as a separate government or receiving its official representatives, "no one of these proceedings will be borne." The implication of that phrase was ominous, and deliberately so. Seward was deliberately provocative in writing that in response to any interference by Britain "we from that hour shall cease to be friends and become once more, as we have twice before been forced to be, enemies of Great Britain."[15]

Lincoln found Seward's letter of instruction to Adams unnecessarily confrontational. Perhaps he remembered Seward's memo during the Fort Sumter crisis about deliberately provoking war with one or more of the European powers, or perhaps he simply saw little benefit in twisting the British lion's tail. He had told Seward back in March that he intended him to have full management of foreign relations, "of which I know so little, and with which I reckon you are familiar." Nevertheless, he now sought to mute some of Seward's more belligerent passages. Rather than declare that British actions would "not be borne," he changed the passage to read merely that they would not "pass unnoticed." As for the threat that British transgression would lead to war, he cut that passage altogether.[16]

Despite Lincoln's efforts, Seward's letter of instruction retained a distinctly bellicose tone, and when it arrived in London, Adams was horrified. His son Henry, who acted as the legation secretary, wrote privately to his brother that it was a "crazy dispatch" and asserted that "if the Chief [their father] had obeyed it literally, he would have made a war in five minutes." Seward's note confirmed Henry's suspicions— shared by many Englishmen—that the secretary of state was still looking for an excuse to go to war with England in order "to divert the Public excitement to a Foreign Quarrel."[17]

Despite Seward's bull-in-a-china-shop diplomacy, British interference in the war on behalf of the Confederacy was extremely unlikely. To be sure, some British leaders saw a possible benefit from the division of its transatlantic competitor into two rival governments, but there was no getting past the slavery issue. For more than a generation, the British had taken the lead in the suppression of slavery and especially the international slave trade. So passionate were British voters on this issue that they were willing to suffer some economic privation if it meant the eradication of American slavery. Consequently, the notion of Britain coming to the aid of a slaveholding republic was no more than a fond but desperate hope of Confederate partisans. Even before Seward's confrontational letter of instruction arrived in London, Her Majesty's government had issued a proclamation of neutrality. While the proclamation did acknowledge the Confederacy as a belligerent, it also warned British subjects against any violation of the Union blockade, even though a blockade barely existed at that time except in name. A few hard-liners in the Lincoln administration were disappointed, but it was the best the North could reasonably hope for, and by September Henry Adams was reporting to his brother that "England has behaved very well. The Southerners were refused recognition and we are no longer uneasy about the blockade." By November, Anglo-American relations had settled into an amicable neutrality—until Wilkes' seizure of Mason and Slidell overturned the apple cart.[18]

LINCOLN FIRST LEARNED of Wilkes' act on November 15 when a telegram arrived from Hampton Roads, where the *San Jacinto*, with Mason and Slidell still on board, had dropped anchor after a short visit to the blockading fleet off Charleston. A public still basking in the good news from Port Royal indulged in another round of national celebration and self-congratulation. Though several of Lincoln's admirers claimed later that the president "at once recognized the dangers and complications that might grow out of the occurrence," most contemporary evidence suggests that Lincoln initially joined in the popular mood. After months of waiting to hear from McClellan that the army was at last ready to move and getting only excuses in reply, it was bracing to hear from someone who, as Charles F. Adams put it, "would do, taking the responsibility of the doing." For a week the papers in Washington and across the North sang the praises of the gallant Captain Wilkes and editorially snapped their fingers at the thought that the British might do anything about it. As the reporter for the *New York Herald* put it, "The arrival of the news . . . completely electrified the lethargic City of Magnificent Distances." While not entirely swept up in the celebration, Lincoln was reluctant to throw cold water on the public mood; there had been so little good news lately.[19]

Most of Lincoln's cabinet shared in the popular enthusiasm, with the single and notable exception of Montgomery Blair. Virtually alone,

Blair argued that the seizure violated America's own long-standing policy on sovereign rights at sea. He was sure that in the end the United States would be forced to release Mason and Slidell and apologize to England. He urged the administration to preempt the inevitable British protest by releasing the prisoners immediately. But in the heady rush of events, such caviling was unwelcome, and Blair's words of caution were overwhelmed by enthusiasm from everyone else. Seward was "jubilant" and "made no effort to conceal his gratification." Welles, ordinarily inclined to be skeptical whenever Seward was "jubilant," basked in the glow of praise for the navy's recent successes, writing his son that "the capture of Mason and Slidell created a sensation almost equal to the taking of Port Royal, and possibly great results may grow out of it." He was right, but not in the way he meant.[20]

If Lincoln had any doubts about Wilkes' act, they centered on its legality, but legal experts all across the North assured him that Wilkes had behaved correctly. Theophilus Parsons, the Dane Professor of Law at Harvard, opined, "I am just as certain that Wilkes had a legal right to take Mason and Slidell from the *Trent*, as I am that our Government has a legal right to blockade the port of Charleston." Of course, at that time the Supreme Court had yet to rule on the legality of the blockade of Charleston. Another authority was Caleb Cushing, who had been Buchanan's attorney general, and who now declared that "the act of Captain Wilkes was one which any and every self-respecting nation must and would have done by its own sovereign right and power." Cushing's opinion, like that of many others, was influenced not only by nationalist enthusiasm but also by anti-British sentiment. Cushing declared that by acknowledging Confederate belligerency, Britain had "taken a step so offensive to our dignity, if not our rights," that it must accept the consequences "as the necessary incidents of her neutrality." In short, Wilkes' violation of British sovereignty was justified because Britain had been insufficiently supportive of the Union cause. Others, such as Richard Henry Dana, the U.S. attorney for Massachusetts, went even further, arguing that the United States could ignore any protests from John Bull because the newly expanded U.S. Navy "could blow him out of the water."[21]

This combination of sanctimoniousness and belligerence dominated the public mood. After Wilkes delivered his prisoners to Fort Warren in

Boston Harbor as instructed, Boston rolled out the red carpet for him. He was feted at a variety of public events, first at a reception in Faneuil Hall, that cradle of American democracy, and then at a celebratory dinner attended by two hundred admirers. The combination of widespread public support, the self-congratulatory mood of his cabinet members, and the assurances of the legal experts convinced Lincoln to suppress his doubts and join in the general celebration. On November 19, the *New York Herald* reported that the president had "declared emphatically" that the prisoners "should not be surrendered by this government, even if their detention should cost a war with Great Britain."[22]

If Lincoln did, in fact, make such a declaration, he was less confident than the experts that Wilkes had behaved in accordance with established maritime law. Sometime that week (the date is uncertain) he wandered into Edward Bates' office and, after folding his long frame into the guest chair, told his attorney general, "I am not getting much sleep out of the exploit of Wilkes, and I suppose we must look up the law of the case." Like the rest of the cabinet (save Blair), Bates had been enthusiastic about the capture of the rebel ministers and assured Lincoln that "the law of Nations is clear upon the point." Not only did Wilkes have a right to seize the men, Bates declared, he had a right to seize the ship as well. But that was the problem—Wilkes had been selective in what he had taken. By taking four men off the ship and declaring them to be contraband, he had acted not only as a naval officer but also as a prize court. Later, Wilkes offered the explanation that because Mason and Slidell carried information in their heads, they constituted the "embodiment of dispatches" and thus fulfilled the definition of contraband materials. Creative as that was, it did not resolve the legal problem, for it was no part of a captain's job to decide what was contraband on board a neutral vessel. His proper course would have been to take the ship as a prize and send it into a prize court, where judges would decide what was contraband and what was not. Lincoln told Bates that "I am not much of a prize lawyer, but it seems to me pretty clear that if Wilkes saw fit to make that capture on the high seas he had no right to turn his quarterdeck into a prize court."[23]

Nevertheless, Lincoln did authorize Welles to send Wilkes a congratulatory letter. Welles had delayed responding to Wilkes' official report in order to ensure that his comments reflected administration policy.

Like the president, Welles recognized that Wilkes "was popular with the country" and that his act "was considered right by the people"; also like his boss, Welles did not want "to repress the national enthusiasm." On the other hand, formal congratulations by the government would transform Wilkes' act from an individual one to one of national policy. Consequently, Welles' brief acknowledgment was carefully worded, though perhaps not carefully enough. It congratulated Wilkes for "the great public service" he had rendered "in the capture of the rebel emissaries," and noted that his conduct had "the emphatic approval of the Department." The letter pleased no one. Seward later argued that by sending it Welles made the government responsible for Wilkes' act. Nor did the letter satisfy Wilkes, for Welles also wrote that Wilkes had erred by not taking the *Trent* as a prize and entrusting its adjudication to a prize court. "The forbearance exercised in this instance," Welles wrote, "must not be permitted to constitute a precedent."[24]

The implied criticism infuriated Wilkes, who had already decided that Welles was both a "damn fool" and a "rogue" who "was entirely unfitted for his position." He now decided that he was a coward as well. Ironically, Wilkes might well have responded to Welles that he had in fact ordered Lieutenant Fairfax to "take possession" of the *Trent*, only to be maneuvered out of it by his subordinate. But he knew that this was no defense, for while commanding officers may certainly take advice from subordinates, they are responsible for all command decisions, and Wilkes accepted full responsibility for this one. "I refused to send the Trent in for confiscation," he wrote, though it was "entirely within my power." He noted that doing so would probably have made him a rich man. If the ship had been condemned by a prize court, as Wilkes insisted it would have been, the value of both the ship and its cargo would have been divided among the crew as prize money, with the lion's share going to the captain. Since the *Trent* was carrying more than $1.5 million, Wilkes stood to make a fortune. Thus it was only his own "decency and self denial" that prevented him from taking the ship, virtues for which he believed he should be praised, not condemned. Moreover, like much of the country, Wilkes thought there was further virtue in defying Britain whatever its reaction. "John Bull would roar and bluster," he insisted later, "but as for going to war, that was entirely out of the question." And if it did come to war, so be it.[25]

While Wilkes' boldness was a refreshing contrast to McClellan's caution, Lincoln understood the difference between boldness and bluster. He was not willing to risk a war to keep Mason and Slidell imprisoned. Before doing anything, however, he would wait for the official British reaction; there was no need to borrow trouble. In the meantime, however, he had to deliver his annual message to Congress when it convened for the winter session on December 2. What could he say about the *Trent*? If he cited it as an administration triumph and the British reaction turned out to be confrontational, it would paint the administration into a corner where the only options were capitulation or war. If he chastised the popular Wilkes and disavowed his seizure of Mason and Slidell, much of the country would be furious with him.

He decided to say nothing at all. In a lengthy message that fills almost twenty printed pages in the *Collected Works*, there is not a word about the *Trent*. He did mention the detention by American naval forces of the *Perthshire*, which had departed Mobile back in the spring before the blockade went into effect and which nevertheless had been stopped by the USS *Massachusetts*. The British owners demanded compensation, and Lincoln recommended that because the incident had been occasioned by "an obvious misapprehension of the facts . . . , an appropriation [should] be made to satisfy the reasonable demand of the owners." It was as close as he came to hinting of a possible policy concerning the *Trent*. The president read a draft of the message aloud to the cabinet on November 29. Welles was no doubt gratified to hear himself praised for his "activity and energy" and for virtually creating a wartime navy and bringing it into service within a few months. "Besides blockading our extensive coast," Lincoln read, "squadrons larger than ever before assembled under our flag have been put afloat and performed deeds which have increased our naval renown."[26]

The next day, Senator Charles Sumner called on the president. Tall, broad-shouldered, and handsome, Sumner had become a martyr to the opponents of slavery back in 1856 when he had been attacked and beaten on the floor of the Senate by South Carolina's Preston "Bully" Brooks for insulting Brooks' kinsman, Senator Andrew Butler. After an almost three-year convalescence (opponents said he was malingering), Sumner returned to the Senate in 1859 and took up his seat as chairman of the Senate Foreign Relations Committee. An Anglophile, Sumner maintained a regular correspondence with a number of Englishmen, including the prominent liberals John Bright and Richard Cobden, and based in part on that correspondence, he was convinced that Britain would not tolerate this insult to her flag. Wilkes had stopped by Sumner's Boston home during his triumphal tour, and Sumner had listened dispassionately as Wilkes presented his case. At the end of it, Sumner dourly predicted that the government would probably not sustain him. Wilkes was offended and told Sumner that "if the Govt did not I was sure the People would."[27]

Now Sumner was back in Washington, where he endeavored to impress upon Lincoln the gravity of the situation. Lincoln knew that Sumner had a tendency to take things seriously—maybe too seriously. When they had first met back in February, Lincoln remarked afterward, "I have never had much to do with bishops where I live, but, do you know, Sumner is my idea of a bishop." Now the bishop was especially solemn. War with England, he insisted, was not at all out of the question, and such a war would be calamitous for the country. It was essential, he declared, to find a face-saving way out. Lincoln took Sumner's concerns seriously, but popular enthusiasm for Wilkes' act remained high. Pacing about his office, he suggested to Sumner that perhaps he could defuse the emerging crisis with a little personal diplomacy. "If I could see Lord Lyons," Lincoln declared, "I could show him in five minutes that I am heartily for peace." Sumner noted that this not only would be a violation of diplomatic protocol but also would infuriate Seward. Sumner suggested that the best way out of this dilemma might be to find some third country—France, or perhaps Prussia—that was willing to act as a mediator. That way, whatever the outcome, both sides would save face. For now, the best option—really the only option—was to await the formal British response.[28]

AS IT HAPPENED, on the very day that Lincoln read his annual message aloud to his cabinet (November 29), the British cabinet was meeting to determine its official reaction to Wilkes' seizure of Mason and Slidell, the news of which had finally reached England two days before. In preparation for the meeting, Lord John Russell, the British foreign minister, had called on Adams to find out if Wilkes had acted under orders or if he had stopped the *Trent* on his own. Adams, of course, had no idea, though he was able to tell Russell that the captain of another U.S. ship charged to look for the rebel emissaries (John B. Marchand of the *James Adger*) had been ordered *not* to interfere with Mason and Slidell if they were found aboard a British-flag vessel. Russell duly reported this to the British cabinet, but in the end the question was moot. It did not matter if Wilkes had acted under orders or not. His seizure of the four men without recourse to a prize court was patently illegal, and the cabinet authorized Russell to send Lord Lyons instructions to demand both their immediate return and a public apology. The United States was to have seven days to respond to this ultimatum. If Lyons did not receive a satisfactory answer within that time, he was to ask for his passport, effectively breaking off diplomatic relations. Meanwhile, the British government would prepare for war.[29]

Before that ultimatum left England, however, it underwent a dramatic and perhaps decisive change. As required, the prime minister sent a copy of it to the queen, who was hosting a dinner party that evening. Her husband, Prince Albert, did not attend the dinner, for he was already suffering from the illness that would soon take his life. He accepted the note, and while the queen hosted her dinner guests, he wrote out some suggested changes. Rather than threaten the United States, Albert's memo suggested that the cabinet might instead encourage the Americans to give "full consideration" to the circumstances of the seizure, after which, it was hoped, they would "spontaneously" decide to release Mason and Slidell. Though the terms remained the same, the tone was entirely different. Victoria assented to the changes, and the note from the Crown led Russell to redraft the ultimatum, which now prominently referred to the "friendly relations which have long subsisted between Great Britain and the United States." Russell even added a private note to Lyons saying that as long as Mason and Slidell were released, the British could be "rather easy about the apology."[30]

Russell might not have been in such a generous mood if he had received Lyons' next dispatch, already en route from America, which contained examples of the belligerent newspaper coverage of Wilkes' escapade. By the time it arrived, however, the modified ultimatum already had been sent. Equally important, even as Russell's note was borne westward on the steamer *Jura*, the frenzied belligerence of the American public had begun to wane. Seward's own truculence began to give way before accumulating evidence that a hard line might actually lead to war. In mid-December, before the arrival of the British ultimatum, Seward received a series of letters from a group of American churchmen traveling in England who reported the intensity of British feeling and the fact that war preparations were clearly under way. At about the same time, he also received a letter from Adams that not only confirmed British preparations for war but also reminded Seward that the current British position—that passengers aboard neutral vessels were not subject to seizure by belligerent warships—was exactly the position that had been asserted by the United States throughout the Napoleonic wars. Perhaps, Adams suggested, the United States could simply congratulate the British for finally coming around to the American point of view.

Many in England, and not a few in America, believed that Seward was still engaged in a conspiracy to manufacture a war with England. Lyons himself believed that Seward was playing "the old game of seeking popularity here by displaying insolence toward us" and that while Lincoln was willing to release the captives, Seward was the great impediment to peace. In fact, it was very nearly the other way around. Seward had abandoned his war-with-Europe gambit with the first shot at Fort Sumter, and he was now nearly frantic in his desire to avoid a European war. It was Lincoln who was reluctant to disappoint the public mood by backing down. As the London *Times* uncharitably put it, he was willing to let "the vessel of the State . . . drift helpless before the gale of popular clamour."[31]

By mid-December, however, that public mood was shifting. As early as December 8, the *New York Times*, very likely influenced by Seward's own metamorphosis, suggested that "if, upon mature reflection, the law should be against us, we shall, in a similar spirit, make the proper reparation." After all, the *Times* piece went on, "the capture of the rebel Commissioners had no political or military value or significance."[32] Indeed, belligerence rapidly gave way to anxiety. As American enthusiasm for war with England waned, rumors began to filter through the street that that war might be coming anyway. Those rumors fueled a plunge of New York stock prices on December 12, the day after Lincoln attended a memorial service on the floor of the Senate for his friend Edward Baker, who had been killed in the debacle at Ball's Bluff.

Two days after that, Charles Wilkes returned to his Washington home on Lafayette Square having completed a triumphal passage overland from Boston. Wilkes lived in the Dolley Madison House, so called because it was where the widow of the fourth president had resided after her husband's death in 1836. The house was only a few hundred yards from the White House, making Wilkes and Lincoln virtual neighbors. A crowd of well-wishers welcomed the sea captain home, and the Marine Band greeted him with a serenade that included "Hail to the Chief." Wilkes played the role of the modest hero, insisting that he had merely done his duty. Buoyed by his triumphal journey and his reception, Wilkes waited only a day or two before calling upon his neighbor the president. He found Lincoln to be "a tall, ill gainly, awkward individual with no manners or address." Judgmental as always, Wilkes saw little that impressed him: "A raw boned western man with a long ungainly stride, small hands, and to all appearances stupid."* Lincoln welcomed Wilkes with his customary smile, shook his hand, and told him that although the navy man had "kicked up a breeze," he admired "the boldness" of Wilkes' act. Wilkes was gratified to hear the president declare that "he intended to stand by me." Certainly, Lincoln admired Wilkes' boldness, but his assurance that he would stand by Wilkes was somewhat disingenuous, and Wilkes may have sensed it. Recalling their conversation years later, Wilkes wrote that despite Lincoln's declared support, "I doubted it at the very time he made the remark." He believed that Lincoln was under Seward's thumb and that the secretary of state "was a very coward in this whole business."[33]

As Wilkes took Lincoln's measure—however inaccurately—Lincoln also had an opportunity to assess Wilkes. If Sumner was a bishop, Wilkes was a fiery evangelist. Supremely confident and utterly unapologetic, he may have reminded Lincoln of the bold and daring David Dixon Porter. Like Porter, Wilkes was perfectly willing to assume authority and to act on it without hesitation. Refreshing as this was, Lincoln may have concluded that Wilkes was just a little too sure

---

*Wilkes' dismissive reference to Lincoln's "small hands" is particularly curious since Lincoln's enormous hands were one of the physical features, besides his great height, that virtually everyone noticed about the president. Indeed, Lincoln's oversize hands have led to speculation that he may have suffered from Marfan syndrome.

of himself. The naval officer would not even consider the possibility that he had made an error, and was utterly dismissive of British threats. Indeed, he seemed to welcome the idea of a war with Britain, reviving the discredited notion that a foreign war would somehow reunify the American Republic. War with England, he wrote later, "would have opened the way to a reconciliation. . . . The leaders of the Confederacy would willingly have seized the opportunity to have entered into terms with the Northern States as they had become aware of the utter uselessness in prolonging the fight and misunderstanding." If Wilkes ventured such notions in his conversation with the president, it could not have elevated him in Lincoln's estimation.[34]

Besides Wilkes, there were others who were disappointed by the waning belligerence of the public mood. Lincoln's political enemies saw that this incident might embarrass and weaken the administration, and sought to fan the flames of bellicosity. On December 16, two days after Lincoln met with Wilkes, Ohio Democrat Clement Vallandigham introduced a resolution in Congress that he hoped would not only regenerate support for Wilkes but also back Lincoln into a corner. One of the most vocal members of the House, Vallandigham was no friend of the administration. Indeed, many doubted that he was a friend of the Union since most of his efforts focused on weakening the government's war effort. Vallandigham disguised his measure as an effort to support the president in resisting British pressure. It praised "the act of Captain Wilkes" and pledged the "full support" of the House for Lincoln in his decision to stand firm despite "any menace or demand of the British Government." In introducing it, Vallandigham declared, "We have heard the first growl of the British lion, and now let us see who will cower."[35]

It was the reputation of the sponsor rather than the language of the bill that exposed it as an effort to embarrass the president. It was still a clever ploy, for few congressmen could afford to vote openly against "upholding now the honor and vindicating the courage" of the nation. To avoid having to do so, Lincoln's friends proposed sending the resolution to the Committee on Foreign Affairs, where, presumably, it would languish until the crisis had passed. Vallandigham protested, but he was voted down 109–16. Disgusted, Vallandigham then predicted that "these men will be surrendered before three months." His fellow

Ohioan Samuel Cox dismissed such histrionics. "I have too much faith in the honor of the people," Cox declared, "to believe that they would ever permit their Government . . . to dishonor them."[36]

By mid-December, a month after he had first learned that Wilkes had stopped the *Trent*, Lincoln had still not settled on a policy concerning Mason and Slidell. He had received lots of advice, much of it unsolicited, including a note from former president Millard Fillmore, who wrote that "either, this Government must submit . . . or take the hazards of a war at a most inconvenient time," but Lincoln had not made a public commitment either way. He still hoped that the expected protests from England, whatever form they might take, could be managed without having to "submit." Lincoln's hope was that he could keep the prisoners and British friendship, too. Everything, therefore, depended on the character of the British response.[37]

THE BRITISH ULTIMATUM reached Lyons' home in Washington a few minutes before midnight on December 18. It was too late to communicate its contents that night, but Lyons called on Seward early the next morning. He was reluctant to make a formal presentation of the note immediately, for as soon as he did, the clock on the seven-day deadline would begin ticking. Lyons therefore told Seward that this was an "unofficial" visit designed to let him know what to expect so that the American government could have a little more time to consider its response. Seward asked if there was some way he could see the note—unofficially, of course—and Lyons agreed. Later that day a messenger delivered a package from Lyons marked "Private and Confidential." Reading the note quickly, Seward saw at once that it decreed Wilkes' act to be "an affront to the British flag and a violation of international law." It also insisted on "full reparation" including "the liberation of the four gentlemen." What it did not say was what the consequences would be for noncompliance. Seward went to Lyons' home to find out, and Lyons told him: the breaking of diplomatic relations as a prelude to war.[38]

What previously had loomed as a potential diplomatic problem was now an imminent crisis. Despite the modifications to the ultimatum urged by Prince Albert (who, as it happened, had died five days earlier), it still left Lincoln almost no middle ground between abject capitulation and war. Based on his conversations with Sumner, with whom he now talked regularly, Lincoln still hoped that mediation, preferably by the French but possibly by the Prussians or even the Poles if necessary, was the best way out of the dilemma, and he drafted a response in which he sought to maneuver into this narrow middle ground. He began by declaring that the United States "intended no affront to the British flag" and that Wilkes had acted "without orders from, or expectation of, the government." But he also declared that the question of whether Wilkes had behaved correctly was something on which reasonable people could disagree. The United States was willing to make reparation, he wrote, if some neutral party could show how Wilkes had erred. For that reason, Lincoln was willing to submit the whole issue "to such friendly arbitration as is usual among nations."[39]

For all its finely wrought reasoning, Seward knew that the president's approach would not meet the requirements of London's ultimatum. He needed more time to bring Lincoln around. When Lyons showed up on Saturday, December 21, to present the note formally, Seward asked him if he could postpone its delivery until Monday, and Lyons agreed. He would deliver the ultimatum officially on December 23, two days before Christmas, which meant that an American answer would be required no later than noon on December 30. Seward scheduled a cabinet meeting for Christmas Eve but postponed it one day to give himself more time to draft a reply. As a result, the cabinet met at ten o'clock on Christmas morning, the timing suggesting much about the sense of urgency.

Seward began the meeting by reading the British note aloud. For most cabinet members, this was the first time they had learned its contents, and it was chilling. Then Seward read the draft reply that he had written. Lincoln did not read his own memo advocating mediation, but he had invited Sumner to the meeting, perhaps in the expectation that the senator would act as his stalking horse in support of that option. Sumner did suggest mediation, but he spent most of his time impressing the cabinet members with his conviction that there was a very real danger of war, and in support of that argument, he read alarming letters from Bright and Cobden, both of them desperate advocates of peace, and both of whom feared that war was imminent. Lincoln's hopes for mediation were dealt a severe blow when a note arrived from the French ambassador, who formally announced his country's support for the British view that Wilkes had violated international law. That removed any possibility of a French mediation; nor did the Prussians appear willing to mediate. The mood in the room grew gloomier as the options narrowed.[40]

As attorney general, Bates had the job of ruling on the legal issues involved, but, clearly rattled, he declared that whatever the legal merits of Wilkes' actions, the fact that all Europe was against them suggested that necessity and not legal precedent must rule their decision. "To go to war with England now," he declared, "is to abandon all hope of suppressing the rebellion. . . . The maritime superiority of Britain would sweep us from all the Southern waters. Our trade would be utterly ruined, and our treasury bankrupt." Almost plaintively, he insisted, "We *must not* have war with England." For all that, Lincoln remained reluctant to accept the notion that he had to surrender Mason and Slidell. His main concern was that it would outrage the American public, who would see the act as craven: "timidly truckling to the power of England," as Bates put it. After all, as Chase noted, Wilkes' crime, if there was one, was "a mere technical violation" of the law. Surely, Chase suggested, "it was not too much to expect of a friendly nation" to "overlook the little wrong." But it would not. Seward insisted that the very survival of the Republic was at stake and that time was running out.[41]

The meeting lasted until two in the afternoon. As the traditional hour for Christmas dinner approached, the only agreement in the room was that Seward would write up his arguments in another draft memo for presentation the next day. Lincoln still appeared to be reluctant to capitulate. As the meeting was breaking up, he drew Seward aside. "Governor Seward," the president said, "you will go on, of course, preparing your answer, which as I understand, will state the reasons why they [Mason and Slidell] ought to be given up." Meanwhile, Lincoln told him, "I have a mind to try my hand at stating the reasons why they ought not to be given up. We will compare the points on each side."[42]

The dour Seward left the meeting believing that the issue was still unsettled and that he had better make a very strong case that would convince his chief. In fact, for all his reluctance, Lincoln had largely accepted the necessity for capitulation. That night at the Christmas dinner he and Mary hosted for some two dozen guests in the White

House, he dropped a number of hints that the administration was likely to let Mason and Slidell go, perhaps preparing the public mind for the coming news. Seward was not at the dinner. He was in his home across Lafayette Park furiously composing a detailed and lengthy memo for the next morning's cabinet meeting.

When the cabinet reassembled on December 26, Seward read his new memo aloud. At its core was the point Adams had made a few weeks earlier when he noted that the current British position on neutral rights was nearly identical to the one the United States had espoused prior to the War of 1812. After a lengthy justification of Wilkes' behavior as "a simple, legal, and customary belligerent proceeding," a justification that was designed to satisfy Wilkes' many admirers at home, Seward acknowledged that Wilkes' failure to take the *Trent* as a prize and submit it to a court for adjudication was a technical error. For that reason, and that reason alone, Great Britain was entitled to reparation because, Seward claimed, the principle at stake was one that had been laid down in 1804 by Secretary of State James Madison, who had declared that "property found in a neutral vessel" must be "carried before a legal tribunal" and not "decided by the captor." Rather neatly, Seward observed that "we are asked to do to the British nation just what we have always insisted all nations ought to do to us." Consequently, Seward concluded, Mason, Slidell, and their secretaries "will be cheerfully liberated."[43]

Though a few members of the cabinet continued to grumble about giving way to British demands—Chase called it "gall and wormwood"—all admired the deft way Seward had turned what was clearly a capitulation into an apparent victory for American principles. Even Lincoln approved. When Seward asked the president about his own proposal for mediation, Lincoln told him, "I found I could not make an argument that would satisfy my own mind . . . and that proved to me [that] your ground was right."[44]

As Lincoln had feared, there was public criticism of the decision, but it was neither as loud nor as widespread as it might have been. Senator John P. Hale, Welles' old nemesis, attacked the decision in the Senate predicting that "if this Administration will not listen to the voice of the people, they will find themselves engulfed in a fire that will consume them like stubble." A few days later, Vallandigham thundered on the floor of the

House that "the American eagle [had] been made to cower before the British lion." His protests, however, were easier to dismiss. His amused colleagues remarked archly how ironic it was that a man who had opposed every warlike preparation to suppress the rebellion should now be so strong an advocate of war with Britain. Though the House agreed (53–45) to call for the publication of the documents and to submit the issue to the Committee on Foreign Affairs, the most representative expression of the House mood came from Benjamin F. Thomas of Massachusetts: "Mr. Speaker, the surrender is made, the thing done. In the presence of great duties we have no time for this luxury of grief."[45]

Within the navy the view was much the same. Wilkes had never been a favorite, and most career officers were quietly satisfied that the government had refused to sustain him. A typical reaction came from Commander Percival Drayton, who wrote to John Dahlgren that Wilkes' behavior was "false to all our traditionary policy of the sea, impolitic, and . . . bullying. The whole matter is to me disgusting and I hate to talk about it. We were very nearly sacrificing every material interest merely to gratify a little hate, and like all bullies when met properly we now sing very small."[46]

After Lincoln and the cabinet approved Seward's memo, its author wasted no time in delivering it to Lord Lyons who was clearly relieved by so prompt and satisfactory a response. Lyons agreed that the American willingness to give up the prisoners "cheerfully" made a formal apology unnecessary, and almost at once good relations between the countries were restored.

THE *TRENT* AFFAIR was Abraham Lincoln's Cuban missile crisis. Though Lincoln's crisis was triggered by an overeager American naval officer rather than a clandestine and premeditated gambit by a hostile foreign power, the ensuing diplomatic standoff was similar in that both Lincoln and Kennedy had to steer a course between apparent capitulation and catastrophic war. In both crises, neither country wanted war; in both crises, neither country wanted to back down. As Kennedy's secretary of state, Dean Rusk, famously put it, the two nations were eyeball to eyeball until somebody blinked. Unlike Kennedy, Lincoln's reluctance to blink was not motivated by a concern that the other side would think him weak; he resisted for fear that a capitulation would depress the public spirit at home at a critical moment in the war. As Bates put it, "The main fear . . . was the displeasure of our own people." In the end, Lincoln sensed not only that there was no other way, but also that the public mood had shifted and that the political cost of capitulation was significantly less in late December than it would have been in mid-November.[47]

In that respect, Lincoln was greatly aided by the absence of a transatlantic telegraph. Such a cable had been laid in the summer of 1858, and in August of that year Queen Victoria had sent the first transoceanic cable message to James Buchanan. But only weeks later the cable parted, and it was not replaced until after the Civil War ended. Throughout the Civil War, therefore, transatlantic messages went by sea. In the crisis provoked by Wilkes' seizure of Mason and Slidell, this proved providential, for the long delays in the transmission of news reports and diplomatic notes acted as a brake on national emotion and allowed both countries to resolve a dispute that might easily have escalated into war. Had the British crafted their ultimatum with full knowledge of the initial belligerent response of the American public and press, it almost certainly would have had a far different tone; had Lincoln been forced to respond to such an ultimatum before the country's infatuation with Wilkes had begun to dissipate, capitulation might well have been politically impossible.

Instead, Lincoln survived the *Trent* affair. In fact, his willingness to bow to necessity may have strengthened his long-term foreign policy in Europe. Britain at once halted its war preparations and, despite some clandestine support of the Confederate navy by British shipbuilders, the British government never again came close to intervention. As Charles Francis Adams expressed it to his son, "The Trent affair has proved thus far somewhat in the nature of a sharp thunderstorm which has burst without doing any harm, and the consequence has been a decided improvement in the state of the atmosphere." As an example of that new mood, the following spring Seward negotiated a new treaty with Lord Lyons concerning the African slave trade that gave British warships the right to search suspected slave ships flying the American flag. Though it surrendered a principle that had been maintained by Americans for half a century, it was ratified unanimously by the Senate. As for Mason and Slidell, when they finally arrived at their diplomatic posts, they were all but ignored by the governments of England and France, and they failed completely to influence the policies of either country toward the Confederacy.[48]

Wilkes, too, survived the crisis. Just as Lincoln had held Porter officially blameless for the confusion surrounding the *Powhatan* during the Fort Sumter crisis, so, too, did he hold Wilkes, if not blameless, then guilty mainly of overeagerness. He did not, however, write Wilkes a formal letter to say so, as he had with Porter. Putting such views in writing, even privately—especially into the hands of a volatile officer such as Wilkes—was taking an unnecessary risk. Perhaps Lincoln accepted the idea that Wilkes had committed only a "technical error" in not seizing the *Trent*, a decision that could be laid at the feet of Lieutenant Fairfax. On the other hand, hindsight suggests that Fairfax's decision may have been the key to the administration's ability to survive the diplomatic crisis that followed. Had Fairfax obeyed Wilkes' initial order to take the *Trent* as a prize, it might have been technically legal, but it would not have made the British any less furious. And it would have eliminated the fig leaf that subsequently allowed Seward to back down in the face of the eventual British protest. Absent that, it would have been harder for the United States to carve out a face-saving policy and the crisis may well have worsened.

Wilkes remained a problem. He was still enormously popular with the public, and he was not the kind of man to remain long in the background. He would have to be given another command. As Welles noted, "when and how to dispose of Wilkes was an embarrassment." For the rest of the war, Lincoln and Welles would try to find appropriate commands for Wilkes before the irrepressible and incorrigible officer finally had to be court-martialed for exceeding his orders. On January 1, 1862, however, as Lincoln and his advisers celebrated the new year, that was still in the future.[49]

At the president's traditional New Year's Day reception, Lincoln patiently smiled and shook hands as he greeted literally thousands of visitors. The cabinet members came first, followed by the senior members of the diplomatic corps. Lincoln's greeting to Lord Lyons went unrecorded, but Chase greeted the British ambassador with the salutation "Pax esto Perpetua," and Lyons responded that he hoped "his conduct had always been that of a Peacemaker."[50]

Lincoln knew that he had dodged a bullet in the *Trent* affair, but he still had much to occupy his mind as he greeted his legions of visitors. The enormous Union army remained idle in its camps; McClellan had fallen ill and was unable to oversee his command; the generals out west apparently were unable to act independently and unwilling to cooperate with one another. To be sure, his naval commanders had been willing to act—Porter, Du Pont, and Wilkes had all made headlines—and there were some tangible successes to show for their efforts: the blockade had become a reality, and the seizure of Cape Hatteras and especially Port Royal had established beachheads for future operations. But these signs of progress, satisfying as they were, were minuscule within the context of the broader war, the end of which could not be foreseen.

In the first ten months of the war, Lincoln had sought to set broad guidelines for his cabinet members and allow them to run their own departments. He had been patient with them—too patient, some thought. More than once he had postponed hard questions until they could be postponed no longer, and consequently, instead of being proactive, he had been forced to react to crises at the last moment. Despite the clarity of his vision and the firmness of his resolve, much of the country, and even some in his cabinet, feared that he lacked the requisite will and purpose for the national emergency. One of those who wanted Lincoln to take a firmer hand was Edward Bates. Bates feared that if the administration did not turn things around in the next thirty days, it would be "shaken to pieces." He wanted the president to seize the moment and be the commander in chief in fact as well as in name—"to take and act out the powers of his place, to command the commanders." Bates was convinced that if the president would "only trust his own good judgment more, and defer less, to the opinions of his subordinates, I have no doubt that the affairs of the war and the aspect of the whole country, will be quickly and greatly changed for the better." In his more despondent moments, Bates wondered if the president had the resolve to do this. On the last day of the year, he confided to his diary: "I greatly fear he has not *the power to command.*" He was wrong about that. Lincoln had the power, but so far he had been reluctant to use it. In the coming year, he would confront that reluctance. Meanwhile, he stood, he smiled, and he patiently shook hands.[51]

1862

CHARTING A COURSE

4

"Rain the Rebels Out"

Lincoln and the River War

LINCOLN BEGAN TO THINK about Union grand strategy almost from the first day of the war. On April 25, 1861, the day the 7th New York regiment marched into Washington to ease fears of a rebel coup de main, Lincoln mused aloud to his secretary John Hay about how the administration could regain control of the crisis. "I intend at present," he declared, "to fill Fortress Monroe with men and stores; blockade the ports effectually; provide for the entire safety of the Capitol; keep them quietly employed in this way, and then go down to Charleston and pay her the little debt we are owing her." At the time, Lincoln was still thinking of the conflict as a kind of police action to pacify an out-of-control minority, but his musings did contain the germ of the holding-and-hitting strategy that subsequently became the Anaconda Plan. He wanted to secure the capital, isolate the South with an effective blockade, then strike with a combined army-navy expedition. What was missing, of course, was a river campaign in the West, a curious omission since Lincoln was both a westerner and a river man. It may be that in April of 1861 he did not yet envision war on a continental scale. When an enthusiastic John Hay asked his boss (whom he privately called "the tycoon") if he could make his military plans public, Lincoln told him: "Not yet."[1]

By the end of the year, with the capital secure and the blockade established, Lincoln had developed a more sophisticated and detailed concept of grand strategy, one that did include a western campaign, and one that he was willing to share with his generals. He began with the simple fact that the Union states had "the *greater* numbers," while the rebellious states, operating with interior lines of communication, had "the *greater* facility of concentrating forces upon points of collision." It seemed evident to him that the way to take advantage of these circumstances was to "menace" the enemy at several different points "at the same time." This would force the rebels to do one of two things: either they would have to concentrate their forces in one place and temporarily abandon the others, or they would have to split their forces into a number of smaller units and try to defend everywhere. If the enemy chose concentration, Union forces should "forbear to attack" the strengthened position and occupy the abandoned sites. If instead the enemy divided his forces into smaller units, they could be defeated one by one. It was a clear-headed and straightforward analysis, but its success depended entirely on effective cooperation by the generals in the field, and as Lincoln already knew, achieving such cooperation was problematic at best.[2]

Lincoln was not eager to coordinate the movements of his generals himself. Unlike his Confederate counterpart, he never cherished visions of donning a uniform and riding to the front, or even moving chess pieces about on a strategic map. That was the role that he expected General Winfield Scott to fill. It had become clear, however, that despite Scott's brilliant success in earlier wars, the current task was beyond him. That was why Lincoln had turned to McClellan, endowing him with command of not only the Army of the Potomac but all Union armies. By January, McClellan had instilled a sense of purpose and direction to the mobilization of the Army of the Potomac, but he had not as yet demonstrated any eagerness to test that army in battle, and his oversight of the nation's other armies was largely pro forma. Worse, McClellan had fallen seriously ill with typhoid fever, leaving a void at the top of the command pyramid.

If that were not bad enough, the evident ineffectiveness and political clumsiness of Simon Cameron convinced Lincoln that he would also have to find a new secretary of war. Cameron had previously suggested that he might be interested in a diplomatic post, and Lincoln used that as a way to ease him out. He recalled Cassius Clay from St. Petersburg with the promise of a field command, and informed Cameron that he was now able to "gratify" him by appointing him minister to Russia.[3] It was not yet clear, however, who could take Cameron's place in the War Department, and meanwhile, with Cameron on his way out and McClellan in his sickbed, there was little energy or direction in the Union war effort. A delegation from eastern Tennessee filled Lincoln's ears with tales of Union patriots "being hanged and driven to despair," and a joint congressional committee met with Lincoln to complain about the absence of a "vigorous prosecution of the war." When Lincoln wrote Major General Henry Wager Halleck, his chief western general, to ask how soon he might be able to begin an offensive, Halleck replied with a lengthy lecture on the principles of war. At the bottom of this unhelpful dissertation, Lincoln wrote: "It is exceedingly discouraging. As everywhere else, nothing can be done." That same day, he dropped in on Meigs, now the army's quartermaster, to whom he felt he could unburden himself. "The people are impatient," the president groaned. "The General of the Army has typhoid fever. The bottom is out of the tub. What shall I do?"[4]

It was under these circumstances that Attorney General Edward Bates began to urge Lincoln to take the strategic reins into his own hands. Typhoid fever often lasted six weeks or more, he noted, and even if McClellan recovered fully, the army could not be without a guiding hand for so long. The entire Union war effort could not stop and wait for one man to get well. Bates even wondered why McClellan had been granted the title of general in chief when the nation already had a commander in chief. Whether Bates touched a nerve or the circumstances simply compelled it, Lincoln saw that someone had to provide direction and leadership, and since apparently no one else was willing or able to do it, he took it upon himself. He even suggested to Orville Browning that "he was thinking of taking the field himself," though it was a measure more of his frustration than of actual intent. What he did do was schedule a meeting of what amounted to a council of war for January 10, inviting Seward, Chase, and Thomas A. Scott (who sat in for the lame duck Cameron), plus two of the army's senior officers: Irvin McDowell, the hapless victim of Bull Run but still the favored candidate of Congress, and William B. Franklin, the senior division commander in McClellan's army.[5]

Lincoln told this group what he had said to Meigs: the country was impatient, the Congress was calling for action, "the bottom appeared to be falling out of everything," and while he was sorry about McClellan's illness, he wondered if it was possible to "do something with the Army of the Potomac." McDowell suggested an advance against Centreville and the old Manassas battlefield; Franklin, who, unlike the president, was privy to McClellan's still-developing plans, urged a move by sea to the York River. Someone wondered aloud if the government could find the number of vessels it would take to transport a whole army to the York River, and Lincoln adjourned the meeting until the next day so that McDowell and Franklin could obtain the answers to such logistical questions.[6]

Lincoln met twice more with this ad hoc war council, expanding it to include both Meigs and Montgomery Blair but not, interestingly, Welles or Fox. Meigs estimated that it might take as long as six weeks to gather the number of ships needed to transport the army to the York River, but Blair supported the amphibious move, fearing that an overland advance toward Centreville would lead to "another Bull Run." Inevitably, word of these meetings leaked to McClellan (who was probably tipped off by Franklin), and when the group reassembled on January 13, McClellan himself was present. He was pale and haggard-looking, but he was out of bed and in uniform. His presence silenced the rest; even Lincoln waited for the general in chief to assume control of the meeting. Instead McClellan was sullen and silent. When Lincoln asked him what should be done, he replied that "the case was so clear a blind man could see it." Chase asked him to be more specific, but he refused to divulge his plans on the grounds that no one in the room could keep a secret. When, at length, Lincoln asked him directly if he had a plan of action for the Army of the Potomac, McClellan said that he did. "Then, General," Lincoln announced, "I shall not order you to give it." And with that, he adjourned the meeting. As long as the commanding general was willing and able to do his job, Lincoln would not wrest it from him. Not yet.[7]

That same day, Lincoln found a replacement for Cameron. The man he chose was Edwin M. Stanton, a Democrat who had served briefly as attorney general in the Buchanan administration. Ironically, Stanton was also the man who had composed Cameron's order to arm slaves as soldiers, the letter that had convinced Lincoln that Cameron had to go. But Stanton had much to recommend him. He was a man of great energy and capacity, and, like Cameron, he was from Pennsylvania, so the geographical balance in the cabinet remained unchanged. Lincoln could only hope that he proved more adept than his predecessor.

Despite McClellan's assurances, two weeks passed without any sign of a movement by the army in Virginia or anywhere else, and partly to prod his generals, but mainly to bring about the simultaneous movement that he believed was essential, Lincoln finally did what Bates had been urging him to do: act as the commander in chief in fact as well as in name. On January 27, he issued an order (significantly superscribed as General Order No. 1) that directed "a general movement of the Land and Naval forces of the United States" one month hence, on February 22, Washington's birthday. On that day, Lincoln declared, the army at Fortress Monroe, the Army of the Potomac, and the army in western Virginia would all advance simultaneously. In addition, Buell's army in Kentucky and the forces at Cairo, Illinois, under Halleck's direction, plus the naval forces in the Gulf of Mexico, would all initiate offensives in the West. Though some scholars have portrayed this order as evidence of Lincoln's strategic naiveté, it was not at all foolish. Very likely, the Confederate army in Virginia and elsewhere would have been hard pressed to react effectively to a Union advance from several directions at once.[8]

It didn't happen. Just as the news of Lincoln's war council got McClellan out of his sickbed, the president's war order ended the general's official silence and prompted him at last to offer a detailed and specific plan of his own. He wrote a twenty-two-page letter, not to Lincoln but to Stanton, in which he offered an alternative to the president's idea of a simultaneous offensive. It was similar to the plan Franklin had hinted at earlier to outflank the enemy by sea, though it changed the army's landing site from the York River to the tiny hamlet of Urbana on the Rappahannock River, from which place, he argued, it would be possible to march to Richmond without having to overcome the rivers and forests of northern Virginia. Lincoln was skeptical, but rather than reject the plan outright, he asked McClellan five questions about it that compelled the general to explain why his plan was better than a direct overland approach. McClellan responded with the first detailed explanation of his strategic ideas, and Lincoln was sufficiently grateful for his candor that he gave his approval. He lifted the February 22 deadline, and McClellan began in earnest to develop what subsequently became the Peninsular Campaign.[9]

Of course, even if McClellan had been successful in Virginia, it would not have achieved what Lincoln still saw as the essential key to Union success: the coordination of all Union armies, east and west. For Lincoln's vision to be fulfilled, the western armies would have had to synchronize their activities with McClellan's advance as well. Moreover, both western armies would be heavily dependent on the river system for transportation and supply. In the West, railroads were useful, but railroads could be wrecked and railroad bridges could be burned, and in any case railroads did not have the capacity of river transport. Whatever happened in the western theater, therefore, would depend not only on the coordination of the two main field armies but also on cooperation between those armies and river gunboats, and the lack of a clear command authority led to a great deal of confusion.

According to tradition, the navy's authority stopped at the high-tide mark. The navy assumed jurisdiction over warships operating on the Potomac, the York, the James, and the other tidal rivers on the East Coast, but Welles assumed that the western rivers were the army's problem. Alas, constructing and commanding gunboats required specialized knowledge that few army officers had, and even fewer were interested in volunteering for such a duty. Welles therefore agreed to send a naval officer to Cincinnati to help the army prepare a riverine force for the western campaign. This created confusion, too, for while navy officers in the West were administratively under the Navy Department, they took their orders from the War Department, and there was no protocol determining which department bore the responsibility for pay and supplies. According to the Constitution, there was only one person in the entire nation who had command authority over both the army and navy of the United States. It was the tall, overworked, and currently discouraged man who occupied the White House. In his effort to effect a coordinated campaign in the West, Lincoln would find that in addition to synchronizing the movements of his generals, he also had to coordinate the army and the navy, a task that proved roughly equivalent to mixing oil and water.

THE MAN GIDEON WELLES SENT to Cincinnati was Commander John Rodgers, whose naval pedigree was strikingly similar to that of David Dixon Porter. Both men bore the names of famous fathers who had served in the War of 1812; both were career officers who had become midshipmen as teenagers. But if their backgrounds were similar, their temperaments were strikingly different. Porter was a brash, self-confident maverick who, like Charles Wilkes, was eager to promote himself and willing to seize any opportunity that might advance his prospects. Rodgers had the manner and aspect of a college professor. He was a quiet warrior whose respect for the traditions of the service kept him solidly in the mainstream and therefore largely in the background. Ironically, while Porter suffered no ill consequences for his brashness and independence, Rodgers would be branded as a troublemaker mainly for doing his job.

Like most naval officers of his era Rodgers' professional goal was command at sea, and he looked upon his assignment to Cincinnati as a kind of banishment, especially since Welles made it clear that while his job was to establish a riverine force, he was to do so "under the direction and regulation of the Army." Nevertheless, Rodgers got to work at once, finding three suitable vessels, which he purchased and began to convert to military use by strengthening their decks to bear the weight of naval armament, reinforcing their thin bulwarks with five-inch oak planks, dropping the boilers from the deck into the lower hold, and rerouting the steam pipes to make them less vulnerable to enemy fire.[10]

These first three river gunboats—*Tyler*, *Lexington*, and *Conestoga*—were destined to play crucial roles in the western campaigns, but when Welles learned what Rodgers had done, he was furious, and he fired off a telegram informing Rodgers that he had overstepped his authority. "The movements on the Mississippi are under the direction and control of the Army," Welles reminded him. Therefore, "All purchases of boats . . . must be made by the War Department." Welles' concern was mainly financial. The gunboats "are not wanted for naval purposes," he asserted. "If they are required for the army," the army should "make requisitions on the War Department." Showing how blind he was to Lincoln's vision of a coordinated offensive, Welles informed Rodgers that "the two branches of service" must not "become complicated and embarrassed" by "any attempt at a combined movement on the rivers of the interior."[11]

Rodgers defended himself by noting that McClellan had approved the purchases, which temporarily mollified Uncle Gideon. Welles even authorized Rodgers to requisition cannon from the navy's Bureau of Ordnance, a circumstance dictated by the fact that the army did not have the kind of gun carriages needed for use on board ships. Welles continued to conceive of Rodgers as essentially an adviser to the army, however, and when in August Rodgers sent him a detailed letter reporting that he had successfully turned the three steamers into gunboats, hired pilots along with engineers and masters, fixed their pay, and begun to enlist crewmen, Welles scrawled a terse note at the bottom: "This whole subject belongs to the War Department." He subsequently declared to a third party that "the gunboats on the Mississippi and Western rivers are under the control and direction of the War Department, with which the Navy has no connection."[12]

Rodgers might have survived Welles' pique if he had managed to get along with the army commander, John C. Frémont, but Frémont became annoyed with him, too. Naval constructor Samuel A. Pook was fabricating half a dozen armored gunboats under army contract, an effort that one authority has dubbed "a Civil War prototype for latter military-industrial linkages in modern America." If so, those linkages were remarkably fragile in 1861. Rodgers' efforts to ensure navy participation in the planning and construction of these gunboats led Frémont to decide that the navy officer was meddling in army business, and he complained about it to Welles. Largely to gratify Frémont, Welles decided to supersede Rodgers with newly promoted navy Captain Andrew Hull Foote, whom Welles had known since boyhood when they had attended the same prep school.[13]

A fringe of white beard and a peculiar curl to Foote's mouth gave him the appearance of a leprechaun, but here as elsewhere, appearances were misleading. Foote was a devout Christian and an opponent of both physical punishment and the grog ration. "Discipline," he declared in a series of general orders to his new command, "to be permanent must be based on moral grounds." He therefore promised "the utmost rigor of the law" for any man found guilty of intemperance or "profane swearing," and he mandated "a strict observance of Sunday," which he hoped would be devoted to "the public worship of Almighty God."[14] Perhaps Welles hoped that Foote would get along better with the army because Foote had briefly attended West Point back in the 1820s, though he had resigned after only six months in order to accept an appointment as a navy midshipman. Now, forty years later, he would try to fill the curious and still largely undefined role of commanding the army's navy.*

As he had with Rodgers, Welles made it clear to Foote that he was "under the direction of the War Department" and that any requisitions for his flotilla must go to the army. By now, however, the weakness— not to say folly—of having navy officers draw on the War Department for logistic support was becoming evident. Though Welles expected that the men of the gunboat flotilla would be paid by the army, Frémont felt no such responsibility, and consequently the men didn't get paid at all. Foote reported that the men were "clamorous" for their pay because their families were "destitute." In addition, Foote lacked a secure source of supplies. He told Welles he was "embarrassed about powder and shot, having been positively refused these both by the Army and Navy." He appealed to Meigs, the army's quartermaster, but Meigs needed approval from the top and advised him to write the secretary of war. Cameron, already a lame duck, had more pressing problems than meeting the needs of some navy officer out west, and ignored him. The fact was that, important as it was, no one accepted responsibility for Foote's orphan command. Foote wrote to Dahlgren at the Washington Navy Yard that "we are without the means of going ahead. . . . If not provided with ordnance materials I can't get the Gun boats along." There was a plaintive note in his comment "May God grant that I never again in this world shall be placed in the painful state I am now in, while the enemy is in sight and we without means of arming & equipping good boats to meet him." As Edward Bates put it in

---

*The "army's navy" included not only the vessels on the western rivers but also hundreds of transport vessels on salt water. Indeed, during the course of the war, the U.S. Army owned or operated a total of nearly four thousand ships, more than half of them chartered transport vessels. This meant that during the Civil War, the army actually controlled more ships than the navy.

his diary, "The boats are under the War Dept, and yet are commanded by *naval* officers. Of course they are neglected—no one knows anything about them."[15]

In addition, Foote was "embarrassed on all sides for want of rank." Despite his forty years of service, the army considered him the equivalent of a lieutenant colonel, and many newly minted army colonels, some of them bearing commissions that were only a few weeks old, assumed they could order his gunboats around pretty much at their whim. Demonstrating some political acuity, Foote did not complain about this to Welles, even though the secretary was his old schoolmate. He wrote instead to Fox. One of Fox's great assets as assistant secretary was that he acted as a friend at court for officers who felt they could not be candid with the judgmental Welles without being accused of complaining. Foote's letters to Fox very likely played a role in Lincoln's decision to create the rank of flag officer, which not only gave Du Pont the rank he needed to command at Port Royal but also gave Foote the ability to deal more effectively with his army counterparts in the West.[16]

For the first nine months of the war, Lincoln did not involve himself with this jurisdictional confusion on the western rivers. In late September, he asked Frémont to dispatch a gunboat to Owensville, Illinois, on the Green River, where a constituent had reported that the town was being threatened by secessionists. Frémont passed the order on to Foote, and Foote sent the *Lexington* up to Owensville.[17] Beyond that, Lincoln did not interfere. In January of the new year, however, as Lincoln contemplated a more assertive role for himself as commander in chief, he learned that a large number of mortar vessels that had been ordered months before and which were intended for the western campaign were still unready because no one seemed to be exercising any oversight of the project. These boats, also called bomb vessels, were essentially flat-bottomed rafts, forty to fifty feet long, each of which boasted in the exact center of its flat deck a single large and very heavy weapon that looked something like a witch's brewing pot. The squat, ugly mortars fired enormous thirteen-inch shells (bombs) in a high arcing trajectory to rain down on enemy fortifications more than two miles away. The mortar boats could anchor around the bend of a river and fire their huge shells over the top of hills or trees to target enemy positions that were out of sight as well as beyond the range of conventional ordnance. Both army and navy authorities acknowledged that they would be useful in the forthcoming river campaign, but since they were neither horse artillery nor really warships, neither service was eager to claim them.

Lincoln may have first considered the capabilities of mortar boats as a result of a visit from David Dixon Porter. Lincoln had not seen the mercurial Porter since the latter had left to take command of the *Powhatan* back in April, but he remembered his bold action on that occasion. When Porter walked into the Navy Department in mid-November, the veteran Commodore Joe Smith looked up and remarked jocularly, "Well, you didn't run away after all!" As always, Porter's timing was impeccable. Like the rest of the nation, the navy was then celebrating the news of Du Pont's victory at Port Royal and Wilkes' capture of Mason and Slidell. In an expansive mood, Welles received Porter cordially and asked him about affairs in the Gulf. Porter was dismissive of departmental plans to blockade the mouth of the Mississippi, and asserted that the navy should instead send an expedition up the river to seize New Orleans.[18]

Welles and others had been contemplating an attack on New Orleans for some time, but most of those who thought about such a campaign believed that the best approach to the city was from upriver since any approach from the south would have to overcome two large stone forts, one on each side of the river, about halfway between New Orleans and the Gulf. As during the Fort Sumter crisis, army authorities were virtually unanimous in concluding that almost any substantial fort could easily destroy wooden warships attempting to pass them. Porter's solution was to use mortar boats to reduce the rebel forts from long range; that would open the way for conventional warships to run past. Welles was intrigued by the idea and took Porter to the White House. For the second time in less than a year, Porter found himself pitching a proposal to the commander in chief.

The notion of seizing New Orleans was not new to Lincoln, but Porter's idea of using mortar boats to do it was. Welles saw that the president was "deeply interested" in the plan, though because of the army's repeated warnings he was "somewhat incredulous as to the feasibility." Porter insisted that assaults on secondary targets could not be decisive; New Orleans was the real target. When Porter had finished, Lincoln leaned back in his chair and said: "This reminds me of a story." As Porter later remembered it, it went like this: "There was an old woman in Illinois who missed some of her chickens, and couldn't imagine what had become of them. Some one suggested that they had been carried off by a skunk; so she told her husband he must sit up that night and shoot the 'critter.'" The next morning the husband came in holding two pet rabbits that he had shot during the night. "Them ain't skunks!" the old woman complained. "Well, then," the husband replied, "if them ain't skunks I don't know a skunk when I sees it." After a good laugh (the president always laughed at his own jokes, and it encouraged others to join in), Lincoln explained that so far in the war the navy had been hunting pet rabbits. Fort Hatteras and Port Royal were all very well, but it was New Orleans—the South's biggest city and most important seaport— that was the real prey, and perhaps it was time to go hunting skunks.[19]

Porter's plan also fit well into Lincoln's overall strategic view of menacing the enemy in several places simultaneously. If Foote's flotilla on the upper river system could advance southward at the same time that a second force pushed upriver, it would compel the rebels either to choose which threat to confront, or else divide their forces in an effort to confront both. Lincoln not only approved the idea, he arranged to meet Welles and Porter at McClellan's headquarters the next day to convince the general to provide forces to occupy the Crescent City once it had been seized. McClellan was chary of the whole idea until he realized that Lincoln was not looking for an assault force of, say, fifty thousand men, but only an occupation force of perhaps ten thousand. Once he appreciated that, he immediately gave his blessing. Subsequently, Welles and Fox decided that David Glasgow Farragut, Porter's foster brother, would command the expedition, and Porter himself would take charge of the mortar flotilla assigned to reduce the rebel forts and allow Farragut's warships to ascend the river. Just as Du Pont had shared command with Thomas W. Sherman in the assault on Port Royal, Farragut would share command with Major General Benjamin F. Butler.

As always, however, issuing the orders did not lead to immediate action. Lacking anything like the Industrial Mobilization Board that emerged in the next century to coordinate the elements of a force buildup, all the efforts aimed at creating two mortar fleets—one for

Foote at Cairo and one for Porter at New Orleans—were necessarily ad hoc and characterized by confusion and misunderstanding. While mortars for the western rivers could be placed on flat-bottom rafts, those intended for the assault on New Orleans had to navigate around Florida to the Gulf on more seaworthy schooners. Welles assigned his brother-in-law George W. Morgan to select appropriate vessels for Porter's squadron in New York. Welles wanted their conversion to have the highest priority, but the foundry in Pittsburgh lagged in producing the enormous mortars, which weighed 17,120 pounds each. Meanwhile, Foote, in Cairo at the other end of the pincer, was having problems of his own with army officials who had no interest in the project. Frustrated, Lincoln ordered Fox to find out what was going on. Fox wired Foote to tell him, "The president desires immediately a full report . . . and full particulars relative to the mortar boats, number in commission, number of mortars mounted, number of mortars ready to mount, etc., the time of completion of all boats, etc." And as if to punctuate the urgency, he added: "Acknowledge this."[20]

In part the confusion in Pittsburgh was a product of Lincoln's decision to replace Frémont with Halleck. Like Cameron, Frémont had exceeded his authority by declaring that the slaves within his command area were free. When Lincoln ordered him to withdraw the proclamation, Frémont dragged his feet and even sent his wife to Washington to lobby for his abolitionist policy. Jessie Frémont's interview with Lincoln was a disaster. Lincoln later declared that "I had to exercise all the awkward tact I have to avoid quarreling with her." On November 2, one day after conferring the title of general in chief on McClellan, he appointed Halleck to replace Frémont in the West. Whatever improvements may have been wrought by the change, it did not advance the production of mortars. Using mortar vessels on the upper reaches of the western rivers had been Frémont's idea, and Halleck was not interested in them. He informed Foote that since the mortar boats could not be completed without further appropriations, all work should stop at once. Foote, who had never thought much of the mortars anyway, was happy to comply.[21]

When he received Lincoln's demand for information about the mortar boats, however, Foote replied at once. Only four mortars had been completed at Pittsburgh, he reported, and they were being sent to New

York for Porter's squadron. No mortars or mortar rafts had been prepared for the western flotilla. Though he didn't say so to Lincoln,
Foote remained skeptical of the queer little vessels. The same day he
replied to Lincoln, he wrote privately to Fox deriding their utility. "I
only wish you could see them," he wrote. "There are no conveniences
for living aboard. They will leak more and more. Some of our best officers have no better opinion of these rafts or boats than I have." Still, if
the White House wanted mortar rafts, it was not his place to stand in
the way. "It is my business to let the Government judge and I am to
obey orders," he concluded. "Let me know what is expected of me
about these Mortar Boats."[22]

Having put his hand in, Lincoln decided to take over management
of the project personally, and to accomplish this, he employed as intermediary a young navy lieutenant named Henry Augustus Wise. It
proved to be a happy association. Though Wise was a cousin of the former governor of Virginia, now a rebel general, he was also a career U.S.
Navy officer and an assistant in the Ordnance Bureau at the Navy Yard
where Lincoln frequently visited. Like Lincoln, Wise possessed the
ability to smooth over potential conflicts between touchy officers of
both services. When Porter wrote Wise to complain that he had not yet
sent the guns he needed for his squadron, Wise sent him a charming
and witty sketch depicting a score of animated naval guns dragging
themselves to Porter's command. Porter was captivated and replied, accurately, "You are an artist." Wise was also an author. Best known by
his literary pseudonym, "Harry Gringo," Wise had published (in 1849)
a witty and irreverent memoir of his role in the Mexican War and his
travels in the South Pacific. Its success led him to write many more humorous stories in the style of Artemas Ward, one of Lincoln's favorites.
Lincoln was certainly aware of Wise's literary pseudonym, and perhaps
because of that there was an easy familiarity in their working relationship. When Wise briefed Lincoln on the problems associated with the
production of mortar rafts, the president told him: "Now I am going to
devote a part of every day to these mortars, and I won't leave off until
it fairly rains Bombs." He directed Wise to tell Foote to get the mortars
ready "at the earliest possible moment," asking at the same time:
"What can be done here to advance this? What is lacking?" Just as Lincoln had asked Scott to send him daily reports on the military situation

in the early days of the war, so now did he order Foote to send him daily reports on the preparation of the mortar boats. "Telegraph us every day, showing the progress, or lack of progress in this matter."[23]

Lincoln also talked to Stanton about the mortars. He told his new war secretary that he was "very much put out" that the War Department was delaying their production, and Stanton promised to look into it. Unwilling to leave it at that, however, Lincoln followed up the conversation by ordering Stanton to "make a peremptory order on the ordnance officer at Pittsburg to ship the ten mortars and two beds to Cairo instantly, and all others as fast as finished, till ordered to stop." In New York, Porter anticipated "much difficulty," since "the fitting out of a mortar fleet" was "a new thing to the Ordnance Department." But to his great surprise, he found that "never during the existence of the O.D. was there more zeal or ability displayed."[24]

By stepping into the vacuum of authority in the western theater, Lincoln became not only the de facto commander in chief but also a kind of chief of staff, with Lieutenant Wise acting as his aide. Wise carried Foote's daily telegrams to the White House the moment they arrived. Wise read them aloud, the president made a decision, and Wise issued the necessary orders. Foote sensed the new urgency at once. "The President," he wired Pittsburgh, "is in a hurry for mortar boats." And if the president wanted mortar boats, he would have them. Over the next few weeks, a flurry of telegrams passed back and forth between Cairo and Washington as Lincoln personally managed the mobilization of mortar boats for the western rivers and for the New Orleans expedition.[25]

Foote remained concerned about the problem of onboard accommodation. After all, the river mortars were simply flat-bottom barges with no hold or cabin; crewmen had to pitch tents on the deck to keep the rain off. "The men must have a steamer for their accommodation," Foote wired. "Shall I purchase or hire a steamer for them?" Wise checked with Lincoln and reported back: "The president directs me to say that he approves [acquiring a steamer] and desires you to go ahead." When Foote sought ammunition for the new craft, Lincoln directed the army's ordinance chief "to supply whatever ammunition may be required." Lincoln told Wise he wanted Foote to have enough shells "to rain the rebels out" and "treat them to a refreshing shower of sulphur and brimstone." When the army balked at paying the salaries of soldiers who transferred into the gunboat service, Lincoln ordered the War Department to pay up. Wise reported to Foote that "Uncle Abe, as you already know, has gone into that business with a will. . . . The wires have not ceased vibrating . . . nor will they until the thing is done."[26]

Lincoln also urged Foote to get on with the preparation of more conventional gunboats. In late January, the president was still hoping that he could get a coordinated national offensive under way by Washington's birthday, and with that in mind, he authorized Foote to make whatever changes he believed were necessary, but only "if the work can *positively* be executed by the 22d of February next." Alas, that deadline became meaningless once Lincoln approved McClellan's movement to Virginia by sea, but it did not ease Lincoln's vexation at the delays that resulted from the complicated and confusing command structure in the West. The president, Fox wrote confidentially to Foote, "was very much exercised in the matter, and I do not blame him."[27]

Lincoln's pique was a product of his perplexity at how service professionals could allow the traditional barriers between the services to deter them from doing what needed to be done. He did not seek out his central role in preparing the mortar squadrons for both Cairo and New Orleans; he assumed the burden because no one else would. Though Bates and Fox continued to insist that it might be best simply to turn the river flotilla over to the Navy Department, Lincoln did not order it. Instead, he showed by example how to overcome the barriers between the services. As Wise put it, "He is an evidently practical man, understands precisely what he wants, and is not turned aside by anyone when his work is before him. From the beginning of this mortar business, he was perplexed to know how to get matters straight, but when he put me on the track I made it clear to him, and since then the machine has been flying along with not a break-down or any risk of a break-up."[28]

ONE WEEK AFTER TELLING WISE that he wanted Foote to "rain the rebels out" of their forts along the western rivers, Gideon Welles arrived at the White House waving a telegram that announced that they had done just that. As it happened, the mortars had played no role in the triumph—

despite Lincoln's efforts, they were still not ready—but the gunboats had achieved a signal victory. Foote reported that after a short, sharp fight, Fort Henry, the principal rebel defense on the Tennessee River, had surrendered unconditionally to his gunboat flotilla. Spurred by Lincoln's order to conduct a coordinated advance by February 22, Halleck had authorized Brigadier General U. S. Grant at Cairo to cooperate with Foote's gunboats in the assault. After being dropped off a few miles below the fort by army transports, Grant's soldiers had approached Fort Henry overland while Foote's gunboats opened fire from the river. Perceiving the weakness of their position, the Confederates evacuated the fort, leaving behind only four score artillerists to battle the gunboats. Four armored gunboats took the fort under fire, and although the *Essex* received a shot through its boiler that scalded a number of men, well-directed fire from the rest of the flotilla overwhelmed the gunners on shore, who raised the white flag.[29]

Lincoln was "joyful" when he heard the news; the "navy boys" had not let him down. Welles wired Foote that his news gave the president "the highest gratification," though his gratification might have been even greater if the operation had coincided with simultaneous advances by Halleck and Buell, not to mention McClellan. Still, a victory was a victory, and this one not only broke the Confederate defensive line in Tennessee, it boded well for future operations, since it was clear that the new river ironclads could more than hold their own against rebel forts. As Albert Sidney Johnston, the Confederate commander in the West, reported to Richmond: "Fort Henry indicates that the best earthworks are not reliable to meet successfully a vigorous attack of ironclad gunboats."[30]

Having kicked down the door, Foote barely paused before sending three gunboats steaming upriver past Fort Henry to pursue the enemy's small flotilla of armed craft, all of which were captured, burned, or sunk. One of the Union gunboats ascended the river all the way to Florence, Alabama, and captured a nearly finished rebel warship (soon converted into the Union warship *Eastport*) along with hundreds of tons of supplies. Another burned the Memphis and Bowling Green Railroad bridge over the Tennessee River, which cut the communications between the Confederacy's two principal field armies in the West and forced both to fall back. Welles was delighted, and praised Foote

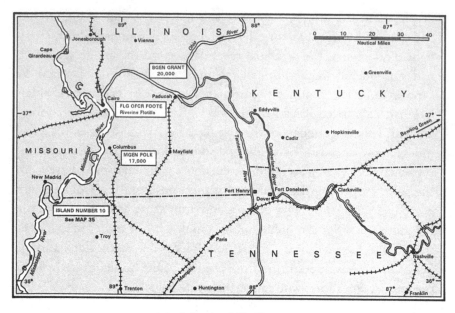

THE WESTERN THEATER, 1862. Map by Bill Clipson, reprinted with permission from *The Naval Institute Historical Atlas of the U.S. Navy* by Craig L. Symonds, © 1995.

for surmounting "great and insuperable difficulties" to create the river force, ignoring the fact that Welles himself had been the author of some of those difficulties. Since January, however, Lincoln's active support for the river flotilla generally, and the mortar boats in particular, had caused Welles to adjust his outlook, and the victory at Fort Henry washed away the last of his reluctance to embrace the riverine flotilla as part of the navy.[31]

The success at Fort Henry also elevated the flotilla in the eyes of the army. Halleck wired Foote congratulations for his "brilliant success," and McClellan, too, took a new interest in the campaign. Prodded by Lincoln, Stanton sent Assistant Secretary of War Thomas Scott out west, and Scott invited Foote to let him know what "additional force and equipment you need." After months of being an orphan, the riverine fleet now had a number of doting parents.[32]

Fort Donelson was next. The rebels had constructed two forts to guard the northward-flowing rivers in central Tennessee and Kentucky: Fort Henry on the Tennessee and a much larger and better-sited fortification named Donelson on the Cumberland River. Halleck was eager to keep the momentum going, and so he ordered Grant to march his force across the short space between the rivers to Fort Donelson, where, presumably, the Grant-Foote team would win another victory. Foote was willing enough, but he was still short of both officers and men, the *Essex* needed substantial repairs, and all his vessels needed to resupply themselves with coal and ammunition, which could best be done at Cairo. The boats would have to backtrack down the Tennessee to the Ohio before steaming up the Cumberland in any case, so a stop at Cairo was not significantly out of the way. Halleck thought Foote was being coy and bombarded him with a series of telegrams—three of them in one day—all urging him to "push ahead boldly and quickly." Grant was more circumspect. "Can you not send two boats from Cairo immediately up the Cumberland?" he asked. Soon thereafter, Foote left Cairo with five vessels.[33]

Lincoln followed developments by telegraph. The early news was encouraging, but then it often was. On February 12—his fifty-third birthday—Lincoln learned that Grant had "invested Fort Donelson from the land side." Three days later Halleck wired that "everything looks well." There was a note of panic, however, in a second telegram that afternoon, in which Halleck insisted, "I must have more men. It is a military necessity." A similar wire arrived that night: "Give me the forces required and I will ensure complete success." This was precisely the kind of pledge that Lincoln had heard too often from McClellan, and he may have been becoming inured to it. Halleck's nervous telegrams from St. Louis had been triggered by news that Foote had made an attack on the fort with his gunboats on February 15 and had been repulsed. Foote reported that he had been on the verge of driving the enemy from his batteries when plunging fire disabled the steering on two of his ships, causing them to drift downriver and out of the fight. Foote himself had been wounded, painfully if not seriously, when a rebel shell exploded near where he was standing. Was the early promise of victory about to be dashed as it had been at Bull Run?[34]

Lincoln sought to reassure his nervous western commander. "You have Fort Donelson safe," he wrote. The only real threat was that the enemy might somehow manage to concentrate against Grant, and to prevent that, Lincoln suggested that Halleck might strike at the bridges and railroads the enemy could use to effect such a concentration. As always, he reiterated that the key to success was "full co-operation" between the Union generals. By the time Halleck received this advice, however, the issue had been decided. The very next day a wire arrived in Washington from Halleck's chief of staff with the news that "the Union flag floats over Fort Donelson." Nearly the entire garrison of some 12,500 men had been taken prisoner. Only Nathan Bedford Forrest's small cavalry command and about fifteen hundred infantry had escaped, including the Confederate commander, Major General John B. Floyd, who fled like a thief in the night.[35]

It was the best news in the war so far. But in contrast to his "joyful" reaction to the news of Fort Henry, Lincoln was unable to join in this celebration. For more than a week, Lincoln's two younger sons, Willie and Tad, had been bedridden with what the doctors called "bilious fever" but which was almost certainly typhoid fever caused by the capital city's pestilent water supply. The president and his wife spent much of their days—and their nights—sitting by their children's beds. Two days after news of the victory at Donelson arrived in Washington, Lincoln staggered out of Willie's room devastated with grief, and in an emotion-strained voice he told his young secretary, "Well, Nicolay, my boy is gone—he is actually gone." And he burst into tears.[36]

Mary Lincoln was inconsolable. Mary Welles, wife of the navy secretary, spent much time at the White House comforting her, and coincidentally cementing the bond between the Lincoln and Welles families. Meanwhile, the war continued. Just as the fall of Fort Henry had opened the Tennessee River for hundreds of miles, the fall of Donelson opened up the Cumberland River. Foote was eager to dash upriver with his gunboats and capture Nashville, but Halleck told him no. He wanted to have an occupation force ready before advancing on the Tennessee capital. Though two gunboats did accompany the occupation force a few days later, Foote was "disgusted." He was convinced that the order to halt "was jealousy on the part of McClellan and Halleck," and he was beginning to think it would be better to cut himself loose from the army. He wrote his wife that once he had all the gunboats and mortar rafts completed and fully manned, he would "not obey any orders except the Secretary's and the President's," adding, "I can well afford to be independent now." That independence was evident in the telegram he sent to Welles declaring that he wanted "no more men from the Army." He complained that the army sent him only the "off-scourings" of the recruits. "I prefer to go into action only half manned than to go with such men."[37]

The victories at Forts Henry and Donelson not only smashed the rebel defensive line in the West, they proved the value of armored gun-boats on the western rivers and the importance of cooperation between the services. The Mississippi was next, and Halleck was eager to em-ploy the proven stratagem of combined operations against Columbus, Kentucky, the so-called Gibraltar of the West. Foote was willing enough, but once again he had to repair his ships, which meant pulling them back to Cairo. Halleck wanted to keep them on the river. Foote complained to Wise that "the generals" were "detaining two boats up the river . . . which I want to repair." Wise took the complaint to Lin-coln, who resolved the dispute in Foote's favor, directing Halleck to send the boats "to Cairo for repairs." When Foote requested some extra anchor chains and four new Dahlgren guns, he sent the request not to Welles but to Wise. Again, Wise took it to the president, who ordered Welles to "have the requisition . . . filled as soon as possible." For all his initial reluctance to get involved, Lincoln was now directing the move-ment of ships and even the dispatch of supplies. Bates had urged Lin-coln "to restore all the floating force of the command of the Navy Department with orders to cooperate with the army, just as the Navy on the sea coast does." That, in effect, is what happened, but mainly it was because Lincoln had effectively taken charge himself.[38]

Lincoln's new role as the commander of the combined forces in the West occasionally required him to soothe some ruffled feathers. When he asked Foote why the *Benton* had not yet been repaired ten days after the fight at Donelson, the flag officer responded defensively. "Could the Pres-ident look at us here," Foote replied via Wise, "his practical and compre-hensive views would at a glance see that our amount of work, with our limited means would call for his commendation rather than surprise at the 'Benton' not being ready." After Wise took the response to the White House and read it aloud to Lincoln, he assured Foote that the president "appreciates your services which meet his entire approbation. . . . We hope you are better of your wounds and be assured your gallant services are properly regarded in Washington."[39]

Despite the tragedy in his personal life, by the end of March Lincoln was beginning to hope that his vision of a simultaneous advance by Union forces might soon be realized. Even McClellan's Army of the Potomac was at last lurching into motion, transferred in the largest military sea lift ever attempted from the Potomac to Fort Monroe at the tip of the Virginia peninsula. On the eve of that departure, Lincoln stripped McClellan of his title as general in chief. Ostensibly his reason was that McClellan would be hard pressed to manage all the nation's armies while he was conducting an expeditionary campaign, but in addition, Lincoln hoped that a new organization might lead to better military coordination. He consolidated three western departments under Halleck's command, and created a new Mountain Department for Frémont.[40]

By March, Union forces were finally on the move everywhere. While McClellan moved to the peninsula, Grant's smaller army, a thousand miles to the west, also used army transports (escorted by the gunboats *Lexington* and *Tyler*) to ascend the Tennessee River to Pittsburg Landing, just above the Mississippi state line, near a little country church called Shiloh; on the Mississippi, Foote partnered with Major General John Pope for a push down the Great Muddy; and a fourth expedition gathered off the mouth of the Mississippi under Farragut and Porter to threaten New Orleans. McClellan's movement in Virginia was unlikely to affect the other three in any significant way, but if Grant, Foote, and Farragut all moved more or less simultaneously, it would fulfill Lincoln's strategic vision and challenge the ability of the Confederacy to defend itself from three directions at once. When Lincoln explained the idea to Bates, the attorney general grasped it immediately and recorded it in his diary: "The enemy is really in a strait. If he move his iron boats up stream to meet Foote, then he leaves the lower river open to Farragut and Porter—and [if] he send them down to meet the gulf force, the coast is clear for Foote."[41]

FOOTE MOVED FIRST. The initial Union target on the Mississippi was to have been Columbus, Kentucky, the highest piece of firm ground on the river between Cairo and Vicksburg. Confederate general Leonidas Polk had considered it so vital he had violated Kentucky's short-lived neutrality to seize it. But the destruction of the railroad bridge over the Tennessee after the fall of Fort Henry had effectively cut it off and compelled the rebels to fall back southward some forty miles (as the river flowed) to Island No. 10, so called because it was the tenth island in the Mississippi River counting southward from its confluence with the Ohio.

The rebels chose this site in part because it was the first defensible position south of the Tennessee-Kentucky line, but also because geography had conspired to render it nearly unapproachable. The island sat in a horseshoe bend of the river, where batteries on the island itself and on the river's eastern bank could cover the approach from upriver for several miles, making an independent attack by Foote's gunboats, as at Fort Henry, problematical. In addition, a series of massive earthquakes a half century earlier had created an enormous swampy backwater called Reelfoot Lake east of the rebel position, which ruled out an overland approach as at Fort Donelson. More than in either previous combined operation, effective army-navy cooperation here would be vital.

Once again, Lincoln kept track of the campaign via the telegraph. While much of the president's attention was focused on McClellan's vast army on the Virginia peninsula, he also kept up with Foote's operations out west. The contrast could hardly have been greater. McClellan's lugubrious messages complained of bad weather, worse roads, and a need for more troops. The news from the West was more upbeat. Every day Wise brought him the latest information sent upriver from Island No. 10 to Cairo and forwarded to Washington by telegraph. Lincoln told Wise to bring him the latest news regardless of the time of day, and taking him at his word, Wise showed up at two o'clock in the morning on March 17 to report that Foote's flotilla was "in line of battle" and "within 2 miles of the enemy." Lincoln may have been especially interested to learn that the mortar boats had fired their first shots in anger that day, lobbing "a few shells to try the range." The next day came news that the firing had begun in earnest, and soon Foote was reporting that the rebel fortifications were being battered "all to pieces," though he also noted that a gun had burst on board the *St. Louis,* killing four sailors. Perhaps for Lincoln's benefit, he added: "The mortars are doing well." Indeed, the next day a mortar shell landed squarely on the Confederates' floating battery, and Foote reported that it "cleared the concern in short meter." After raising expectations of another quick victory, a few days later Foote reported: "This place, Island

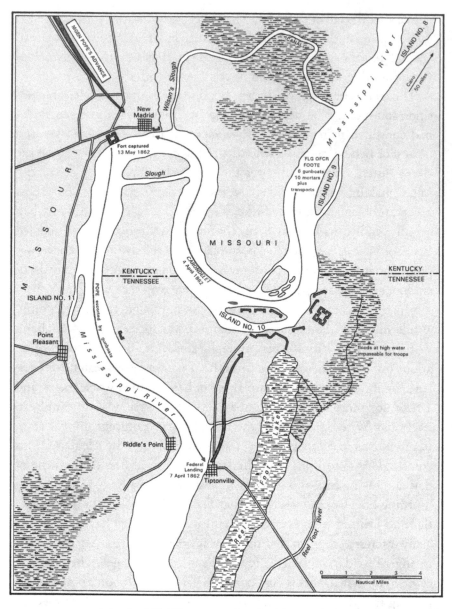

ISLAND NO. 10. Map by Bill Clipson, reprinted with permission from *The Naval Institute Historical Atlas of the U.S. Navy* by Craig L. Symonds, © 1995.

No. 10, is harder to conquer than Columbus." Indeed, he did not think it could be taken at all without a land assault from the rear.[42]

For more than two weeks, Foote's mortar rafts rained down "sulphur and brimstone," to use Lincoln's phrase, on the rebel defenses. At the same time, however, Foote was looking for a way to by-pass the rebel fortifications altogether. Halleck wanted him to get at least a few of his ironclads downriver to New Madrid, Missouri, on the west bank where Major General John Pope was seeking protection for his transports so that his army could cross the river and attack the rebels from the rear. Foote even tried to carve a canal through an old slough in the hope of finding a way around the enemy strong point. Meanwhile, there was no apparent movement either in Virginia or the West.

Then all of a sudden there was a tidal wave of news. On April 6, Foote reported that one of his ironclads, Henry Walke's *Carondelet*, had run past the batteries at Island No. 10 "without injury" and arrived safely in New Madrid. Another vessel made the run the next night, and together the two gunboats successfully escorted Pope's army across the river. The cabinet was in session on April 8 when news arrived that Island No. 10 had surrendered. At almost the same moment, another telegram brought news of "the most terrible battle of the war." The telegraph operator at Cincinnati reported that a rebel army had attacked Grant's force at Pittsburg Landing "in overwhelming force." Not until the next day did Lincoln learn that after being driven to the banks of the river on April 6, Grant had counterattacked the next day, and that the battle at Shiloh Church was a Union victory. There was more: two days later Lincoln learned that the enemy had abandoned Fort Pulaski, guarding the entrance to Savannah, which, along with the capture of Fernandina, Jacksonville, and St. Augustine the month before, virtually closed the coasts of Florida and Georgia.[43]

The good news from the West and from the coastal navy may have encouraged Lincoln to take a slightly harder line with McClellan, who was still stalled on the Virginia peninsula battling the mud and his own fears. Union forces were successful elsewhere, so why not in Virginia? Lincoln confessed to his friend Orville Browning that "he was becoming impatient and dissatisfied with McClellan's sluggishness of action." In an effort to prod his reluctant general, Lincoln wrote him pointedly on April 9: "It is indispensable to *you*, that you strike a blow." The next day, Lincoln issued a "Proclamation of Thanksgiving" for the victories elsewhere.[44]

Meanwhile, Union forces on the Mississippi continued their advance. On April 17, Wise brought Lincoln a note that the mortar boats had opened fire on Fort Pillow, near Memphis, and they had "cleared the river of all vessels, the shells falling in the rebel camp." Surely Foote's gunboats would now speed southward to take Memphis and then on to New Orleans. With luck, they would meet Farragut's squadron coming upriver from the Crescent City.[45]

IT TOOK LONGER THAN EXPECTED for Farragut to get his big oceangoing warships over the sandbars of the Mississippi Delta—so long, in fact, that Fox began to wonder if they had picked the wrong man for the job. Farragut wrote Fox to ask for more shallow-draft steamers, and when Fox read the request, "a cold shudder" passed through him. In a letter to Porter marked "Private," Fox asked him candidly if they had made "a mistake in our man," suggesting that "it is not too late to rectify our mistake," presumably by replacing Farragut with a more aggressive commander. Porter may have seen an opportunity here, for instead of defending his foster brother, the forty-eight-year-old Porter suggested that the sixty-year-old Farragut was in over his head. "Men of his age in a seafaring life are not fit for the command of important enterprises," he wrote, "they lack the vigor of youth." Porter portrayed Farragut as addleheaded and confused. "What his plans are I don't know," Porter wrote. "He talks very much at random at times, and rather underrates the difficulties before him, without fairly comprehending them." "Too much time has been lost in getting these ships ready. . . . He erred in not requiring greater promptitude in his captains. . . . It is very difficult for a man of his age finding himself commanding so large a force for the first time in his life." In case Fox missed the point, Porter followed this up with another letter a week later in which he wrote that Farragut "is full of zeal and anxiety, but has no administrative qualities, wants stability, and loses too much time in talking."[46]

Fox did not have time to react to Porter's curious condemnation of Farragut before he saw a southern newspaper carrying the story that New Orleans had fallen to the Yankees. He showed the paper to the president, and though there was no news from official sources, Lincoln could dare to hope. Confirmation came two days later. Under Porter's direction, Lincoln's mortars had pounded away at Forts Jackson and St. Philip for four days, but despite inflicting a lot of physical damage, they had not been able to neutralize the forts. Farragut would wait no longer. Though Porter had suggested to Fox that his foster brother was "not a Nelson or a Collingwood," Farragut took the bit in his teeth and steamed past the forts at 2:00 A.M. on April 24, triggering a middle-of-the-night pyrotechnic eruption as the gunners in the forts fired at the dark shapes on the river and the ships fired at the muzzle flashes on the ramparts. Farragut did not plan to shoot it out with the forts, however. Like Walke at Island No. 10, his goal was to get past them uninjured. The rebels sent fire rafts downstream, one of which briefly set Farragut's flagship, the *Hartford*, on fire. They also attacked with their small flotilla of gunboats, including the much-feared, but finally ineffective, ironclad *Louisiana*. The fire on the *Hartford* was extinguished, the enemy gunboats were routed, and Farragut's warships steamed safely past the forts.[47]

Barely pausing to inspect the damage, Farragut left Porter behind to keep an eye on the rebel forts and continued upriver to New Orleans. The next day he anchored off Jackson Square and demanded the surrender of the city. There was no resistance. Confederate authorities had all but stripped New Orleans of soldiers in order to concentrate against Grant at Pittsburg Landing, and the small number of troops that remained decamped as soon as Farragut's ships anchored off the city. Though the civil population shouted epithets and shook their fists, it was all sound and fury. Captain Theodorus Bailey led a small group of marines through a crowd of angry and frustrated civilians to the custom house to raise the American flag. The fall of the South's largest city was a body blow to the rebellion. In the decade before the war, more maritime traffic had flowed out of New Orleans than from Mobile, Charleston, Savannah, and Richmond combined.[48]

Farragut's occupation of the river doomed Forts Jackson and St. Philip as well. Cut off from their only line of supply and support, they had no choice but to surrender, which allowed the army transports carrying Major General Benjamin Butler's army of occupation to ascend the river and take control of the city. Farragut's original notion of running past the forts, and not Porter's (and Lincoln's) notion of demolishing them first with mortar fire, had proved successful.

The fall of New Orleans did not lead to an immediate conquest of the Mississippi. Farragut took his oceangoing steamers up to Vicksburg, but after determining that the city was unassailable without a contingent of ground troops, he returned downriver to New Orleans. On receipt of this news, Lincoln plunged from hope to despair. He had expected—indeed, he had specifically ordered—Farragut to continue northward to Memphis to join with Foote's squadron, and he had already notified Foote (through Fox) that Farragut would appear in Beauregard's rear "at once." Then on May 16 Lincoln learned that Farragut had instead returned downriver. With Lincoln's approval, Fox wrote to Farragut, "This retreat may be a fatal step as regards our western movements. . . . It is of paramount importance that you go up and clear the river with the utmost expedition. . . . There is not a moment to be lost." Lest there be any doubt about the source of these orders, Welles followed Fox's letter with one of his own two days later in which he told Farragut that "the President of the United States requires you to use your utmost exertions (without a moment's delay and before any other naval operations shall be permitted to interfere) to open the River Mississippi and effect a junction with Flag Officer Davis."[49]

There were delays at Memphis, too. Panicked by the rebels' surprise attack at Shiloh, Halleck had ordered Pope's army to abandon its movement down the Mississippi and join Grant at Pittsburg Landing. Foote was so disappointed, he complained about it to Welles. He was convinced that if Pope had stayed, they could have had Fort Pillow "in four days" and "Memphis in two days afterwards."[50] Instead, Foote never did see the fall of Memphis. The wound he had received at Fort Donelson and a gradual weakening of his general health compelled him to ask for relief. Reluctantly, Welles sent Captain Charles Henry Davis to stand in for him. Welles intended Davis' appointment to be temporary, but Foote found he could not return to active duty, and the assignment became permanent. With Davis in command, and aided by a ram fleet under the army's Colonel Charles W. Ellet Jr., the Union river squadron defeated an overmatched Confederate squadron in the Battle of Memphis on June 6—the only purely naval engagement on the western rivers during the war—which led to the capture of Memphis as surely as Farragut's run past the river forts had ensured the fall of New Orleans.

Meanwhile, prodded by Lincoln's direct order, Farragut returned to Vicksburg and ran past the batteries on the bluff to anchor in the bend of the river just north of the city. On July 1, he was joined there by Davis' flotilla. Though Vicksburg itself remained in rebel hands—its capture would take another year—the Union naval pincers had come together. Two weeks later, Congress passed an act formally transferring the western gunboat flotilla from the War Department to the Navy Department, and Welles was happy to claim the river fleet as his own.

DESPITE THE INHERENT DIFFICULTIES of coordinating combined operations hundreds of miles apart, each of them a thousand miles from the capital, Lincoln had not only managed to achieve cooperation but also validated his strategic vision. As he had foreseen, simultaneous attacks at different places had compelled the rebels to choose what to defend. Hoping that the river forts would contain the threats to Memphis and New Orleans, they had concentrated their armies for an all-out attack on Grant at Shiloh, and though they had come close, their gamble had failed. Grant survived their furious attack at Pittsburg Landing, and both Memphis and New Orleans fell to the navy. With their fall, Tennessee and Louisiana were reclaimed for the Union.

Though the junction of Union navy forces above Vicksburg in July did not signal permanent control of the Mississippi, at both the northern and southern ends of the river, Union forces had established a grip they would never relinquish. Indeed, the Confederacy never fully recovered from the reverses of these four months, and at least some of the credit belonged to the Union president, who was beginning to act the role of commander in chief in fact as well as in name. Though he would never claim it—it was not in his character to do so—he could take quiet gratification in the knowledge that the important victories in the Mississippi River Valley were due, at least in part, to his influence and involvement. The experience would encourage him to take further steps in his evolution as commander in chief.

5

"It Strikes Me There's Something in It"

Lincoln and the *Monitor*

IN THE FALL OF 1861, long before the capture of New Orleans or Memphis, and even before the resolution of the *Trent* affair, a visitor named Cornelius Bushnell showed up at the White House bearing a letter of introduction from Seward. In those simpler times, it was possible for visitors simply to present themselves and have a reasonable expectation that they would get in to see the president. A note from Seward, however, was a golden ticket, and Bushnell was immediately ushered into Lincoln's office. The president greeted him warmly, as he did most visitors, and asked what he could do for him. Bushnell replied that he had recently been to Brooklyn to see the Swedish-American inventor John Ericsson, who had entrusted him with a plan for a new kind of warship, and he presented Lincoln with the model of a unique naval vessel with a flat bottom and a flat deck, almost like one of the river mortar boats, though instead of being squared off, it was pointed at both ends. In the middle of this raft-like deck was an armored cylindrical tower containing two large naval guns. The tower itself was designed to rotate so that the big guns could point in any direction regardless of the heading of the ship. Even more than the mortar rafts, this new vessel was clearly outside the mainstream of warship design.[1]

Lincoln was fascinated by technology. While much of his attention to the mortar vessels was a product of his concern about the lack of military progress in the West, it also derived from his interest in innovative machines of war—or machines of any kind, for that matter. Lincoln was then, and remains today, the only American president ever to hold a patent. Significantly, perhaps, it was a patent for maritime—or at least riverine—use. In 1848, while traveling up the Detroit River with Mary aboard the passenger steamer *Globe*, he observed along with the rest of the passengers that another steamer, the *Canada*, had run itself fast aground on a sand bar. The officers and crew of the *Canada*, in an effort to free her, had placed "empty barrels, boxes and the like" under her to try to lift her off the bar. It occurred to Lincoln that perhaps river steamers could be equipped with flotation devices—rather like water wings—that could be inflated to lift boats over such obstacles. When he returned to Springfield, he put pencil to paper and sketched out his idea. The result was an invention titled "Manner of Buoying Vessels," which won him U.S. Patent 6,469.[2]

As president, Lincoln manifested his interest in technology in a number of ways, including his habit of making frequent visits out to the Washington Navy Yard. His first such trip took place on May 9, just two months into his presidency, when he attended a musical concert there, listening to a lengthy program of military marches and sentimental ballads by the band of the 71st New York Regiment. Before leaving, he asked the yard's commanding officer, John A. Dahlgren, if he could witness the firing of one of the new eleven-inch naval guns of Dahlgren's own design. Often called soda bottle guns because their fat breech and tapered gun tube gave them the appearance of a bottle lying on its side, they weighed eight tons each and were, at that time, the largest weapons in the nation's arsenal. Dahlgren was both pleased and flattered, and he immediately arranged a test firing.

It was a spectacular demonstration. The gun crew fired the big weapon three times. John Hay, who was with the president, was impressed by the thunderous crash, the brilliant muzzle flash, and the leaping rebound of the massive gun, followed instantly by the sight of an eleven-inch shell skipping across the water "throwing up a 30 ft. column of spray at each skip" toward the target. This was called firing by ricochet and was the most reliable way of hitting a floating vessel since the gunners could simply aim the weapon at the target without having to calculate the range. Dahlgren was gratified, and Lincoln impressed, when all three shots struck home. It was, Hay wrote, a scene "both novel and pleasant." Almost as an afterthought, he added: "The Prest. was delighted."[3]

Thus when Bushnell presented Ericsson's plan for an armored vessel, the president was immediately intrigued. It is possible to imagine him bending over the table to examine the design. Though the vessel depicted had only two guns, they were big Dahlgren guns like the ones Lincoln had watched being fired at the Navy Yard.* They were enclosed in a cylindrical tower that was composed of eight layers of overlapping one-inch iron plate, and the turret itself, which rested on a brass ring embedded in the ship's deck, could rotate. The crew's quarters, officers' staterooms, and engine spaces were all below the water line. Lincoln saw at once that the defensive power of that armored tower combined with the offensive power of those two enormous guns made this a formidable vessel indeed. Bushnell was gratified that Lincoln was "greatly pleased with the simplicity of the plan." The president was so impressed, in fact, that he agreed to meet Bushnell at the Navy Department the next day to urge its adoption.[4]

The group that Bushnell sought to convince, with Lincoln's help, consisted of three senior naval officers—all captains—and was known popularly as the Ironclad Board. Welles had created it in response to news stories about Confederate efforts to construct an ironclad warship of their own. When the U.S. Navy had abandoned the Gosport Navy Yard in a disgraceful panic back in April, it had left behind the large oceangoing screw steam frigate *Merrimack*.† After they occupied the yard, the Confederates raised it, placed it in dry dock, purged the salt water from its engines, cut away its masts and scantlings, and began to erect a wooden casemate on its undamaged hull with the evident intention of covering that casemate with armor plate. Welles got

---

*Ericsson's plan for the *Monitor* specified two 12-inch Dahlgren guns, but no guns of that size were immediately available, and so the vessel went to sea with two 11-inch guns taken from the USS *Dakotah*.

†The correct spelling of both the ship and the river for which it was named is *Merrimack,* but most nineteenth-century observers, including northern newspapers, dropped the final "k." Moreover, even though the vessel was rechristened CSS *Virginia* after its transformation, northerners, including Lincoln, continued to refer to it as the *Merrimac.*

"occasional vague intelligence" of this process, mostly from the newspapers, and decided it would be wise to prepare a countermeasure. An appropriations bill was quickly passed and signed, and Welles put out a call for proposals that would be evaluated by a board of three senior navy captains—the Ironclad Board.[5]

Bushnell had submitted one of the seventeen proposals that reached the board, but a number of navy officers had suggested to him that the vessel he proposed was so heavily burdened with armor, it might not float.* To obtain expert testimony that it would, Bushnell took his plan to Brooklyn to seek out the man everyone agreed was best qualified to assess it: the Swedish-born inventor John Ericsson. For his part, Ericsson was still nursing a grudge for the government's poor treatment of him after the explosion of a gun on board the USS *Princeton* back in 1844. Ericsson had designed the *Princeton*, the world's first screw propeller warship, but during a public relations cruise on the Potomac, one of its big guns had exploded at the breech, killing both the secretary of state and the secretary of the navy along with four others. Though Ericsson had not designed the flawed gun, the Navy made him the scapegoat for the disaster. Nevertheless, when Bushnell showed up at his door seventeen years later, Ericsson willingly examined the plan he had brought and, after a few calculations, assured Bushnell not only that the vessel would float but also that its armor would repel shot up to six inches in diameter. Then Ericsson asked Bushnell if he would like to see a plan for "a floating battery absolutely impregnable to the heaviest shot or shell." Bushnell declared that he would, and Ericsson brought out the model for the harbor defense battery that eventually became the USS *Monitor*. Excited, Bushnell asked if he could show it to the authorities in Washington, and Ericsson agreed, which is how it came to Lincoln's attention.[6]

---

*The vessel for which Bushnell was acting as agent eventually became the USS *Galena*. It proved a dismal failure. A conventionally rigged sloop-of-war with an extreme tumblehome coated with iron shingles, she proved remarkably clumsy and inefficient. Most of her rigging was removed once she was commissioned, and because her armor proved ineffective, it too was eventually removed, which was far worse. She ended the war as a rather ugly wooden steam sloop.

Lincoln was as good as his word. At eleven the next morning, he met Bushnell at the Navy Department to offer support for Ericsson's novel design. In addition to the board members, there were several other officers in the room, drawn, no doubt, by news that the president was in attendance. Fox was there, too, though not Welles, for he was still en route from Hartford. The officers were impressed by the novelty of Ericsson's design; certainly it was unlike any of the other proposals they had received. But novelty is not necessarily a virtue to men who have spent a half century or more as part of a system that prides itself on tradition. After a few noncommittal murmurings from the assembled officers, Lincoln spoke up. He did not order the board to adopt the proposal; that was a decision for the proper authorities to make. Instead he expressed his opinion in a characteristic way by declaring: "All I can say is what the girl said when she put her foot into the stocking. It strikes me there's something in it."[7]

Lincoln did not stay for the full meeting. Nor was he there the next day when Welles, now returned from Hartford, presided over the ongoing discussion. Charles Henry Davis, who was destined to replace Foote in command of the Mississippi Squadron but who at this point was serving as one of the three board members, had not been present to hear Lincoln, and he was the most skeptical. Davis was very much a product of the Old Navy. He even looked the part, affecting the epaulettes and gold braid of his rank and sporting a splendid walrus mustache that gave him the aspect of a character from Gilbert and Sullivan. He was suspicious of Ericsson, whom he associated—unfairly—with the explosion on the *Princeton*, and he was suspicious, too, of the revolutionary design of his proposed vessel. It simply did not fit Davis' conception of what a warship should look like. At the end of the day's discussions, he told Bushnell that he could safely "take the little thing home and worship it." It would not be idolatry if he did so, Davis said, "because it was made in the image of nothing in the heaven above or on the earth below or in the waters under the earth."[8]

The skepticism of the board members sent Bushnell back to Brooklyn. When Ericsson asked him what the officers had thought of his design, Bushnell was not entirely forthcoming. He said that they were impressed by the "genius" of it but that there were a few technical questions about it that Bushnell could not answer. "Well," Ericsson replied, "I'll go. I'll go tonight." It was a significant concession on his part to be willing to give the government another chance.[9]

When Ericsson appeared before the board ready to answer their technical questions, he was annoyed to encounter hostility instead. Aware of the president's interest, Welles had asked the board members to be circumspect, but their latent suspicion was evident. The elderly Commodore Joe Smith, who chaired the board, suggested that surely such a curious vessel would be unstable in a seaway. Ericsson denied it, and his detailed and technical explanation was so passionate that it silenced the critics. Even Davis was impressed. Still, it took the board three meetings to come to a conclusion. Welles was partly responsible for overcoming what he called "prejudices, ignorance and fixed habits and opinions" of the board members, and he maneuvered the discussion toward a favorable conclusion. He asked Ericsson how much it would cost to build his armored battery. Clearly prepared for the question, Ericsson answered promptly: "Two hundred and seventy-five thousand dollars." This was but a fraction of the million and a half dollars that Congress had appropriated, and less than the cost of either of the other two finalists. Welles may have feared the outcome of a secret ballot, so he turned at once to the board members and asked them one by one "if they would recommend that a contract be entered into." They did. Welles then turned back to Ericsson and told him to get started; a contract would be forthcoming.[10]

Welles told Ericsson that the new ship had to be ready for action in one hundred days, and though it was afloat in ninety-three days, several components that Ericsson had entrusted to subcontractors were not ready until February 1862. That month (at about the time that Foote was attacking Fort Henry out in Tennessee) Welles was busy at his desk when "a negro woman who resided in Norfolk" and who claimed to have new information about the *Merrimack* arrived at his office in Old Navy. She told Welles that the *Merrimack* "was nearly finished, had come out of the dock, and was about receiving her armament." From the bosom of her dress she produced a letter that provided details of the rebels' progress. There was not a lot Welles could do with the information except urge more haste in the completion of Ericsson's ironclad, which the inventor had named *Monitor*. Finally, on March 3, Ericsson turned the *Monitor* over to the government, and Welles ordered it to leave for Hampton Roads as soon as possible. Suggesting how much importance he attached to this one little ship, he sent both Fox and Henry Wise to Hampton Roads in advance of the craft to meet it upon its arrival.[11]

FIVE DAYS LATER, as Lincoln waited for news of Foote's assault on Island No. 10, Stanton charged into his office with a telegram from John E. Wool, the Union army commander at Fort Monroe. Stanton read it aloud: "The *Merrimack* came down from Norfolk to-day . . . , sunk the *Cumberland*, and the *Congress* surrendered. The *Minnesota* is aground and attacked . . . , the *St. Lawrence* just arrived and going to assist. . . . Probably both will be taken." The telegram ended with the ominous prediction that "the *Merrimack*, *Jamestown*, and *Yorktown* will pass the fort to-night." Stanton told Lincoln that he had already notified the other members of the cabinet of this disaster and that they were on their way to the White House.[12]

The news from Hampton Roads was chilling on several levels. If one enemy ship could destroy an entire Union squadron, it could not only raise the blockade but make McClellan's move to the Virginia peninsula impossible, thus wrecking the Union's grand strategy for the spring campaign. If it were truly indestructible, it might steam unhindered anywhere it wanted to go, appearing off the major cities of the Atlantic coast to set them afire or hold them for ransom. Stanton outlined these dire prospects for Lincoln even before Seward and Chase arrived, and when Welles appeared, they turned to him as one to ask what, if anything, could be done. Welles replied laconically, "I knew of no immediate steps that could be taken." He noted that Louis M. Goldsborough, the on-scene commander, was away on an expedition to the North Carolina sounds. There were other competent officers there, of course, but the news from Wool suggested it was unlikely that any of the navy's traditional warships could stand up to the *Merrimack*. The one good piece of news he could provide was that "our own iron-clad battery" had left New York on Thursday and should arrive at any moment. In fact, he was momentarily expecting a communication about it from Fox.[13]

Welles' report did not quell the sense of shock—even panic—in the room. Stanton in particular was "almost frantic," pacing "up and down the room like a caged lion." He claimed that "the Merrimac . . . would destroy every vessel in the service, could lay every city on the coast under contribution, could take Fortress Monroe." He thought it "likely" that it would come up the Potomac to "disperse Congress, destroy the Capitol and public buildings, or she might go to New York and Boston and destroy those cities." Clearly the government would have to recall Goldsborough from North Carolina at once and abandon Port Royal; they would have to notify the governors of all seaboard states to take measures to protect their ports. "Not unlikely," he said, looking out the window at the Potomac, "we shall have a shell or cannonball from one of her guns in the White House before we leave this room."[14]

In response to this flood of alarm, Welles affected a calmness that was at odds with his normal volatility. He suggested that the secretary of war was getting ahead of himself. After all, he noted archly, the *Merrimack* could not possibly go to Washington, New York, and Boston all at the same time. Sending warnings to the governors would only create a sense of alarm without offering any real help. Besides, Welles told him, a deep-draft vessel such as the *Merrimack*, covered as it was with heavy armor, would not be able to ascend the Potomac beyond Kettle Bottom Shoals, fifty miles downriver from the capital, nor could it challenge Goldsborough's force in the shallow waters of the North Carolina sounds. And finally, Welles concluded, there was the *Monitor*. A skeptical Stanton asked Welles how many guns this *Monitor* carried. "Two," Welles told him, "but of large calibre." At that, Stanton's face took on a "mingled look of incredulity and contempt [that] cannot be described," and he turned away in disgust. The tension between the two men rose to a dangerous level, and Lincoln stepped in to prevent the men from saying things that could not be forgotten.[15]

Seward, too, interceded. He agreed with Welles that perhaps they were "given away too much to our apprehensions." There was really no alternative, he said, but to wait and hear what Ericsson's battery could accomplish. At that, Stanton abruptly left, going out, as it proved, to send warning telegrams to Boston and New York on his own authority and to make other preparations as well. Lincoln, too, soon left. With his civilian advisers in open disagreement, he wanted the views of a serving officer, and his frequent visits to the Washington Navy Yard had convinced him that Dahlgren was just the kind of competent professional whose advice would be crucial in this crisis. He called for his carriage and headed for the Navy Yard accompanied by his friend Orville Browning, who had filled Stephen Douglas' Senate seat after Douglas' sudden death the previous June.[16]

Dahlgren was a slim and "delicate featured" man who was exactly Lincoln's age but looked at least a decade younger. A newspaper had recently described him as being "perhaps forty years of age." It also noted that "his thin nostrils expand as he talks with a look of great enthusiasm." It was that enthusiasm, in addition to Dahlgren's interest in technology, that drew Lincoln to him. Arriving at the Navy Yard, Lincoln and Browning found Dahlgren in his office. Lincoln told him that he had "frightful news," and he explained what had happened. The president asked Dahlgren if the *Merrimack* could, in fact, steam up the Potomac to Washington. Welles had claimed the big ship could not get over the Kettle Bottom Shoals. What did Dahlgren think? Dahlgren thought it was doubtful, but after checking with the local pilots who knew the river better than he did, he reported that they believed "a vessel drawing 22 feet of water" could pass the Kettle Bottom Shoals, where, according to the pilots, "24 feet can be had." Lincoln asked Dahlgren to come with him back to the White House, and Dahlgren climbed into the carriage. Dahlgren noted that "the President was not at all stunned by the news, but was in his usual suggestive mood." En route, Lincoln asked him about Stanton's prediction that the rebel ironclad could lie off New York or Boston and hold those cities for ransom. Dahlgren said it was possible that "she could go to New York, lie off the City, and levy contributions at will."[17]

Back at the White House, Dahlgren, Meigs, and others joined the cabinet in a kind of war council. Charles Wilkes showed up, too, and was bemused to find everyone "in a scare . . . except Mr Lincoln who sat with his legs hanging over the arms of a large Arm chair." "Stanton," Wilkes noted, "appeared to assume control." Stanton urged the president to act at once to protect the capital by blocking the Potomac River, and Lincoln asked Dahlgren how this might be done. Dahlgren suggested erecting batteries, including several mortars, at Giesboro Point, just below the mouth of the Anacostia River, or blocking the shallows at Kettle Bottom Shoals by sinking ships laden with ballast. This second option would be a desperate act, for it would cut the nation's capital off from the outside world, but, after all, these were desperate times. With Stanton's urging, Lincoln authorized Dahlgren to make the preparations, but told him not to act on them yet, and Dahlgren returned to the Navy Yard. Wilkes thought that "Mr. Lincoln seemed to me to be the only one who was calm and placid and appeared willing to await the further progress of events."[18]

Welles continued to argue that the *Merrimack* would not be able to ascend the river, and that in any case they should wait to hear what effect the Ericsson battery might have on the rebel ironclad, but Wilkes thought that Welles was "entirely ignored by the rest of the meeting." Stanton was utterly dismissive of the chances of "any little vessel of two guns against a frigate clothed with iron." Nor, he added, did he have "much confidence in naval officers for such a crisis." He told Welles that he had already sent warning telegrams to northern governors, and that he had contacted Cornelius Vanderbilt, who owned a number of large steamers and who "was a man of resources and great energy" to ask him what to do. In doing so, Stanton clearly implied that the opinion of Cornelius Vanderbilt was more valuable in a crisis than that of Welles or any of his clearly helpless naval officers.[19]

Dahlgren, meanwhile, was busily assembling several dozen boats along the riverfront in Washington and Georgetown for use as block ships. Stanton authorized Dahlgren to buy as many boats as he needed and "to draw on any of the regiments or forts for men, guns, or munitions." He even authorized Dahlgren to appropriate privately owned vessels—the government would make it up to the owners later—and that afternoon Stanton went to the Navy Yard to oversee the effort personally. Then, late that afternoon, a note arrived at the Navy Yard for Stanton informing him that "the Merrimac did not go to sea but has put back to Norfolk." A cryptic sentence at the end of the note said: "The message reads as if she had had an encounter with the Erricson [*sic*]."[20]

Confirmation came a few hours later. Lincoln was in the telegraph office just before seven o'clock, when a message arrived from Fox that Ericsson's *Monitor* had met the *Merrimack* in Hampton Roads and fought her hull to hull for four hours, "part of the time touching each other." At the end of the fight, just before noon, "the Merrimack retired." Lieutenant John L. Worden had been temporarily blinded when a rebel shell had struck the pilothouse, but his wound did not appear to be life-threatening. The steam frigate *Minnesota* had been "somewhat injured," but the *Monitor* itself was "uninjured and ready at any moment to repel another attack." It was the best possible news, and as he returned to the White House, Lincoln must have walked with a lighter step. For all his surface placidity, Welles, too, felt a great relief, and late that night he ordered Dahlgren to "suspend operations for . . . sinking boats or placing obstructions in the Potomac."[21]

Stanton, however, was not convinced that was the end of it. When he and Welles encountered each other the next day (Monday, March 10) in Lincoln's office, he wanted to know by what authority Welles had countermanded his orders to block the Potomac. Welles said that the navy had spent much of the fall and summer keeping the Potomac open by clearing the southern bank of enemy batteries. He observed that the army had not been much help in this effort, but that thanks to the navy, the river was still open, and it was the river traffic that kept both the capital and McClellan's army supplied. If the river were blocked, both would be cut off entirely. He would not do it, he declared challengingly, unless the president ordered it.[22]

Once again Lincoln stepped in, almost literally, to keep the two men apart. Characteristically, he tried to defuse the rising tension with humor. He joked that "Mars"—meaning Stanton—wanted "exclusive control of military operations." But not satisfied with that, Mars also wanted a navy, and had begun to improvise one. Lincoln decided that Stanton could go ahead with his preparations. The boats "might be loaded and sent down the river," but they were not to be sunk in the channel until it was known for certain that the *Merrimack* was on its way. Moreover, whatever expense was involved would have to be paid by the War Department. "Mars," Lincoln concluded, must not "cripple Neptune."[23]

Stanton was neither amused nor deterred. He contacted Cornelius Vanderbilt again, asking him how much money he wanted to build an ironclad warship that would prevent the *Merrimack* from getting out of Hampton Roads. Vanderbilt was flattered by Stanton's evident confidence, and two days later he arrived in Washington to see Lincoln. He offered to make the government a gift of the *Vanderbilt*, the enormous passenger steamer named for him, claiming that she was "the best ship in the world." Unwilling to be ungracious, Lincoln replied:

"We will take her." Vanderbilt then said, "I have another ship, the next best one in the world. I will have her completely iron armored, if you desire it, and when she is done you shall pay me a reasonable price for her." Stanton told him to go ahead by all means, though no one, apparently, bothered to bring Welles into the discussion or even to tell him about it.[24]

Relieved as he was with the *Monitor*'s success, Lincoln continued to worry about the *Merrimack*'s potential for mischief. He wondered if instead of blocking the Potomac to keep the *Merrimack* out, it might be possible to block the Elizabeth River to keep her in. If the proper vessels could be procured, he wished the navy to try it. Meanwhile, he ordered Welles to ensure that the *Monitor* was "not too much exposed." Fox wrote back to assure him that "the Monitor will take no risk excepting with the Merrimack."[25]

As for the *Monitor*'s wounded commander, Wise brought Worden back to Washington and put him up on the second floor of his own home. The next day, Wise accompanied Welles to the White House to give the president a "very spirited" eyewitness report on the battle, and news of Worden's condition. After he finished, Lincoln declared, "Gentlemen, I am going to see that feller." He got up at once, and Wise accompanied him on the short walk to his home. After climbing the stairs to the second floor, Lincoln entered the darkened bedroom and saw Worden stretched out on the bed, his swollen and lacerated face blackened by burns where it was not covered by bandages.

Wise told Worden who his visitor was: "Jack, here's the President, who has come to see you."

Unable to see, Worden struggled up onto one elbow and extended his hand. "You do me great honor, Mr. President, by this visit."

Clearly moved, Lincoln replied, "No, sir, you have done me and your country honor and I shall promote you."[26]

Lincoln's confidence in Ericsson's peculiar little vessel had been validated. Its success in Hampton Roads also reestablished Ericsson's credentials with the government and led to a series of contracts for the construction of several dozen more monitors. Indeed, the Union endured a bout of what some called "monitor fever" as Welles, Fox, and others enthusiastically embraced armored vessels on the monitor design as the key to success in the naval war. Ericsson even took it upon himself to lecture Lincoln about the future of warfare. "The time has come Mr President," he wrote, "when our cause will have to be sustained not by numbers, but by superior weapons." In fact, of course, it would be sustained by both. In the summer of 1862, however, Ericsson sketched out for the president a vision of future war that would come to define "the American way of war." He predicted that "by a proper application of mechanical devices alone will you be able with absolute certainty to destroy the enemies of the Union."[27]

WITH THE IMMEDIATE THREAT of the *Merrimack* apparently neutralized, McClellan's grand amphibious movement to Fort Monroe could go ahead as planned. During a two-week period beginning on March 17, a total of 389 ships, almost all of them chartered army transports, delivered 121,000 men, 15,000 animals, 1,200 wagons and ambulances, and 44 artillery batteries to Fort Monroe on the Virginia peninsula. It was an enormous logistical feat and one particularly well suited to McClellan's organizational abilities. Alas, McClellan's actions once he arrived at Fort Monroe suggested that he somehow believed that the movement itself would so discourage the enemy that the rest of the campaign would be mostly a matter of letting the ripe fruit fall into his lap.[28]

Worse, Lincoln learned that despite his many assurances, McClellan had left the national capital nearly bereft of troops. Lincoln had agreed to McClellan's seaborne end run only on the condition that McClellan left Washington "entirely secure." But the local commanders reported that they had too few soldiers, and those they did have were raw recruits hardly to be depended on if the enemy mounted a serious attack. Shocked, Lincoln ordered that Irvin McDowell's First Corps, the last element of McClellan's command to embark, be held back for the protection of the capital. McClellan was "astonished" when he learned of this, and he wrote melodramatically that he had received the news at the front "while listening to the rebel guns." McClellan protested that the enemy in Virginia was "in large force" and "being reinforced daily." He reported that it now seemed likely he would have to fight the enemy's whole force—as if he had previously expected otherwise—and he asked that Lincoln not compel him to undertake this monumental task "with diminished numbers." He complained that he had barely eighty-five thousand men to take on the huge enemy army.[29]

Lincoln was less susceptible to this kind of blackmail than he once had been. He telegraphed back that "I think you better break the enemies' line . . . at once. They will probably use *time*, as advantageously as you can." And a few days later he wrote McClellan a long letter that was both encouraging and gently admonitory. In the interim, he had learned of the victories at both Island No. 10 and at Shiloh, and that may have led him to be more forceful than usual with his reluctant general. "After you left," Lincoln wrote, "I ascertained that less than twenty thousand unorganized men, without a single field battery, were all you designed to be left for the defense of Washington. . . . My explicit order that Washington should, by the judgment of *all* the commanders of Army corps, be left entirely secure, had been neglected." Lincoln also took issue with McClellan's complaint that he had too few soldiers to meet the enemy. He noted that McClellan's own returns showed him with 108,000 men, though he now claimed he had only 85,000. "How can the discrepancy of 23,000 be accounted for?" He ended with a not-so-veiled warning: "I have never written you, or spoken to you, in greater kindness. . . . *But you must act.*"[30]

No doubt feeling betrayed, even martyred, McClellan turned to the navy for help. He believed that the enemy line stretching across the peninsula from Yorktown to the Warwick River was too strong for a frontal attack but that the navy could easily outflank it and force a Confederate retreat. Alas, the navy was no more helpful than Lincoln. When Fox asked Goldsborough if he would be "willing to place himself under the orders of General McClellan" for this emergency, the flag officer replied that "he would never under any circumstances place himself under the orders of an officer of the army." Goldsborough did say he would gladly *cooperate* with McClellan, but his actions suggested otherwise. He sent a half dozen vessels to open fire on the Gloucester Point batteries, but after a brief and halfhearted bombardment, he withdrew them, declaring it too dangerous, even though none of the ships had received any damage. McClellan wanted Goldsborough's ships to run past the batteries at night the way Farragut had run past Forts Jackson and St. Philip on the Mississippi. Goldsborough, however, was no Farragut. Fearful of another sortie by the *Merrimack*, he kept most of his big ships in Hampton Roads and behaved as if his primary function were to maintain the fleet undamaged. Under such circumstances—short of troops (as he saw it) and with an uncooperative navy—McClellan decided that instead of attacking the enemy line "at once," as Lincoln had urged, he had no choice but to settle down to a regular siege—a tactic well suited to his particular talents, but one sure to prolong the campaign.[31]

BACK IN WASHINGTON, the capital was strangely quiet now that the army had left. As one New York journalist noted, "Until recently the town was filled with military. An innumerable caravan of army wagons was always moving in the streets, and the hotels were bedlams of noise and confusion. To-day the strangers who arrived are wondering at the dulness [sic] which prevails." In the midst of this interlude, Lincoln received a visit from Count Henri Mercier, the French minister. A few days earlier, the French frigate *Gassendi*, which had been a witness to the battle of ironclads in Hampton Roads the month before, had dropped anchor in the Potomac off the Navy Yard, and Mercier had come to invite the president to visit her. Because Franco-American relations had been strained by the *Trent* affair and by American suspicion of French sympathy for the rebel government, Seward encouraged the visit. Lincoln was perfectly willing, not only because of the benefit it might bring to foreign relations but also because, as he said, "he was not very familiar with war vessels, and would like to see how the French frigate looked."[32]

Lincoln and Seward took a carriage to the Navy Yard, where Dahlgren escorted them down to his barge, manned by half a dozen sailors. Dahlgren took the tiller himself, and the barge bearing the official party was "pulled rapidly out towards the ship." The *Gassendi* was completely dressed with flags and the yards were "manned"—that is, the French crew had lined up along the yardarms in tribute to their visitor. As the president's barge approached, a large American flag was broken out at the mainmast, and when Lincoln reached the deck of the big frigate, the first shot of a twenty-one-gun salute banged out near the bow. The ship's captain and his officers, all decked out in their best uniforms, greeted Lincoln at the gangway. The captain, Jules Gauthier, invited the official party to his cabin for a light refreshment of (what else?) champagne. Then came a tour of the vessel. A reporter from the

New York Herald observed that Lincoln was "his usual, quiet, homely, unpretentious" self during the tour, and that he "chatted affably" with those members of the crew who could speak a few words of English. Then, the tour over, Lincoln was escorted back to the gangway and he took his leave as another twenty-one-gun salute began. The *Herald* reporter assured his readers that the whole visit was "a happy augury for the future amicable relations of the two countries."[33]

What the *Herald* reporter did not relate was that once Lincoln had settled himself back in Dahlgren's barge, he suggested they row around to the bow of the frigate instead of returning directly to the Navy Yard. "I should like to look at her build and rig from that direction," he said. Dahlgren dutifully pushed the tiller over and the little barge headed for the *Gassendi*'s bluff bow. Above them, however, the twenty-one-gun salute was still in progress, and those in the boat could hear the gunnery officer counting off the seconds between the shots: "Un, deux, trois . . ." Then, almost directly above the president's head, came "the flash and deafening roar of a cannon." The shots were blanks, of course, but flame, smoke, and bits of sacking flew from the muzzle with explosive force. Dahlgren didn't wait for the next shot. Pulling the tiller hard over, he called out to the boat's crew: "Pull like the devil, boys! Pull like hell!" Through it all, Lincoln sat "impassively," and he never mentioned it afterward.[34]

A FEW DAYS AFTER this close encounter with naval gunnery, Lincoln decided to go down to Fort Monroe and see for himself how things were going. He had concluded that McClellan needed prompting, and his experience as an activist commander in chief during the western river campaign may have encouraged him to consider a more hands-on role in Virginia. He left Washington on Monday evening, May 5, with Stanton, Chase, and an army general with the unlikely name of Egbert Ludovicus Viele, who had recently returned from the capture of Fort Pulaski near Savannah. They boarded the new revenue cutter *Miami* (which Chase called "a staunch little steamer") and started down the Potomac in the dark. It was drizzling rain, and since the navigational lights were unreliable, after only about fifteen miles the pilot refused to go any further, insisting that they anchor and wait for daylight.[35]

As a revenue cutter, the *Miami* was officially part of the Treasury Department, and Chase took it upon himself to act the part of host. The official party gathered in the central cabin for dinner, where "a shaded lamp suspended from the ceiling threw a cheerful light on the table," and afterward they engaged in a lengthy discussion of the military situation. Stanton was concerned about being away from the office. He had received an enquiry from a field general that he hadn't entirely understood, and, pressed for an answer, he had told the general to "go ahead." Now he worried that he might have approved an unwise maneuver. Lincoln consoled him with the thought that surely what Stanton *meant* was that if it was a good idea, *then* the general should go ahead. As was often the case, it reminded him of a story. There was a horse for sale back in Illinois, the president began, which was reputed to be very fast. A large crowd of potential purchasers had gathered to inspect it, and the owner hired a boy to ride it up and down "to exhibit its points." A suspicious bidder pulled the boy aside and asked him if the horse had a splint. "Well, mister," the boy replied, "if it's good for him he has got it, but if it isn't good for him he hasn't." Lincoln and his party finally turned in sometime in the early morning, though the president had a hard time folding his frame into the bed assigned to him in his tiny cabin.[36]

At first light they got under way again, and soon they were passing Kettle Bottom Shoals. Lincoln was leaning against the railing watching the passing shoreline when the long string of ballast-laden barges and scows placed there two months before by Stanton's directive came into view. Someone in the party asked about them, and Lincoln declared, "Oh, that is Stanton's navy." He might have let it go at that, but apparently he decided to have a bit of fun at Stanton's expense. "That is the squadron Welles would have nothing to do with and about which he and Stanton had the dispute. It was finally decided, I believe, that the War Department might have a fleet of its own to fight the 'Merrimac' and there it is." Stanton, who in Viele's opinion "courted antagonism with a spirit of uncompromising defiance," did not see any humor in the president's remark. He replied defensively that he simply thought it was best to "provide for an emergency." He should have said nothing at all, for his comment reminded the president of another story.[37]

There was in Illinois, Lincoln said, a "respectable lawyer" who was well known for a curious physical characteristic. He had breasts that were "enormous, more protuberant than those of many females." When a colleague suggested to him that such a deformity could be of no possible use, the man disagreed. He insisted that if he were abandoned on "an uninhabited island, with no other human being but a nursing infant, he had no doubt Providence would furnish, through him, nourishment for the child." Just in case anybody missed the point, Lincoln then declared that the man had made this declaration "with as much apparent sincerity as Stanton showed when he urged a navy composed of canal boats to stop the Merrimac."[38] This time Stanton wisely made no further comment.

The *Miami* reached the mouth of the Potomac at midday and entered the heavy chop of the Chesapeake Bay. Since it was noon, the stewards began to serve lunch, and the distinguished party sat down to eat. Lincoln's stomach betrayed him almost at once, and, announcing that he was too ill to eat, he stretched out on a ship's locker. The others tried to continue with their lunch but did so only with difficulty. As Chase remembered it, "The plates slipped this way and that—the glasses tumbled over and slid and rolled about—and the whole table seemed as topsy-turvy as if some Spiritualist were operating upon it." Soon Stanton, too, gave up on lunch and left the room hurriedly. When he returned, he lay down on a locker near the president. Chase and General Viele went topside.[39]

It was full dark by the time the *Miami* came within sight of Fort Monroe, at the tip of the peninsula formed by the York and the James Rivers. Viele remembered that "the outlines of the grand old fortress were dimly visible along the horizon as we approached, and around and about it in the adjacent waters was a cordon of floating videttes, whose thousand lights glimmered like stars in the mirrored surface." Fort Monroe was the largest and most powerful of all the coastal fortifications constructed by the Army Corps of Engineers between 1819 and 1834 as part of the Second System of coastal fortifications. It had remained in Union possession despite its location in Virginia because, while the Buchanan administration had dithered over Fort Sumter, Major General John Wool had quickly sent reinforcements into Fort Monroe. Since then it had been a thorn in the side of the Confederacy. Wool, at age seventy-eight (two years older than Scott), was the oldest general in the war to hold a field command. Nevertheless, when the *Miami* dropped anchor off the fort late on the evening of May 6, he came out in a small tug to greet the president. Lincoln roused himself to greet the gaunt, almost cadaverous general who combed his thin hair forward in a vain attempt to cover his balding head. As Lincoln talked with Wool, someone suggested that it might be appropriate for them to call on Goldsborough on board his flagship the *Minnesota*, and so Lincoln, Wool, and the rest of the official party climbed down into the tug and headed across the dark water toward the bluff side of the big steam frigate.[40]

As the tug came alongside, it became evident that the only way to board the *Minnesota* was by steps built into the side of the frigate, steps that were so shallow that only one's toes could gain a purchase. There were thin guide ropes on either side, but in the full dark, the climb up the side of the warship looked daunting. Etiquette required that the president go first; aware of that, Lincoln stepped on the thwart of the tug, grabbed the ropes, and made his way up without incident. Once on board, Lincoln met the commander of the North Atlantic Blockading Squadron, Louis Malesherbes Goldsborough. He was not physically impressive: a stocky, even plump, short-necked fifty-seven-year-old with small eyes and a scraggly beard, though in the middle of the night after a long day of seasickness the president was probably not focusing on Goldsborough's appearance. He was pleased to note that the big *Minnesota* was a much more stable platform than the little *Miami*, and he happily accepted Goldsborough's invitation to sleep aboard.[41]

LINCOLN WAS UP EARLY the next morning, eager to see the fort and the area of operations in the light of day. From the deck of the *Minnesota*, he looked around the roadstead, seeing half a dozen regal-looking warships at anchor plus the unimpressive but nevertheless fascinating stump of the *Monitor* turret. There was, in addition, the silhouette of the enormous side-wheel steamer *Vanderbilt*, which Stanton had chartered from its namesake owner and which now boasted a new reinforced bow ram made of heavy timbers covered with iron plate. Goldsborough stood beside Lincoln and pointed out the pertinent military features of the roadstead, including the scene of the famous duel of the ironclads two months before, and the location of the rebel batteries, which were clearly in sight at Sewall's Point. As Lincoln studied the enemy fortification across the water, he asked Goldsborough why

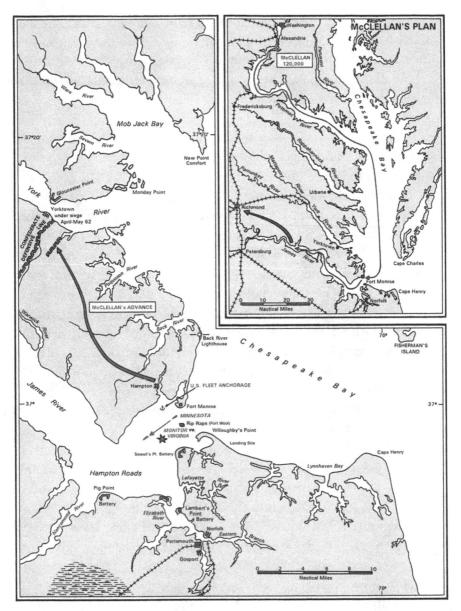

THE VIRGINIA PENINSULA AND HAMPTON ROADS. Map by Bill Clipson, reprinted with permission from *The Naval Institute Historical Atlas of the U.S. Navy* by Craig L. Symonds, © 1995.

the navy tolerated the continued presence of those batteries. The flag officer had no good answer to that, and he agreed at once to organize a "demonstration"—a kind of reconnaissance in force—to test them. Lincoln had come to Fort Monroe to see if he could prod his reluctant general, but he saw that prodding was likely to be necessary in other quarters as well.

While Goldsborough went off to set things in motion, the official party made a round of visits in the roadstead. At Stanton's suggestion, they visited the *Vanderbilt* first. Though Cornelius Vanderbilt had offered his big side-wheel steamer to the navy at the outset of the war, Welles had turned him down because its deep draft made it unsuitable for blockade duty and it was too profligate with coal for any other use. Thanks to Stanton, however, the big ship now rested at anchor in Hampton Roads ready to run down the *Merrimack* if it ever again came out into open water. Lincoln was interested in the jury-rigged bow ram, which he inspected carefully, and the immense paddlewheels, each of which weighed over a hundred tons and which were held together by a complex web of iron rods. After breakfast ashore the official party reboarded the tug and went out to see the *Monitor*.[42]

The six-foot-four-inch Lincoln was an incongruity on board the little ironclad. His manner, too, was different from that of most visitors. Whereas others gushed ("like a bottle of soda water," one said) about the mechanical marvel, Lincoln was quiet and introspective, and asked practical questions. His guides were surprised and impressed that "he was well acquainted with all the mechanical details of our construction." He shook hands with all the officers, including its new commanding officer, William N. Jeffers, and before he left, he asked that the crew be assembled. He walked past them, hat in hand, looking into their faces, and then thanked them for their service. As he left, they offered up three cheers.[43]

That afternoon, Lincoln had the rare opportunity of witnessing an operation he had set in motion himself. Goldsborough had designated five steamers, plus the *Monitor*, for the "demonstration" against Sewall's Point, and to observe it, Lincoln and his entourage boarded the tug and went out to a battery on what was called the Rip Raps: a small, man-made island about a third of the way between Fort Monroe and Sewall's Point. That battery had initially been named Fort Calhoun after the South Carolina senator and onetime vice president, but Calhoun's association with the doctrine of state nullification made the name unseemly amidst civil war, and it was renamed Fort Wool once the conflict began. Now Lincoln stood on its ramparts to watch the action he had suggested. Just before noon the great ships were in motion—the big steamers, led by *Seminole*, drew up their anchors, black smoke spewing from their stacks, and moved, very slowly it seemed, toward the objective. They began firing eleven-inch shells at the rebel battery, the white smoke from the guns mixing with the black smoke from the stacks. One of the shells carried away the enemy flagstaff. Some brave soul in the rebel battery climbed up onto the ramparts with another Confederate flag, which he waved defiantly until another shell from the *Seminole* ended his bravado. The little *Monitor* also got under way, and its big guns joined the bombardment: "a belch of smoke, followed in a few seconds by a report like distant thunder." A few of the guns at the Rip Raps joined in. As Lincoln watched, "the small [rebel] battery at the extreme point was silenced," and the Union guns shifted their fire to another battery about half a mile nearer to Norfolk. Lincoln may have wondered, if the navy's guns could so easily silence the enemy shore batteries, why Goldsborough had waited until now to do it.[44]

As Lincoln watched, a larger puff of black smoke "curled up over the woods" behind Sewall's Point, and almost in unison, those watching from the ramparts declared, "There comes the Merrimac." Sure enough, from around the point the iron monster itself appeared. Its progress was glacial, and before it had fully emerged, Lincoln and his party were already back on board the tug and en route to Fort Monroe. From the deck of the tug Lincoln watched the *Merrimack*'s slow emergence. The wooden ships of the U.S. fleet pulled up their anchors and began to move away. They were under strict orders—Lincoln's orders, in fact—to avoid battle with the *Merrimack* and to leave it to the *Monitor* and the *Vanderbilt* plus the two or three other vessels that had been modified with heavy bow rams. The *Monitor* held its ground, offering battle, and soon there was "a clear sheet of water" between the two ironclads. But at that point, as Chase noted, "the great rebel terror paused—then turned back."[45]

The silencing of the Sewall's Point battery was gratifying, but rather than bask in this limited success, Lincoln at once sought to take advantage of it. After reviewing the soldiers in their camp site near Hampton, he reboarded the tug and asked its captain to lay him alongside the *Monitor*. There, he deferentially asked Jeffers if "there would be any military impropriety" if he got his ship under way without orders from Goldsborough, and if not, would he please conduct a reconnaissance of Sewall's Point to see if the works had, in fact, been abandoned, and to "report to him the result." Back on the *Minnesota*, Lincoln suggested to Wool that if the works ashore had been neutralized, it might be possible to land an armed force there in order to approach Norfolk from the rear. Wool was hesitant. He claimed that there was no satisfactory landing site in the vicinity, and after all, there was still the *Merrimack* to worry about. A few officers suggested that perhaps troops could be sent instead to Burnside in North Carolina, who could approach Norfolk from the south. It may have seemed to Lincoln that nearly all his officers—of both services—favored an indirect approach when a direct approach was available.[46]

That afternoon, however, Chase returned from a cruise on the *Miami* to tell Lincoln that he and General Wool had found "a good and convenient landing place" on the south shore of the roadstead safely away from the *Merrimack*'s anchorage. The news provoked Lincoln to call for a chart of the area, and after conversing with a local pilot, he thought he identified an even closer landing site. He told Chase he "wished to go and see about it on the spot." Thus it was that the president of the United States and two of his cabinet members led a naval reconnaissance mission to the Virginia shore. Lincoln and Stanton boarded the small tug along with "some 20 armed soldiers from the Rip Raps," and Chase followed in the larger *Miami*. Being of shallower draft, the tug went closer to the shore. Several horsemen appeared on the beach, and, concerned for the president's safety, Chase asked by signal if the *Miami* should open fire on them. Lincoln said no, and the tug soon retreated out of range.[47]

Back at Fort Monroe, Wool agreed to conduct an amphibious landing near Sewall's Point, though he preferred the beach that he had visited with Chase to the one Lincoln had reconnoitered, and Lincoln deferred to him. He didn't care which landing site the army used, so long as something happened. Wool issued the pertinent orders, and aides ran off in all directions to designate the units and arrange for the transports. At the same time, Lincoln also sought to support McClellan's push up the peninsula. That, after all, was the reason Lincoln had come to Fort Monroe in the first place. As it happened, however, the rebel army had evacuated the Yorktown line the day before Lincoln left Washington, and now McClellan was busy orchestrating the pursuit. Because of "the present state of affairs," McClellan declared that he was far too busy to leave his command and see the president, though he did ask if it was possible for "the Galena and other gunboats to move up James River." He was still hopeful that a naval thrust up the James would outflank the rebels.[48]

Lincoln put the question to Goldsborough that night. It was quite late by the time Goldsborough came ashore, and the president had already retired, though he insisted on seeing Goldsborough regardless of the time. Propping himself up in bed, Lincoln emphasized the importance of supporting McClellan's advance, declaring that it was urgent that the *Galena*, and perhaps the *Monitor*, too, be sent up the James River as soon as possible. Goldsborough hesitated, saying that before he could do that, he would have to bring other vessels around from the York River in order to ensure continued superiority in Hampton Roads. At this, Stanton, who had also entered the room, lost his temper and "in the most impatient and imperious manner insisted that it should be done instantly." Again acting as the soothing intermediary, Lincoln merely reiterated that the mission was an urgent one, and allowed Goldsborough to save face by asking him which officer he thought should command the expedition. Goldsborough named John Rodgers, who was now captain of the *Galena*, and so Rodgers was sent for. Asked by the president if he was willing to lead an expedition up the James, Rodgers, of course, replied that he was. Lincoln thanked both naval officers for their support, and Stanton left to assure McClellan by telegraph that an expedition under Captain Rodgers would be sent up the James at once.[49]

EVERYONE WAS UP EARLY the next morning. As Rodgers prepared to take the *Galena* upriver to support McClellan, the amphibious expedition aimed at Norfolk also got under way. Some five thousand soldiers, many of whom Lincoln had reviewed the day before, marched down from Hampton and embarked in canal boats at the Fort Monroe docks. Wool begged Stanton to be allowed to lead the attack personally, and Stanton agreed. Lincoln, Stanton, Chase, and Viele all went along as well. Lincoln was very much caught up in the moment. One soldier recalled seeing the president "rushing about, hollering to someone on the wharf." The landing itself was haphazard as troops splashed ashore from the several rowboats and congregated above the beach. Chase and Viele went ashore with the troops, though Lincoln and Stanton remained aboard ship and soon returned to Fort Monroe.[50]

Ashore, there was much confusion as the troops cautiously moved inland. Chase was appalled by the chaos, and he questioned Wool forcefully about it. Wool declared that much of the confusion came about because officers were concerned about violating the chain of command and consequently hesitated to act unilaterally. Fed up with such punctiliousness, Chase ordered Viele "in the name of the President of the United States" to take command of the advance and march toward Norfolk. Slowed briefly by a destroyed bridge, the Union soldiers soon encountered an abandoned enemy camp. The barracks were still smoldering, and the rebels had left behind twenty-one heavy guns. Cheered by this bloodless victory, the Union troops marched on. A few miles short of Norfolk, they encountered a deputation of civilians, including the mayor, who had ridden out in a carriage to surrender the city. Only later did any of the Union command team begin to suspect that the mayor's elaborate surrender ceremony was intended to allow the last of the evacuating Confederates to make good their escape.[51]

Lincoln was much concerned when he heard that Chase had gone ashore with the troops, and he was relieved to see his Treasury secretary again at eleven o'clock that evening. He was even more pleased to learn that Norfolk had been taken, and "he fairly hugged General Wool." Lincoln was delighted and offered congratulations all around, though privately he may have wondered if the expedition would have taken place at all if he had not been there to prod Goldsborough and Wool into action. Certainly Chase thought the whole campaign was a result of the president's efforts. "I think it quite certain that if he had not come down," Chase wrote home, Norfolk "would still have been in possession of the enemy." What neither Lincoln nor Chase knew was that the rebels had planned to abandon Norfolk in any case once the Confederate army had evacuated the Yorktown line. Still, the experience may have confirmed Lincoln in his growing view that professional expertise might be less valuable in war than a clear head and an energetic spirit.[52]

The next morning (Sunday, May 11), as Lincoln was preparing to return to Washington, Goldsborough came in with astonishing news: the rebels had blown up the *Merrimack*. With Norfolk in Union hands, the big rebel ironclad had lost its base. Because it drew nearly twenty-two feet of water, it could not escape up the James River to Richmond. Its crew managed to reduce its draft to eighteen feet, but the river pilots told its new commander, Josiah Tattnall, that he had to reduce it another foot, and Tattnall was out of time. Unwilling that his ship should fall into the hands of the Yankees, he ordered it destroyed, accomplishing what neither the *Monitor* nor the *Vanderbilt* had been able to do. It is possible that with a few extra days, Tattnall might have found a way to lighten the *Merrimack* the extra foot needed to allow it to escape upriver. Instead, the fall of Norfolk, a product of Lincoln's personal intervention, compelled him to order its destruction.

"So has ended a brilliant week's campaign of the President," Chase wrote home. As in his management of the river campaign in the West, Lincoln found that by taking the lead and showing how progress could be made, he could inspire his commanders to be more assertive with the enemy. He had inspired the sailors, too. "The sailors all unite in saying he is 'a trump,'" wrote the reporter for the *Washington Star*, and "they also express the opinion that the success of the movement is due to the energy infused into it by 'Uncle Abe.'" For his part, Lincoln made no claims about the role he had played in the campaign, nor was there a public relations official to trumpet it to the public. He had no interest in claiming credit; he merely wanted progress.[53]

Alas, Lincoln had begun to wonder if the kind of progress needed could be achieved with men such as Wool and Goldsborough in command. Despite his eagerness to command the landing force, Wool had dithered in uncertainty once ashore, and though Goldsborough had eventually sent his ships into action, it was only after Lincoln had prodded him to do so. Welles had chosen the fifty-seven-year-old Goldsborough to replace the sixty-four-year-old Silas Stringham partly because Goldsborough had a reputation for ferocity. Some of that reputation, however, derived from Goldsborough's terrible temper rather than his aggressiveness. After observing him firsthand, it concerned Lincoln that Goldsborough acted as if his primary function was to ensure the efficient maintenance of the fleet rather than to attack the enemy. Goldsborough may have sensed that he had not impressed the president during his visit, for there was a note of anxiety, even apology, in a plaintive note to Lincoln about the operation. "I supposed I was carrying out your wishes in substance if not to the letter." Sensing that Goldsborough needed reassurance, Lincoln provided it: "You are quite right," he wrote, that "the movement was made in accordance with my wishes," and he thanked Goldsborough for his "courtesy and all your conduct so far as known to me during my brief visit here."[54]

Lincoln's concern about Goldsborough's suitability for his job could wait, however, for there were more important issues to consider at the moment. McClellan's campaign against Richmond was just beginning in earnest, and on top of that, Lincoln returned to Washington only to learn some very troubling news that suggested he would now have to confront an even more difficult problem—indeed, the most difficult problem of the war: the future status of the southern slaves.

6

"We Cannot Escape History"

Lincoln and the Contrabands

LINCOLN RETURNED TO WASHINGTON on May 13. The *New York Times* reporter observed that the president was "in high spirits, and greatly refreshed and invigorated by his sojourn to the seat of war." That same reporter also noted that "in the new character of General and Commander he has added immensely to his popularity." Lincoln's high spirits were soon depressed by news that in his absence Major General David Hunter, commanding the Department of the South, had declared martial law in South Carolina, Georgia, and Florida—the three states within his command—and, further, that Hunter had announced that all persons "heretofore held as slaves" in those states were now "forever free."[1] One can imagine Lincoln sighing in frustration as he read that order, for not only were such issues well beyond the authority of a department commander, but also Lincoln saw that this declaration could rupture the fragile political coalition that sustained his administration. From the moment of his election, Lincoln had been compelled to walk a political tightrope between abolitionists, who regularly and earnestly urged immediate emancipation for all the slaves, and War Democrats, who insisted that slavery was incidental to the war and who viewed any move toward emancipation as revolutionary. Hunter's order—like Cameron's and Frémont's earlier proclamations—put him on the spot. Lincoln knew there was no escaping this issue in the long run, but he had hoped to keep it in abeyance a while longer.

In part, Hunter's order derived from a complication that had emerged along the South Atlantic coast. There Flag Officer Du Pont presided over the South Atlantic Blockading Squadron from his flagship *Wabash*, anchored in Port Royal Sound near Hilton Head Island, where Hunter made his headquarters. The largest of Du Pont's several squadrons (nine ships) was off Charleston, and smaller squadrons patrolled the waters off southern ports from St. Augustine, Florida, to Georgetown, South Carolina. At all these places, the interaction between the blockading fleet and the enslaved persons living along the coast created a new dynamic. Naval officers exploring the coastal inlets found that "the negroes . . . came down to the shore with bundles in their hands, as if expecting to be taken off."[2]

A particularly dramatic encounter took place off Charleston on May 13, the day Lincoln returned to Washington. Early that morning, lookouts on the USS *Onward* noticed a steamer coming out of Charleston Harbor. Several of the blockading vessels beat to quarters before someone noticed that the vessel was flying a white flag. It turned out to be the Confederate dispatch vessel *Planter*, used by the rebel commanders in Charleston to carry messages around the harbor. Instead of its regular commander, however, the *Planter* was under the control of its pilot, a slave named Robert Smalls. Left alone on board by the rebel officers, Smalls quietly got up steam at 4:00 A.M. and, with his wife and child plus twelve other slaves on board, took the boat out into the harbor. He donned the coat and hat of the *Planter*'s captain and made the proper recognition signal as he passed Fort Sumter in the predawn darkness, then he steamed out of the harbor to the blockade fleet and freedom.* Smalls' bold feat made headlines in the North and drew attention to the issue of black refugees along the South Atlantic coast.[3]

Another encounter between the blockading ships and southern slaves took place a week later when a small Union flotilla under Commander

---

*Smalls became the pilot on the blockade vessel *Crusader*, but he served as a volunteer without pay. Not until 1863, when Union policy caught up with reality, did Smalls get either recognition as a pilot or the $50 a month that went with it. Eventually, Smalls was confirmed as the captain of the *Planter*, in which capacity he earned $150 a month.

John B. Marchand ventured up the Stono River, ten miles south of Charleston. After steaming upriver for half a dozen miles in the *Unadilla* (the first of the ninety-day gunboats that Welles had authorized the year before), Marchand was returning toward the open sea when the sound of screams from the riverbank drew the attention of every man on board. Marchand saw "a stampede of slaves on the cotton and corn fields to the south of the river." They were running flat out as if in fear for their lives. "One Negro woman we saw hurrying down to the water's edge with eight little children," Marchand wrote in his journal, "one of them sucking her breast, another she had on her shoulder, two others were holding only her scanty dress, and the other four little ones, at top of speed and almost naked, flocked around and materially impeded her progress." Behind them was a small body of Confederate cavalry "charging at full speed among the flying slaves." Marchand watched in horror as "the cavalry fired their pistols on all sides amongst the Negroes." At once he ordered his gunboats to open fire. With the explosion of the first shell, the rebel horsemen "went scampering in every direction," a sight which Marchand found extremely gratifying. While the cavalry fled, the group of slaves, mostly women and children, some seventy or eighty in number, all crowded down to the bank of the river. Obviously, Marchand could not leave them there, so he dropped anchor and sent boats to bring them on board.[4]

From them, Marchand learned that the appearance of his gunboats in the river the day before had convinced the local planters to move their slaves to the interior. The master had promised them they could stay in their homes, but when the men had finished their work, the cavalry had suddenly appeared and driven them off the island and onto the mainland. Aware of this, and unwilling to be next, the women and children had left their cabins and hidden in the nearby woods. The cavalrymen found them and chased them to the river. The refugees told Marchand they did not want to go inland to be put back to work on the fields. Clearly, however, they could not stay aboard the warships. To Marchand, the solution was self-evident: "I must colonize them." He landed them at a secure location where they could be protected from rebel cavalry by intervening swamps and by the gunboats, and over the next week several hundred more refugees joined them. Marchand visited his colony regularly, dropping off supplies and checking to see how the colonists were doing. Sympathetic as he was to their plight, Marchand was not free of the race prejudice that was nearly universal in the nineteenth century. When he stopped to look in on them a week later, he noted in his journal, "They were a happy set of darkies enjoying themselves in doing nothing."[5]

Similar colonies sprang up all along the Atlantic coast. At Port Royal, Du Pont established a colony on North Edisto Island, where between seven hundred and nine hundred displaced blacks were settled under the navy's protection in the first week of occupation. A month later there were more than fourteen hundred.[6] Though the Fugitive Slave Law was still technically in effect, Benjamin Butler had devised a clever legal construction to circumvent it. The year before when a few escaped slaves had shown up at Fort Monroe, Butler had refused to return them to their master because the rebels had used them to work on military entrenchments, drive wagons, and do other jobs that supported the illegal rebellion. Butler explained that this made them, in effect, "contraband of war," just like captured military equipment. Such a construction allowed Butler to refuse to send them back to their masters without overtly challenging the principle of slave property, and soon the escaped slaves were routinely being called "contrabands."*

Clever as this was, Butler's construction was not a complete or final solution. By the spring of 1862, when Marchand established his colony on the Stono River, there were so many contrabands in camps along the South Atlantic coast, they threatened to overwhelm the ability of the Union navy to supply them. Charles Francis Adams Jr. wrote his ambassador father from Port Royal, "We have now some 7,000 masterless slaves within our line and in less than two months we shall have nearer 70,000, and what are we to do with them?"[7]

Seeking an answer to that question, Du Pont appealed to Gideon Welles, who replied that this untapped source of manpower should not be allowed to remain idle. Because it would not be "proper" to employ the contrabands without compensation, he authorized Du Pont to "enlist them for the naval service," though he also declared that they were

---

*Ironically, it was in precisely this context that Charles Wilkes had insisted that Mason and Slidell were "contraband of war" when he took them off the *Trent* the previous November.

to have "no higher rating than boys, at a compensation of $10 per month and one ration per day."[8] There is no evidence that Welles checked first with the president before issuing his orders to Du Pont, but it is noteworthy that while Lincoln had repudiated and later dismissed Cameron for announcing a policy of enlisting blacks for the army, he remained silent in response to Welles' declaration. For one thing, black men had served in the United States Navy since the days of John Paul Jones, and although the enlistment of runaway slaves was a bit different, it did not challenge the existing social order in the same way that arming black soldiers would. Lincoln may have sensed that the general public would react more benignly to the notion of black men serving aboard warships at sea than they would to the specter of black men with rifles in their hands on land. In addition, with the Confederacy promising to execute any Negro found with arms in his hands, Lincoln concluded that it would be better "to employ them where they would not be liable to be captured," such as aboard ship.[9]

Chase was eager to turn the problem of black refugees into an opportunity. He appointed Edward L. Pierce to be the agent in charge of the contrabands at Port Royal, and when Pierce visited Washington, the Treasury secretary arranged for him to meet with the president. Pierce wanted to discuss the plight of the contrabands along the South Atlantic coast, but Lincoln cut him short. Pierce concluded that the president was uninterested in the problem, though he also acknowledged that Lincoln's anxiety about the health of his sons, then fighting for their lives against typhoid fever, was likely a factor in the president's apparent disinterest. As Pierce was leaving, however, Lincoln called him back and scribbled a note for him authorizing Chase to "give such instructions in regard to [the] Port Royal contrabands as may seem judicious." Lincoln, in effect, gave Chase carte blanche to increase and extend the refugee encampments.[10]

One of Lincoln's favorite stories, which he told on several occasions, concerned the Irish priest who, when offered a swig of whiskey, declared that his piety would not allow him to drink it, but that if somehow a wee dram were added to his coffee "unbeknownst to him" he would not object to it. When Lincoln allowed the sympathetic Chase to assume supervisory control over the coastal contraband camps, he was surely aware that Chase would encourage an expanded program of support for the refugees, including the introduction of schools and even the distribution of land. Lincoln did not initiate these programs, but he did not object if they occurred "unbeknownst to him."

Lincoln could not remain silent about Hunter's proclamation of freedom, however. Refusing to send escaped slaves back to their rebel masters—even providing for their care and support—was one thing, but declaring that all the slaves in a three-state region were free was quite another. Lincoln saw that he had no choice but to declare Hunter's order "altogether void," though not everyone in his cabinet agreed. Chase argued in vain that at least Hunter should be allowed to explain the reasons for his order. Significantly, however, even as Lincoln overturned Hunter's declaration, he also signaled that the power of emancipation by fiat was not out of the question, only that it belonged to the president rather than to his field commanders. "Whether it be competent for me, as Commander-in-Chief of the Army and Navy, to declare the Slaves of any state or states free," Lincoln wrote to Hunter, "and whether . . . it shall become a necessity . . . to exercise such supposed power are questions which . . . I reserve to myself."[11]

In issuing this order, Lincoln successfully postponed the moment of decision, but he would not be able to do so indefinitely. The influx of contrabands along the South Atlantic coast and Hunter's proclamation reminded him that at some point, and sooner rather than later, he would have to come to grips with the nation's most intractable problem. In the end, the contraband problem was a political question, not a naval one, but it was the question that was at the heart of the war itself, and the one on which all other issues depended.

LINCOLN HATED SLAVERY. "If slavery is not wrong, nothing is wrong," he declared in 1864, adding: "I can not remember when I did not so think, and feel." But Lincoln also knew that he could not simply wave a magic wand to make slavery go away. A decade earlier he had told an audience in Peoria, "If all earthly power were given me, I should not know what to do." One thing was clear, however: whatever he chose to do would be within the law, and certainly within the Constitution. At his core Lincoln was a politician, not a revolutionary; he believed in the efficacy—and the sanctity—of the political process. Slavery was the Gordian knot of American history, but Lincoln was no Alexander. He would not slash through that knot with the sword of war; his instinct was to untie it one strand at a time. For most of his political career, he had hoped that a national policy confining slavery to those states where it already existed would undermine its long-term economic viability and lead to its eventual demise—that was the fundamental belief underpinning his consistent opposition to the expansion of slavery into the western territories. He acknowledged that such a gradualist approach might well take several generations before slavery was finally eliminated, but he saw no other legal way to do it.[12]

In addition, Lincoln also understood better than most of his contemporaries that the issue of black freedom involved two related, but in the end very different, problems. The first was emancipation itself, a complicated and volatile issue in its own right. But the second problem was even more volatile—even explosive—and that was defining the social and political status of the former bondsmen in a post-emancipation America. Lincoln knew that many of those who opposed slavery in principle were nevertheless horrified by the idea of racial equality. For all his genuine humanity and his optimism about the future of the country, Lincoln was fundamentally pessimistic about the future of race relations in the United States. Lincoln's political pole star was the Declaration of Independence with its assertion that "all men are created equal." But he knew that in nineteenth-century America this was little more than an abstraction. His sensitivity to the nuances of public opinion in his native Illinois had convinced him that the vast majority of white Americans would simply not tolerate blacks as equals. As James Gordon Bennett, the mercurial editor of the popular *New York Herald*, put it in 1862: "That the negro should be as free as white men, either at the North or at the South, is out of the question."[13]

As far back as 1854, during the debates over the Kansas-Nebraska Act, Lincoln had acknowledged the intractability of America's race problem. Though he had been a member of the American Colonization Society, he admitted that sending all of America's slaves to Africa was virtually "impossible." On the other hand, freeing them and keeping them in the country "as underlings" hardly changed their condition. "What next?" he asked rhetorically, as if he were arguing the case with himself. "Free them and make them politically and socially, our equals? My own feelings will not admit of this; and if mine would, we well know that those of the great mass of white people will not." He did not defend or justify the existing racial prejudice; he merely acknowledged it. "A universal feeling," he noted, "whether well or ill-founded can not safely be disregarded." Four years later, in his debate with Stephen Douglas, he declared, "There is a physical difference between the two [races], which in my judgment will probably forever forbid their living together upon the footing of perfect equality."[14]

In part, of course, Lincoln's remarks were politically motivated. He knew he could not win election, even in Illinois—maybe *especially* in Illinois—by supporting what his political enemies called "amalgamation." But in part, too, they reflected a genuine confusion about how— or even if—freed blacks could be integrated into white America. Hunter's untimely proclamation reminded him that the momentum of war had made emancipation in his lifetime a genuine possibility. But neither he nor anyone else had a clear plan that was both humane and realistic about what to do with the former slaves once they were free. Would they become citizens? Serve on juries? Vote? And more urgently, would they be allowed to bear arms in the military? In the cultural context of 1862 these were revolutionary, even radical, notions. Most Americans recoiled at the thought of blacks as citizens of the Republic. Consequently, though abolitionists and other progressives urged Lincoln to strike at slavery at once, he hesitated. His vacillation was in part a product of his concern for the fragility of his political coalition, but in part, too, it was because he had no answer to that second crucial question: if blacks were not to be slaves, what *would* they be?

Just as he had procrastinated during the Fort Sumter and *Trent* crises in the hope that time and circumstance would suggest a solution, Lincoln now hesitated to put forward a proactive policy on the dominant issue of his generation in the hope that events might show him a way forward. Lincoln used a parable to explain it to a visitor: "A man watches his pear-tree day after day, impatient for the ripening of the fruit. Let him attempt to *force* the process, and he may spoil both fruit and tree. But let him patiently *wait*, and the ripe pear at length falls into his lap." When a group of citizens visited the White House in January 1862 to urge him to end his temporizing and boldly announce a progressive policy, he put them off in a characteristic way by telling them a story. In recording the story in his diary, the class-conscious George Templeton Strong may have exaggerated Lincoln's midwestern twang: "Wa-al," Lincoln began, "that reminds me of a party of Methodist parsons that was traveling in Illinois when I was a boy thar, and had a branch to cross, ye know, because the waters was up. And they got considerin' and discussin' how they should git across it, and they talked about it for two hours, and one of 'em thought they had to cross one way when they got there, and another another way, and they got quarrelin' about it, till at last an old brother put in and says, says he, 'Brethren, this here talk aint no use. I never cross a river until I come to it.'" The visitors felt obliged to join the president in laughing at the story, but even as he laughed, Lincoln knew that the river—his personal Rubicon—was getting closer, and that a decision about both emancipation and the future political and social status of the freed slaves could not be postponed much longer. As he would acknowledge in his State of the Union address at the end of the year: "We cannot escape history."[15]

ABSORBING THE CONTRABANDS into the blockade fleet caused scarcely a ripple either among the public at large or within the navy. Historically, free blacks had made up some 15 percent of the navy's enlisted force. During the 1850s, the figure had dropped to only about 5 percent; now it would grow again back up to 15 percent. Naval officers, always eager for more hands, generally welcomed the contrabands on board as simply so many more strong backs, and the white sailors welcomed them, too, mainly because the newcomers were generally assigned "the dirtiest, most strenuous, and most physically demanding jobs," thereby relieving white sailors of those duties. A few blacks rose above the rank of "first class boy"—Robert Smalls was eventually confirmed as captain of the *Planter* at a salary of $150 a month—but most performed the endless menial tasks inherent to a ship of war. White officers and men alike took a certain delight in using the enemy's slaves against them. One captain on the blockade acknowledged that "the question of what is to be done with the slaves, is a knotty one," but, he added, "we have nothing to do better than to weaken their masters, and strengthen ourselves by holding on to all we can lay our hands on, and this I for one have no scruples in doing, obeying as I am the most positive direction of the Secretary of the Navy."[16]

In part, this reaction derived from the sailors' horror at seeing slavery up close. Du Pont himself, though he was from the slaveholding state of Delaware, was shocked by the reality of slavery along the South Carolina coast, a reality that put the lie to the rosy picture of the institution that had been presented publicly by southerners for more than a decade. "All those sweet-potato patches, garden trucks, fowls, all of which the 'Negro was allowed,' is simply a falsehood," Du Pont wrote privately to his brother. "They had had nothing." Du Pont was happy to employ contrabands on board his ships, but he saw at once that this was hardly a solution to the refugee problem, for the navy could not employ them all. "They can't be worked as slaves," Du Pont wrote, "yet such is the degradation in which they have been kept that they are like children [and] must be controlled. Who is to have this authority? Who is to clothe and feed [them]? Who is to get the crops?" Whatever the answers to these questions, they would have to be found soon, for as Du Pont reported, "they are starving and *naked*." Almost in desperation, he asked, "What is to be done?" It would prove the most difficult and sensitive question Lincoln had to confront as commander in chief.[17]

As Du Pont's squadron labored with mixed success to make the blockade impermeable, the constantly expanding contraband colonies along the coast exacerbated the problem of supply. At New Bern and Roanoke Island in North Carolina, as well as at Port Royal and all along the barrier islands of South Carolina and Georgia, thousands of former slaves settled into their makeshift camps. Du Pont had his hands full just managing his large force—grown now to thirty-eight warships—without worrying about how to organize, police, supply, and defend the crowded contraband camps. In order to allow the contrabands to defend themselves from rebel raids, he authorized the issuing of some old flintlock muskets to the men in the camps. This was well ahead of government policy which still forbade the acceptance of black soldiers for the army, but neither Lincoln nor anyone else in the government objected. As often happens in war, reality in the field forced new policy considerations in the capital. Indeed, the need to find a solution to the refugee problem on the coast led to proposals that were well ahead of anything being considered in Washington. Major General Ormsby Mitchel, who replaced Hunter in command of the Department of the South in September, suggested settling the contrabands permanently into cooperative plantations on the offshore islands.* To protect them, he suggested "the formation of black regiments" that could occupy the coastal forts when white regiments moved inland. He argued that "if the black population should prove itself able to occupy hold and defend, the territory given into its charge by the Government, then shall we then have indeed reached the solution of the great problem; and the question 'what shall be done with the liberated Slaves?' will have been satisfactorily answered."[18] Indeed. But would the country accept such an answer?

THESE CIRCUMSTANCES ENCOURAGED LINCOLN to give serious consideration to a proposal first put forward in the fall of 1861 by a Philadelphia shipper named Ambrose W. Thompson. Thompson had acquired title to several hundred thousand acres of land straddling the Central American isthmus from the Lagoon of Chiriqui on Panama's Mosquito Coast in the Gulf of Mexico to the Gulf of Dulce on the Pacific in what is now southern Costa Rica. Seeking to make a profit from his investment, he offered to lease naval bases to the federal government at both ports and construct a railroad between them. He insisted that large coal deposits in the area would enable him to supply the navy with fuel at about half the prevailing price.[19] In addition to these tangible benefits to the navy, Thompson's plan became tied up with the question of emancipation and racial policy when he suggested that former slaves could be used to colonize the region, mine the coal, and thus make them not only self-supporting but also active contributors to the war effort. Indeed, almost at once the idea of establishing Chiriqui (as the site came to be called) as a colony for former slaves soon outstripped the initial object of acquiring naval facilities and cheap coal.

Welles was skeptical about the whole project, distrusting the entrepreneurial Thompson, whom he considered a charlatan, but Lincoln was intrigued, and he asked his brother-in-law Ninian Edwards to look into it. Edwards responded enthusiastically, confining his comments to

---

*Mitchel was a Kentuckian who was a late convert to abolitionism. Though most of his progressive (not to say radical) ideas were eventually adopted, he did not live to witness their implementation, since he died of yellow fever only a month after assuming command.

the "main object" of supplying the navy with coal, and noting only in passing that Thompson also proposed "to lease land for colonization purposes." Lincoln, however, was more interested in the potential of Chiriqui as a colony for freed slaves. Aware of Welles' skepticism, he delegated the issue to the secretary of the interior, Caleb Smith, authorizing him "to carry the contract into effect." Soon afterward, Du Pont's victory at Port Royal and the influx of contrabands to the navy's coastal enclaves gave an urgency to the issue. At about the same time, the senior Frank Blair (father of Montgomery Blair and Frank Blair Jr.) weighed in, writing to Lincoln that the Chiriqui project was a virtual cornucopia of national blessings. The elder Blair argued that at a single blow the deal would obtain ideal naval ports on both oceans, produce an isthmian railroad, provide virtually unlimited cheap coal for the navy, and secure "a million acres of land for the colonization of American Freemen in Homesteads and freeholds."[20]

The notion of colonizing freed blacks outside the United States was hardly new. Lincoln himself had been for many years a member of the American Colonization Society, co-founded by his political idol Henry Clay back in 1816. Those whites who supported colonization insisted that they were motivated by benevolent impulses, but most white abolitionists—and virtually all blacks—saw it as a kind of banishment rooted in virulent racism. Moreover, the logistics of such a project were daunting. Even if all of the American ships then afloat were employed in constant rotation, they could not relocate the entire black population of America to another region as fast as the population itself increased. In short, the overseas colonization of America's black population was a practical impossibility.

Yet Lincoln saw a number of benefits in Thompson's proposal. There was, of course, the fact that it would secure U.S. interests in the Central American isthmus and gain valuable bases for the navy. More important, however, Lincoln believed that an overseas colony could be an attractive alternative for those former slaves who might find life in a post-slavery America intolerable. Lincoln feared that the racism that he knew to be endemic not only in the South but also in his own Midwest might easily create conditions for "free" black Americans that were only marginally better than slavery. Creating a sanctuary for them in Central America at least gave them a choice. And as far as Lincoln was concerned, it would be a choice. He never supported the idea that *all* former slaves should be deported or that *any* should be transported against their will. Still, if a colony for free blacks existed, it would at least provide them with an option. Then, too, the possibility of black colonization overseas would assuage the fears of some northerners that emancipation would trigger an influx of unsupervised former slaves into their towns and cities.[21]

Meanwhile, Lincoln continued to move cautiously and incrementally toward an emancipation program for the slaves in the border states, those slave states that had remained in the Union. In his view, legal emancipation was possible, but only if it met three criteria: it must be gradual rather than abrupt, it must compensate the owners who would be deprived of their property, and it must be sanctioned by the voters. Only then, in his view, would emancipation pass constitutional muster. All three of these elements were evident in the bill that Lincoln sent to Congress in March (three days before the *Monitor* met the *Merrimack* in Hampton Roads). Lincoln's bill committed the nation to cooperate with any state that adopted a program for the "gradual abolishment of slavery." It was virtually unprecedented (and some said unconstitutional) for a president to propose legislation, but Lincoln knew how he wanted the bill to be worded. He was careful not to intrude on the prerogative of state governments. States could choose to participate or not, but those that did would receive "pecuniary aid" to compensate the owners for their loss of property. Lincoln calculated that the expense of buying up all of the 432,622 slaves in the border states at $400 "per head" would cost the government about the same as eighty-seven days of war, and he argued that a successful program of compensated emancipation would shorten the war by at least eighty-seven days. Lincoln made it clear that, in his view, "gradual, and not sudden emancipation, is better for all," though there was a veiled warning in his observation that if "resistance continues, the war must also continue," and anything could happen in wartime, for "it was impossible to foresee all the incidents, which may attend and the ruin which may follow it." It was not a threat, simply a reminder that the momentum of history could resolve the issue in ways as yet unplanned and unforeseen.[22]

Lincoln's emancipation plan was carefully calibrated to be progressive without being draconian. The abolitionist Thaddeus Stevens thought it "the most diluted, milk-and-water gruel proposition that was ever given to the American nation." Yet even this careful dipping of an abolitionist toe into the pool of public opinion proved that it was further than most Americans were willing to go. Border-state men evinced no interest in selling off their slaves, and northern men opposed it for fear that the freed slaves would migrate north. There was some public support. Henry J. Raymond, editor of the *New York Times* and a loyal Republican, called it "a master-piece of practical wisdom," and Bennett in the *Herald* declared that the president's message was "so simple, so just, so profound and comprehensive that we may pronounce it as reaching the final solution and settlement of the most perplexing difficulty in our political system." A day later, however, Bennett had second thoughts and decided that Lincoln's proposal was perhaps not "the final solution" after all. "There is an important question upon which Mr. Lincoln does not touch in his Message," Bennett wrote in his front-page editorial, "but which is intimately and inseparably connected with the whole subject, and that is, what is to be done with the emancipated negroes?" Lincoln hardly needed Bennett to remind him, but as yet he had no satisfactory answer to the question, and in the end, Lincoln's proposal for border state emancipation came to nothing.[23]

A month later, in April 1862, Lincoln signed a congressional act abolishing slavery in the District of Columbia. This bill had originated in the Congress and, significantly, it included an appropriation of $100,000 "for colonization." In fact, an amendment to require *compulsory* emigration and overseas colonization was barely defeated in the Senate when Vice President Hamlin broke a 19–19 tie. Lincoln did not sign the bill at once. He worried about its legitimacy since it did not provide the citizens of the District a vote on the issue.* But in the end, he did sign it, convinced that the Constitution gave Congress explicit and direct authority over the District.[24]

Of course, none of this helped him resolve the issue of dealing with the tens of thousands of refugee contrabands along the coast and else-

---

*Back in 1849, during his one term as a congressman from Illinois, Lincoln had introduced a bill for the emancipation of slaves in the District of Columbia. It called first for a popular referendum on slavery within the District, after which the government would buy all slaves in the District from their masters at full market value.

where. Even in his own cabinet there were sharp divisions about how to handle that question. When the emancipationist-minded Chase proposed that the administration "establish a military government over the sea islands," the more conservative Bates objected that the proposal was "an abolition contrivance, to begin the establishment of a negro country along that coast." Contrivance or not, the negro colonies were already there, and with each passing day they became more permanent. Already Du Pont was encouraging the contrabands to plant crops for the next year's harvest. Though Lincoln knew he would have to resolve the issue eventually, he continued to delay, deciding on this occasion to "leave the whole matter to the War Dept."[25]

MEANWHILE, LINCOLN KEPT HIS EYE ON MILITARY EVENTS in Virginia, where McClellan continued his glacial advance. The most worrisome news was from the Shenandoah Valley, where Confederate Major General Thomas "Stonewall" Jackson was marching up and down the valley almost at will. On May 25, Jackson drove the small Union army of Nathaniel P. Banks from Winchester and sent him fleeing pell-mell for the Potomac River with the rebels in hot pursuit. Lincoln had never sought the role of chess master in this war, but as he looked at the map it seemed evident to him that Jackson had stuck his neck into a noose. The audacious rebel commander was well north of both Frémont's army in western Virginia and McDowell's corps near Fredericksburg. If these Union forces cooperated—and if they moved swiftly—they could trap Jackson in the lower valley and destroy him. Loath as he was to intervene in the direction of military operations, Lincoln saw that there was no one but himself who was in position to achieve the kind of coordination that was needed. Encouraged by his recent success in orchestrating the capture of Norfolk, he assumed effective command, issuing telegraphic orders to both Frémont and McDowell to send forces to the Valley. Frémont was to approach from the south to block Jackson's retreat, while James Shields' division of McDowell's corps advanced from the east. Instead, Frémont decided to approach from the west leaving Jackson an escape route, and appreciating his danger just in time, Jackson's men performed a heroic feat of marching, some of them covering forty-two miles in a single twenty-four-hour period, to slip between the closing pincers.

Lincoln was disappointed, particularly with Frémont, but the experience also taught him that it was easier to draw lines on a map than it was for living soldiers to duplicate those maneuvers. Carl Schurz, who was both a Republican political adviser and a division commander in Frémont's army, was bold enough to point this out to him. Lincoln's order, Schurz wrote to the president in a private letter, was "based upon an imperfect knowledge of facts," and consequently, "it was absolutely impossible to carry out." If Lincoln took the lesson to heart, he also saw that if he did not assume the role of coordinating the armies in the field, someone else must do so.[26]

On the last day of May, the Confederate army outside Richmond under Joseph E. Johnston launched a counterattack against McClellan's forces near a small crossroads called Seven Pines. Though the Union army mostly held its ground and inflicted heavy losses on the attackers, the carnage horrified McClellan and confirmed him in his conviction that he was greatly outnumbered—why else would the enemy be so bold as to attack?—and made him more cautious than ever. Worse, from McClellan's point of view, Lincoln's decision to send part of McDowell's corps to the valley had deprived him of expected reinforcements.

Soon McClellan was under attack again. During the last week of June, he was struck again and again by the rebel army, commanded now by Robert E. Lee since Johnston had been wounded at Seven Pines. During what became known as the Seven Days Battles, Lincoln spent most of his days, and some of his nights, in the War Department telegraph office hoping for good news, or at least hoping not to hear bad news. On June 25, McClellan reported that another great battle was in the offing, that he faced two hundred thousand enemy soldiers, and that if disaster occurred, the fault would lie not with him but with those who had refused to send him the reinforcements he needed. Lincoln wired back urging McClellan to "save your army at all events" and promising to send reinforcements as fast as he could. He also wired Goldsborough asking him to "do what you can" to support the army. The president's determination was evident in his grim declaration to Seward that "I expect to maintain this contest until successful, or till I die, or am conquered, or my term expires, or Congress or the country forsakes me."[27]

McClellan did save his army, though in doing so he surrendered the initiative in the campaign. Reaching the James River on the last day of

June, he boarded the *Galena* and conferred with Commander Rodgers. Still convinced that he was hugely outnumbered, he asked Rodgers where he could bivouac his army to place it under the protection of the river gunboats. Rodgers recommended Harrison's Landing, near Berkeley Plantation, and McClellan issued the necessary orders. He also renewed his complaints that the government had failed to support him. "I have lost this battle because my force was too small," he wailed in a telegram to Stanton. "I again repeat that I am not responsible for this." Lincoln's willingness to absorb McClellan's complaints and respond with encouragement was severely tested. Desperate to prevent a complete meltdown by his field commander, the president responded soothingly to McClellan's intemperate telegrams, telling him that "all accounts say [that] better fighting was never done" and offering him "ten thousand thanks" for his efforts. Lincoln knew that, whatever his faults, at that moment McClellan was the indispensable man.[28]

For the second time during the campaign, Lincoln decided to travel to the battlefront and assess things for himself. He left on July 7—a Monday—and headed south on the steam sloop *Ariel*. After an uneventful trip, the president reviewed the troops at Harrison's Landing, examined the entrenchments, and talked with the army's senior officers. He was taking the temperature of the army and of its commanders. It was during this visit that McClellan handed him the subsequently infamous Harrison's Landing letter containing the general's views "concerning the existing state of the rebellion." What those views were soon became clear. McClellan objected to any plan to emancipate any slaves whatsoever. "All private property and unarmed persons should be strictly protected," he lectured the president, and in particular, "Military power should not be allowed to interfere with the relations of servitude." Whatever the president's private thoughts about the appropriateness of McClellan's letter, he kept them to himself.[29]

As Lincoln's doubts about McClellan grew stronger, he also began to have doubts about Goldsborough. That very week Congress passed a resolution of thanks to Goldsborough for his role in the capture of Roanoke Island back in February, and four days later it created the rank of rear admiral, which was to be bestowed on up to nine senior officers, including Goldsborough. Yet that officer's behavior continued to cause concern. Lincoln recalled his refusal "to place himself under the orders of General

McClellan," his unwillingness to seize the initiative in Hampton Roads, and his reluctance to send warships up the James River. Since May, in fact, Goldsborough had behaved as if his principal job were the administrative supervision and maintenance of his large fleet, grown now to sixty-five ships. Worried that Goldsborough might not provide McClellan the active support the general claimed he needed, Lincoln approved Welles' decision to send the volatile and flamboyant Charles Wilkes to the James River to assume command of an independent flotilla. Though he would be within Goldsborough's command area, Wilkes would report separately to the Navy Department. His primary responsibility, Welles told him, was to cooperate with McClellan.[30]

Goldsborough was "offended" by this order, which effectively stripped him of a dozen of his front-line warships, and when the newspapers speculated that Wilkes' appointment suggested that the government was dissatisfied with the navy's performance, Goldsborough complained to Welles about the "scurrilous and unmerited attacks" on him by "the public prints." Stung by the "vile and vulgar writings" in the press, and concerned, too, about the health of his namesake son back home, he asked "to be relieved from my present position." Whereas previously Lincoln might have tried to soothe his prickly naval commander by offering him "ten thousand thanks," he said nothing when Welles replied simply that "the Department will order an officer to relieve you at an early day." Welles had decided that while Goldsborough had "some capacity," he had "no hard courage." It took almost three months to find a replacement, during which time Goldsborough acted as caretaker for the fleet. "I keep perfectly quiet and say nothing," he wrote to his wife. "Importunity on my part would not be graceful." In August, Goldsborough got his promotion to rear admiral (along with Farragut and Du Pont), and in September he was relieved as commander of the North Atlantic Blockading Squadron by acting Rear Admiral Samuel Phillips Lee to spend the rest of the war performing routine administrative duties.[31]

Wilkes proved to be more cooperative with the army than Goldsborough had been. He reorganized the anchorage off Harrison's Landing and ensured a regular flow of supplies to the army. Much like Du Pont, however, Wilkes also fell under the spell of McClellan's charm. Little Mac graciously welcomed Wilkes to his headquarters and openly shared his views of the campaign, something he had declined to do with the president. McClellan had previously told Lincoln that he could take Richmond if the president would send him fifty thousand more men. When Lincoln replied that he didn't have fifty thousand men to send, McClellan interpreted that as an order not to advance. Now Little Mac told Wilkes that he was eager to take Richmond but that he was under positive orders from Washington not to try it. Wilkes was infuriated that McClellan was "anxious to renew the attack" and was prevented from doing so only by "the evident imbecility" of his civilian masters in Washington.[32]

While McClellan and Wilkes swapped stories of Lincoln's "imbecility," Lincoln himself remained committed to achieving effective cooperation not only between the army and the navy but among all commands. Aware that he was not the man to do it, and equally aware that it would have to be someone other than George B. McClellan, on July 11 he ordered Major General Henry Halleck to turn his command over to Grant and come east. Halleck was the second western general summoned to Washington that summer since Lincoln had previously approved the creation of a new field army in Virginia under the command of Major General John Pope, the conqueror of Island No. 10. Halleck's first major act as general in chief was to order McClellan to evacuate the peninsula and return to northern Virginia. McClellan was disgusted, though perhaps not surprised. When he shared the news with Wilkes, the navy officer was at least as angered as McClellan. Wilkes immediately telegraphed Welles that recalling McClellan was "the most suicidal act that any administration could commit" and that it would "entirely ruin the Union cause." He insisted that "the moment I receive the additional vessels the Department is to supply me, . . . Richmond can be taken." Wilkes asked Welles to "lay these views before the president," which Welles did. But Lincoln was experienced now with commanders who were sure that as soon as they were reinforced, success was certain. The order stood.[33]

EVEN DURING THESE WEEKS of epochal military events, Lincoln never ceased to ponder the over-arching twin questions of emancipation and black freedom. As McClellan fended off Lee's furious attacks outside Richmond, the president decided that the time had come to embrace emancipation as a war measure. He still had no answer to the question of what would become of the freed slaves afterward, but he recognized that events were now threatening to race ahead of policy. Already Congress was debating a Second Confiscation Act, which would declare free all the slaves owned by rebels and traitors. Hannibal Hamlin later claimed that the president discussed emancipation with him at the Soldiers' Home as early as June 18, prior to the Seven Days' Battles. Whether or not that conversation ever took place, a month later, after he returned from his visit to Harrison's Landing, Lincoln raised the issue with two members of his cabinet. On July 13, he attended the funeral of Edwin Stanton's infant son, a particularly melancholy event given that the president had lost a son of his own only five months before, and during the ride out to the cemetery, Lincoln confided to Seward and Welles his belief that the time had come to announce that if the rebels did not soon capitulate, he must declare slavery at an end. It was, Lincoln said, a "military necessity" and "essential for the salvation of the Union." Both Seward and Welles were taken aback by the president's announcement since he had previously avoided the issue so carefully. They each responded that it was so momentous a step they wished to think about it before replying, which was very likely exactly why Lincoln had brought it up with them.[34]

Lincoln also revived the Chiriqui scheme. Thompson was positively utopian in pushing his proposal, asserting that his company would provide "Hospital stores, medicines, Physicians, Schools & c." to ensure a fully self-sufficient colony. The coal mines would provide good, well-paying jobs, and the company would assist in the construction of homes and towns. Because the bill emancipating blacks in the District of Columbia had appropriated a small sum for colonization, Lincoln appointed the Reverend James Mitchell to head a new Office of Emigration in the Interior Department with instructions to recruit some free blacks from the District to make up the initial group of colonists. The thought was that if some well-established and educated free blacks made up the first wave of emigrants, they could ease the transition for the newly emancipated slaves who would follow them. Mitchell, however, found little enthusiasm for emigration within Washington's free black population, and he reported to Lincoln that the "colored residents of the District" were not inclined to leave. It was necessary,

Mitchell suggested, for the president to educate these free blacks to the idea that "an escape from their present relation to the American people is a *duty and a privilege*."[35]

Thus prompted, Lincoln invited—or rather summoned—a deputation of free blacks to the White House on August 14. It was a historic moment, for it was the first time that a U.S. president had met with a group of African Americans in the White House other than as servants.* After a few preliminaries, the president explained to his visitors that Congress had placed a sum of money at his disposal to support the colonization of free blacks overseas. He told them it had long been his "inclination" to support such a program, and now it was his duty as well. Lincoln suggested that both races suffered from the obvious physical differences that existed between them, and given that, it was better that the races be separated. He acknowledged that they had suffered "the greatest wrong inflicted on any people," but he also told them that they had to be realistic. The fact was that there was virtually no chance, even as free men, that they would ever achieve genuine equality within American society. "On this broad continent," he noted, "not a single man of your race is made the equal of a single man of ours." It was not right, he said, but it was "a fact with which we have to deal." And given that fact, it would be better for them if they found new homes. He then praised the "great natural resources and advantages" of Chiriqui, where there was "opportunity to the inhabitants for immediate employment."[36]

The visitors were not convinced, though their spokesman promised the president that they would "hold a consultation" about it. It may be, however, that this delegation was not Lincoln's real audience. Interestingly, and perhaps significantly, Lincoln had made sure to include a reporter from the Associated Press at the meeting, which is how his remarks found their way into several eastern newspapers the next day. Lincoln almost certainly hoped that Chiriqui could become a sanctuary for some of America's black population. In addition, he also may have hoped that his remarks would ease the fears of northerners. Republican candidates from the northern states were already being assailed with the

---

*The five men were Edward M. Thompson, John F. Cook, John T. Costin, Cornelius Clark, and Benjamin McCoy.

charge that an emancipationist policy "will work great harm in the coming election." One congressional candidate wrote to beg the Republican governor of Illinois, Richard Yates, to "get the President or Sec of War to publish, that there is no intention to send negroes into free states." Sensitive as he was to the political mood, Lincoln may have lectured Washington's free blacks on the virtues of emigration in order to reassure the northern electorate that colonization was still on the table.[37]

Lincoln may have felt the need to do so because events were moving swiftly, the momentum of change having assumed a power of its own. In July, Congress had passed the Second Confiscation Act, which not only freed all slaves in the hands of the army, including those along the Atlantic coast, but also authorized Lincoln "to make provision for the transportation, colonization, and settlement . . . of such persons of the African race . . . as may be willing to emigrate." Five days after that, Lincoln took the plunge, reading the draft of an Emancipation Proclamation to the full cabinet. He was not asking for their approval, he told them, for he had made up his mind to act. He did, however, seek their advice about the wording. The cabinet was mostly supportive, if somewhat surprised. Only Seward, who, along with Welles, was aware that the president had been considering such a step, ventured to speak against the timing of the announcement. He noted that issuing such a document now, after the recent collapse of the Peninsular Campaign, would suggest desperation on the part of the government: "the last shriek on the retreat," as he put it. Better, he argued, to wait for a victory, and then announce the new policy. Lincoln heard him out but was prepared to go ahead nonetheless until a late-night visit from Seward and his political guru, Thurlow Weed, convinced him of the wisdom of waiting.[38]

His patience was not perceived as a virtue in all quarters. Horace Greeley used an editorial in his influential *New York Tribune* to chastise the president for what he called a "mistaken deference to Rebel Slavery." Deciding that it was necessary to respond, Lincoln did so with a public letter in which he insisted that emancipation was secondary to union and was, in fact, a means to achieve it. Lincoln ensured that the letter was widely circulated at the time, and it has been widely quoted since. In its key sentence, he declared: "If I could save the Union without freeing any slave I would do it, and if I could save it by freeing all the slaves I would do it; and if I could save it by freeing some and leaving others alone I would also do that."[39] This, of course, was less than forthright, for Lincoln had already made up his mind to declare free all the slaves held in rebel areas ("freeing some and leaving others alone") as soon as his armies produced a victory. But the letter to Greeley, like his public support for colonization, gave Lincoln political cover. His official position was that whatever he did, he did for the Union, and moreover, that whites need not fear the social revolution that alarmist Democrats foresaw as the consequence of emancipation. Lincoln had decided that answering the question of what to do with the freed slave after emancipation could wait. What he needed now was a military victory that would allow him to announce the new policy.

INSTEAD OF A VICTORY, there came news of another defeat. On August 30, Major General John Pope's new Army of Virginia suffered a humbling rout on the ground of the old Bull Run battlefield. Lincoln was devastated. What did this string of defeats mean? "God wills this contest," he mused to himself in one of those private memos he sometimes used to clarify his thoughts. "He could give the final victory to either side any day. Yet the contest proceeds."[40] Lincoln's agony was compounded by rumors that McClellan had failed to offer Pope any substantive support and had thereby contributed to his defeat. Stanton and Chase renewed their arguments that Lincoln must dismiss McClellan. Lincoln was no more pleased with his general than they were, but he also saw that McClellan's popularity with the soldiers was a valuable asset in the current national mood. For all his faults, he remained the indispensable man. Against the advice of most of his cabinet, on September 1 Lincoln put McClellan in command of all the troops converging on Washington from Manassas and from the peninsula.

McClellan reorganized the army, a task for which he was particularly suited, and started westward to confront Lee's army, which had crossed the Potomac and moved into Maryland. Lincoln haunted the telegraph office, his eagerness for news evident in the series of almost daily wires he sent to McClellan asking simply: "How does it look now?" Even in the midst of this crisis, however, he continued to push Thompson's Chiriqui scheme in the cabinet. His perseverance was curious since by now several of the Central American governments had gotten wind of the scheme and protested the establishment of an American colony in their midst. As a result, the cabinet voted to kill the plan. Despite that, a week later Lincoln signed a contract with Thompson's company and ordered that Thompson be paid the first installment of $50,000. In all, Thompson was to be paid a total of $200,000 to transport ten thousand emigrants to Chiriqui, where they would be settled onto two thousand homesteads ranging in size from sixty acres for a family of five to twenty-five acres for a single man.[41]

A week later, news of the victory at Sharpsburg, along the banks of Antietam Creek, reached Washington, and as soon as it became clear that this was indeed a victory, though not as complete a one as he might have wished, Lincoln determined to issue his proclamation. He met with the cabinet on September 22, and after sharing aloud a humorous short story by Artemus Ward, he became serious. "When the rebel army was at Frederick," he announced, "I determined, as soon as it should be driven out of Maryland, to issue a Proclamation of Emancipation." He had made a promise, he said, "to myself, and"—a slight pause here—"to my Maker." "The rebel army is now driven out, and I am going to fulfill that promise." Then he proceeded to read the document. Seward suggested that the passage referring to colonization should be modified to make it clear that "the colonization proposed was to be only with the consent of the colonists," and Lincoln agreed. Later that day, the document became public, and the die was cast.[42]

Within days Lincoln was reviving his emigration scheme. He told his cabinet that it was "essential to provide an asylum for a race which we had emancipated, but which could never be recognized or admitted to be our equals." Bates agreed, but since he believed "the negro would not go voluntarily," he argued that blacks would have to be compelled to leave. No, Lincoln insisted. It was worthwhile, maybe even necessary, to offer the freed slaves an alternative—Lincoln's word, *asylum*, was deliberately chosen—but it was completely unacceptable to compel them to go. "Their emigration," he insisted, "must be voluntary and without expense to themselves." In this exchange it was clear that for Lincoln, colonization was not a means of ridding America of black faces but rather a humanitarian undertaking to allow them to escape the racism that he knew to be endemic in the Republic, and to enable them to become landowners. In the words of the editor of the *National*

Republic, Jacob Van Vliet, who wrote to Lincoln in support of the plan, it would "instantly take thousands of these poor, houseless, homeless, friendless beings, from the depths of poverty, and place them in a land where there is no prejudice against them." Of course, for all its benevolent intentions, none of this took into consideration the fact that there was virtually no enthusiasm for emigration on the part of the blacks themselves.[43]

That fall marked the end of both Lincoln's emigration scheme and of McClellan's command of the army. On October 6, the countries of Honduras, Costa Rica, and Nicaragua all formally protested the plan to establish an American colony in Central America. In the face of such universal opposition, and lacking any enthusiasm from free blacks, Lincoln authorized Seward to assure the foreign governments that the United States had changed its mind. There would be no colony for freed slaves, no overseas sanctuary, at Chiriqui or anywhere else in Central America. A month later, on November 5, the president finally dismissed McClellan, giving command of the army to Ambrose Burnside.

If Lincoln had few regrets about firing McClellan, he did regret having to abandon his colonization scheme. For many more months, well into 1864, he continued to hope that he might establish a kind of pilot program for willing black emigrants. During his annual State of the Union message in December, Lincoln declared, somewhat disingenuously, that "applications have been made to me by many free Americans of African descent to favor their emigration." That was not quite true, of course, since the enthusiasm for emigration had been entirely on his part. But Lincoln also had to report that "several of the Spanish-American republics have protested against the sending of such colonies," and "under these circumstances, I have declined to move any such colony to any state." Even then he did not surrender the idea altogether. Perhaps to keep the door open for voluntary emigration, or to ease northern fears of black migration, or both, he expressed the hope that "ere long, there will be an augmented, and considerable migration" to Liberia or to Haiti.[44]

In that, of course, he was wrong. Even after the failure of Reconstruction in the 1870s, black Americans showed little enthusiasm for emigration. Liberia was the most popular site for black emigrants, but from a black population of four and a half million, only about three thousand actually moved there in the ten years after the end of the war.

Despite a hundred years of de facto and de jure apartheid, the eventual solution to America's race problem did not lie in emigration or separation. Lincoln feared that whites would never accept blacks as citizens. His assumption proved correct during his own abbreviated lifetime, and, in fact, during the lifetime of anyone then living. But "never" is a very long time, and in the end, the solution to the difficult question of what to do with the freed slaves was a domestic one. It was, as Lincoln wrote in the summer of 1863 while contemplating Reconstruction in Louisiana, for "the two races" to "gradually live themselves out of their old relation to each other."[45]

TWO WEEKS AFTER Lincoln's Annual Message, there was more bad news from Virginia. Burnside had been defeated at Fredericksburg and the army had suffered horrible casualties. Lincoln was again plunged into despair. "It appears to me the Almighty is against us, and I can hardly see a ray of hope," he told Orville Browning. For the sake of the army he pulled himself out of his despair to send the soldiers a letter congratulating them on "the courage with which you, in an open field, maintained the contest against an entrenched foe." Such courage, he wrote, "will yet give victory to the cause of the country, and of popular government."[46]

It had been a difficult year for the country—and for its president. The lengthy casualty lists from Shiloh, from the peninsula, from Antietam, and now from Fredericksburg had each been wounds to Lincoln's heart, and the death of his beloved Willie had cut even deeper. In an implied rebuke of his administration, the Democrats gained twenty-eight House seats in the fall elections, though Republicans and Unionists still held a majority. Of course, there had been progress, too. Much of Tennessee, Louisiana, and western Virginia, had been recovered; the Union navy controlled most of the Mississippi River as well as great chunks of the southern coastline; the blockade grew tighter and the European powers continued to keep their distance; the rebel offensives in Kentucky and Maryland had been turned back; and the nation had responded willingly, even enthusiastically, to Lincoln's call for three hundred thousand more volunteers. Crucially, the September announcement of impending emancipation had not derailed the Union war effort.

In securing these gains, Lincoln had become a more activist commander in chief than he had intended, or even imagined, at the war's outset. He had played an important role in coordinating the river war out west; he had personally helped orchestrate the capture of Norfolk. Elsewhere in Virginia, he had appointed corps commanders, directed the movement of troops in the pursuit of Stonewall Jackson, and sequentially encouraged, coddled, chastised, and finally replaced George B. McClellan. Most important of all, he had redefined the nature of the war itself by striking at the core of the national schism: the institution of slavery. In each case, he had listened to the advice of others, but in the end all of the important decisions were his own.

As the unhappy year came to an end, Lincoln remained concerned about the long-term prospects for free blacks in a white America. He had delayed embracing a policy of emancipation by fiat, clinging to a belief that gradual and compensated emancipation supported by a vote of the people would not only meet the constitutional test but also be more certain. In addition, he did not want to invoke emancipation until he could answer the essential follow-on question: what would happen to the former slaves in a post-emancipation America? He abandoned only with reluctance the notion that colonization was a viable solution, or even a partial solution, to the nation's race problem. He still did not know what the solution would be, for he could not see that far into the future. What he did see was that the war was creating a new dynamic, accelerating the pace of social change so much that (as he had noted in March) "it was impossible to foresee" all that might result.[47]

A hint of a solution was embedded in the Emancipation Proclamation sitting on his desk and waiting to be signed. That document, studded with legalese and lacking entirely the Shakespearean poetry of which he was capable, included a paragraph toward the end stating that the newly emancipated blacks were to be "received into the armed service of the United States." Though their initial role would be limited to garrisoning forts, it was a crucial declaration nonetheless. Lincoln was aware that once black Americans had served in the army, the nation would incur an implied debt that at some point would have to be acknowledged, though the form and timing of that acknowledgement remained hidden behind the curtain of history.[48]

At his annual New Year's Day open house, the president once again greeted the thousands of visitors who lined up at his door, and afterward he retired upstairs to sign the final version of the Emancipation Proclamation. As he approached the table, he noted that his right hand, strained from all that shaking of hands, was trembling. "I never, in my life, felt more certain that I was doing right," he told Seward. "My whole heart is in it." But he feared that if he signed the document with a shaking hand, future generations would examine the signature and think he had hesitated. He stood there a moment massaging his sore writing hand, then declared, "But, any way, it is going to be done," and taking the pen in his hand, he bent over the table and subscribed his name in a bold hand.[49]

1863

TROUBLED WATERS

7

"The Peninsula All Over Again"

Lincoln, Charleston, and Vicksburg

SIEGE. Lincoln's experience with George McClellan during 1862 had made the word an imprecation. After the failed Peninsular Campaign, the president associated sieges with delay, expense, and a lack of will; almost any tactic was preferable to a siege. Moreover, despite Lincoln's involvement with combined operations on the Tennessee and Cumberland Rivers as well as in Hampton Roads, McClellan's insistence that any and all reinforcements to him must come by sea led Lincoln to make a mental association between "combined operations" and "siege warfare." This contributed significantly to Lincoln's reaction to the important strategic initiatives in 1863 at Charleston and Vicksburg and colored his relationships with the admirals in charge of those campaigns.

As Lincoln began the new year, he was sensitive to the fact that there had been far too much instability in the army's field leadership during the first two years of the war, especially in the Eastern Theater. It was not by design. Lincoln did not enjoy hiring and firing generals. He preferred to support his field commanders while they conducted the war, but ill fortune and the impatience of the public had dictated otherwise. McDowell had come to grief at Bull Run; McClellan on the peninsula; Pope at the Second Battle of Bull Run; and Burnside at Fredericksburg. Lincoln had granted McClellan a second chance, and Little Mac had partially redeemed himself with the bloody though incomplete victory at Antietam. After that, however, he reverted to type, and Lincoln had finally replaced him with Ambrose Burnside.

In an effort to justify Lincoln's trust, Burnside attempted a turning movement against Lee only a month later, ordering the army into motion on the night of January 20. Unfortunately for that unlucky commander, a cold rain drenched the soldiers and ruined the roads, and the movement collapsed in a disastrous tragedy of errors. This infamous "mud march," even more than the disaster at Fredericksburg, turned most of the army against Burnside, and the hapless army commander felt compelled to ask Lincoln either to sustain him by firing his critics or to replace him. Lincoln opted for the latter, selecting Joe Hooker as the army's new commander. The president knew there were risks inherent in such an appointment, for Hooker was a self-confident, even brash officer, but Lincoln decided that a man with too much confidence was better than one with too little. He appointed Hooker and hoped for the best.

The navy's command structure was only marginally more stable. On the western rivers, Rodgers had given way to Foote, who gave way to Davis, who in October 1862 gave way to David Dixon Porter, a man who shared many of the same strengths—and weaknesses—of Joe Hooker. Porter was talented and energetic, but he was also self-promoting, boastful, casual with the truth, and lacking in what Welles called "high moral qualities." Lincoln knew from personal experience that Porter could be a loose cannon, but that did not prevent him from listening carefully when Porter showed up in Lincoln's office in the fall of 1862. Learning that Welles had scheduled him to go to St. Louis to inspect gunboats, Porter had decided he had nothing to lose by calling on the president personally to plead his case for what he considered a more suitable assignment. Seward was with the president when Porter arrived, and there was some initial banter among the three about the spring of 1861, when they had come together to try to save Fort Pickens. The president took advantage of Porter's visit to pump him for a firsthand account of the river war. Porter related Farragut's run past the forts below New Orleans in dramatic detail, and explained why the subsequent movement upriver had not succeeded in capturing Vicksburg. He described that city's dominating location atop a high bluff overlooking a hairpin turn in the river with low swampy ground to its front, and offered several ideas about how it might be taken. He even may have suggested (as he did privately to Fox) that the city could have been captured earlier but for "a want of energy." As always, Lincoln listened carefully and was impressed that Porter not only seemed to know exactly what needed to be done but was apparently eager to go and do it. Porter later claimed that before he left, the president reassured him that "you shall be in Vicksburg when it falls."[1]

That afternoon, Lincoln initiated a conversation about Vicksburg with Fox. The assistant secretary doubted that the steady but unimaginative Charles Henry Davis, who had stepped in to replace the ailing Foote, was sufficiently energetic to mount a determined campaign against the rebel citadel. Davis' request to be continued in command was half-hearted at best: "I have no doubt that when I have collected my means and matured my plans," he wrote to Welles, you "will be satisfied with my efforts if not with my success." It was hardly a ringing call to action, and it inspired little confidence in Washington. Indeed, Welles had already selected Davis to be chief of the new Bureau of Navigation with authority over the Naval Observatory, the Hydrographical Office, and the Naval Academy, an assignment well suited to Davis' interests and abilities. But if Davis came to Washington, who would assume command on the Mississippi? Though Porter believed for the rest of his life that his selection was the result of Lincoln's personal intervention, it is not clear who first suggested him: Lincoln, based on the visit just concluded, or Fox. The latter seems likely, for Fox and Porter carried on a gossipy, almost conspiratorial correspondence, and Porter had recently suggested to Fox that "Davis . . . deserves to lose his command."[2]

Whoever proposed Porter's name, Welles made the appointment, and he did so very much aware that it was something of a risk. Not only was it certain to disappoint virtually all of the navy's captains that a mere commander was bequeathed an admiral's flag—even that of an acting rear admiral—but also there was the question of Porter's volatile personality. The day he made the appointment, Welles confided to his diary: "It is a question, with his good and bad traits, how he [Porter] will succeed. . . . If he does well I shall get no credit, if he fails I shall be blamed." When Porter left for the West, Welles wrote: "This is an experiment, and the results not entirely certain." In approving Hooker and Porter for these commands, Lincoln seemed to be saying that he preferred energy to caution, and that high moral qualities mattered less in a commander than results. "What I now ask of you is military success," he wrote to Hooker in January, "give us victories." He hoped for no less from Porter.[3]

The trend toward younger and more assertive officers was evident among commanders of the North Atlantic Blockading Squadron as well. There, Stringham (age sixty-four) had given way to Goldsborough (age fifty-seven), who gave way to Samuel Phillips Lee (age fifty). Lincoln's Lee (as his biographers have dubbed him) was a distant cousin of the rebel army commander, but more important, he was married to Montgomery Blair's sister, which made Fox, Blair, and Lee all brothers-in-law. Of course, Captain Lee had solid credentials as well as family connections. He had commanded a vessel in Wilkes' Great Exploring Expedition two decades earlier, and more recently he had commanded the *Oneida* during Farragut's run past Forts Jackson and St. Philip on the Mississippi, and had led the advance upriver to demand the surrender of Vicksburg, a demand that had been haughtily rejected. Now, like Porter, he assumed the rank of acting rear admiral in order to supersede the tired and dispirited Goldsborough.[4]

As for Charles Wilkes, whose independent command of the Potomac River Flotilla had triggered Goldsborough's request to be relieved, Welles dispatched him on yet another independent assignment to hunt down the Confederate commerce raiders that were wreaking havoc in the West Indies. Wilkes' particular quarry was the CSS *Alabama*, which most Union officers referred to as "No. 290"—the designation under which she had been constructed in the Birkenhead Shipyard at Liverpool, England. Like Porter and Lee, Wilkes was designated an acting rear admiral and received command of a "Flying Squadron," composed of five ships, that was to cruise the area between Key West and the Windward Islands searching for rebel raiders. If elevating Porter over the heads of several dozen senior officers invited criticism, putting Wilkes in command of a squadron operating where it was likely to interact with ships of foreign registry was perilous, as subsequent events would prove.

Elsewhere the naval command structure was more stable. Farragut—Porter's older foster brother—still commanded the West Gulf Blockading

Squadron on the lower Mississippi, and Du Pont kept a steady hand on the helm of the South Atlantic Blockading Squadron, grown now to fifty ships, from his anchorage at Port Royal. Both Farragut and Du Pont were line officers. While the Navy Department had officially assimilated line and staff officers in 1859, most serving officers still made a mental distinction between those who were in line to command ships and those who provided specialized support, such as surgeons, pursers, chaplains, and engineers. A relatively new category of officer, best personified by John A. Dahlgren, was the scientific warrior, whose technical talents were crucial to the new kind of war that was being fought, but who spent little time at sea and whose expertise might or might not translate into effective command leadership.[5]

Dahlgren, like Porter still a navy commander, took over the Washington Navy Yard after Franklin Buchanan resigned his commission in April 1861. Though the law restricted the command of navy yards to captains, Lincoln confirmed Dahlgren in his position in gratitude for his stalwart behavior during that emergency, securing a change in the law to allow Dahlgren to stay on. "He held it when no one else would," Lincoln declared, "and now he shall keep it as long as he pleases." In the ensuing months, Lincoln's frequent visits to the Navy Yard to witness the testing of one or another experimental weapon, or simply to escape the White House for an afternoon, made Dahlgren part of the president's inner circle. It was significant that during the panic over the anticipated arrival of the *Merrimack* in March 1862, Lincoln had abandoned his civilian advisers in the White House and ridden out to the Navy Yard to consult with Dahlgren.[6]

Elevated to head the Bureau of Ordnance, Dahlgren reveled in his status as friend of the president, but he was frustrated by the knowledge that as long as he stayed at the Navy Yard, even as a bureau chief, he might never advance beyond his current rank. He made particular note of the fact that Porter, who was junior to him in the commander's list, now flew an admiral's flag, and he was bold enough to mention it to Lincoln. The president told Dahlgren that he was ready to promote him to captain as soon as Welles sent his name forward, but Welles dragged his feet. It was navy policy that promotion was to be earned by winning battles at sea, and Welles believed that promoting an individual for either his scientific contributions or his political connections set a terrible precedent. When Congress established the rank of rear admiral in August the legislation decreed that such promotions were to go to men who had earned them in battle. Almost at once, Dahlgren began to lobby for an active sea command. On the same day that Lincoln agreed to send Porter west to lead the Mississippi Squadron, he received a letter from Dahlgren asking for command "of the sea forces that are to attack the Charleston forts." Dahlgren knew that this task had been assigned to Du Pont, but either naively or disingenuously, he suggested that "as Admiral Du Pont has reaped so many laurels, I am sure he would not object." Lincoln wished to gratify Dahlgren if he could, and he broached the idea with Welles that same day.[7]

Welles had nothing against Dahlgren per se, nor was his confidence in Du Pont unbounded. He worried that Du Pont had "too much finesse and management" and that in particular he tended to resort "to extraneous and subordinate influences to accomplish what he might easily attain directly." In addition, Welles suspected that Du Pont was encouraging a kind of naval clique, a group of officers personally loyal to him, in much the same way that McClellan had encouraged a personal following among the army's generals. Nevertheless, the attack on Charleston would be the capstone of Du Pont's campaign, and to push him aside and entrust it to a mere commander who had no significant sea service simply because he was a friend of the president was unthinkable.[8]

In spite of that, Welles sent Foote, still battling poor health, to Port Royal to try the idea out on Du Pont, who was, unsurprisingly, "astounded" and more than a little offended by the proposal. Du Pont concluded at once that the idea had sprung from Dahlgren himself, who, Du Pont believed, was "a diseased man on the subject of preferment and promotion." Du Pont worked himself up into a bit of snit, observing that it had been Dahlgren's own decision to become an ordnance specialist, a career path that allowed him to avoid decades of onerous sea duty. In consequence of that decision, Du Pont complained to Fox, "he was licking cream while we were eating dirt" (though "swallowing sea spray" might have been a more suitable phrase). "Now he wants all the honors belonging to the other but without having encountered its joltings." Du Pont didn't object to having Dahlgren join his squadron—he could be "one of my captains," he told Foote—but Du Pont had no intention of stepping aside to give Dahlgren command of the fleet or allowing him to command the forthcoming attack. Foote saw that there was no way to gratify both Du Pont and Dahlgren, and he reported as much to Welles, who in turn told the president.[9]

It is not clear whether Lincoln was displeased by this response, but he showed an uncharacteristic willingness to let Welles bear the brunt of Dahlgren's disappointment. The president reiterated that he would be happy to give Dahlgren "the highest grade" available—presumably an admiral's rank—if Welles would simply ask him for it. When Dahlgren mentioned this to Welles, the navy secretary tried to reason with him, suggesting that gaining rank by such means would not add to his reputation. Instead, Welles offered him command of one of the new monitors and a temporary assignment as Du Pont's ordnance officer, but only if he would agree to return to the bureau after the attack on Charleston. Dahlgren declined. He may have tried to exert a form of blackmail: aware that both Lincoln and Welles considered his expertise in ordnance vital to the war effort, he suggested that if he was expected to earn his promotion at sea, he would have to resign his post at the Bureau of Ordnance. Welles did not yield. "I am compelled," he wrote in his diary, "to stand between the President and Dahlgren's promotion." Of course, it is possible that Lincoln counted on him to do exactly that. He was the president, after all; he simply could have overruled Welles. The secretary's firm stand meant that Lincoln could continue to demonstrate his friendship for Dahlgren without upsetting the command structure of the Navy Department as he had done with Porter's appointment.[10]

The failure of Dahlgren's gambit meant that while Porter went west to target Vicksburg, the attack on Charleston would be led by Du Pont, who, whatever his faults, was the navy's most accomplished and respected senior officer. The attack on Vicksburg would necessarily be a combined operation (as Porter had noted, gunboats could not climb cliffs two hundred feet high), but Welles and Fox hoped that the assault on Charleston would be conducted by the navy alone. That winter, while Hooker reorganized the dispirited Army of the Potomac along the banks of the Rappahannock, Lincoln looked to the navy—to Porter at Vicksburg and Du Pont at Charleston—to boost the flagging morale of the Union.

PUBLIC MORALE WAS AT A LOW EBB for a number of reasons. While the Emancipation Proclamation had angered some, conscription, war weariness, and the absence of any evident progress dispirited almost everyone. The unhappiness was especially palpable in Lincoln's native Midwest. There, the War Democrats were wavering, and the Peace Democrats—called Copperheads by their enemies—complained that Lincoln's war was an "utter, disastrous, and most bloody failure." It was against this background that Lincoln agreed to endow Major General John A. McClernand, an Illinois War Democrat, with the command of an independent army to cooperate with Porter's river squadron in the campaign against Vicksburg.[11]

McClernand was a "political general" who had served several terms in Congress before the war. Though he had performed satisfactorily as a volunteer general in the campaigns for Forts Henry and Donelson and at Shiloh, his greatest asset was his status as a staunch War Democrat in a key western state. Now he offered to raise a new army and use it to seize the key rebel citadel on the Mississippi. Though it was certain to cause complications—McClernand would operate independently of Grant, and he was senior to William T. Sherman—it was an offer Lincoln could hardly refuse. Besides, at that time Lincoln believed that McClernand was at least as proficient as any of his other western generals, though he did worry that McClernand was "too desirous to be independent of every body else." Before he sent Porter on his way, Lincoln told his new admiral that McClernand was "a natural born general." Porter did not know McClernand, but he told Gideon Welles that he was happy that his army counterpart was not a West Point man, since they were "pedantic and unpractical." It was an opinion he would soon have cause to reconsider.[12]

While McClernand spent most of the next two months recruiting his army, Porter spent those same months surveying, reorganizing, and enlarging his command, converting it from an army flotilla to a navy squadron in accordance with the new legislation. In addition to absorbing army vessels into navy service, Porter added a total of fifty-four new ships, and by the end of the year his squadron was the largest in the navy, greater in number, if not in total tonnage, than Farragut's, Lee's, or Du Pont's.* Welles worried about the mounting expenditures but decided that it was important "to sustain all reasonable demands." He knew that Vicksburg was high in the president's priorities; Lincoln had recently declared that Vicksburg was "the key" not only to controlling the Mississippi but also to the war itself. Fox echoed Lincoln's view when he wrote Porter, "The opening of the river as early as possible is the imperative act to be considered above even the capture of Charleston."[13]

Porter struggled to find men for his enlarged squadron. Under the previous arrangement, the navy had paid civilian volunteers a dollar a day to do much of the shipboard work, but now that the squadron was a navy command, Porter was unwilling to continue to pay "lazy deck hands" to do work that could be done better by navy men. Sailors, however, were in short supply, and to fill up his growing squadron, Porter turned to contrabands. At Porter's urging, Welles authorized the enlistment of more black sailors. As in the saltwater navy, Welles insisted that their rating be no higher than landsman, though once they were shipped, he agreed that they could be promoted to seaman, fireman, or gunner, and that upon "the termination of enlistment" they would "retain their advanced rating." Once again, this was well in advance of administration policy concerning black soldiers, and these western black sailors would be more visible to the civil population than those serving on the blockade.[14]

Porter reveled in the alarm his mixed-race crews caused among the southern white population. "It takes all the fight out of them," he wrote to Fox. "Take away their niggers and you stop the war." He bragged to

---

*In the process of restructuring the Mississippi Squadron, Porter had to rename more than a dozen vessels that bore the names of ships already in service. In doing so, however, he chose particularly nonmartial names: *Terror* became *Ivy*, *Spitfire* became *Hyacinth*, *Intrepid* became *Fern*, and *Resolute* became *Myrtle*. The *New York Herald* mocked the new names as inappropriate for warships.

Fox, "The Squadron is chock full of niggers, including women and children. I take all that come."* While Porter's language reflected typical nineteenth-century attitudes, he was well ahead of his peers in arguing that "they are better than the white people here," though his comment was more likely a reflection of his scornful view of southern whites than a product of his admiration for blacks.[15]

One organizational problem that continued to frustrate Porter was the status of the so-called ram fleet. This curious force was the brainchild of the engineer and bridge-builder Charles W. Ellet Jr., who back in the spring of 1862 had proposed buying a handful of river steamers, reinforcing their bows with heavy timbers, and sending them against the enemy as rams under his own command. Welles thanked him for his idea and sent him packing. Not to be so easily put off, Ellet took his suggestion to the War Department, where Stanton thought it was a fine idea and gave Ellet a commission as an army colonel. Ellet deputized more than a dozen of his relatives as his subordinates, and at the Battle of Memphis in June, his ram fleet played a key role in breaking up the enemy river squadron, giving Charles Henry Davis his only victory of the war. Ellet himself died not long after that battle, bequeathing command of the ram fleet to his brother Alfred. Now Alfred Ellet was unwilling to have his command subsumed within Porter's squadron. When Porter tried to give him orders, Ellet claimed he was not subject to the navy's chain of command. Porter adopted a carrot-and-stick strategy in dealing with Ellet. The carrot was an offer to keep Ellet's command intact as a semi-autonomous "marine brigade" within the navy's command structure; the stick was his warning that any vessel operating on the rivers without navy orders would be "brought to and detained by any naval commander who might meet them operating on the river."[16]

Like all jurisdictional disputes between the services, this one could be resolved only by the president, and the two service secretaries took

---

*In their eagerness to assist the Yankees, many underage contraband boys volunteered for national service, and it became common for officers, and even some enlisted men, to take "a boy" on board as a personal servant. In language that strikes the modern ear with sinister implications, Porter told Fox, "If you want a nice boy say the word and you can get him."

their competing views to Lincoln. Welles insisted that the ram fleet be turned over to the navy; Stanton was adamant that it belonged to the army. Both men became emotional, but Welles, for once, managed to keep his temper, while Stanton did not. Whatever impact that had on the president, Lincoln sided with Welles in the dispute and told Stanton that the ram fleet must be turned over to Porter. Porter exulted that "the organization of the squadron is now entirely naval," but Fox reminded him of what was at stake. "The President is just and sagacious," he wrote, but the key was success. "Give me success; nothing else wins."[17]

All this time, Porter had heard nothing at all from McClernand, and he began to wonder if that officer actually had an army. As for Grant, Porter was suspicious of him, too. "I don't trust the army," he wrote to Fox in November, "it is very evident that Grant is going to try and take Vicksburg without us," adding, somewhat smugly, "but he can't do it." Porter's suspicions were assuaged a month later when he finally met Grant. The quiet, stern-looking general was very different from what he had expected. There was no frivolity, no West Point pretension, about him. Sherman, too, was a surprise, telling Porter that he would "do anything possible to advance the cause of our country, and more especially to comply with any request made by Admiral Porter." Completely disarmed, Porter responded in kind, writing Sherman that "I wish to cooperate with the army in every way."[18]

The plan, as Grant explained it, was for his own army to march southward from Memphis, drawing to him the principal rebel force under John C. Pemberton. At the same time, Sherman would move down the Mississippi with thirty thousand men, escorted by Porter's gunboats, to attack Vicksburg. By ascending the Yazoo River just north of the city, Porter could put Sherman's men ashore behind the enemy fortifications. It was a true combined operation that incorporated Lincoln's idea of attacking the enemy at different points simultaneously. Moreover, if Porter's gunboats could ascend further up the Yazoo to the Yalobusha and Tallahatchie Rivers, it would put them on the flank and rear of Pemberton's army and cut it off from Vicksburg. Sherman would take Vicksburg, and Pemberton would have to retreat eastward. As for McClernand, well, perhaps the three of them could resolve the issue before he arrived.[19]

Alas, all three elements of this plan unraveled in December when Grant's army was cut off from its supply base by a rebel cavalry raid on Holly Springs, Sherman's men were turned back from the heights north of Vicksburg, and Porter's gunboats failed to ascend the Yazoo far enough to outflank the enemy. The loss of the ironclad *Cairo* to a rebel mine in the Yazoo showed that there were new dangers on the rivers, and Porter endured a grievous personal blow when Lieutenant Commander William Gwin, one of his favorites, suffered a mortal wound.[20]

This bad news from the West coincided with a crisis in Lincoln's cabinet. Chase and Seward, playing power politics, each sought to gain an advantage by discrediting the other, and Lincoln had to use all his political skill to hold his administration together. When McClernand wrote privately to Lincoln charging Halleck with "utter incompetency" for allowing Grant to hijack his soldiers, Lincoln begged him not to press the issue and to focus on the work at hand. "I have too many family controversies, (so to speak) already on my hands," the president responded, "to voluntarily, or so long as I can avoid it, take up another."[21]

There was some good news. On New Year's Eve, the Union army of Major General William S. Rosecrans successfully fought off a furious attack by a rebel army along the banks of Stones River near Murfreesboro in middle Tennessee, and two days later, on January 2, Rosecrans fended off a second attack. Soon afterward, the rebel army fell back to Tullahoma, halfway to the Alabama line. There was no effective pursuit, however, and it was hard to determine if this victory—if it was a victory—had secured any important advantages.

McClernand finally showed up north of Vicksburg. With Grant still falling back to Memphis from central Mississippi, the newcomer superseded Sherman in command of the Union forces there. McClernand was wise enough to ask Sherman for his ideas about what to do next, and Sherman proposed temporarily abandoning the attack on Vicksburg in order to reduce a rebel fortification called Fort Hindman on the Arkansas River. When he made the suggestion, Sherman assumed he would command the expedition himself, but McClernand at once adopted it as his own. By this time, Porter and Sherman had developed a compatible working relationship, even a friendship, and both men saw the newcomer as an outsider. This created a frisson of tension as Union forces moved upriver to Fort Hindman.[22]

The attack on Fort Hindman, though ultimately successful, did little to improve the command relationship. Porter thought that McClernand failed to give the navy its due, and he complained to Welles that "Army officers are not willing to give the Navy credit." Grant, still in Memphis, wanted to know what McClernand was doing at Arkansas Post in the first place. He wired Halleck that "McClernand has . . . gone on a wild-goose chase to the Post of Arkansas." Grant did not know at the time that the campaign had been Sherman's idea, a fact that Porter, too, conveniently ignored. Annoyed by McClernand's failure to give him and the navy sufficient credit, Porter wrote caustically to Welles that the whole expedition had been "rather a waste of time."[23]

Lincoln's hopes for progress in the West were again disappointed. From Washington, Grant's unproductive probes along the rivers north of Vicksburg seemed hesitant and halfhearted. McClernand, now relegated to a role as one of Grant's corps commanders, wrote directly to Lincoln to tell him that it was probably best "to invest the place and leave it to fall by siege." Porter agreed that there was now no alternative to "a tedious siege."[24]

For Lincoln, this was terrible news. His experience with McClellan had so scarred him that he was now suspicious of anything that even looked like a siege. Aware of the Union's numerical and technological superiority, he could not understand why so many of his commanders favored maneuver and sieges over a direct approach. Knowing the president's state of mind, Fox wrote Porter: "I dislike to see you all set down for a long siege at Vicksburg." He tried to energize the western admiral by holding out the prospect of promotion and medals: "You did well at Arkansas Post," Fox wrote, "and we shall get you a vote of thanks for it." But the big prize, Fox reminded him, was Vicksburg: "If you open the Father of Waters you will at once be made an admiral; besides we will try for a ribboned star."[25]

For the next two months, as Porter's gunboats explored the sluggish backwaters of the Yazoo River and Steele's Bayou to little apparent effect, Grant put men to work digging a canal across DeSoto Point. Lincoln had little faith in any of these operations beyond "a general hope" that Grant knew what he was doing. As week after week passed with no evidence of progress, he all but gave up on Grant and Porter. He even authorized the army's adjutant general, Lorenzo Thomas, to make a change in command—presumably by elevating McClernand—if he thought it would accelerate matters. Meanwhile, he hoped for progress elsewhere.[26]

IF THE CAMPAIGN AGAINST VICKSBURG was now to be "a tedious siege," Welles and Fox were more determined than ever that the assault on Charleston would be entirely different. Since the first days of the war, Lincoln had anticipated reclaiming the city of Charleston for the Union. His ambition in that respect was symbolic rather than strategic. Like the president, Welles acknowledged that "the place has no strategic importance," though he also knew that "there is not another place our countrymen would so rejoice to see taken." Charleston was where the first shot of the war had been fired; it was the ideological and psychological heart of the rebellion. Fox still chafed at the memory of his failure to reinforce Fort Sumter back in the spring of 1861, and he spoke for many in the North when he wrote to Du Pont that "the fall of Charleston is the Fall of Satan's Kingdom."[27]

Charleston (like Vicksburg) boasted a peculiar geography that made a direct assault by either army or navy forces problematical. As Charlestonians liked to say, their city stood where the Ashley and Cooper Rivers flowed together to form the Atlantic Ocean, and it was surrounded by marshy inlets that made an overland approach difficult. Moreover, the city itself was separated from the ocean by a broad estuary surrounded on all sides by forts and batteries, including Fort Sumter, which made a strictly naval assault equally daunting. To solve this strategic puzzle, the Union's best hope was to rely on a combined operation. In that respect, Charleston's history should have been instructive. In 1776, during the American Revolution, the initial British assault against the city had pitted half a dozen Royal Navy warships against the patriots' coastal forts—Fort Moultrie in particular—and it had failed. Four years later, a combined attack by Royal Navy and British army forces had been successful.

Indeed, the initial Union campaign against Charleston in 1862 looked remarkably like the one British forces had employed in 1780. Following up on Marchand's successful reconnaissance of the Stono River in May, several of Du Pont's vessels landed three thousand Union soldiers on the north bank of the Stono very near the spot where the

THE SIEGE OF CHARLESTON. Map by Bill Clipson, reprinted with permission from *The Naval Institute Historical Atlas of the U.S. Navy* by Craig L. Symonds, © 1995.

British had landed eighty-two years earlier. These forces were to cross James Island and assail rebel-held Fort Johnson from the rear (as the British had done). Once in control of that fort, Union gunners could bombard Fort Sumter's weakly defended gorge wall, and the suppression of Fort Sumter would open the way for the navy to steam into the harbor. The army's premature and uncoordinated assault on a rebel battery near the village of Secessionville in June halted the overland advance, and the army subsequently evacuated James Island.[28]

Du Pont thought the army's decision to evacuate was a terrible mistake, but Welles was not particularly disappointed, for it revived his hope that the attack on Charleston, like the capture of Port Royal, could be a purely naval one. Charleston was more heavily fortified than Port Royal, to be sure, but the success of Ericsson's *Monitor* in Hampton Roads in March had convinced Welles that ironclads in general, and monitors in particular, were virtually impervious to conventional ordnance. Welles was sure that if Du Pont had a few monitors, they could steam boldly into Charleston Harbor, pass Fort Sumter, and anchor in the inner harbor. There, they could compel the outer forts to surrender or suffer having the city shelled into submission. In urging this approach, Welles had multiple goals. Not only would it chastise the city that personified rebellion and treason, it would also validate Welles' good judgment in sponsoring the monitor class of warships, and it would gain new accolades for the navy. As Fox put it in a letter to Du Pont: "I feel that my duties are two fold; first, to beat our southern friends; second to beat the Army."[29]

For his part, Du Pont was unconvinced that a purely naval attack on Charleston Harbor was practical or even possible. In fact, he was not particularly impressed by the new monitors, for despite their defensive strength they carried only two guns each. Even a half dozen monitors could bring only twelve guns to the fight. And in any case, Du Pont believed that Charleston's geography made it impossible for ships to run past the protecting forts as Farragut had done on the lower Mississippi or as Walke had done at Island No. 10. Because the inner harbor was ringed by other fortifications, even if his ships successfully passed Sumter, there was no sanctuary for them once they were inside. Du Pont described Charleston Harbor as a cul de sac, like a porcupine turned inside out; there simply was no such thing as running past the batteries. But while

Du Pont shared these doubts with his wife and with his political ally Henry Winter Davis, a sometime Know-Nothing congressman from Maryland, he was unwilling to appear a reluctant warrior to the administration. Consequently, as his biographer has written, he "failed to counter the expectations of his civilian masters forthrightly."[30]

Lincoln's expectations were influenced by Welles and Fox. Like them, Lincoln was a champion of new technology, and he shared at least some of their confidence in the capability and invulnerability of the monitors. It was bracing to hear Welles declare confidently that with a few ironclads, Du Pont "could go right into the harbor, with little or no risk, and destroy the Forts, batteries, and the town itself." In addition, such a direct approach was a refreshing contrast to McClellan's indirect—and, in Lincoln's view, unnecessarily complex—strategic plans.[31]

Du Pont had a chance to make his case on October 16 when he called on Lincoln in the White House during a brief trip away from the blockade. Their conversation took place at the peak of Lincoln's annoyance with McClellan's obstreperousness. Surprised, and somewhat taken aback, when Lincoln began by offering a critical assessment of McClellan's command, perhaps intending it to be a cautionary tale, Du Pont squandered his opportunity. He did not mention his desire for more ironclads, and more important, he failed to outline his concerns about the tactical plan. Instead he emphasized the "moral effect" that the presence of his squadron off the coast had on the enemy. "The iron grip we had on the coast," he assured Lincoln, "falsified the declarations of the chief promoters of the rebellion." He begged that "the government should not lose sight of us."[32]

Du Pont did share his concerns with Fox, whom he considered an ally, during the return trip to Port Royal. Fox accompanied him as far as Hampton Roads, and Du Pont took advantage of the opportunity to emphasize that the attack on Charleston should be a joint one involving a substantial body of soldiers. Fox readily agreed, promising that ten thousand to fifteen thousand soldiers would be sent to Port Royal at once. But there was no meeting of the minds. Fox thought Du Pont wanted a body of troops to take possession of the city after the navy captured it, like Butler's troops at New Orleans. Du Pont knew he had failed to make his case when Welles wrote him in January to tell him that five ironclads were being sent to him "to enable you to enter the harbor of Charleston and demand the surrender of all its defenses." Rather than try to explain his views again, Du Pont merely replied: "I shall endeavor to execute its [the department's] wishes."[33]

This misunderstanding derived in part from Welles' near-absolute confidence in the efficacy of the monitors, and in part from Du Pont's reluctance to be fully candid with his civilian masters for fear of being considered weak-willed. Rather than contradict Welles' optimistic assumptions directly, Du Pont instead sent him a series of reports emphasizing the difficulty of the approach and the strength of the enemy defenses, hoping that Welles would read between the lines and give him more discretion. Welles correctly intuited the message behind Du Pont's constant requests. The navy secretary told him bluntly that "if after careful examination you deem the number of ironclads insufficient" for the capture of Charleston, the attempt "must be abandoned." At the same time, however, Welles prodded him by writing that "the Department will share the responsibility imposed upon commanders who make the attempt." The implication was clear: if Du Pont and his captains feared for their careers or their reputations, Welles was willing to accept the responsibility for failure. Du Pont did not respond directly to this suggestion, but his litany of requests and complaints continued. He reported that his machinery was breaking down for lack of oil. He was short of almost everything, coal in particular, but also "sugar, coffee, flour, butter, beans, and dried fruit." By the end of January, these reports began to remind Welles, and Lincoln, too, of the kinds of letters that McClellan used to send.[34]

The first of the new monitors, larger and improved versions of the original, arrived in Port Royal in late January, and by the end of the month Du Pont had five of them, plus the giant *New Ironsides*, an ocean-going armored frigate that carried fifty big guns.* Lincoln kept track of the growth of Du Pont's ironclad force, and he expected imminently to

---

*The new *Passaic*-class monitors were not only larger than Ericsson's original *Monitor* but also more heavily armed. Each carried one new 15-inch Dahlgren gun, as well as one 11-inch gun. These 15-inch guns were the largest naval guns deployed in the nineteenth century, and only an inch smaller than the largest U.S. Navy guns on World War II battleships. Du Pont had witnessed a demonstration firing of a 15-inch gun at the Navy Yard during his visit to Washington in October and was impressed. It was not enough, however, to change his mind about the limited offensive capability of monitors.

hear news of an ironclad attack on the city. Instead, the next word from Charleston was that on the last day of January two small Confederate ironclads, diminutive clones of the dreaded *Merrimack*, stole out of Charleston Harbor in a morning fog and temporarily chased off the Union blockading fleet. Beauregard trumpeted this success as the lifting of the blockade. Du Pont was defensive, insisting that the triumphal rebel reports were hugely exaggerated, but privately, he wrote his wife that the episode may have been salubrious, since the rebel sortie might finally "open Mr. Fox's eyes" to the difficulties he faced at Charleston.[35]

Two weeks later, Brigadier General John Gray Foster, who commanded the soldiers that were to cooperate with Du Pont in the attack, arrived at the White House to brief the president on the forthcoming operation. Stanton and Halleck were there to represent the army, and Fox (though not Welles) was there to represent the navy. Foster told the president that the attack was to be a combined operation in which his soldiers landed on Morris Island, the southern headland, and erected batteries there to reduce Fort Sumter. Once Sumter was neutralized, Du Pont's warships then could enter the harbor safely. Characteristically, Lincoln was mostly a silent observer, but Fox became agitated almost at once, and he interrupted Foster to declare that it had been long settled that the attack was to be spearheaded by Du Pont's monitors. Indeed, he could barely conceal his frustration that the army seemed to be contemplating another siege. Turning to Halleck, Fox asked him: "What would be the result of the ironclads reaching a position off the city?" Halleck replied that the enemy would immediately have to evacuate James Island. Fox turned back to Foster to ask bluntly: "Why attack the forts?" Foster had to admit that "if we could get to the city it would be no use."[36]

Lincoln followed this exchange with interest. He was at least as suspicious as Fox was of sieges, and he suggested that perhaps Fox should go down to Charleston personally to make sure that Du Pont understood the plan, since apparently there was still some confusion about it. Fox agreed to go, but Welles worried that sending him on such an errand would "touch Du Pont's pride" and "do more harm than good." Lincoln's desire to send Fox to Charleston suggested that his faith in Du Pont had seriously eroded. For a day and a half he considered sending Fox there regardless of its impact on Du Pont's feelings. He called Fox over to the White House early the next morning and they had a private conversation about it while Lincoln was shaving, which Fox found somewhat awkward, telling his wife that it reminded him of the receptions held by Louis XIV. In the end, Lincoln decided that Fox did not have to go, but that he should send Du Pont a pointed letter, and so Fox wrote to Du Pont: *"The idea of a siege meets with such disfavor that the President wished me to go down and see you,"* underscoring the sentence for emphasis. He made it as clear as he could that the administration expected Du Pont to execute a purely naval attack. He advised Du Pont "not to take these soldiers too closely into your counsels in a purely naval matter." And he iterated the plan as it was understood in Washington: "It seems very clear that our course is to go in and demand the surrender of the forts, or the alternative of destruction to their city." If that didn't work, then, but only then, it might be time to think about a siege. He described the attack as he saw it unfolding in his mind's eye. Imagine, he wrote, "carrying in your flag, supreme and superb, defiant, and disdainful, silent amid the 200 guns until you arrive at the centre of this wicked rebellion and then demand the Surrender of the forts." He reminded Du Pont that "the President and Mr. Welles are very much struck with this programme," and begged Du Pont "not to let the army spoil it."[37]

This episode marked the moment when Lincoln began to wonder if Du Pont was not simply a maritime version of George McClellan. The admiral had been rock solid in organizing the blockade, and his capture of Port Royal had been swift and sure, but his constant requests for more ironclads, his gloomy reports, and especially his apparent preference for a lengthy siege rather than a bold dash into the harbor all sounded eerily familiar. As Du Pont no doubt hoped, his reports lowered expectations in Washington, but they also lowered Du Pont's standing with the administration. Welles noted that, like McClellan, "Du Pont shrinks, dreads, the conflict he has sought," yet at the same time he was "unwilling that any other should undertake it." Welles concluded that Du Pont was simply being protective of his reputation. "I am disappointed," Welles confided to his diary, "but not wholly surprised." The president agreed. That same day, Dahlgren noted in his diary that "Abe is restless about Charleston."[38]

Lincoln's restlessness may have contributed to his decision two days later to ask Welles to promote Dahlgren from commander to admiral, skipping the rank of captain altogether. Previously, Lincoln had told Dahlgren that he would promote him only if Welles requested it; now he simply told Welles to do it. Welles remained opposed—Dahlgren did not have the sea service to justify it—but he dutifully submitted Dahlgren's name, along with that of Charles Henry Davis, to the Senate, which confirmed both men. Dahlgren's elevation rankled many in the service. The wife of one senior officer wrote her husband that Dahlgren's promotion "defeats the object of making Admirals & makes it too cheap." Cheap or not, the promotions of Davis and Dahlgren gave the country a total of six admirals: Farragut, Goldsborough, Du Pont, Foote, Davis, and Dahlgren, in that order of seniority. Interestingly, however, four of the six, including Dahlgren, held largely administrative positions; only Farragut and Du Pont commanded squadrons. Porter, Lee, and Charles Wilkes also commanded squadrons as acting rear admirals, but they remained statutory captains. Indeed, Porter was elevated to captain by the same legislation that made Dahlgren an admiral. A few days later, Dahlgren called on Welles to thank him for the promotion, but Welles told him candidly that it was not his doing, that he had advised against it, but that the president had insisted. Perhaps by now Lincoln wished he had acceded to Dahlgren's initial request to command the naval assault on Charleston.[39]

Du Pont, meanwhile, decided to test the new monitors by sending a few of them to attack Fort McAllister on Ogeechee Sound south of Charleston. Three monitors pounded the earthwork fort on January 27, and four of them did so again on February 1. Lincoln asked for a copy of the report, which he presumably read with his usual care. The good news was that the monitors were as tough as advertised; the *Montauk* took sixty-one direct hits and remained essentially undamaged. On the other hand, the monitors did not inflict any perceptible damage on the fort. From Du Pont's point of view, this proved his claim that for all their invulnerability, the monitors had limited offensive punch. What Welles perceived, however, was that "the turret vessels are strong and capable of great endurance." Once again there was no meeting of the minds.[40]

Welles decided to send an observer down to assess the monitors for himself, and the man he chose was Alban Stimers, a thirty-six-year-old career navy engineer who had been aboard the original *Monitor* during its duel with the *Merrimack*, and who was now the number two man at what was generally called the Monitor Bureau, charged with overseeing the monitor construction program. Stimers went along as an observer in yet a third attack on Fort McAllister on March 3. Once again the monitors hammered away at the enemy earthworks, and once again, while they escaped unscathed themselves, they were unable to silence the enemy guns.

Du Pont was frustrated that this evidence of the monitors' limited capability had no apparent impact on expectations in Washington. He wrote his wife, Sophie, "The president ought to know but does not that the work on the defenses of Charleston have gone on without intermission for twenty-three months." Apparently it did not occur to him that if the president "ought to know" but did not, it was because Du Pont had not told him. A few days later, he wrote his friend Winter Davis that "if the President knew what was involved in a failure he would never think of such a thing." Looking back at it later, Du Pont acknowledged that he might have stated his views "in more emphatic terms" and he justified his failure to do so by claiming that having laid out "all the facts . . . before the Department for its judgment and decision," he had done all that anyone should expect. Instead of forthrightly telling the president what he needed to know, he was content to send broad hints about the difficulties and adopt a martyr's role.[41]

A week later, on March 12, Lincoln dropped in at the Navy Department, where Stimers, just back from Port Royal, was discussing his visit. Like Welles, Stimers was professionally invested in the success of the monitors, and he was eager for them to demonstrate their prowess. Consequently, he portrayed Du Pont as timid and uncooperative. He told Lincoln that he had attended a council of war aboard Du Pont's flagship where the planning had focused, once again, on how the army could seize the rebel shore batteries before Du Pont made any effort to run into the harbor.[42]

Lincoln thought this sounded like "the Peninsula all over again" and, somewhat alarmed, he asked Stimers if this meant "we were going into a *siege*." He suggested that Du Pont's "long delay," and especially his "constant call for more ships, more ironclads, was like McClellan calling for more regiments." He told Fox that if Du Pont wasn't going to use the monitors at Charleston, perhaps they should be sent instead to Farragut on the Mississippi. Only "with difficulty" did Fox talk him out of it, and afterward Fox wrote Du Pont to tell him about the president's suggestion, no doubt hoping that it would spur the admiral to quicker action. Privately, Lincoln told Welles that "he was prepared for a repulse at Charleston." "The President," Welles wrote in his diary, "who has often a sort of intuitive sagacity, has spoken discouragingly of operations at Charleston during the whole season. Du Pont's dispatches and movements have not inspired him with faith; they remind him, he says, of McClellan." After that, Welles wrote Du Pont to tell him that he could have two more monitors, giving him a total of eight, but he was to understand that he was not to wait for the army, nor was he to engage the rebel forts; he was to run past them and take command of the harbor. Even then Welles was not sanguine that the orders would have much impact. Taking his cue from Lincoln, he wrote in his diary that "Du Pont is getting as prudent as McClellan."[43]

As Lincoln had feared, the public was becoming impatient. The *New York Herald* editorialized, "The operations against Vicksburg and Port Hudson thus far have resulted only in failures. . . . Our land and naval forces assigned to the work of reducing Charleston . . . appear to be waiting for 'something to turn up.' . . . General Hooker still remains fast in the mud on the Rappahannock." Given this situation, Lincoln wrestled with his depression. In February, Dahlgren noted that "the President never tells a joke now," and in March, a week after Stimers' visit, when Lincoln again visited the Navy Department, Dahlgren was shocked by his appearance. "He looks thin and badly, and is very nervous," Dahlgren wrote. Even more disturbing, Lincoln seemed not himself. He "complained of everything," insisting that "they were doing nothing at Vicksburg and Charleston." He was distressed that "Dupont was asking for one iron-clad after another, as fast as they were built." He thought "the canal at Vicksburg was of no account, and wondered that a sensible man would do it." Dahlgren tried to cheer up his friend, putting an optimistic spin on the reports. But the president was inconsolable and expressed the fear that "the favorable state of public expectation would pass away before anything was done." Then, almost as if by force of will, he dragged himself out of his mood, "leveled a couple of jokes at the doings at Vicksburg and

Charleston," and left. Dahlgren's final comment in his diary that night was: "Poor gentleman."[44]

LINCOLN DID NOT WAIT PASSIVELY in the White House to hear from Du Pont. On April 4, along with his wife and son Tad, he boarded the steamer *Carrie Martin* in the midst of a snowstorm for a visit to Hooker's army, which was still encamped near Falmouth on the north bank of the Rappahannock. He reviewed the newly reorganized cavalry corps, some ten thousand strong, and admired the soldiers in their new blue uniforms, the rows of glittering bayonets testifying to Hooker's revitalization of the army. Of course McClellan had revitalized the army too—it remained to be seen what Hooker would do with it.[45]

When he returned to Washington on April 11, Lincoln saw a telegram from Hampton Roads reporting that one of Du Pont's ships, the *Flambeau*, had touched there en route to Washington with dispatches from the admiral. Apparently, the initial attack on Charleston had been repulsed. There were no details, however, and Welles ordered the captain of the *Flambeau* to hurry on to Washington with Du Pont's report. Lincoln went to the Navy Department at noon the next day, but the *Flambeau* had not yet docked, so he returned to the White House. That afternoon, Welles came to see him with Du Pont's report in hand and read it aloud to Lincoln and to Charles Sumner, who was also present. Du Pont reported that he had intended to pass Fort Sumter and attack its weaker northwest wall, but "the nature of the obstructions compelled the attack from the outside." The fight, he wrote, was "fierce and obstinate" but also indecisive, and toward evening Du Pont had ordered a withdrawal, intending to renew the action the next day. Instead, the damage reports of his several ironclad captains convinced him that doing so would have "converted a failure into a disaster," and he called it off. He added the observation that "Charleston can not be taken by a purely naval attack."[46]

Lincoln was disappointed but not surprised. It was, he said, "very much as he expected it to be." Welles was disappointed, too, but he was also angry that Du Pont had stopped to fight it out with Fort Sumter. He had expected him to pass Fort Sumter and the other batteries, "not stop to encounter them." The repulse was personally embarrassing as well, for Welles had lost face in his rivalry with Stanton, who, in

Welles' imagination, took the news somewhat smugly. For Lincoln, however, the important information was that Du Pont had terminated the attack. The president knew from his recent visit to Falmouth that Hooker was planning to cross the Rappahannock soon to inaugurate the spring campaign, and Grant's operations against Vicksburg were reaching a critical stage. In accordance with his strategic vision, Lincoln wanted Du Pont to maintain a credible threat at Charleston to prevent Beauregard from sending reinforcements to either Virginia or Mississippi. In the hope that it was not too late, Lincoln sent a telegram to Du Pont urging him to "hold your position inside the bar near Charleston, or if you have left it, return to it, and hold it until further orders." He did not order him to renew the attack—he left that to Du Pont's discretion—but he wanted the Confederates to think that the attack might be renewed at any time. It was important, Lincoln wrote, to keep up the demonstration "for a collateral and very important object."[47]

It was too late. Before he received these messages, Du Pont had already withdrawn the battered ironclads back to Port Royal. The regular blockading ships remained on station, but they were outside the bar and posed no immediate threat to the city. Du Pont knew the administration would be disappointed, but he was determined not to submit to any criticism. In his view, he had given sufficient warning that the obstacles were great and his own resources limited. To his wife, he wrote, "I will stand no reproof. I have served too long and too faithfully, and too loyally to the administration, to the country, and to the cause to stand for that and if I am censured, I will ask for a court." When he received Lincoln's telegram, he complained that its "tenor and tone" implied "a censure," and somewhat petulantly requested that "the Department will not hesitate to relive me by any officer who, in its opinion, is more able to execute that service in which I have had the misfortune to fail—the capture of Charleston." He no doubt expected this remark to elicit further assurances of the administration's confidence. In that, he would be disappointed.[48]

THAT SAME DAY, a thousand miles to the west, David Dixon Porter ran his river ironclads past the Vicksburg batteries. His achievement did not seem particularly significant at the time. Other Union vessels had run past those batteries before: Charles Ellet's nineteen-year-old nephew, Charles Rivers Ellet, did it in the *Queen of the West* in February, and a few days after that one of Porter's ironclads, the *Indianola*, did so as well, though both ships were subsequently lost to the enemy.* Moreover, the idea for Porter's maneuver came not from Porter himself but from Grant and, quite independently, from Lincoln himself.

Grant concluded that the lengthy and tedious effort to outflank Vicksburg via the rivers and bayous north of the city was played out, and that the best chance of getting behind the city was to cross the river south of it. Lincoln's purpose was quite different. The president wanted a naval force on the stretch of river between Vicksburg and Port Hudson, Louisiana, two hundred miles to the south. That section of the Mississippi included the mouth of the Red River, which the Confederates were using to bring supplies to the eastern theater from Arkansas and Texas. Before Porter had left Washington for his new command, Lincoln had spread out a map of the West and pointed to the Red River. "Here," he said, "is the Red River which will supply all the Confederates with cattle and corn to supply their armies." It was to halt that flow of supplies that the *Queen of the West* and the *Indianola* had run past Vicksburg in February, and in March, Farragut ran a few of his deep-water ships into that stretch of river from the south, though he had lost the steamer *Mississippi* during the run past Port Hudson. Lincoln thought the loss of one ship was a small price to pay for cutting off rebel commerce from the West, but Farragut could not hold his position indefinitely because he had no way to keep his vessels coaled. Consequently, Lincoln wanted Porter to send some of his ships past Vicksburg to take their place.[49]

Porter made the run on April 16, each of his ironclads towing a coal barge. Though it triggered a lively exchange with the enemy batteries,

---

*Charles Rivers Ellet, at nineteen, was the youngest full colonel in the U.S. Army. His youthful enthusiasm may have led him to push too far too soon up the Red River, where he ran the *Queen of the West* onto a mud bank under the guns of a rebel battery. The Confederates seized it and subsequently used it to capture the *Indianola*. Disgusted, Welles asked Porter if he should be prepared for news of "additional disgrace and disaster." Porter, however, used an old coal barge, which he modified to resemble a powerful ironclad, and sent it drifting past Vicksburg. In a panic, the Confederates blew up the *Indianola* to prevent its recapture by this dreaded false ironclad.

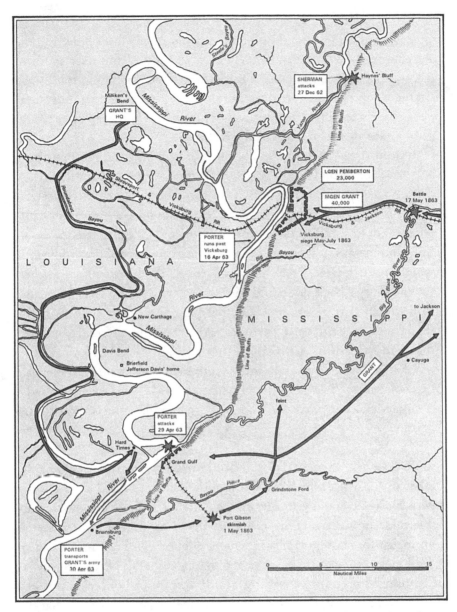

THE VICKSBURG CAMPAIGN. Map by Bill Clipson, reprinted with permission from *The Naval Institute Historical Atlas of the U.S. Navy* by Craig L. Symonds, © 1995.

no one was killed, and only a dozen were wounded. The army transport *Henry Clay* was lost, but that, too, without any loss of life, and the
next morning, Porter was securely in command of the river south of
Vicksburg. Grant's army was already in motion, marching southward
on the western side of the river. Porter and Grant would rendezvous at
the aptly named Hard Times Landing, from which place Porter would
ferry Grant's soldiers across to the east bank.[50]

In mid-April, the outcome of all this marching and maneuvering
was unclear. Welles told Porter that "this successful movement . . .
reflects great credit upon yourself," but neither he nor Lincoln saw at
the time how crucial the move would become in the ensuing campaign. Indeed, Lincoln now wanted Porter and Grant to bypass Vicksburg and move south to assist Banks in the capture of Port Hudson. It
was only much later, after Grant had crossed the Mississippi, marched
to Vicksburg's back door, and forced its capitulation, that it became
evident that Porter's run past Vicksburg had been a key element in the
final triumph. Until then, there seemed to be little difference between
Du Pont's assertion that "Charleston can not be taken by a purely
naval attack" and Porter's claim that "there is no possible hope of any
success against Vicksburg by a gunboat attack." Porter even sounded a
bit like McClellan when he wrote, "My main object is to meet with no
defeats."[51]

WHATEVER THE EVENTUAL RESULT of Porter's run past Vicksburg, the
relative ease with which he accomplished it contrasted dramatically
with Du Pont's failure to run into the harbor at Charleston, and further undermined Du Pont's insistence that a handful of ironclads were
no match for shore fortifications. As evidence, Du Pont forwarded to
Washington the reports from each of his captains, all of them supporting his decision not to renew the attack. But instead of seeing this as a
validation of Du Pont's good judgment, Welles saw it as proof that the
admiral's loyal captains were willing to parrot his explanations. Mc-
Clellan's generals had always backed him up, too. After reading the reports, Welles summarized them this way: "It is the recommendation of
all, from the Admiral down, that no effort be made to do anything."
Fox's disillusionment with Du Pont was evident in his private note to
Porter: "Our ironclads at Charleston were only dented, yours have

been perforated through & through . . . yet we get no dispatches from you that they are failures and that nothing can be done." When one of Du Pont's captains wrote that monitors were suitable mainly for harbor defense and were not effective offensive weapons, Welles took it personally and concluded that the officer was a "dupe" of Du Pont and that his letter was part of a conspiracy designed to prove that "the Secretary is a knave, or a blockhead, the tool of knaves." Welles could not understand how he had been so mistaken about Du Pont.[52]

As for Lincoln, despite the mental association he now made between Du Pont and McClellan, he was not yet ready to give up on his admiral. During a visit to the Navy Department on April 21, he expressed wonder at Du Pont's readiness to assume that his letter constituted a censure. Admirals, it seemed, were as touchy as generals. He was not angry at Du Pont, he said, and indeed was in quite a good humor. After chatting amiably with Fox and Dahlgren, he stood up and said: "Well, I will go home; I had no business here; but, as the lawyer said, I had none anywhere else." Dahlgren was pleased that "Abe" was telling jokes again.[53]

In the end, Du Pont was the author of his own downfall because of his reaction to a newspaper article that appeared in the *Baltimore American* on April 15. The article was signed by Charles C. Fulton, the postmaster at Port Royal, who had been on board the steamer USS *Ericsson* during Du Pont's attack on the Charleston forts. Though Fulton had witnessed the fighting from a distance, most of his information had been supplied by Stimers, who sought to protect the reputation of the monitors by criticizing Du Pont's poor management of the engagement. Fulton wrote (inaccurately) that the fire from the monitors had "pierced and crushed" the walls of Fort Sumter, that "in three hours more the fort would be compelled to surrender," and that the monitors had been virtually undamaged. Worse, he declared that Du Pont had been terrified by "ghost" obstructions and that his captains were ready and eager to renew the attack, only to be overruled by their timid commander. The attack had failed, Fulton wrote, because "the great work has been intrusted to incompetent hands." The article infuriated Du Pont, and when he learned that Stimers had been Fulton's source and that Stimers had subsequently repeated these lies to others in public, he ordered Stimers arrested.[54]

On April 30, Welles received a bitter and rambling twenty-page letter from Du Pont that took issue with Fulton's erroneous assertions. What struck Welles, however, was not how unfairly the admiral had been treated, but that Du Pont seemed to be far more upset by the public criticism than he was by the failure of the attack. Du Pont was right about the article—it was an unfair and biased piece of journalism—but it was no worse than much of what had been printed about Lincoln in the past two years. Instead of inspiring Welles to fly to Du Pont's defense, the complaining letter convinced him that Du Pont was not the man he thought he was. "I fear he can no longer be useful in his present command," Welles wrote in his diary, "and I am mortified and vexed that that I did not earlier detect his vanity and weakness."[55]

Two days later, on Saturday, May 2, Lincoln was working alone in his office when Henry Winter Davis called on him. Davis was not a political enemy of the president's, but he was not quite an ally, either. A cousin of Lincoln's friend and political adviser, David Davis, this Davis had spent most of his political life as an anti-immigrant Know-Nothing, and he had officially supported John Bell in the 1860 election. In spite of that, Lincoln had briefly considered him for a cabinet position in order to include a representative from the border state of Maryland. Fearing that Davis' Know-Nothing roots would be a detriment, however, Lincoln had instead picked Montgomery Blair. Now Winter Davis came to see the president as Du Pont's champion. He insisted that Du Pont was being done an injustice by the public press, and said that Lincoln should allow Du Pont's official report to be published so that the facts could exonerate him.[56]

Lincoln patiently summarized the history of the campaign against Charleston. He explained that he had expected Du Pont to move against Charleston in the fall. That had been delayed when Du Pont said he first needed to make a trial of the monitors against Fort McAllister. Lincoln had next expected an attack in January or February. That had been delayed when Du Pont said that he needed more monitors, which the department supplied. Then in March Du Pont had insisted that the monitors needed new layers of iron plate "to strengthen the decks." That, too, had been provided. The president insisted that throughout all this, he had retained full confidence in Du Pont.

But he had been surprised and disappointed, Lincoln said, when after all that delay and all that effort, Du Pont had called off the attack after only three hours. He had expected "that the attack might last for days or even weeks and be a gradual process." He was even more concerned by Du Pont's quick withdrawal from the harbor since it was important "to secure a continued menace" of the city "while operations proceeded elsewhere." He did not hold Du Pont at fault; he took out the letter he had written to Du Pont telling him that "no censure upon you . . . is intended" and read it aloud to Davis. Lincoln did say that he was concerned that Du Pont seemed to be more worried about his reputation than about making progress in the war, and, of course, there was the troubling testimony from Stimers, who reported that the monitors had suffered only superficial damage and that all of them save the *Keokuk*, which foundered, had been fully repaired by noon the next day.

At that, Davis interjected that "Mr. Stimers' statement . . . is false" and that in fact Stimers had been "the chief instigator" of all the calumnies that were being unfairly heaped on Du Pont. Stimers was so invested in the success of the monitors, Davis insisted, that he sought to make Du Pont a scapegoat for their shortcomings. He charged that the Navy Department (meaning, of course, Welles and Fox) had been determined to make the attack a purely naval one in order to gain accolades for the monitors, whereas Du Pont had wanted to work with the army in a combined campaign. Lincoln said he had begun to suspect that the Charleston operation had become something of a navy "pet," but he claimed to be surprised to hear that Du Pont had preferred a joint attack. This was not entirely true, of course, for Lincoln had been present when first Foster and then Stimers had mentioned Du Pont's preference for joint action, though at the time, when Foster had mentioned a "combined operation," what Lincoln heard was "lengthy siege." The news that Du Pont "had never thought the [naval] attack wise" was, however, a genuine surprise. If that was the case, Lincoln asked, why hadn't Du Pont told him? Davis replied that he supposed Du Pont was "waiting to be invited" to discuss it. He assured the president that "from the beginning" Du Pont had regarded the undertaking as desperate: "a Balaclava charge."

Lincoln assured Davis that he "would examine the [full] report as soon as he got it," and "if the public interest would permit," it should be published," though he also noted that if the report exposed some weaknesses in the monitors, "it may not be prudent to say so much to the enemy just yet." In a follow-up letter to the president two days later, Davis suggested that, at the very least, someone in the Navy Department should repudiate Fulton's scurrilous article, for its official silence seemed to sanction it. Nevertheless, Lincoln's ability to charm his visitors was evident in Davis' report to Du Pont that "my confidence in the honesty and substantial good sense of the President increases on every interview."[57]

In the end, Du Pont's report was not published, nor did the Navy Department repudiate Fulton's vicious article. Nor did Lincoln come to Du Pont's defense. Welles had already made up his mind that Du Pont had to go, Fox agreed, and Lincoln did not intervene. He would not champion an officer who waited to be asked before explaining a critical problem, or who was more concerned about his public image than military success. "Give us victories," Lincoln had told Hooker three months before, and that was still the yardstick by which he assessed his commanders. Of course, a replacement for Du Pont would have to be found, and that would take some time—in the end, it took six weeks. In the meantime, Lincoln had other, more pressing concerns, for on the same day that Winter Davis begged for fair treatment for his friend Du Pont, Stonewall Jackson's corps slammed into Hooker's army near the wilderness crossroads at Chancellorsville.

LINCOLN SPENT MOST OF THE NEXT SEVERAL DAYS in the War Department telegraph office trying to determine what was happening in the tangle of wilderness fifty miles to the south. "We have heard nothing . . . since your short dispatch to me of the 4th," he wired to Hooker on the morning of May 6. But he did not want to distract his general in the midst of a fight. "I know you will do your best," he wrote. "Waste no time unnecessarily, to gratify our curiosity." Then, just before noon, Major General John A. Dix at Fort Monroe sent a wire reporting that captured rebel newspapers were carrying the story that Lee had beaten Hooker and that the Yankee army had retreated back across the Rapidan. Hooker confirmed it at four-thirty that afternoon.[58]

Lincoln was devastated. Noah Brooks, who was in the room when the news arrived, recalled that the president turned ashen and walked up and down with his hands clasped behind his back, muttering, "My God! My God! What will the country say?" For a short while Lincoln hoped that this might be only a temporary setback. "I would be very glad of another movement," he wrote encouragingly to Hooker the next day. As if to inspire him, he forwarded the news, just received, that Grant had captured Grand Gulf, south of Vicksburg. He also noted that exchanged prisoners were claiming that Richmond was bereft of troops, and that a captured enemy dispatch revealed that Lee's losses had been "fearful." He was grasping at straws. After talking with Hooker face-to-face during another flying visit to the army, Lincoln accepted the fact that there was nothing to be gained by renewing the fight along the river line, and he told Hooker he would be satisfied if he simply kept "the enemy at bay" and "put your own army in a good condition again." At Chancellorsville, as at Charleston, a commander of whom much had been expected had, after long preparation, suffered a disappointing defeat.[59]

8

"I Shall Have to Cut This Knot"

Lincoln as Adjudicator

IT WAS NOT ALL BAD NEWS. Though the reports from the Army of the Potomac were devastating, those from the West were more positive, even electrifying. After his capture of Grand Gulf, Grant marched inland, brushed aside a rebel force under Joseph E. Johnston, and captured the Mississippi state capital, Jackson, on May 14. He then turned west toward Vicksburg's back door, defeating the main Confederate army of John C. Pemberton at Champion Hill on May 16, and soon his forces were closing in on the city. Assaults on the Vicksburg defensive lines on May 19 and May 22 were unsuccessful, however, and Grant settled in for a siege. Despite Lincoln's abhorrence of sieges, the almost breathless pace of the campaign left him feeling optimistic. On the day Grant captured Jackson, Dahlgren noted in his diary, "The President . . . was full of jokes and we had some hearty laughs." Though only a month earlier Lincoln had expressed doubt about Grant's seemingly endless maneuverings, he now wrote a friend that Grant's campaign was "one of the most brilliant in the world."[1]

Meanwhile, Lincoln again found himself playing referee in a series of disagreements between his secretary of state and his secretary of the navy. From the outset, Seward and Welles had taken opposing sides on many, if not most, of the issues before the cabinet, and like jealous siblings, each appealed to Father Abraham to sustain them. Usually,

Lincoln brought the two men together and let them hash it out, but on occasion he played the role of arbiter, meeting separately with each man to let him explain his position, weighing and measuring the power of their arguments, then deciding for himself. On other occasions, Lincoln sought a middle ground between them. Seward prevailed in most of these clashes, leaving Welles to complain to his diary about the mysterious influence that "the trickster" had on the president. There was more than a hint of jealousy in Welles' notation that Lincoln allowed the "assuming and presuming, meddlesome, and uncertain" Seward to influence the president's "wonderful kindness of heart." In the spring of 1863, the disputes between Seward and Welles focused mostly on America's precarious relationship with England. As a question of diplomacy, it was a subject that fell squarely within Seward's domain as secretary of state, but the source of the friction was the conduct of U.S. Navy officers on the high seas, and that, Welles insisted, was his responsibility.[2]

Their first quarrel that spring concerned the authorization of American privateers. Despite administration protests against Confederate privateers back in 1861, Congress authorized Union privateers in March 1863, granting to Lincoln the power to issue letters of marque. Seward was enthusiastic about it. He believed that sending out private armed vessels would remind the English of how much they had to lose by risking war with the United States and act as a restraint on British behavior. Seward also suggested that American privateers would slow down, if not entirely halt, Confederate blockade running. He even imagined that privateers might hunt down and destroy Confederate commerce raiders, such as the *Alabama* and *Florida*, that were savaging northern commerce. As the *New York Herald* put it: "The seas will swarm with heavily armed, swift steam vessels of war, which will render our blockade so effectual that all intercourse between the rebels and foreign Powers will entirely cease, while the Alabama and Florida will be captured as surely as they exist." Welles found such expectations not only absurd, but insulting. Just as Stanton had implied the previous spring that steamers belonging to Cornelius Vanderbilt were more likely to provide an effective deterrent to the *Merrimack* than navy warships, so now did Seward suggest that private letter-of-marque ships would be more successful than the navy in hunting down the *Alabama*. To

Welles, such an assertion was ridiculous. "The idea that private parties would send out armed ships to capture the Alabama," he wrote, "was too absurd to be thought of for a moment."[3]

In the midst of this dispute, Charles Sumner, who so reminded Lincoln of a bishop, came to see Lincoln in the White House. As chairman of the Senate Foreign Relations Committee, Sumner, too, was deeply concerned about relations with England. He had recently received letters from Richard Cobden and the duke of Argyle, two of his regular English correspondents, who feared that Anglo-American relations were once again deteriorating, and he was convinced that Seward's privateering scheme would only make things worse. Though Sumner was a giant of a man, nearly as tall as Lincoln and powerfully built, he was intimidated by the diminutive secretary of state and allowed Welles to lead the opposition. When he arrived in Lincoln's office, he had just been to see Welles who had shown him a letter that he had written to Seward attacking the whole notion of privateers. Sumner was so impressed by it he rushed over to the White House to urge Lincoln to read it for himself. Lincoln did just that, crossing Lafayette Square on foot, his long strides eating up the short distance, to knock on Welles' door.[4]

As it happened, Welles had already sent the letter and he hadn't kept a copy, but he summarized it for the president from memory. It started out by declaring bluntly that "to issue letters of marque would in all probability involve us in a war with England," because Union privateers would attack "neutral vessels intended to run the blockade," and most of them flew the British flag. Welles reasoned that privateers were motivated by profits, not patriotism, which would prevent them from engaging armed vessels such as the Alabama. Indeed, it was more likely that some of them, "like wolves among sheep," would end up attacking U.S. shipping. Welles agreed that something needed to be done to signal the British that the United States would not tolerate continued violations of neutrality indefinitely, but authorizing privateers was not only likely to cause trouble but also might well lead to war and, in doing so, end up aiding the rebels.[5]

Lincoln listened carefully, letting Welles do most of the talking. Nodding in apparent agreement, he did not commit himself, and near the end of the visit, he steered the conversation to other topics. But Welles had made his point. When, a few days later, Seward brought up the case of a Prussian citizen named Sybert, who had volunteered to take a private armed vessel out to sea to do the work of a "whole squadron of naval vessels," Lincoln was cool to the idea and turned Sybert's application over to the Navy Department "to be disposed of." In the end, Lincoln decided that there was little to be gained, and much to lose, by instituting a program of Union privateering.* Whatever benefit the threat of privateers might have on British behavior, there was simply too much risk. He was determined to fight only one war at a time.[6]

That determination also influenced Lincoln's handling of another dispute between Seward and Welles about the treatment of captured blockade runners. Once again Seward was motivated primarily by how the navy's behavior affected America's relations with Britain, though this time he was eager to assuage the British rather than intimidate them. Welles was concerned about England, too, but he was a stickler for existing law and established procedure, and he resented any involvement in matters of navy protocol by the secretary of state. The roots of their dispute stretched back to the previous fall, and, unsurprisingly perhaps, the man at the center of it was the mercurial Charles Wilkes.

Before Wilkes left the James River for the West Indies in command of a five-ship "Flying Squadron," he had persuaded Welles to grant him the rank of acting rear admiral. Welles felt obliged to gratify him since it was the same title borne by David Dixon Porter on the Mississippi and Samuel Phillips Lee at Hampton Roads, and Wilkes was senior to both of them on the captain's list. In appointing Wilkes to his new command, Welles wrote him that "much must necessarily be left to your judgment and discretion"—two words not generally associated with Charles Wilkes—and enjoined him to "observe and respect the rights of neutrals." In particular, he was to avoid "giving unnecessary offense." More welcome, perhaps, was Welles' reminder to Wilkes that his principal job was "upholding and maintaining the honor of our flag." Here was a duty that Wilkes could embrace enthusiastically. After he wrote

---

*Welles reveled in his rare victory over Seward, but it is possible that Seward was pleased simply to make the point that the United States had at least *considered* employing privateers. He hoped that fact alone might give British authorities pause when they calculated how much they risked by openly assisting the Confederacy.

the orders, Welles noted prophetically in his diary that Wilkes "has given great trouble and annoyance to the Department heretofore and will be likely to give us more trouble."[7]

Concerned that the rebel raider *Alabama* might be heading for Bermuda, Welles suggested that Wilkes consider sending one or two of his vessels there. Instead, Wilkes went there himself with three of his five ships. He arrived at the principal Bermuda port of St. George on September 27, ten days after the Battle of Antietam, and five days after Lincoln announced the Emancipation Proclamation. From the outer roadstead he could count seven steam vessels at the wharves, all of them obvious blockade runners, and all of them flying the British flag. Since the laws concerning the use of neutral ports required the warship of any belligerent power to remain in port for at least twenty-four hours after the departure of any potential foe, Wilkes took only two of his ships into the harbor, leaving the USS *Sonoma* outside so that it could legally chase down any vessel that tried to leave.[8]

Wilkes was a little annoyed not only because British authorities tolerated the presence of those blockade runners but also because, contrary to custom, the British did not hoist a flag at the fort when he entered the harbor. Aware of Welles' determination to get along with the British, he let it go—for now. He had a convivial meeting with the colony's governor-general, Harry St. George Ord, and got permission to coal his ships from a pre-positioned coal supply, even though neutrality laws forbade either side from using neutral ports as regular coaling bases. After this auspicious start, however, relations soon soured.

The first confrontation was over Wilkes' positioning of the *Sonoma* in the middle of the main ship channel, where it could mark any vessel that came in or out. It was, in effect, a kind of blockade. Two days later, a small boat approached the anchored *Sonoma*, and a British Royal Navy lieutenant from HMS *Desperate* came on board to inform the *Sonoma*'s captain, Thomas H. Stevens, that he could either go into the inner harbor or leave the area, but he could not anchor here in the "fairway." Stevens thought the officer's manner "brusque," and he responded in kind, informing the British lieutenant that he would anchor where he pleased, and that he took orders only from his own admiral. The lieutenant departed, and both men reported the conversation to their superiors.[9]

Wilkes approved Stevens' response, told him "to stay where he was," and the next morning, he took himself to the consul general's residence to protest. The *Sonoma* would come into port, Wilkes informed him, when the *Tioga* had finished coaling and was ready to go out to take her place. Very well, Ord replied, but in that case the *Sonoma* would not be allowed to coal at St. George because by taking a position off the port entrance, she violated both the spirit and the letter of the law concerning the use of neutral ports for coaling ships. Thinking this unreasonable, Wilkes ignored him and coaled the *Sonoma* anyway. Ord informed Wilkes that "this could not be permitted," though he did not interfere.[10]

Wilkes replied to Ord's note the way he responded to every challenge: he went on the offensive. He reminded Ord of the presence of those seven steamers, all clearly engaged in illicit trade with the rebels; he protested the fact that the British had failed to raise a flag at the fort upon his arrival; he denied that Stevens in the *Sonoma* had blocked the main ship channel because the entrance into St. George was "an open roadstead." But what really provoked Wilkes' ire was that while reviewing the neutrality laws, Ord—perhaps incautiously—had used the phrase "I have to instruct you . . ." Ord was perfectly correct on the issues, but Wilkes was infuriated that a foreign official presumed to "instruct" an American admiral about anything. "This I cannot permit!" Wilkes wrote. "My government has alone the power of instructing me." Ord's remark, he declared, was "entirely uncalled for." Ord decided not to make an issue of it, though he did forward the exchange to the British Foreign Office.[11]

Wilkes concluded that the British at Bermuda were "all a pack of secessionists." It seemed to him that the British offered "every assistance and aid" to the rebel blockade runners and cruisers, while insisting on the strict letter of the law for Americans. Well, two could play at that game. Wilkes demanded that the British render the salute they had neglected to offer upon his entrance. He was amused when Ord blamed the oversight on the fort's commander, Major William Monro, who in turn blamed it on a hapless gunnery sergeant. Eventually the proper salute was rendered, and after a strained three days, Wilkes departed St. George. He left two of his ships outside the port to watch the blockade runners still in the harbor, and steamed off in his flagship, the *Wachusett*, for the Bahamas, and another confrontation with British authority.[12]

Arriving at Nassau on November 20, Wilkes steamed deliberately into the roadstead, completely ignoring the pilot boat that came alongside. The pilot called across that the *Wachusett* "could not anchor at or off this port without first obtaining the governor general's permission." Wilkes ordered his executive officer to reply that "he should anchor if he saw fit to do so without any reference to the governor general's wishes or prohibitions." He did not go into the harbor, however, and dropped anchor outside in the roadstead. When the pilot reported the American's remark to the senior British naval officer in the harbor, Captain Malcolm of HMS *Barracouta*, Malcolm was furious. He protested Wilkes' behavior to the U.S. consul at Nassau, Samuel Whiting, and declared that if Wilkes tried to anchor without permission, "he should fire upon them at once." Whiting tried to mollify him by suggesting that he should not take the word of "a drunken Bahama pilot," but Malcolm clearly thought otherwise.[13]

Two days later, Wilkes got under way, steaming past the entrance to Nassau, and almost at once the *Barracouta* also got under way. Apparently, Malcolm was waiting to see if Wilkes would try to enter the harbor without permission. Spotting the *Barracouta* and divining its intentions, Wilkes ordered his crew to quarters, cast loose the guns, and prepared for action. When the *Barracouta* got within a quarter of a mile, Wilkes stopped his engines and waited to see what the British vessel would do. Neither ship attempted to communicate with the other. "We could distinguish the crew at quarters and quietly awaited his further action," Wilkes reported afterward to Welles. The two ships lay side by side for most of half an hour before Malcolm blinked: the *Barracouta* wore around and headed back into port. Wilkes congratulated himself that he had faced down a bully. He reported to Welles, "I shall be overcautious to avoid being the first to break the peace; you may be assured of this, but if anyone should take upon themselves to break it, or do insult to our flag, they must take the consequence."[14]

Eventually news of these encounters worked its way through the diplomatic channels from the West Indies to Lord Lyons in Washington, which led Lyons to complain to Seward that Wilkes was "contemptuously" violating the rules of war. Not only did the American admiral place a warship in the ship channel at St. George, but he had behaved "offensively and unlawfully" toward the governor. Seward passed the note to Welles, who responded by urging Wilkes to cultivate "a mutual friendly feeling" with the British and "extend all customary courtesies to the British authorities on sea and land." There was no tone of chastisement in his letter. Rather, Welles expressed sympathy with Wilkes that his "patience and forbearance may be tried," and he told him that he counted on his "intelligence" to avoid trouble. Indeed, so far Welles' principal concern was not Wilkes' behavior toward the British but the fact that his "Flying Squadron" had made no captures.[15]

Welles was more annoyed by Wilkes' incessant calls for reinforcements. In virtually every letter, at least twice a week, Wilkes complained that his force was too small to do the job he had been assigned. He protested that he had but five ships to patrol more than a thousand miles of open ocean. Moreover, the ships he had were too old, too slow, and altogether inadequate either to halt the flow of illegal trade out of St. George and Nassau or to contend with the rebel cruisers. He reported that his flagship, the *Wachusett*, broke down an average of once every four days. He asked Welles to take some ships off the blockade and add them to his squadron. Welles wouldn't do it. He explained to Wilkes that the blockade was the main effort, and that his "Flying Squadron" was supplementary. Wilkes found this reply shortsighted and wrongheaded. "It is utterly impossible," he wrote, "for you or the country to expect" anything of such a tiny force. "If my force had been increased, when requested, with suitable vessels, it [the capture of the *Alabama*] would have been a certainty." All this had a familiar ring to it. On the James River, too, Wilkes had asserted that the fall of Richmond was "a certainty," if only he were given reinforcements. As for complaints about his behavior, Wilkes proclaimed that he had never "afforded any ground for the misrepresentations" of the British. He concluded: "I have nothing further to say upon the subject."[16]

Welles did not send more ships for Wilkes' command, but he did order Lieutenant Charles Baldwin in the giant side-wheel steamer *Vanderbilt*, acquired for the government by Edwin Stanton during the

Merrimack crisis, to join the search for the rebel raiders *Florida* and *Alabama*.* Welles ordered Baldwin to operate independently of Wilkes' command, but in late February, Baldwin approached St. Thomas in the British West Indies while Wilkes' *Wachusett* happened to be anchored in the harbor. With the *Vanderbilt* still in the offing, a British-flag steamer, the *Peterhoff*, chose that moment to leave port. Instantly suspicious, but unable to pursue it himself due to the twenty-four-hour rule, Wilkes signaled for the *Vanderbilt* to follow her out to sea, then board and search her. Baldwin dutifully followed the *Peterhoff*, stopped it about five miles outside the harbor, and sent over a boarding party. The *Peterhoff*'s captain assumed it would be a routine check since another U.S. Navy ship had stopped and inspected him only a few days earlier. This time, however, the boarding officer found the *Peterhoff*'s papers to be "not quite satisfactory." Though she obviously carried a large cargo, her manifest listed only seven boxes of tea, and despite having several passengers on board, she had no passenger list. Baldwin detained the vessel while he sent a report of these facts to Wilkes, who at once ordered that the ship be seized as a prize of war and sent to Key West for adjudication.[17]

Like the *Trent* affair more than a year before, Wilkes' seizure of the *Peterhoff* triggered a crisis that threatened to rupture Anglo-American relations. First, Wilkes had directed the capture while anchored in a neutral harbor. Although he had not effected the capture personally, he had ordered it, and that could easily be construed as a violation of the neutrality laws. Second, the *Peterhoff* had been cleared by British customs for Matamoros, Mexico, across the Rio Grande River from Brownsville, Texas. While a reasonable person might suspect that its goods could subsequently be transshipped across the river into Confederate territory, technically and legally it was a ship that was proceeding from one neutral port to another.† What proved in the end to be most

---

*Ordinarily the command of a large ship such as the *Vanderbilt* would go to a captain, but Cornelius Vanderbilt himself asked that Lieutenant Baldwin be given the command.

†The use of Matamoros as a quasi Confederate port was not new. In February 1862, the British-owned steamer *Labuan* was anchored in the mouth of the Rio Grande loading cotton when it was seized by the USS *Portsmouth*. The British protested this as an illegal seizure because although the *Labuan* was flying the Confederate flag and taking on a Confederate cargo, it was technically in Mexican waters.

difficult, however, was British concern about the mail on board the *Peterhoff*. Even if the ship were contraband (which the British denied), and even if her seizure were legal (which they also denied), the British insisted that the mail she carried in sealed mailbags should be delivered unopened.

Their expectations were the product of a note that Seward had written the previous fall. Still smarting from the *Trent* affair, and determined to maintain good relations with the British, Seward had composed a note to Welles suggesting "the expediency of instructing naval officers that . . . the public mails of every friendly or neutral power" should be forwarded at once to their "designated destination." Welles resented Seward's attempt to insert himself into Neptune's domain and told him that the existing protocol was more than sufficient. The orders which Welles had sent out the previous summer enjoined all naval officers who made captures to "preserve all the papers and writings found on board and transmit the whole of the originals unmutilated to the judge of the district to which such prize is ordered to proceed." Having set Seward straight, Welles assumed that was the end of it. But without telling Welles, Seward had shared his note with Lord Lyons' attaché, William Stuart, who forwarded it to Lord John Russell, the British foreign minister, who read it on the floor of the House of Commons. Consequently, when the *Peterhoff* case reached the New York prize court, the British consul refused to allow the court to open the mailbags to obtain the ship's cargo manifest or its official papers. When told that the prize court had jurisdiction over the mails, the consul protested to Lyons, who protested to Seward, who went to see Welles. At Welles' home, Seward asked the navy secretary to telegraph the prize court judge and instruct him to allow the British consul to take charge of the mails. Welles refused to do it.[18]

Welles told Seward that the law on this issue was quite clear: A ship's papers—all its papers—were to be sent to the court in order to determine whether it was a legitimate prize of war. The mail on the *Peterhoff*, Welles told him, "was properly and legally in the custody of the court."

"But . . . mails are sacred," Seward expostulated. "They are an institution."

"That would do for peace," Welles replied, "but not for war."

It was obvious to Welles that the British wanted the mail precisely because it contained ship's papers that would expose the *Peterhoff* as a blockade runner. If the courts were denied access to the mailbags of suspected blockade runners, every such vessel would simply seal up its cargo manifests in the mail bags and proceed with impunity. Seward countered that he had already made "an arrangement" with the British Legation; it would cause enormous problems if he abrogated his promise now. Unmoved, Welles replied that Seward had no authority to make such a promise. In his diary that night, an annoyed Welles wrote: "The Secretary of the Navy does not receive orders from the Secretary of State." But Seward had an ace to play, and that was his relationship with the president.[19]

A FEW DAYS AFTER RETURNING from his visit to the army at Falmouth in April, Lincoln was in his office at the White House when Seward came in to explain that there was a new difficulty with the British concerning captured mail. The British press was suggesting that the seizure of the *Peterhoff* was a deliberate provocation "to exasperate England and bring about war." It was important to patch things up, Seward declared, before another crisis blew up in their faces. Lincoln urged Seward to resolve the issue as necessary to preserve peace. The next day, however, an annoyed Gideon Welles stormed into Lincoln's office. Welles was piqued that Seward had "gone privately to the President" to support his "unauthorized acts" concerning the *Peterhoff*, and, as before, he had written a letter to Seward to explain his argument. This time, however, he did not wait for Lincoln to ask if he could read the letter; Welles had brought it with him. And with Lincoln's permission, he proceeded to read it aloud.[20]

In it, Welles acknowledged that naval officers were "restricted and prohibited from examining or breaking the seals of the mail bags." They could, at their discretion, make the mail available to a representative of the country where the ship was registered, but any papers relating to the vessel, its cargo, or its destination were, by law and by policy, under the jurisdiction of the court. To be sure, Seward had sent him a note the previous fall "suggesting" that captured mails should be forwarded to their destination, but Welles had rejected the suggestion. "The idea that our Naval officers should be compelled to forward the mails found on board the vessels of the insurgents," Welles read, "was so repugnant to my own convictions that I came to the conclusion it was only a passing suggestion." He had no idea at the time that Seward had shared the note with Lord Lyons, which was the source of the current misunderstanding. He concluded that the U.S. Navy "has acted strictly in accordance with the law and with his instructions in the matter of the Peterhoff's mail."[21]

Lincoln affected great surprise. He reached out for the letter and read it himself. After he finished, he looked up at Welles and said his object was "to keep the peace," for obviously "we could not afford to take upon ourselves a war with England and France," but he had been unaware of the particular circumstances. He told Welles to go ahead and deliver the letter to the secretary of state, who would, no doubt, "bring the subject to his attention for further action." Indeed, Lincoln asked Seward to respond formally to Welles' note, which he did two days later. In that response, Seward reminded Lincoln that he had shared the contents of his October note with the president and that Lincoln not only had approved of it orally but also had written "Approved" across the bottom of it. Because of that, "the views therein expressed were then communicated to the British Government by authority of the President." That made them national policy, a policy from which it was now impossible to retreat.[22]

After the cabinet meeting the next day (Tuesday, April 21), Lincoln asked Seward and Welles to remain behind. He wanted them to find common ground, if there was any; he wanted, as he said, to get "the right" of it. Because the subject was "novel" to him, he wanted to hear both sides. Seward went first. He dwelt on the historical sanctity of private mail and suggested that one of the reasons the British had reacted so strongly to the *Trent* affair was because the *Trent* was a mail packet. Moreover—and decisively, as far as Seward was concerned—the administration had already pledged to deliver the mails on captured ships, and the nation could not renege on that pledge without risking its relationship with Britain. Welles was unimpressed. "The whole subject belonged to the courts," he insisted, "which had, by law, the possession of the mails." What Seward was claiming, he declared, was that a private agreement, made by him alone, without consultation with the cabinet or ratification by the Senate, had the force of a treaty. Even the president, he insisted, could not change the law unilaterally.[23]

Lincoln ventured the thought that "perhaps the Executive had some rights on this subject," but, lawyer that he was, he wanted to know the precedents of the case. The *Trent* incident was not analogous, he declared, for the *Trent* was a mail packet and not a blockade runner like the *Peterhoff*. But what about the sanctity of sealed mailbags? What precedent was there for opening sealed bags and reading other people's mail? He told them he would send each of them a set of questions ("interrogatories") to help him understand the issue. Seward insisted that "there was not time. . . . Lord Lyons was importunate in his demands." But on this, as on most decisions, Lincoln refused to be rushed, and that night he sat down and wrote out his set of questions to which Seward and Welles were to supply written responses. Just as he often forced himself to commit his own views to paper in order to distill and clarify them, he frequently asked his advisers to do the same. In particular, he wanted to know what legal precedents either man could cite, and he asked them to summarize the "dangers and evils" that could result from forwarding the mails in this case.[24]

The replies came in the next week. They were lengthy and detailed, and Lincoln studied them carefully. Seward continued to emphasize the danger of provoking a rift with Britain, and strongly implied that a failure to satisfy the British on this issue might lead to an open rupture. Welles insisted that "the decision of the Secretary of State . . . is not controlling" in matters of prize cases adjudicated in a public court. It was a judicial issue, and until the courts passed judgment, it was not up to the secretary of state or any other official to act. Legally Welles may have been correct, but, as Seward pointed out, insisting on the letter of the law risked disaster. Moreover, in a paper that ran to more than thirty pages, Welles did not cite a single specific precedent to prove the court's jurisdiction over the mail on captured ships. Lincoln would not overturn Seward's pledge unless he had incontestable legal precedent. The risks were just too great. He told Charles Sumner that "we should have war with England if we presumed to open their mail bags, or break their seals or locks. They would not submit to it, and we were in no condition to plunge into a foreign war on a subject of so little importance." Recognizing that his advisers had staked out utterly incompatible positions on the issue, Lincoln declared emphatically: "I shall have to cut this knot."[25]

This time, rather than bring them together, Lincoln confronted his bickering secretaries separately. He was sensitive to the fact that it would be easier for one of them to give way if he did not have to do so in front of the other. He called Welles to the White House on May 15, the day after Grant's capture of Jackson in far-off Mississippi. Disappointed that Welles had not included any precedents in his lengthy brief, he wanted to know if "the courts ever opened the mails of a neutral government."

"Always," Welles replied, "when the captured vessel on which mails were found were considered good prize."

"Why then," Lincoln queried, "do you not furnish me with the fact? It is what I want, but you furnish me with no report that any neutral has ever been searched."

Welles replied that the right to search had never been questioned. The mails often provided the best evidence of a ship's guilt or innocence, and opening the mail was the equivalent of ascertaining the facts.

"But if mails ever are examined, the fact must be known and recorded," Lincoln said patiently. "What vessels . . . have we captured where we have examined the mails?"

All of them, Welles insisted.

"What was the first vessel taken?"

"I do not recollect the name."[26]

Even Lincoln's legendary patience may have been challenged by this exchange. In the end, he asked Welles to search the court records in Philadelphia, New York, and Boston to see if any of them contained a specific case where the mails on a captured vessel had been opened. Welles set several men to work searching the files, but the results were ambiguous. Even though doing so was routine, there was no controlling case in which the court specifically authorized in writing the seizure of mail.[27]

Though Lincoln's attorney general, Edward Bates, agreed that the law backed Welles' interpretation, Seward encouraged Delafield Smith, the attorney general in New York, to order that the mail from the *Peterhoff* be turned over to the British. Bates issued an order to stop it, but it was too late. Once again allowing the inertia of events to decide policy, Lincoln let it go. Both Bates and Welles fumed that "the trickster" Seward had once again dragged the president into his schemes. "The mail of the Peterhoff is given up," Welles complained to his diary, "but that is not law, and the law must be sustained [even] if the Secretary of State is humiliated."[28]

In effect, Lincoln chose conciliation over confrontation. He had sided with Welles on the issue of privateers, and now he effectively sided with Seward on the issue of the mails, but in both cases, he chose the policy that was less likely to provoke difficulties with Britain. Welles and Bates might be correct about the legal status of mail on captured ships, but that would hardly matter if it led to war. Sumner thought Lincoln was "horrified" at the idea of war with England, affecting more concern now than he had during the *Trent* crisis back in the fall of 1861. The actual risk of war may have been slight; Lord Lyons subsequently told Sumner that he never intended his request to be a demand. But Lincoln would not take the chance. Welles was disappointed, and he was convinced that, once again, Lincoln had been "humbugged" by Seward.[29]

Lincoln also took action to ensure that neither Wilkes nor some other overeager navy captain provoked another crisis with England. Seward brought Lord Lyons out to the Soldiers' Home to chat with Lincoln about the problem. Seward explained that gratifying the British on these kinds of issues would strengthen the hand of Lord Palmerston, who was being criticized at home for having recognized the blockade. Lincoln was reluctant to overrule Welles in his management of the navy, but he saw that for the sake of good Anglo-American relations, it was necessary in this case to "put in the strength of his hand." A few days later, he sent Welles a curious letter that was clearly the product of two minds. The first half of the letter, almost certainly written by Seward, enjoined Welles to instruct his various ship commanders to "avoid the reality, and as far as possible, the appearance, of using any neutral port, to watch naval vessels, and then to dart out and seize them on their departure." Nor were navy ships to "detain the crew of a captured neutral vessel." After itemizing the new instructions, the tone of the letter then changed abruptly. Indeed, it seemed to begin anew. "My dear Sir," it read, "it is not intended to be insinuated that you have been remiss in the performance of the arduous and responsible duties of your Department, which I take pleasure in affirming has, in your hands, been conducted with admirable success." Almost certainly,

Lincoln took Seward's peremptory draft and added some praise to help the medicine go down. In his diary that night, Welles preened that "the President takes occasion to compliment the administration of the Navy in terms most commendatory and gratifying," and Welles subsequently sent new orders to all squadron commanders specifying that "foreign subjects captured in neutral vessels . . . are entitled to immediate release."[30]

THERE WAS STILL THE QUESTION of what to do, if anything, about Wilkes. His error—if it were an error—in ordering the seizure of the *Peterhoff* was a relatively minor indiscretion, but it was part of a worrisome pattern. When Napoleon Collins in the USS *Octorara* seized the British-flag steamer *Mont Blanc* off Sand Key, a spit of land claimed by the British, Lincoln ordered the vessel released to its owners and told Welles to make sure that Collins knew he had "incurred the displeasure of the President." Collins responded that he had seized the *Mont Blanc* "in accordance with the verbal instructions of Admiral Wilkes," and noted that Wilkes had continued to declare his support for the act "even after the vessel had been restored to the owners."[31]

Nor was that the worst of it. Welles, and even Lincoln, might have been willing to tolerate Wilkes' seizure of questionable prizes. Lincoln was always more tolerant of overzealousness than timidity, and given that, Wilkes' bold stand against British diplomats might have been forgiven. Wilkes' fatal error was that he overstepped his authority within the Navy Department. Still eager to expand the size of his own command, when the *R. R. Cuyler* and *Oneida* appeared in the West Indies on temporary duty, Wilkes simply incorporated them into his squadron. Welles peremptorily ordered him to send them to Farragut, who needed them for the blockade of Mobile, but Wilkes dragged his feet. When Welles asked him directly why he did not obey the order, Wilkes responded that "I perhaps owe you an apology." But what he offered instead was an excuse. He was, he said, in "hot pursuit" of the *Florida* and the *Alabama* and needed these ships to "blockade and search the various harbors where" those ships "might have taken refuge."[32]

The final straw, however was Wilkes' virtual hijacking of the *Vanderbilt*. After seizing the *Peterhoff* on Wilkes' order, Baldwin took the big side-wheel steamer into the harbor at St. Thomas, and as soon as Wilkes got a good look at her spacious cabins and broad deck, he at once abandoned the cranky *Wachusett* and made the *Vanderbilt* his new flagship. Baldwin was under orders to patrol the waters near Fernando de Noronha, off the coast of Brazil where it bulged into the Atlantic, for Welles expected, not without reason, that the *Alabama* would have to pass that way. Instead Wilkes moved on board and retained the *Vanderbilt* in the Caribbean. As it happened, the *Alabama* spent most of the next six weeks cruising the area off the Brazilian headlands where Welles had ordered Baldwin to operate, making no fewer than twelve captures of American ships in April and May. All that time, Wilkes on the purloined *Vanderbilt* was cruising from Martinique to Barbados and from St. Thomas to Venezuela. It was later established that Wilkes spent fifty days out of those two months at anchor.[33] An annoyed Gideon Welles convinced himself that if Wilkes had not usurped the *Vanderbilt* for his own comfort and convenience, the depredations of the *Alabama* might have been brought to an end.*

Thus when Seward called on Welles in May in the wake of the *Peterhoff* controversy to ask "if anything could be done with Wilkes," Welles was in no mood to defend his wayward admiral. Though Seward had initially proposed Wilkes for the assignment, he now suggested that "unless . . . we are ready for a war with England," he would have to be replaced. This time Welles agreed with "the trickster," and that same day he took steps to replace Wilkes with a less troublesome officer. He worried a little about the public reaction, for Wilkes was greatly admired by a certain segment of the public, and his dismissal would coincide with the announcement of Du Pont's removal from command. Still, whatever the public reaction, Welles consoled himself that it was his duty.[34]

AND WHAT OF DU PONT? When Lincoln met with his war cabinet later that month (Stanton and Halleck for the army, Welles and Fox for the navy), he mostly listened as his advisers considered future operations at

---

*The captain of the *Alabama*, Raphael Semmes, agreed. After the war, he wrote in his memoir, "If Mr. Welles had stationed a heavier and faster ship than the *Alabama* . . . little of the eastward of Fernando Noronha, and [another] off Bahia, he must have driven me off, or greatly crippled me in my movements" (Raphael Semmes, *Memoirs of Service Afloat* [Baltimore: Kelly, Piet, 1869], 640).

Charleston. Halleck was opposed to renewing the attack, but Fox, still smarting from his lost opportunity two years before and determined to redeem the navy's honor, was eager to have another crack at it. He pressed the case for it so earnestly that Lincoln felt obliged to give way. Welles declared that if they did make another attempt at Charleston, it would have to be under someone other than Du Pont, since that officer's lack of confidence in a naval attack was "demoralizing others." "If anything is to be done," Welles asserted, "we must have a new commander." Like Wilkes, Du Pont would have to be recalled.[35]

It is curious that Du Pont and Wilkes should have been linked in the public mind by the timing of their dismissals. Du Pont was a stalwart pillar of the naval establishment, deeply professional but also progressive in his views. He was well liked, even admired, by the entire officer corps. Wilkes, on the other hand, was boisterous, bullying, self-important, and thoroughly disliked by all but a very few of his fellow officers. Yet from Welles' point of view, both men had fallen into the habit of complaining about insufficient resources, and both seemed more concerned about their personal reputations than military success. Wilkes was at least aggressive, but his boldness often bordered on rashness, and produced more complications and difficulties than successes. Nevertheless, Welles knew that the dismissal of these two men, at virtually the same time, would become grist for both the public press and official courts of inquiry.[36]

Lincoln stayed out of it. He had been disappointed by Du Pont's willingness to abandon the attack so quickly, and by the admiral's obsessive concern for his reputation. His opinion of Du Pont was not improved by a letter he received from David Hunter, who begged the president to release him from the obligation to "cooperate with the navy," since it was evident that "Admiral Du Pont distrusts the ironclads so much that he has resolved to do nothing." As for Wilkes, just as Lincoln had proved willing to sacrifice troublesome or ineffective generals in order to promote the war effort, he was also willing to sacrifice Wilkes in order to maintain good relations with England.[37]

Nor did he urge any particular candidate as a possible replacement for either man. Their dismissals created openings for two new squadron commanders, and Dahlgren was candid, almost embarrassingly so, in pressing his requests for active service. Welles was acutely aware that Dahlgren was "the choice of the President," but he continued to insist that Dahlgren lacked the experience to justify a fleet command, and he was certain that "there would be general discontent [in the navy] were he selected." Absent presidential pressure, Welles decided to send Captain James Lardner to replace Wilkes in the West Indies, and for the South Atlantic squadron, he sent for his old boyhood chum Andrew Hull Foote.[38]

Foote had left his Mississippi River command due to ill health and was now serving as chief of the Bureau of Equipment and Recruiting. Since then, however, his health had improved, and Welles had already queried him about taking over from Du Pont. At first Foote declined for fear of wounding Du Pont's sensibilities, but once Welles made it clear that Du Pont was going to be replaced in any case, Foote agreed to take the job. Then in an effort to gratify the president, Welles asked the admiral what he thought about having Dahlgren as his second in command. Foote said he would be pleased to have Dahlgren under him but doubted that Dahlgren would agree to it. He was right. When Fox broached the idea, Dahlgren not only declined, he declared that he would not go at all "unless he could have command of both naval and land forces." Welles thought Dahlgren was making a terrible mistake. Here was a great opportunity for him to justify his recent promotion and silence the whispering in the navy about his having obtained that rank with no significant sea service. Perhaps aware of that, Dahlgren suggested a kind of compromise. It was bad business, he suggested, to have two admirals share the command of one fleet, but if the command could be divided, making the ironclad portion of the fleet independent of the squadron, with special responsibility for the attack on Charleston, he would agree to take it.[39]

Welles and Fox thought this might break the logjam, and they suggested that Dahlgren go see Foote in New York and try the idea out on him. Foote was suffering from terrible headaches when Dahlgren arrived, but he greeted him warmly and expressed pleasure at the notion of Dahlgren commanding the ironclads. So it was settled. Foote would have the squadron, Dahlgren would have the ironclads, and Major General Quincy Adams Gillmore, who had played a key role in the capture of Fort Pulaski, off Savannah, would command the troops on shore that would cooperate in a renewed attack on Charleston.[40]

Then fate played a hand. That very week, Foote's health, never very strong since his wound at Fort Donelson, began to deteriorate rapidly. The headaches got worse, and Foote took to his bed. His whole constitution seemed to break down. He was suffering from liver failure, one of the manifestations of Bright's disease. All through the month of June, as Lee's Army of Northern Virginia moved west into the Shenandoah Valley and then north across the Potomac into Maryland and Pennsylvania, Foote's condition worsened. It was, Welles wrote to his son, "a great calamity to the country." By June 20, it was clear that Foote was not going to recover, and Welles informed Dahlgren that he would now very likely succeed to command of the fleet after all. Dahlgren was in New York at Foote's bedside a few days later when, "by some effort," the old admiral roused himself from unconsciousness and clearly said: "Dahlgren, yes!" Then, as if anticipating Welles' concerns, he gasped out: "Who will fight for Dahlgren?—Dahlgren's boys," before he lapsed again into unconsciousness. They were very nearly his last words, for he died the next day.[41]

So Dahlgren would get his sea command after all. Though Welles told him that "in giving [you] this command I was consulting the wishes of the President," it was Du Pont's fall from grace, Dahlgren's persistence, and the dying wish of Foote that made it apparently inevitable. Welles knew there would be problems with the appointment. He warned Dahlgren that due to Du Pont's popularity and Dahlgren's own lack of sea experience, the officers of the fleet would very likely resent him. Some might even refuse to serve under him and ask for transfers, and if so, they should be accommodated. Welles also told him that his appointment was a temporary one. He was to capture Charleston, then return to the Ordnance Bureau. In the meantime Henry Wise would take charge of the bureau.[42]

LINCOLN WAS PLEASED, but he had other, far more immediate concerns, for Lee's army was advancing deep into Pennsylvania. On the day Foote died, elements of the rebel force had reached as far north as Carlisle, Pennsylvania, and as far west as York, a hundred miles north of Washington. Far more important than who would command at Charleston was the question of who would command in Pennsylvania. Hooker's uncertain reaction to Lee's invasion was worrisome. Back in the spring when he had accepted the command, Hooker had asked Lincoln if he could report to the president directly. It was an implied disparagement of Halleck, but Lincoln allowed it. Now when Hooker offered his resignation to Lincoln in protest of Halleck's refusal to let him evacuate Harpers Ferry, expecting, no doubt, that Lincoln would refuse it and support him, Lincoln instead accepted it, naming George Gordon Meade as the army's new commander.

For the next week, Lincoln haunted the War Department telegraph office and focused almost exclusively on the news from Pennsylvania. J. E. B. Stuart's cavalry cut the telegraph line on June 25, and Lincoln suffered through several days of uncertainty. Then just past midnight, in the first few hours of July 4, a telegram from a newspaper reporter in Hanover, Pennsylvania, claimed that "the most terrific battle of the War" was being fought near the town of Gettysburg. As it happened, the reporter was from Connecticut and was known to Welles, who vouched for his reliability. A more formal dispatch arrived later that morning from Meade, who reported that the battle had gone well. Then other news cascaded in: the rebel army had been beaten and Lee was in retreat. It was enough to encourage Lincoln to issue a public statement announcing that the army had covered itself "with the highest honor" and won "great success."[43]

The extent of that success was still unclear. Lincoln hoped that Meade would seize the moment and complete the defeat of Lee's wounded army, but within a few days it became evident that it was not likely to happen. Lincoln was distressed to see a copy of Meade's congratulatory letter to his soldiers urging them "to drive from our soil every vestige of the presence of the invader." The phrasing struck Lincoln like a slap. *"Great God!"* he exclaimed. *"Is that all?"* The object was not to drive the enemy from "our soil"—for it was *all* "our soil"—but to destroy the enemy army and end the rebellion.[44]

Joy turned to despair, then turned to joy again only a day later. Lincoln was in the White House on July 7 looking over a military map with Salmon P. Chase and "one or two others" when a jubilant Gideon Welles came in with a telegram from Porter, who reported that Grant had captured Vicksburg and with it Pemberton's entire rebel army. Lincoln was ecstatic. His first thought was to get the news to Meade as soon as possible. Just as he had tried to inspire Hooker by telegraphing him news of Grant's capture of Grand Gulf, so now he hoped to inspire Meade with news of the fall of Vicksburg. He picked up his hat to return to the telegraph office, but then stopped and turned back to Welles. Throwing his arm around his navy secretary, Lincoln declared expansively: "What can we do for the Secretary of the Navy for this glorious intelligence? He is always giving us good news.* I cannot in words tell you my joy over this result. It is great, Mr. Welles, it is great!"[45]

Once again, the joy did not last. A week later Lincoln learned that Lee's army, wounded but intact, had crossed safely back over the Potomac River into Virginia, and his elation collapsed again into despair. After the news from Vicksburg, he had allowed himself to imagine that one more hard blow might not only ruin Lee's army but also end the war. Instead, the Army of the Potomac had once again found reasons not to attack, and Lee's army had escaped. As he walked over to the War Department with Welles, Lincoln stopped suddenly and turned to his navy secretary. "What does it mean, Mr. Welles?" he asked, in obvious anguish. "Great God, what does it mean?" When Welles suggested that instead of depending on Halleck to issue orders to the armies, Lincoln should do so himself, Lincoln calmed down. "Halleck," he said quietly, "is a military man, [and] has had a military education." When Welles argued that the president had a clearer view of what needed to be done than Halleck did, Lincoln's face grew "clouded." He did not express the thought, but it is possible that he was contemplating both the limited capacity of his senior general and the possibility that he might have to assume even more command authority himself. Later that afternoon, Welles found him lying on a sofa in the War Department "overwhelmed with the news" of Lee's escape.[46]

In this mood, Lincoln sat down to write Meade a letter. "I do not believe you appreciate the magnitude of the misfortune involved in Lee's escape," he wrote. "He was within your easy grasp, and to have closed upon him would, in connection with our other late successes,

---

*Stanton resented the fact that Porter, who had more direct access to the telegraph lines, had usurped Grant's right to send the good news himself. It was one more example of the rivalry not only between the army and the navy institutionally but also between Stanton and Welles personally.

have ended the war. As it is, the war will be prolonged indefinitely." But Lincoln never sent the letter. As he often did, he wrote out his thoughts to purge himself of his anguish, then returned to the job at hand. It would serve no purpose to chastise Meade now, after he had won an important victory less than a week into his command tenure. So Lincoln put the letter in an envelope and put it away.[47]

He did write to Grant, not only to congratulate him for his triumph at Vicksburg but also to confess that back in the spring, he had begun to doubt his western general. Even after Porter had run past the city and Grant had struck inland, Lincoln had thought they were making a mistake. He had hoped that Grant and Porter would bypass Vicksburg and continue south to attack Port Hudson. Now, however, the wisdom of Grant's movements was made manifest, and Lincoln told him so: "I now wish to make the personal acknowledgement," he wrote, "that you were right, and I was wrong."[48]

As for Porter, as Fox had promised, the fall of Vicksburg made him a rear admiral—no longer merely an acting admiral. With Foote's death and Porter's promotion, the number of American admirals remained at six.* Porter was convinced that Lincoln had promoted him over Welles' objections. Like both Du Pont and Wilkes, Porter believed that the soft-spoken Lincoln was a staunch supporter and that the blunt and sometimes caustic Welles was the font of his difficulties. In fact, it was Welles who asked Lincoln for the nomination, believing that for all his faults Porter was "brave and energetic," characteristics most needed just now. Lincoln assented to the nomination, but he was less enthusiastic about Porter's suitability for high command. Nevertheless, Lincoln's ability to soothe and charm convinced Porter that the president was his champion, just as Welles' tendency to annoy and irritate convinced him that the navy secretary was his foe.[49]

AT CHARLESTON, meanwhile, Dahlgren superseded Du Pont on July 6, just days after the twin successes at Gettysburg and Vicksburg, and he infused a new vigor into the fleet almost at once. In a significant

---

*In order of seniority, they were Farragut, Goldsborough, Du Pont, Davis, Dahlgren, and Porter. Another half dozen men served as acting rear admirals, and another eight were listed in the *Navy Register* as rear admirals on the retired list.

Gideon Welles and Gustavus Vasa
Fox ran the Navy Department during
Lincoln's presidency. Welles was a
literal-minded, no-nonsense former
Democrat from Connecticut who often
played "bad cop" to Lincoln's "good
cop" when dealing with navy officers.
Welles also distrusted the motives and
political maneuvering of Secretary of
State William Henry Seward, whom he
suspected of trying to take advantage of
Lincoln's good nature. Fox was a former
navy lieutenant who came to Lincoln's
attention during the Fort Sumter crisis
and for whom Lincoln created the post
of assistant secretary of the navy. In that
capacity, Fox acted as a kind of chief
of naval operations, an office that did
not exist until the twentieth century.
Lincoln appreciated Fox's temperament
and ability and wrote to Welles that Fox
"is a live man whose services we cannot
well dispense with." (Welles, Library
of Congress; Fox, Naval Historical
Collection)

Lincoln frequently rode out to the Washington Navy Yard to witness the testing of new weapons, visit with the commander, John A. Dahlgren, or just to get away from the White House for a few hours. Lincoln was fascinated by technology in general and naval technology in particular, and he was an early supporter of ironclad warships, including John Ericsson's *Monitor*. (Naval Historical Collection)

This cartoon from *Harper's Weekly* depicts Seward delivering a letter of marque to a clearly annoyed Britannia. Seward hoped that the threat of American privateers would convince the British to moderate their behavior; Welles was just as convinced that it would lead to a confrontation and perhaps war. Though Lincoln often sided with Seward on questions of diplomacy, this time he backed Welles and declined to institute a privateering program. (Naval Historical Collection)

THE LETTER OF MARQUE.

Postman Seward (*to old Mother Britannia*).—"Letter of Marque from Mr. Lincoln—guess there's a Check in it!"

Charles Wilkes was the stormy petrel of the U.S. Navy during the Civil War. He entered the war with a well-earned reputation for cupidity and obstinacy, and lived up to it during the war. His most notorious act was stopping the mail packet *Trent* while in command of the USS *San Jacinto*, an act that nearly led to a disastrous rift in Anglo-American relations. Lincoln had to balance Wilkes' popularity for twisting the British lion's tail against the consequences of British hostility. In the end, Lincoln's patience and pragmatism allowed him to escape the crisis. Wilkes, however, went on to commit other troublesome acts, and in 1864 he was suspended from the service by a court-martial. (Naval Historical Collection)

USS *San Jacinto* (at right) stopping the British packet *Trent*. (Naval Historical Collection)

Andrew Hull Foote was a schoolboy friend of Gideon Welles, a devout Christian, and a fierce disciplinarian. When he replaced John Rodgers in command of the western river flotilla, he found there was no established protocol for combined army-navy operations. Filling the void, Lincoln took over personal management of the production and distribution of mortars for both the river flotilla and the Gulf Squadron. The mortar rafts were first used in the combined attack on Island No. 10 in the Mississippi. Though the mortars proved less strategically effective than hoped, Lincoln had demonstrated how to break down the historical barriers between the services. (Naval Historical Collection)

Bombardment of Island #10. (U.S. Naval Institute)

Lincoln's mortars were also placed on schooners and used in the Union attack on the forts guarding New Orleans on the lower Mississippi. David Dixon Porter had argued that the mortar's thirteen-inch shells would destroy the rebel forts and allow conventional U.S. Navy ships to run past them up to the city. The huge shells did not destroy the forts, however, and in the end, Porter's foster brother, David Glasgow Farragut, had to run past the forts in the pre-dawn darkness of April 24, 1862. (U.S. Naval Institute).

Farragut's fleet running past the Mississippi River forts below New Orleans. (U.S. Naval Institute)

A print composed and circulated in late 1862 depicts the Union's naval leaders: Foote occupies the place of honor in the center surrounded by (clockwise from top) Du Pont, Porter, Davis, Farragut, Worden, and Goldsborough. (Naval Historical Center)

David Dixon Porter was a brash, self-promoting, and not always truthful officer, but he was also energetic, aggressive, and bold. Lincoln tolerated his weaknesses for the sake of his strengths. Porter was also lucky, often in the right place at the right time to gain important commands. In April 1863, he led a portion of the Mississippi River Squadron past the Vicksburg batteries, a move that proved crucial to the eventual capture of the city. He ended the war in command of the North Atlantic Blockading Squadron. (Naval Historical Collection)

Porter's fleet runs past Vicksburg, April 16, 1863. (U.S. Naval Institute)

In the early weeks and months of the war, Samuel Francis Du Pont was the nation's most highly regarded naval officer. His service on the Blockade Board and especially his capture of Port Royal on the South Carolina coast in November 1861 confirmed his status as the navy's most dependable admiral. Soon, however, his reluctance to execute a naval attack on the Charleston forts and his constant calls for more and more ironclads led Lincoln to think of him as a nautical George McClellan. After the failure of Du Pont's attack at Charleston in April 1863, Lincoln concluded that Du Pont was more concerned for his own reputation than the mission. (U.S. Naval Institute)

Lincoln's favorite admiral was John A. Dahlgren. The ordnance expert replaced Du Pont in command of the South Atlantic Squadron. Welles believed that Dahlgren lacked the seagoing experience to justify promotion to admiral or fleet command, but Lincoln made Dahlgren an admiral anyway, skipping him over the rank of captain altogether. Soon afterward, Du Pont's dismissal and Foote's death placed Dahlgren in command of the South Atlantic Squadron. (Library of Congress)

Attack on Port Royal, November 7, 1861. (Naval Historical Collection)

Attack on Charleston, April 7, 1863. (Naval Historical Collection)

Lincoln told Welles that "there had not been, take it all in all, so good an appointment in either branch of the service, than Farragut." David Glasgow Farragut did what Lincoln's admirals at Charleston would not: charge past protecting forts to cut them off and render them useless, doing so both at New Orleans in 1862 and at Mobile Bay in 1864. In addition, Farragut stayed completely out of politics, telling an audience at Cooper Union in New York, "I meddle not with politics." (Farragut, Naval Historical Collection; Mobile Bay, U.S. Naval Institute)

Attack on Mobile Bay, August 5, 1864. (U.S. Naval Institute)

Samuel Phillips Lee was well connected. He was a third cousin of Robert E. Lee, and his wife was the sister of both Frank Blair Jr., a corps commander in Sherman's army, and Montgomery Blair, Lincoln's postmaster general. Designated an acting rear admiral in 1862, Lee was still an acting admiral in 1864. Eager for promotion, he encouraged his influential relatives to press Lincoln on the issue. Lincoln would not be pressured, however, and Welles insisted that Lee must secure some marked victory to justify his promotion. Lee hoped to win that victory against the forts guarding Wilmington, but instead David Dixon Porter took over his command and conducted the assault on Fort Fisher in January 1865. (Naval Historical Collection)

Attack on Fort Fisher, January 13, 1865. (Naval Historical Collection)

Abraham Lincoln, commander in chief of the army and the navy. (Library of Congress)

gesture, he moved his flag headquarters from the large and comfortable *Wabash* to the stuffy and cramped monitor *Catskill*. He did so at great personal sacrifice, for Dahlgren (like Lincoln) was prone to seasickness, and in the cramped confines of the *Catskill* he succumbed almost at once. In spite of that, within hours of assuming command, he was meeting with Major General Gillmore to plan a new assault on the Charleston forts. The new plan was nearly identical to the one Du Pont had proposed almost a year before—the one that Fox had mocked and dismissed as unnecessarily complicated: The army under Gillmore would occupy Morris Island and establish batteries there to bombard Fort Sumter, which would clear the way for the navy to enter the harbor. It would be more difficult now because the Confederates had strengthened their fortifications on Morris Island. Despite that, the renewed campaign suggested, initially at least, how effective combined operations could be when there was genuine cooperation.[50]

Gillmore's soldiers clambered ashore on the southern tip of Morris Island, while four of the monitors, including the *Catskill* with Dahlgren on board, enfiladed the enemy defenses from the sea. The big eleven- and fifteen-inch shells from the monitors drove the defenders from their entrenchments and allowed the Union troops to overrun the southern half of the island. Gillmore's jubilant soldiers marched northward along the sandy beach while Dahlgren's monitors paralleled their march offshore. The advance halted at Fort Wagner, an enormous sand earthwork that straddled the width of the narrow barrier island. The fort's big guns threatened the monitors, too. The *Catskill* was struck sixty times, and though it suffered no serious damage, Dahlgren himself had a close call when a direct hit on the pilot house loosened a bolt and sent it flying past him.[51]

Gillmore first tried to seize the rebel fort by a coup de main. After pounding the fort with a massive bombardment on July 18, he ordered George C. Strong's brigade to conduct a frontal assault along the length of the narrow island. Dahlgren watched it from the pilot house of the *Catskill*, though the attackers were soon obscured in the falling darkness, and Dahlgren had to guess from the location of the muzzle flashes what was happening on shore. He could not fire his big guns for fear of hitting Union soldiers. Only later did he learn that, spearheaded by the African American 54th Massachusetts regiment, the attack had succeeded in reaching the walls of the battered fort, but despite great heroism and horrific losses, it lacked the impetus to secure the objective. Dahlgren concluded that "the General evidently has not force enough."[52]

Gillmore agreed, and he asked Dahlgren if he could supply a column of "sailors and marines" for another try. Dahlgren replied that he was already shorthanded, and so Gillmore wrote to Halleck to ask for reinforcements. Halleck had never been enthusiastic about the attack on Charleston, and he was annoyed to receive such a letter. He scolded Gillmore, telling him he never would have approved the campaign in the first place if he had known it would require more troops. Dahlgren, however, had also written to Welles about Gillmore's need for troops, and evincing a newfound enthusiasm for combined operations, Welles sent Fox to Halleck to ask if the army could spare some soldiers for Charleston. If Halleck was annoyed by Gillmore's request, he was incensed to hear the same request from the navy. He suggested somewhat testily that perhaps Fox should take care of the navy and let the army take care of itself. Welles thereupon went to see the president.[53]

Lincoln was working in the oval White House library when Welles came in to complain about Halleck's lack of cooperation. Welles argued that the campaign against Charleston never should have been initiated if the government did not intend to support it and see it through. Welles suggested that it was apparently the policy of the army chief "to wait until Gillmore was crushed and repelled, and then to try and regain lost ground." Lincoln did not disagree. He had finally concluded that for all Halleck's theoretical knowledge, he lacked the forcefulness to prosecute the war aggressively. The problem, of course, was that reinforcements for Gillmore must come from somewhere else, presumably from the Army of the Potomac, and in the midst of the campaign season (it was late July) it seemed to Lincoln that Meade was going to want all the men he had.

Somewhat archly, Welles asked him "if he really believed Meade was going to have a battle."

"Well, to be candid," Lincoln replied, "I have no faith that Meade will attack Lee—nothing looks like it to me."

"Why, then . . . not send a few regiments to Charleston?" Welles asked.

"Well . . . I will see Halleck," the president replied. "I think we should strain a point. May I say to him that you are going to strengthen Dahlgren?"

"Yes. . . . But it would be better that you should say you ordered it, and that you also ordered the necessary army increase."[54]

Halleck resisted. He betrayed his conservative and defensive mindset by claiming that "to withdraw troops from General Meade would endanger the safety of his army, and open the North to another raid." Nevertheless, he grudgingly agreed to send an additional ten thousand men to Charleston from elsewhere, half of them African American units.[55]

Despite these reinforcements, Gillmore did not try another frontal assault against Wagner, and decided instead to initiate a formal siege. An engineer by training who had graduated first in his West Point class of 1849, he was most comfortable and confident when solving engineering problems. He therefore set his men to work constructing across the island what was called a "parallel": a line of entrenchments just beyond artillery range from Wagner. This would serve as the starting point for a series of such lines, each several hundred yards closer to the objective. It was a precise and predictable form of warfare that dated back to the seventeenth century, and while it was almost certain to be successful in the end, it was also likely to consume months. The previous fall, Lincoln had worried that Du Pont's preference for a combined operation would lead to a "lengthy siege." Now, though Du Pont was gone, that was exactly what had happened.

Dahlgren continued his manic activity. Even as the siege on Morris Island progressed in accordance with time-honored protocols, Dahlgren's monitors were in action virtually every day, pounding away at Fort Wagner, Fort Sumter, and other targets of opportunity. He responded with alacrity to all of Gillmore's requests for fire support, but the constant activity was wearing on the monitors, on the men inside them, and on Dahlgren himself, whose health continued to deteriorate. On August 17, Gillmore and Dahlgren began a sustained and coordinated artillery bombardment of both Wagner and Sumter that lasted more than a week. On the first day of the bombardment, a shell from Sumter smashed into the roof of the pilothouse of the *Catskill*, killing Dahlgren's chief of staff, Captain George W. Rodgers. When Lincoln heard that "Captain

Rodgers" had been killed at Charleston, he hurried over to the Navy Department, where he was only partially relieved to learn that it was George Rodgers of the *Catskill* who had been killed and not his cousin, the more prominent John Rodgers of the *Weehawken*.[56]

The level of cooperation between the army and the navy in these attacks was unprecedented, surpassing even the cooperation between Grant and Porter at Vicksburg. These were not independent units that simply happened to be on the same side; at Charleston the army and navy constituted a truly unified force. Indeed, the partnership between Gillmore and Dahlgren was so close that their ship-to-shore flag signals during the bombardment of August 17 resembled a conversation.

> GILLMORE: What do you think of our morning's work?
>
> DAHLGREN: Sumter appeared to be damaged a good deal. What is your opinion?
>
> GILLMORE: Are your ironclads out of action for the day or are they going in again?
>
> DAHLGREN: If the fire from Wagner disturbs you, I will send some monitors up to silence her again.
>
> GILLMORE: One of my officers reports that the enemy are mounting a heavy gun on the sea face of Wagner.
>
> DAHLGREN: I will send some monitors up to stop it as soon as the men have had a little rest.[57]

By the end of August, Wagner had been silenced, and Sumter badly battered. On September 7, the rebels evacuated both Fort Wagner and Battery Gregg, at the northern tip of Morris Island. In theory, this was the moment for Dahlgren's monitors to charge into the harbor and put the city under their guns, but a number of factors stayed Dahlgren's hand. The constant activity had taken a toll on the monitors: their smokestacks were perforated, their bottoms were covered with so much sea growth they could barely make three knots, most of them needed an engine overhaul, and four of them had only one working gun. Moreover, the crews were exhausted, stretched to the breaking point by the constant shelling and the oppressive August heat inside iron vessels. Obstructions in the ship channel barred their entrance to the inner harbor, and there was still Fort Moultrie to deal with. When Stanton visited in early September, he concluded that with the army in possession of Morris Island, "it will not pay to go farther." Given all that, Dahlgren enquired of Welles what his next objective should be.[58]

Welles' reply showed how much his views had shifted over the summer. Bowing to Stanton's view that the army's possession of Morris Island effectively closed the port, he decided that sending the monitors into the harbor now would achieve no strategic purpose. Better, he decided, to wait until the ironclad fleet could be reinforced again. He wrote Dahlgren, "The Department is disinclined to have its only ironclad squadron incur extreme risks when the substantial advantages have already been gained." Doing so now, he concluded, would be "merely a point of honor."[59]

It was a victory of sorts, though despite Fox's initial hopes, the navy reaped no headlines for "the fall of Satan's kingdom." Indeed, since both the city and Fort Sumter—ruined as it was—continued to fly the rebel flag, there were no headlines at all beyond now-routine notices such as "The Bombardment of Sumter Still Going On." For all his energy and activity, Dahlgren had not been able to succeed where Du Pont had failed. Moreover, Dahlgren paid a heavy price for his unremitting efforts. He continued to suffer horribly from seasickness. In an effort not to lose face with the veterans, he tried to keep up appearances, but by late August he was suffering so severely he could barely sit in a chair. When Gillmore came on board in early September to coordinate plans, Dahlgren had to greet him from his bed. He confided to Henry Wise that "some days I could hardly walk across the cabin." In his diary, he confessed that he felt his "life was passing away."[60]

The honeymoon between the navy and the army was ending, too. When Dahlgren asked Gillmore to shell Sumter again in late September, the general responded with a five-page lecture explaining that there were no enemy guns left to shell in Sumter. Dahlgren replied that he was not worried about artillery, but about sharpshooters in the fort who were interfering with Union boat crews trying to dismantle the obstructions in the ship channel. There was a hint of anger, as well as disillusionment, in Dahlgren's complaint that "having expended my means for sixty days in helping *him* to clear Morris Island, he demurs at the first step in help of me!" The two commanders patched up this quarrel, but criticism in the newspapers about the lack of progress at Charleston soon led them to turn on each other.[61]

In October, Gillmore sent General Alfred H. Terry and Colonel Joseph R. Hawley to Washington to complain about Dahlgren's growing incapacity. They were brutally candid with Welles, telling him that Dahlgren was "incompetent, imbecile, and insane." With Lincoln they were more circumspect, perhaps aware that the president considered Dahlgren a special friend. Lincoln may have surprised them by asking why they were not shelling the city of Charleston. They replied that they were saving their fire for work against the forts. Welles discounted much of the army's criticism of Dahlgren as service jealousy, and attributed the rest of it to the fact that Dahlgren was simply ill and overworked, but he admitted that Dahlgren's particular skills lent themselves more to his previous position as chief of the Bureau of Ordnance than his new job as fleet commander.[62]

That same month, Henry Wise, who had replaced Dahlgren in the Ordnance Bureau, told Lincoln's secretary John Hay that Dahlgren was in "wretched health, dyspeptic, distraught, and overworked," and when Lincoln heard about it, he sent Hay down to Charleston to see for himself. Hay was shocked by Dahlgren's appearance, and even more by his physical and mental condition. Hay thought not only that Dahlgren was "giving way under the strain of his position" but also that "his brain seems to be a little affected." Dahlgren's subordinates reported that he kept mostly to himself, and when he did meet with his officers, he sometimes forgot what he was saying in midsentence. He would call a council of war and then forget the purpose of it. Hay confided to his diary that "his dispatches have lost coherence. The business of the fleet is in chaos." Four days later, he concluded sadly, "Altogether it seems as if we must admit that his career at Port Royal is up to this point a failure."[63]

For all that, Dahlgren's persistence, and particularly his effort to keep the government informed, kept him in good stead with both Lincoln and Welles. In the six months between July 6, when he took command, and the end of the year, Dahlgren sent more than 350 official reports to the capital—an average of two a day. He seldom missed an opportunity to remind Washington what he was doing. When Lincoln wrote to ask him about an anti-torpedo device that an inventor had suggested, Dahlgren replied that it was certainly worth a trial. But he also took the opportunity to report to the president that his monitors were blocking every channel and "interdicting absolutely all access" to the port of Charleston, "so that neither men, ordnance, nor supplies of any kind can get in, nor can cotton get out to pay for them." He estimated that the threat posed by his monitors kept "20,000 to 25,000 of their best troops . . . in abeyance in the vicinity," preventing them from being used elsewhere. He may not have captured the city, but he wanted Lincoln to understand that he was, in his own words, "rendering invaluable service."[64]

Despite the reports of his "insanity," Dahlgren's energy and loyalty satisfied Lincoln and Welles that they had the right man on the spot. Whatever his weaknesses, physical or otherwise, Dahlgren understood the importance of keeping Washington fully informed. He could not give Lincoln the victory he hoped for, but the contrast between Du Pont's tiresome complaints and Dahlgren's conscientious reports was striking. In any case, there was no going back now. Having "thrown away" Du Pont, Welles—and Lincoln—would stick by Dahlgren to the very end.

9

"Peace Does Not Appear So Distant as It Did"
Lincoln and Wartime Politics

LINCOLN'S HOPE that the victories at Gettysburg and Vicksburg might herald a swift end to the war went unfulfilled. In Virginia, Lee regrouped and even managed to reinforce his army, bringing its strength back up to sixty thousand men. Though much of his offensive potential had been squandered in the summer campaign, he remained as dangerous as ever on the defensive, and Meade evidenced little eagerness to challenge him. In the West, Union Major General William Rosecrans maneuvered the rebels out of Chattanooga, but gratifying as that was, the western Confederate army remained intact and poised for a counterstroke. At Charleston, the campaign had bogged down into a siege despite Dahlgren's manic energy. Nevertheless, by the late summer of 1863, Lincoln could write a public letter asserting, "The signs look better. . . . Peace does not appear so distant as it did."* While this was unquestionably good news, it also meant that in the fall of 1863, even as Lincoln continued to deal with problems of military strategy,

---

*It was in this public letter to James C. Conkling that Lincoln offered his well-known paean to the navy's role in the war: "Nor must Uncle Sam's Web-feet be forgotten. At all the watery margins they have been present. Not only in the deep sea, the broad bay, and the rapid river, but also up the narrow bayou, and wherever the ground was a little damp, they have been, and made their tracks."

he also began to confront the complex political issues that would have to be addressed in a postwar America.[1]

Lincoln's domestic arrangements that summer and fall were Spartan. He spent his nights not in the White House but in a two-story cottage at the Soldiers' Home in the rolling hills a few miles north of the city. Like most government officials, Lincoln sent his family off to more temperate climes during the oppressive summer months. Mary and their youngest son, Tad, went to the White Mountains of New Hampshire during July and August, but Lincoln himself stayed in Washington—it was, after all, the prime military campaign season. He arose early each morning and after a breakfast that typically consisted of an egg and a cup of coffee, he rode into the city escorted by a small cavalry guard, arriving at the White House at "precisely eight o'clock." There he met John Hay, who usually had his correspondence arranged for him in neat piles. Lincoln either answered the letters personally or instructed Hay how to deal with them. Then, after about two hours, he sat down to read the papers. It was important to Lincoln to keep abreast of public opinion, and he read both the friendly press and the opposition papers. In addition to the *Daily National Intelligencer*, Lincoln paid special attention to Horace Greeley's often critical *New York Tribune*. Asked once how he felt reading Greeley's diatribes against him, Lincoln made light of it: "It reminds me of the big fellow whose little wife was wont to beat him over the head without resistance," he said. "When remonstrated with, the man said, 'Let her alone. It don't hurt me, and it does her a power of good.'" Lincoln also read Henry Raymond's *New York Times*, generally perceived as an organ of the Seward-Weed faction of the party, and James Gordon Bennett's *New York Herald*, occasionally clipping articles of particular interest to file away in his desk.[2]

Beginning at eleven, Lincoln received visitors in his office, the walls of which were covered by campaign maps and an oil painting of Andrew Jackson. That painting was noteworthy not only because Lincoln himself was a former Whig, a party that had been formed to oppose Jackson's presidency, but also because in his current circumstances, Lincoln had come to identify with Jackson's bold stand against the Nullifiers in 1833. The president sat with his back to the window as he received his visitors, listening carefully and sympathetically to each, before rising to see them on their way. Many of them sought employment, and for some he wrote short notes, often a variation on "If you can do so consistent with the public interest, please appoint him to the office he requests." Or "If this appointment can consistently be made, I shall be glad." Even when Lincoln was unable to grant a particular request, most of his visitors left his office with an enhanced opinion of the chief executive.[3]

On those days when he managed to see all of his visitors, Lincoln generally took up his hat and left his office to visit the various departments of government, dropping in unannounced simply to see what was going on. One twenty-first-century business expert has likened this to the modern business school practice known as MBWA, "management by walking around."[4] Lincoln dropped in most often on the State or War Department, but he was also a frequent visitor to the Navy Department, where he chatted with Welles or Fox and whoever else happened to be there. Returning to his office by five, he rose from his desk around six, again took up his hat, and went out the back to meet his cavalry escort for the ride back to the Soldiers' Home. There he would dine, read, work on his public and private correspondence, and finally sleep in the marginally cooler air.

Lincoln filled his days with such quotidian activities because there was so little news from the front. Though it was the peak campaign season, Meade showed no eagerness to take advantage of the long days and the abundant grass to inaugurate a new campaign, and August passed into September without a major movement by either side. Perhaps aware of how this looked, Meade wrote to Halleck seeking guidance. He was convinced that he could not engage Lee except "under very disadvantageous circumstances," and even then the results were not likely to yield any strategic advantage. Meade concluded that he was "reluctant to run the risks involved without the positive sanction of the government." Halleck took Meade's letter to Lincoln, who was disappointed not only that Meade seemed to need further cosseting but also because Lincoln had appointed Halleck as general in chief precisely so that he could provide the kind of guidance that Meade now sought, and yet here was Halleck asking Lincoln what should be done. Rather than rebuke either man, however, Lincoln sat down to express his views—again—about grand strategy.[5]

He began with a clear-eyed assessment of army strength. By Meade's own estimate (an accurate one), Lee now had "not less than forty thousand infantry" with him, having sent off a number of units to other theaters, while Meade had nearly ninety thousand. Lincoln recognized that acting on the defense gave an army a significant advantage, so ninety thousand men attacking forty thousand did not necessarily ensure success. But by that same calculation, Lincoln wrote, Lee's reduced army could presumably be stalemated by keeping forty thousand Union soldiers in front of him, "leaving us fifty thousand to put to other use." It was essentially the same argument he had made to Halleck back in January 1862 when he had suggested that Union armies should "menace" the enemy at several different points at the same time and "forbear to attack" their strengthened positions while exploiting the weakened areas. In that way, the Union could take advantage of its numerical superiority without simply trying to overwhelm the rebels with sheer numbers. Lincoln made it clear that he was not eager for Meade "to fight the enemy slowly back into his intrenchments at Richmond," in a grinding campaign that occupied many months and cost many thousands of lives.[6]

The night after he sent these thoughts off to Halleck for Meade's benefit, Lincoln was asleep in his room at the Soldiers' Home when a messenger woke him up to hand him a dispatch containing the news that Major General William S. Rosecrans had been attacked in northern Georgia and was engaged in a desperate fight. Lincoln tried to go back to sleep, but, unable to do so, he got up, dressed, and went into the city. The next day he was at his usual post in the War Department telegraph office when another dispatch arrived that was more encouraging. Part of the army, at least, was making a valiant stand. Apparently, elements of Lee's army from Virginia had traversed five states by rail to join the western rebel army and concentrate on Rosecrans. It occurred to Lincoln that if Lee was thus weakened, perhaps there might be an opportunity for Meade in Virginia. Halleck, however, disputed this view; after all, he reminded the president, it was essential to defend the capital. To Welles, who had joined Lincoln in the telegraph office, the president complained, "It is the same old story of this Army of the Potomac. Imbecility, inefficiency—don't want to *do*—is defending the Capital."

Having heard this tale before, Welles asked him bluntly: "Why not rid yourself of Meade . . . ?"

In reply, Lincoln asked, "Who among them is any better . . . ?"

During this exchange, Lincoln wondered aloud why his admirals gave him far fewer problems than his generals, and suggested that "perhaps naval training was more uniform and equal than the military."

No, Welles said, perhaps thinking of Du Pont and Wilkes. "We had our troubles, but they were less conspicuous." He did allow that the navy had been fortunate in picking Farragut and Porter for positions of high responsibility, and, feeling generous, added: "Du Pont had merit also," though he expressed it in the past tense.

Lincoln agreed only in part. He conceded that "there had not been, take it all in all, so good an appointment in either branch of the service as Farragut," but he was less sure about the others. Du Pont, he still believed, was essentially a naval McClellan, and as for Porter, Lincoln described him as "a busy schemer, bold but not of high qualities as a chief"—a less generous evaluation than Welles', but a more accurate one.[7]

Eventually the telegraph brought the news that Rosecrans had managed to save the army by falling back into Chattanooga. It was not victory, but at least Lincoln was able to get some sleep. Over the next several days, Rosecrans consolidated his position in Chattanooga while the rebels occupied the high ground south of the city to inaugurate a kind of siege. Rosecrans had clearly lost the initiative, and he now seemed to focus exclusively on hanging on to Chattanooga and keeping his army fed. Lincoln feared that he had also lost his nerve. To John Hay he remarked that Rosecrans was "confused and stunned like a duck hit on the head." Eventually, in addition to sending Rosecrans twenty thousand reinforcements under Joe Hooker, Lincoln decided that Grant should assume command of the western theater and go to Chattanooga personally to instill some energy and direction into the defense there. That fall, while Gillmore and Dahlgren conducted a siege of Charleston, it would be Grant's job to lift the rebel siege of Chattanooga.[8]

MEANWHILE, the fallout from the dismissal of Du Pont and Wilkes continued to roil the political waters. Welles had expected that Du

Pont would be the more troublesome public opponent because of his "cunning" and "immense wealth," but Wilkes, too, proved a difficult and persistent adversary. Welles had received a letter from Jane Wilkes back in June asking if the rumor that her husband was to be recalled was true. While she would be happy to have him home, she wrote, she fired a warning shot in suggesting that if necessary her husband would "fully vindicate himself before his Country." On July 6, the same day that Dahlgren reported aboard the *Wabash*, Wilkes walked into Welles' office to ask directly why he had been superseded. Welles told him it was because of protests from the British. It was, he said, a matter of diplomacy, one in which the Navy Department had to gratify the State Department. Wilkes thereupon went to see Seward. Disingenuously, Seward told him that diplomacy had nothing to do with it, that for his part he was entirely satisfied with Wilkes' conduct, and he was unaware of why he had been recalled. Wilkes concluded that his fall was due entirely to the personal enmity of the secretary of the navy, whom he referred to privately as a "fool," an "imbecile," and "completely incompetent." Welles put him on the retired list at half pay and ignored him until Wilkes went public in December.[9]

Meanwhile, there was Du Pont to deal with. Officially, Du Pont had been relieved at his own request, since after the failure of the April attack he had told Welles that the department should replace him if it found an officer who could capture Charleston. He had not expected Welles to take him literally, however, and he probably found some satisfaction in the fact that his replacement had not, after all, been able to capture Charleston. Now shunted aside, he saw himself as a victim of Welles' unrealistic expectations, Alban Stimers' poison tongue, and Charles Fulton's vitriol. He was particularly bitter toward Fox, whom he had once considered an ally but whose faithlessness was now revealed. In hindsight, he decided that he had sensed it all along, writing his wife that "I had [it] *in my bones* early that Fox would be a traitor to me."[10]

For all his progressive views, Du Pont was fundamentally a nineteenth-century man, and as such felt a compulsion to defend his professional honor. Welles thought Du Pont was obsessed—even "deranged"—on the issue of his public reputation, but he was no more so than most officers of his generation. What Du Pont wanted was a public exoneration, and since Welles refused to publish his official reports, he looked to the trial of Stimers for his redemption. He calculated that the witnesses called to disprove Stimers' slanders would also prove that the failure of the attack back in April had been due not to the "incompetent hands" of its commander but to the Navy Department's insistence that he rely solely on the flawed monitors.[11]

Welles was not about to let that happen. He would not allow Du Pont to orchestrate a court-martial in Port Royal where all the presiding officers and all of the witnesses would be part of Du Pont's chain of command, and he certainly would not allow anyone to offer public testimony about the weaknesses of the monitors. He could not order Du Pont to withdraw the charges against Stimers, but in lieu of a court-martial he ordered a court of inquiry, and rather than hold it at Port Royal he ordered it moved to the Brooklyn Navy Yard. Finally, Welles chose officers for the court who were either public advocates of the monitors, inimical to Du Pont personally, or both. When John Hay met the members of the court, he characterized the group as having "a very large infusion of fogy . . . fine old fellows with nine stripes on the coat sleeve." Du Pont was disgusted, and he concluded that Stimers "is now to be whitewashed."[12]

It was worse than that. The court met intermittently over the summer, gathering depositions from several officers, and it convened that fall. Du Pont gave his testimony in early October, and a week later there was some awkwardness when both he and Stimers were guests of honor at the Brooklyn Navy Yard to witness the launching of Ericsson's newest monitor, the *Manhattan*.* Meanwhile, in his court testimony not only did Stimers refuse to back down, but his defense essentially was that everything he had said about Du Pont was true, and he repeated it for the record, insisting "that the Monitors had received no serious injury; that they could be repaired in a few hours; that the trial [at Charleston] ought not to condemn them." He claimed that his special expertise in the field of armored warships, gained from his experience as a member of the crew of the original *Monitor* in its fight with the *Merrimack*, gave him insight that Du Pont lacked, since the admiral's limited knowledge

---

*Suggesting the metamorphosis of the monitor class, the new *Manhattan* was more than twice as long as the original *Monitor*, displaced nearly twice the tonnage, and carried two 15-inch guns.

of ironclads "derived from casual inspection and the reports of others." He asserted that his arrest and trial was nothing more than "an effort to justify a failure of Rear Admiral Dupont."* The court apparently agreed, and concluded that "in their opinion there is no necessity or propriety of further proceedings in this case."[13]

Disappointed that his "last hope of justice at the hands of the Department" was now "extinguished," Du Pont wrote Welles a long, self-justifying letter. If he could not get satisfaction from the court, he was determined to challenge the "insulting imputations" that Welles had made about his service and, by implication, his character. In tendentious detail, he listed the several efforts he had made to inform the department of the limitations of the monitors, and the repeated urgings he had received from Washington to avoid a combined operation and mount a purely naval attack. He was correct in his facts, but his letter betrayed a sea lawyer's tendency to mine the past in order to pick out those events that put his service in a favorable light.[14]

Du Pont's letter infuriated Welles. Although back in July the navy secretary had written Du Pont a pro forma letter of congratulations for his "safe return," and had even gone so far as to offer "high appreciation of your services and of the ability that you have exhibited," he now sat down to vent his anger at Du Pont's temerity. He claimed he had "neither the time nor the inclination to enter into a controversy or review" of Du Pont's tenure of command, but then he proceeded to do exactly that, producing a five-thousand-word letter in which he blasted the admiral in language so confrontational it is impossible to avoid the conclusion that he meant to be deliberately insulting. Welles cited Du Pont's "constant complaints—the distrust that painfully pervaded your correspondence—your distressing personal anxiety about yourself, that seemed to overshadow public duty—your assaults upon editors instead of assaults upon rebel batteries," among many other failings. He implied that Du Pont was not only incompetent but cowardly, and he

---

*Stimers got his comeuppance when a subsequent investigation revealed that he had made unauthorized changes to Ericsson's plan for light draft monitors for use on the western rivers. Stimers' changes made the vessels so heavy they would not float. Repairs cost the government $10 million, and the episode ruined Stimers' reputation.

concluded that "you were not relieved one moment too soon." Rather than try to soothe his disgruntled admiral, Welles sought to put him in his place.[15]

It was no doubt a therapeutic exercise, and after purging himself, Welles probably should have folded up the letter and put it in a drawer, as Lincoln had done with his letter to Meade after Gettysburg. Instead he sent it, and he did so without consulting Lincoln, who almost certainly would have been shocked by such a mean-spirited missive. After Du Pont shared its contents with several of his friends, many of them urged him to show it to the president to expose Welles' viciousness and to elicit presidential support. Winter Davis was especially eager for him to go to Lincoln, arguing that the president was a fair and just man who would do whatever was necessary to rectify the situation. Others were less sure. Du Pont's wife and several of his fellow officers told him that Lincoln was too much under the thumb of Fox to give Du Pont any redress. One officer wrote Du Pont that Lincoln "still looks upon Fox as the impersonation of naval wisdom, and upon Dahlgren as the exemplar of naval skill." Another wrote, more accurately, that Lincoln "is honest, and sincerely desirous to do justice, but he has not much time for investigation, and feels bound to support his Cabinet." In the end, Du Pont decided not to take Welles' letter to the president. Instead he determined to "set my teeth and abide results," a course of action that would have served him better if he had adopted it sooner. For all practical purposes, Du Pont's fifty-year naval career was ended. He remained a rear admiral on the navy list, but he never again held an important assignment.[16]

WELLES HAD HOPED that a naval success at Charleston would generate favorable newspaper coverage for the Navy Department. Instead the most prominent navy news that fall featured the continuing rampages of the Confederate commerce raiders, in particular the *Florida* and the *Alabama*. In a public letter, the merchants of New York took Welles to task for leaving their trade "unprotected." They insisted that "the loyal merchants and shipowners of the country are entitled to have a more energetic protection of their interest." The *New York Herald*'s outspoken editor, James Gordon Bennett, complained that it was "galling to the national pride that four or five fleet Anglo-rebel cruisers should be allowed to drive our commerce from the seas," and he assailed Welles for "the neglect, the carelessness, the incompetency, and the utter imbecility of the Navy Department."[17]

The public criticism had deep roots extending back to the previous year when the *Florida* and the *Alabama* had been built in Liverpool under the pretense that they had been ordered by a neutral government. Charles Francis Adams protested this obvious fiction, but he made little headway with the British government. Despite his objections, the *Florida*, constructed under the name *Oreto* to bolster the fiction that she was being built for Italy, left Liverpool in March 1862 with English officers and crew. A Confederate special agent, James D. Bulloch, arranged to have it met in the West Indies by another vessel that carried guns and ordnance to be transferred onto the *Oreto* near a remote cay in the Bahamas. A group of Confederate officers headed by navy Captain John N. Maffit replaced the English officers and turned the *Oreto* into the CSS *Florida*. Maffit's planned cruise of destruction was delayed by an outbreak of yellow fever, however, and Maffit was forced to run for a friendly port. With only eighteen men on board, and ill himself, he put into Cardenas, Cuba. The Spanish government would not let him stay there indefinitely, however, and Maffit decided to head for Mobile, where he could refit and take on a full crew.[18]

On September 4, 1862, Commander George Preble, the senior U.S. Navy officer of the blockading squadron off Mobile, spotted the smoke of an approaching steamer. It made boldly for the entrance to the harbor flying the British flag. Preble ordered his flagship *Oneida* to close with it, and when he got near enough, he hailed the deck. There was no answer, and Preble punctuated his request by firing a shot across its bow. The ship neither answered nor stopped but continued to steam on toward the entrance to Mobile Bay. Preble would have been justified in opening fire, but, recalling departmental warnings about not provoking the British, he fired two more warning shots before he finally fired for effect. When he did, the *Florida* dropped its English colors, but it did not return fire. In fact, it could not do so since in addition to its undersized crew, the *Florida* had no rammers or sponges on board. Several of Preble's shots struck home, killing or injuring more than half the *Florida*'s small crew, but none of the shots succeeded in stopping the *Florida*, and it escaped under the guns of Fort Morgan into Mobile Bay.[19]

Preble reported the incident to Farragut, who was both distraught and disgusted that an enemy warship had run right through the Union blockading squadron in broad daylight. He wrote to Welles that the incident was "mortifying," and complained that "there never was a finer opportunity for stopping a vessel." In his frustration, he added: "Why Captain Preble did not fire into her after she failed to stop or answer his hail, I cannot imagine." Aware that this episode would become fuel for the anti-administration newspapers, Welles was at least as annoyed as Farragut, and he took Farragut's report to the president.[20]

The timing of Welles' visit was unfortunate for Preble, for it was just three days after the Battle of Antietam, and Lincoln was unhappy with McClellan's stubborn refusal to pursue Lee's wounded army. When Welles suggested that Preble's dereliction of duty "must not go unpunished," Lincoln snapped: "Dismiss him, if that is your opinion." Welles hesitated. Preble bore the name of one of the most distinguished families in the history of the U.S. Navy. His grandfather, Edward Preble, had been the hero of the Barbary Wars and the role model for a whole generation of naval officers. Seeing Welles' uncertainty, Lincoln seized the moment. "I will do it!" he declared, and he ordered Welles to inform Preble that "by direction of the President," he was dismissed from the navy forthwith. Like those officers who had abandoned the U.S. Navy to enter Confederate service, Preble's name was "stricken from the rolls of the Navy," a fact that was announced on board all U.S. Navy ships. In dealing with personnel matters, Welles had generally played the "bad cop" and Lincoln the "good cop," but on this occasion, the roles were reversed.[21]

Both Preble and Farragut were shocked by Lincoln's "summary and severe punishment." Farragut wrote that no doubt Preble "deserved some censure," but considering the government's sensitivity about giving offense to the ships of other nations, he thought Preble's hesitancy to fire into a vessel flying the British flag was understandable. Preble himself wrote to Lincoln that "I do not believe you would do intentional injustice to anyone, yet you have done me the most cruel injustice." Others agreed. Preble was popular, and several officers wrote Welles to support his request for a court of inquiry.* The case became political in January 1863 when the Senate Naval Affairs Committee petitioned for a reconsideration. By now, Welles may have been having second thoughts, and he wrote Lincoln that while he still believed Preble's dismissal had been justified, he was resubmitting the case to Lincoln for possible clemency. On February 12, 1863—his own fifty-fourth birthday—Lincoln restored Preble to his former rank. He reiterated that the commander had been "guilty of inexcusable neglect" for allowing the *Florida* to run into Mobile, but because it had been "an error in judgment" rather than a crime, Lincoln wrote, Preble could be forgiven.[22]

By this time the *Florida* was already back at sea. It escaped out of Mobile in January, running out through the blockade squadron at three in the morning during a northwest gale. Commander George Emmons in the *R. R. Cuyler* gave chase but soon lost her in the darkness. Over the next eight months the *Florida* captured and burned some twenty-two Union merchant ships until it steamed into the harbor at Brest, France, for a refit in August. Welles sent the *Kearsarge* in the hopes of trapping it there, but since neither France nor England would allow U.S. Navy vessels to use their ports for such a purpose, it was both logistically impractical and politically difficult for the *Kearsarge* to stay there indefinitely.[23]

The career of the *Alabama*, under Confederate navy Captain Raphael Semmes, was even more devastating, and caused the administration serious political difficulties. Though merchants across the North urged Welles to send more cruisers to look for the *Alabama*, Welles considered that "an act of folly." He was convinced that maintaining the blockade—imperfect though it might be—was of greater strategic importance than scattering vessels across the world's oceans in pursuit of a handful of commerce raiders. He had, of course, sent some

---

*Preble finally got his day in court, but not for another decade. In April 1872, the U.S. Navy granted him his court of inquiry. One of the witnesses was Maffit himself, who testified that Preble's shells did horrible damage to his ship, as "shell and shrapnel were bursting all around us," and that only "the superior speed of the Florida enabled me to pass" safely into the harbor. After deliberation, the court concluded that Preble "did all that a loyal, brave, and efficient officer could do to capture or destroy her" (*Official Records of the Union and Confederate Navies in the War of the Rebellion* [Washington, DC: Government Printing Office, 1894–1922], 1:464, 468).

ships out to look for the *Alabama*—that had been the primary mission of Charles Wilkes' "Flying Squadron," and he had ordered the *Vanderbilt* to patrol for the *Alabama* off the Brazilian headland. Wilkes' appropriation of the *Vanderbilt* had foiled that design, and Welles convinced himself that the subsequent depredations of the *Alabama* were largely a product of Charles Wilkes' cupidity in preventing the *Vanderbilt* from completing its assigned mission.[24]

The navy's apparent incompetence was underscored in December when a U.S. Army transport vessel, the *Fulton*, captured the blockade runner *Banshee* off North Carolina. Bennett's *New York Herald* was acidly gleeful in announcing that while the *Banshee* had successfully eluded many *navy* ships while making several runs in and out of Wilmington, North Carolina, it had finally met its match in an *army* transport. Bennett renewed his attack on the Navy Department and again called for Lincoln to remove Welles from the cabinet. Welles complained privately to his diary that "those who are most ignorant complain loudest," and refused to let it sway him from his focus on the blockade. "Unreasonable and captious men will blame me," he wrote, "take what course I may. I must, therefore, follow my own convictions."[25]

Welles could take such a position because, despite the public criticism, Lincoln continued to stand behind him. It might have gained Lincoln some respite from the complaints if he had asked Welles to step aside, but the president knew not only that it would be unfair but that it would be only a matter of time before the critics found reason to criticize Welles' successor, whoever he might be.

THE WAR AT SEA was very much on Lincoln's mind as he composed his annual message to Congress in December. He began by congratulating the country on avoiding a foreign war. He did not specifically mention either Charles Wilkes or the *Peterhoff* case, but he did note that "questions of great intricacy and importance have arisen out of the blockade," and he was pleased to report that "they have been . . . accommodated in a spirit of frankness, justice, and mutual good will." The prize courts, he declared, "by the impartiality of their adjudications, have commanded the respect and confidence of maritime powers." As for the depredations of the rebel raiders, he blamed them on "a class of semi piratical vessels, built, armed, and manned abroad, and with no recognized nationality."

While preparing his remarks, Lincoln wrote that "these predatory rovers have as yet escaped our cruisers," though he expressed a hope that recent negotiations with the British would prevent them from allowing any more raiders to leave their shores. After writing that, it occurred to Lincoln that since those negotiations were still ongoing, it might be best not to bring them up at all, and he struck the paragraph from his message.[26]

Welles wrote his own report with the expressed intention of doing "wrong to no one," and, indeed, it was relatively benign in its treatment of the two admirals he had effectively dismissed. Du Pont, he wrote, had "expressed a willingness to relinquish the position" at Charleston. This was technically true, of course, but it completely glossed over the bitter tensions behind his removal. As for Dahlgren's lack of progress since then, Welles employed the passive voice to note merely that "delays and difficulties intervened" at Charleston, so "it was not deemed advisable to attempt a passage up to the city." Welles praised David Dixon Porter's "activity, energy, and readiness of resources" on the Mississippi, and he even had some good things to say about Wilkes. "That officer," Welles wrote of Wilkes, "by his energy and decision, contributed to break[ing] up one of the several lines of illicit traders organized to convey supplies to the rebels." But Welles also blamed Wilkes for the navy's inability to find or capture the *Alabama*. "Acting Rear-Admiral Wilkes on falling in with the Vanderbilt . . . detained her in his possession so long as to defeat the object and purposes of the department," he wrote. "The unfortunate detention of the Vanderbilt wholly defeated the plans of the Department."[27]

When Wilkes read that in the papers, he concluded that Welles' criticism touched upon his honor, and, like Du Pont, he insisted—even demanded—that his own reports be "laid before Congress for my full justification." Welles had no intention of doing any such thing; the navy was not a debating society in which officers got to dispute departmental reports in public. Besides, this was not a matter of differing opinions—Wilkes had clearly violated his orders. Welles wrote back to Wilkes to set him straight: "You prevented the orders of the Department from being carried into execution," and "in doing it you were guilty of a grave offense." As far as Welles was concerned, that was the end of it. Unlike Du Pont, however, Wilkes was not one to set his teeth and abide results. He was convinced that Welles was using him as a scapegoat to excuse his own failures. A week later, a copy of Wilkes' letter of protest to Welles appeared prominently in the *Philadelphia Inquirer* and the *New York Times.*[28]

It was against navy regulations to send official correspondence to the press without permission, and Welles asked Wilkes if he had been the source of the published letters. Wilkes "coolly" denied it. Welles probably should have let it go, but he was a stickler for rules and regulations. "I do not wish to be severe," he wrote, "but he cannot be permitted to go unrebuked." Unable to prove Wilkes guilty of corresponding with the press, he charged him instead with violating orders when he was still on active duty, and he convened a court-martial.[29]

The central charge was that Wilkes "did enter upon and take possession and control of the United States steamship of war Vanderbilt." For good measure, Welles added a lengthy list of other crimes, including insubordinate conduct, negligence, carelessness, the use of disrespectful language, refusal to obey a lawful order, and conduct unbecoming an officer. Wilkes fought back. He argued before the court that Welles had preferred charges against him "for manifest personal motives," and that since the court had no jurisdiction over personal matters, it should adjourn at once. When that gambit failed, he claimed that the members of the court had been selected to ensure his conviction, and because of that "a fair trial cannot be had." He named Paulding and Goldsborough in particular as personal enemies—Paulding because Wilkes had publicly criticized his failure to relieve the Gosport Navy Yard back in 1861, and Goldsborough because Wilkes had superseded him on the James River in 1862. The court rejected that argument as well. Wilkes then challenged the evidence against him, claiming that official orders amounted to "hearsay," and that testimony by any officer junior to him should not be admitted. When that failed, he prolonged the trial for days by conducting a lengthy and detailed cross examination of every witness. His legal tactics did not endear him to the court, and in the end it found him guilty, sentencing him to be publicly reprimanded and suspended from the navy for three years.[30]

Lincoln made no public comment, but he was aware of the proceedings. Wilkes' attorney was Orville Browning, no longer a U.S. senator but still a close friend of the president. Browning talked to Lincoln about the case at least three times during the trial, and along with

Thomas Ewing, another of Lincoln's old friends, he approached Lincoln to ask about the possibility of a presidential pardon. The president put both men off for almost a year, telling Ewing that he was "not ready to decide" the case and that he did not want Ewing or anyone else to come in and "scold" him about it. The day after Christmas, however, when Ewing again showed up at the White House, Lincoln told Welles he was thinking of commuting Wilkes' sentence. Welles remained opposed. "It is a misfortune," Welles wrote in his diary, "that the President gives his ear to a class of old party hacks like Ewing who are paid to come here and persuade the President to do wrong. All this President has the sagacity to see but hardly the will to resist." In the end, Lincoln reduced Wilkes' suspension to a single year.* Since the court's verdict was not handed down until April 1864, however, that one year lasted until the war was over. Like Du Pont, Wilkes would not see any more active wartime service. It is not clear that Lincoln had any further involvement in the case. In his *Autobiography*, Wilkes claimed that the president wrote him "a highly complimentary message to the effect of thanks," but if Lincoln wrote such a letter, it has not survived.[31]

THE UNSEEMLY DENOUEMENT to the naval careers of both Samuel Francis Du Pont and Charles Wilkes was due almost entirely to Welles' judgmental worldview, and differed dramatically from the way Lincoln handled most of the generals he had to dismiss. The president seldom criticized anyone directly, even when he felt compelled to dismiss them, and he never employed the kind of confrontational language that Welles used in writing to Du Pont. The closest Lincoln ever came was in the fall of 1862 when he read a report from McClellan that the horses of his army were fatigued. Lincoln was in the telegraph office when the message arrived, and in an instinctive response he shot back a question: "Will you pardon me for asking what the horses of your army have done since the Battle of Antietam that fatigue anything?" The passage has

---

*Lincoln's inability to resist granting pardons was endemic throughout his administration. In many cases he changed death sentences to imprisonment, and reduced prison sentences to last only for the duration of the war. The same month he reduced Wilkes' sentence, he also commuted the executions of more than a dozen soldiers, all of whom had been found guilty of desertion or cowardice.

been widely quoted by historians as a clever riposte, but its sarcastic tone was uncharacteristic of Lincoln, and it is possible he regretted sending it almost as soon as it left his hand. He knew that he was more likely to produce good results by encouragement than by hectoring.[32]

More typical was his reply to General Samuel R. Curtis in 1863 during the Du Pont controversy when he wrote to tell Curtis that he could not gratify his request for a command. Curtis was a friend and political ally who had been accused of corruption. Lincoln did not believe the charges but concluded that, given the circumstances, it would be unwise to appoint him to a command. "I did not mean to cast any censure upon you," Lincoln wrote to Curtis, "nor to indorse any of the charges made against you by others. With me the presumption is still in your favor that you are honest, capable, faithful, and patriotic." If Welles had penned those two sentences in his letter to Du Pont, even after relieving him of command, it very likely would have ended the squabble, made Du Pont a staunch ally, and saved him for future service. Welles could not do it. In his world, the facts were the facts and that was all there was to it. In taking such a stance, however, he permanently alienated a possibly useful officer.[33]

With the single exception of McClellan, Lincoln managed to maintain the loyalty, and even the admiration, of most of his disappointed generals. A month after dismissing Hooker from command, he wrote to Meade asking if he would accept Hooker as a corps commander. "I have not thrown General Hooker away," the president wrote, and indeed, Lincoln later sent Hooker west with a corps command to participate in the relief of Chattanooga. By contrast, Welles did "throw away" both Du Pont and Wilkes, neither of whom ever saw active service again.[34]

Welles' treatment of Charles Wilkes can be usefully compared to Lincoln's treatment of John A. McClernand. Grant had tolerated McClernand longer than he believed was good for the service, mainly out of deference to the president. After the fall of Vicksburg, however, McClernand released a copy of his General Order No. 72 to the newspapers. His crime was the same as Wilkes: he violated department rules by forwarding an official letter to the press without the approval of his commanding officer. And his purpose was the same: he wanted to get his own version of the story to the public. It did not help that McClernand's report exaggerated the role of his own corps to the detriment of others, especially

Sherman's. Grant demonstrated both shrewdness and political sensitivity by sending a trusted staff officer, Colonel John A. Rawlins, to Washington to ascertain just how committed the president was to McClernand. Lincoln liked and trusted McClernand, but he did not want to impose his personal choices on Grant against his will. He apparently assured Rawlins of this, for soon afterward, Grant dismissed McClernand from his command. Declaring himself "more jealous of my honor than my life," McClernand demanded a court-martial that would clear his name. Grant refused. McClernand thereupon did what Du Pont would not: He appealed to the president to see that he was "fairly dealt by."[35]

The request put Lincoln in a bind. While he did not want to antagonize McClernand, who had been—and still was—a valuable ally in the war effort, neither was he willing to overrule Grant. In the end, he sided with Grant, but even while refusing McClernand's request, the president made a point to praise his service to the country: "Grateful for the patriotic stand so early taken by you in this life-and-death struggle of the nation," Lincoln wrote, "I have done whatever has appeared practicable to advance you and the public interest together." He declared that Grant's decision "pains me, not less than it does you," but he insisted that he could not interfere in the command of the western armies, for to do so would "magnify" the problems in the field, and "could not but be of evil effect." He concluded rather enigmatically that "he who has the right needs not to fear," and he signed the letter "Your friend as ever." It worked. McClernand expressed gratitude for the president's "kind letter" and thanked him for "the friendly assurances it contains." If Welles had written such a letter in response to Wilkes' complaints, the navy would very likely have avoided a messy and public court-martial.[36]

Welles' tendency to chastise, however, was as instinctive as Lincoln's was to soothe, for he believed it was his duty to insist on rigorous accountability. When his brother-in-law George Morgan asked him if he didn't think it was "time to bury all differences," Welles responded that "you evidently suppose that I have something personal in court martialing Wilkes." Not so, he insisted. Wilkes had brought it all upon himself. "I bore with his conduct what few would have borne" until "no alternative was left but a court." Whether or not that was true, Welles' pettifoggery and his refusal to coddle men who, in his view, valued their own reputations above their service to the country dragged the navy through the public press in a series of indecorous courts-martial that did nothing to advance the war effort. He never regretted it, and blamed it all on the admirals themselves. "I treated both Dupont and Wilkes as light as was possible," he insisted in a letter to his son, "but shall likely have the ill-will of both." He was right. For the rest of their lives the two men excoriated Welles at every opportunity in both their private letters and in their public memoirs.[37]

Significantly, however, neither Du Pont nor Wilkes blamed Lincoln for their difficulties, though both men believed that he allowed Welles and Fox to make too many independent decisions. Lincoln's willingness to listen sympathetically, his refusal to directly criticize his subordinates, and his ability to salve wounded egos with kind words convinced both disappointed admirals that the president was their friend, even when he acquiesced in their dismissals. It was one of Lincoln's great gifts that almost everyone who left his office, even if he failed to accomplish whatever mission had brought him there, did so with a powerful sense of the president's personal concern for his problem. Partly this was due to Lincoln's natural empathy, but it was also a measure of his political skill.

Perhaps the most astute comment about this particular aspect of Lincoln's personality came from Sophie Du Pont, the admiral's loyal wife. When Du Pont was trying to decide if he should take Welles' mean-spirited letter to the president, Sophie convinced him it would do no good because, she declared, Lincoln would treat him the same way he had treated "another officer much aggrieved who appealed to him—pat him on the shoulder and say, 'Well, well, my dear Admiral, it *is* a hard case, I own, but you see, in times like these, of war and trouble, when we have such difficulty to get along, each one must be willing to suffer something for the country, etc., etc.'" If Lincoln never used those exact words, they nevertheless captured the spirit of his management style as well as his convictions. Sophie meant the comment to be a criticism, suggesting that Lincoln put politics ahead of justice. In fact, of course, it reflected his determination to put the good of the country ahead of personal ambition. He expected his admirals—and his generals—to tolerate inconvenience and disappointment for the good of the cause. The broader goals of Union and victory were more important than anyone's personal trials, including his own.[38]

EVEN AS HE CONTINUED to prosecute the war, Lincoln remained very much a political animal, sensitive to the shifting, sometimes fickle currents in the public mood. Lincoln kept a close eye on the elections that fall in Pennsylvania, Ohio, and New York for signs that his fragile coalition was holding. He was pleased and relieved when he learned on October 13, 1863, that the election returns in both Pennsylvania and Ohio were favorable to the Union cause. Early in the day, Chase wired him from Ohio promising "complete victory" and projecting a ten-thousand-vote margin over the Democrats. By the afternoon, new estimates showed a margin of twenty thousand votes, and by the end of the day the editors of the *Cincinnati Gazette* were predicting a sixty-thousand-vote victory. Two weeks later, Seward wired him that New York, too, was holding firm.[39]

Heartening as this news was, the more serious political threat came from within Lincoln's own party. Conservative Republicans supported the president so long as it was evident that his primary goal—indeed, his only goal—was saving the Union. They were lukewarm to the idea that the party should ensure the permanence or universality of emancipation, and most of them opposed the proposition of granting citizenship or other civil rights to the former slaves. More progressive Republicans, such as Chase, pressed Lincoln not only to make emancipation permanent and universal but also to make a commitment to civil rights for blacks. Lincoln was entirely committed to emancipation in the rebellious South, and encouraged programs by which the border states could undertake voluntary emancipation, but he made no specific commitments either way about civil rights for blacks. On this, as on other issues, Lincoln kept both branches of his party in the fold by postponing the moment when he had to choose between them.

In a cabinet meeting later that winter, Lincoln told a story about a black preacher who told his parishioners that there were "two roads for you" and they must "be careful," for one road led "straight to hell," and the other went "right to damnation." Upon consideration of this warning, the parishioner responded: "Josh, take which road you please, I go troo de wood." Similarly, on the twinned issues of Reconstruction and black citizenship, Lincoln chose neither the conservative road nor the radical one, each of which was sown with political land mines, but attempted to thrash his way through the middle wood. Lincoln had not entirely given up on the idea of colonization, but he knew, too, that colonization could serve only as a safety valve for those freedmen who sought overseas sanctuary. He was very much aware that most of the freed slaves would necessarily remain in America, and eventually he, as president, would play the key role in defining their legal status within the Republic.[40]

That issue—defining the legal status of freedmen—threatened to fracture Lincoln's party even as it celebrated its election victories in October and November, and it led to some jockeying for position among those who sought to succeed Lincoln as president. On the very day that Lincoln delivered his poetic dedicatory speech at Gettysburg in November, the *New York Herald* reported that "the political pot is beginning to boil," and noted that Lincoln faced a serious challenge for renomination within his own party. Half the men in Lincoln's cabinet had been his rivals for the nomination in 1860, and only Bates and Seward had abandoned their ambitions in that regard. Not only had Seward become a staunch supporter and admirer of Lincoln, but he had split with his Machiavellian political adviser, Thurlow Weed. Chase, on the other hand, made little secret of his undiminished ambition, and the Treasury secretary campaigned quietly in Washington and openly in New England and Ohio. In addition, at least half a dozen generals were in the hunt. McClellan looked to be the favorite of the Democrats, and some in the Republican Party agreed with James Gordon Bennett when he wrote that in the midst of war, "it is evident . . . that our next president must be a military man." Bennett suggested nominating either Nathaniel P. Banks or Grant. Among Lincoln's closest associates, only Seward, Stanton, and Welles were innocent of ambition for the presidency, though they frequently squabbled over other matters. Consequently, even as he managed the war, Lincoln remained sensitive to the political fire in his rear. As Bennett put it, "The fears of Mr. Lincoln's advocates are that he may be slaughtered in the house of his friends."[41]

At least none of the navy's high-ranking officers posed a political threat. The most popular of them was Farragut, who arrived in New

York that fall. When Farragut was introduced at a giant rally outside Cooper Union, the crowd "rose to its feet as if instantaneously animated by the same impulse, and broke out into one loud, hearty, prolonged cheer." Resplendent in full uniform, Farragut bowed and smiled, but when called on to make a speech, he replied: "I was invited here this evening not as a politician but as a naval officer . . . , to see the unanimity and the Union feeling which prevails here. But I must leave politics to you, my fellow citizens. I meddle not with politics in the way of speeches. . . . I will endeavor to do my duty on the sea while you do yours here." It was exactly the kind of public statement Lincoln might have scripted for him if he could, and it drew sustained applause from the audience.[42]

Characteristically, Lincoln was able to make light of the fact that several of his closest advisers, both civil and military, were actively maneuvering for his job. Pressed to comment about national politics at another public meeting in November, he, like Farragut, declined to make a speech, but as was often the case, he was willing to tell a story. This one was about "the Widow Zollicoffer's Darkey," and this is how the reporter of the *New York Herald* recorded it:

> The widow, while making her jam, was called away to a neighbor who was about increasing the population. (Loud laughter.) "Sam, you rascal," she said, "you'll be eating my jam while I'm away." Sam protested he'd die first; but the whites of his eyes rolled hungrily towards the bubbling crimson. "See here, Sam," said the widow, taking up a piece of chalk, "I'll chalk your lips, and then on my return I'll know if you've eaten any." So saying, she placed her fore finger heavily over the thick lips of her darkey, holding the chalk in the palm of her hand, and not letting it touch him. Well, when she came back, Sam's lips were chalked a quarter of an inch thick, and she needed against him no other evidence. (Laughter.)

Like most of Lincoln's stories, this one had a message, and in case anyone had missed it, Lincoln remarked that

> it is much the same about the Presidency. (Renewed mirth.) A good friend of mine declares that he wouldn't take it at any price; but his

lips were thickly chalked when he came back from Ohio. (Great merriment, in which Mr. Chase joined heartily.) So were General Fremont's out in Missouri when he pushed his "emancipation order;" and General Butler's were not only chalked, but had the jam on, and had it thick. Secretary Seward once chalked very badly, but had given it up as of no use since his quarrel with the machine proprietor of his own state [Weed]. (Loud laughter.) Mingled chalk and jam might be seen on the lips of General Banks; while the same compound formed quite a paste around the orifice through which his good friend Governor [Horatio] Seymour [of New York] supplied the wants of nature. (Roars of laughter.) He had never seen chalk on the lips of Secretary Stanton or General Henry W. Halleck; but, with these exceptions, there was scarcely a man connected with the army who did not chalk his lips. (Continued mirth. . . .)[43]

With so many potential rivals, Lincoln appreciated Welles not only for his efforts in managing the navy but also for the fact that he didn't chalk his lips.

THE NEXT DAY, Lincoln was ordered to his bed when his doctor determined that he had contracted a mild case of what was then called "varioloid" and which is now called smallpox. It was not life-threatening, but Lincoln had to curtail his activities. From his sickbed he learned that Joe Hooker had driven the rebel forces from atop Lookout Mountain, west of Chattanooga, effectively breaking the rebel siege of the city, and a few days later, Grant drove the enemy away from Chattanooga altogether after a spectacular assault straight up Missionary Ridge. Lincoln fired off a telegram to Grant thanking him for the victory and reminding him to "remember Burnside," who himself was besieged in Knoxville. It was not necessary. After Missionary Ridge, the rebels abandoned Tennessee, their main army falling back into northern Georgia, where it went into winter camp. In Virginia, too, the armies went into camp, and the campaign season came to an end.[44]

Much had been accomplished. The Mississippi River once again flowed, in Lincoln's felicitous phrase, "unvexed to the sea"; Lee's extended raid into Pennsylvania had been turned back and his army badly weakened; Grant had not only captured Pemberton's rebel army at Vicksburg virtually intact but also mauled Bragg's army at Chattanooga and driven it into Georgia. While the rebel flag still flew at Charleston, the city had been effectively closed to illicit trade. To be sure, the war was not over: two great rebel armies—one at Dalton, Georgia, now under Joseph E. Johnston, and the other waiting behind the line of the Rappahannock and Rapidan Rivers in Virginia under the always dangerous Robert E. Lee—remained intact and in the field. Nevertheless, by the end of 1863 it was possible to believe that the war would not last forever.

Almost as good as this military news was a series of reports about a resurgence in Union sentiment across the Confederate South. From Mississippi, Lorenzo Thomas reported "a growing Union feeling" in that state; a few days later Edmund Fowler, an expatriate Alabamian, told Lincoln that pro-Union candidates had won election to the legislature there; and on October 30, Unionists met in Fort Smith, Arkansas, to discuss reunion. Lincoln had always believed that there was a large latent Union element in the Confederacy, and now he dared hope that reunion might be at hand. Such hopes were premature in the fall of 1863, but they did encourage Lincoln to begin to piece together a plan for postwar reconstruction of the rebellious states.[45]

On December 8, the same day he delivered his annual message to Congress, Lincoln took his first steps toward defining a postwar America in a "Proclamation of Amnesty and Reconstruction." To any citizen willing to take an oath of allegiance (an oath the president wrote himself), Lincoln offered a "full pardon" and the restoration of all property "except as to slaves." Despite rumors (or hopes) that Lincoln might backslide on the question of emancipation, the prescribed oath pledged all citizens to support not only the Constitution but also "all proclamations of the President made during the existing rebellion," including the Emancipation Proclamation. Lincoln also declared that new state governments could begin to organize as soon as a number of qualified voters equal to 10 percent of those who had voted in the last presidential election took the new oath of allegiance, a condition that soon gave Lincoln's plan its popular label as "the Ten Percent Plan."[46]

Lincoln remained deliberately vague about the precise status of the former slaves in these reconstructed states: he was still seeking the middle ground (taking to the woods) on these sensitive issues. His sensitivity to what the public, both North and South, would tolerate compelled him to proclaim only what was likely to command the support of the broad majority of white citizens. Consequently, he did not specify citizenship, suffrage, or any other civil rights for the former slaves, and the only program for which he openly declared his support was public education. This was partly because Lincoln valued free public education as the means by which the landless poor could make something of themselves, but in addition he very likely calculated that the notion of freed slaves going to school would be less worrisome to the white population than the specter of blacks breaking out of their traditional roles as landless laborers. Lincoln therefore declared that he would support any state provision that recognized the "permanent freedom" of the former slaves and which provided for their education, even if it remained "consistent with their present condition as a laboring, landless, and homeless class."[47]

Once again, Lincoln had perceptively gauged the public mood. Hay thought "the immediate effect" of Lincoln's proposal was "something wonderful." "Men acted as if the millennium had come." Lincoln's strong position against slavery captivated the radicals and completely cut the ground from under Chase's presidential bid. At the same time, his caution in specifying limited civil and property rights for the freedmen eased the fears of conservatives. Of course, this Ten Percent Plan was no more Lincoln's last word on Reconstruction than the Chiriqui scheme represented his last word on black settlement. It was simply all that circumstances would allow in December 1863. In his private correspondence, he offered a number of hints that he might be willing to go further as circumstances allowed. In a letter to a southern planter who asked how the government would react if plantations began to employ freed slaves under "fair contracts," Lincoln responded that he "would regard such cases with great favor," adding that, as a matter of principle, he should treat the freed slaves "precisely as I would treat the same number of white people in the same relation and condition."[48]

The prospect of eventual peace also led Lincoln to consider the legal status of the defeated rebels. From the beginning, he had insisted that the United States remained a single country, and he was eager to reembrace the truly repentant, especially those who had been either coerced into rebellion or merely swept along by the current of events. The same inclination that led him to issue pardons or to commute the sentences of those accused of treason or cowardice also led him to offer pardons to the former rebels. If the country was ever going to come together, it must begin by forgiving, not punishing. The more generous his terms, he hoped, the sooner the war might end. On his own, he initiated a secret mission to the coast of Florida, arming John Hay with a sheaf of blank amnesty forms and sending him to Dahlgren at Port Royal, who escorted him to the Florida coast in an effort to establish a reconstruction government there. Hay failed to get 10 percent of the voters to sign on ("the President's 10th," Hay called it), and without that Lincoln decided he could not proceed. Meanwhile, the president urged even those who had always been loyal to take the oath. "It does not hurt them," he wrote to Tennessee's Unionist governor, Andrew Johnston; it "clears all question as to their right to vote, and swells the aggregate number who take it."[49]

Success at Gettysburg, at Vicksburg, and at Chattanooga, plus partial success at Charleston, all contributed to Lincoln's new optimism that the war might be entering its final phase. Necessarily, he had focused more attention on military affairs than on naval affairs during the year, giving Welles and Fox a free hand to manage the war at sea, and his laissez-faire approach had produced results. Porter had justified his self-confidence; Dahlgren had proved his zeal; Farragut had demonstrated his loyalty. There was more stability in the naval high command. The loss of Foote had been a blow; the loss of Du Pont and Wilkes, merely inconvenient.

Lincoln's end-of-year comments about the navy were revealing. In his annual message, he made particular note of the rapid emergence and increased importance of the armored fleet. Of the 588 warships carried on the navy's list in December 1863, 75 of them were armored, with more and bigger ironclads on the way. Lincoln saw armored warships as the key to naval supremacy not only in the current war but also in the postwar world. Anticipating the arguments of Alfred Thayer Mahan a generation later, Lincoln wrote, "Our country has advantages superior to any other nation in our resources of iron and timber, with inexhaustible quantities of fuel in the immediate vicinity of both, and all available and in close proximity to navigable waters." Although "other governments have been making large expenditures . . . with a view to attain naval supremacy," it seemed likely to him that "this government is destined to occupy a leading position among maritime powers." After he wrote this passage, however, he (or perhaps Seward) decided that the British might construe it as too direct a challenge to their maritime supremacy, and he deleted it, replacing it with a slightly less confrontational sentence: "The events of the war give an increased interest and importance to the navy which will probably extend beyond the war itself."[50]

Before this Mahanian vision could be fulfilled, however, there was still the war to be won.

1864

FULL SPEED AHEAD

10

"A Worthy Object"

Lincoln and the Red River Campaign

THE NEW YEAR BEGAN AMIDST A SURGE OF OPTIMISM. Like many others, Lincoln hoped—even expected—that 1864 would be the year the war ended. After the spectacular Union triumphs of the previous year, it seemed impossible that the secessionists could hold out much longer. Lincoln's hopes soared in May when it appeared that Grant had won a slugfest in the tangle of Virginia undergrowth known as the Wilderness, and he began to believe that the war might be brought to an end that summer. Lincoln closely followed the news of Grant's operations in Virginia and, as much as he could, Sherman's in Georgia, but he focused as well on the looming election. In his own mind, the military campaigns and the national election were inextricably linked. Just as a perceived lack of progress in the war could affect the outcome of the election, Lincoln feared that his own failure at the polls would mean defeat in the war. Even more than usual, war and politics intertwined in the winter and spring of 1864.

One military campaign that demonstrated this clearly was the combined operation that spring by Major General Nathaniel P. Banks and Rear Admiral David Dixon Porter to advance up the Red River to Shreveport, Louisiana, the first step toward an invasion of east Texas. Though obviously a military campaign, the rationale behind it derived less from military considerations than from economic, diplomatic, and political factors, and it illuminated the variety of pressures that informed Lincoln's decision making.

The initial pressure that encouraged Lincoln to look toward Texas was the North's hunger for southern cotton. If oil is the "black gold" of the modern world economy, with obvious consequences for policy makers and war planners, cotton was the "white gold" of the nineteenth century. From the beginning of the war, Confederate officials had insisted that cotton was their secret weapon. The world's need for cotton was so great, they believed, the lack of it would compel the powers of Europe to support the southern bid for independence lest they lose access to it. On the basis of that assumption, southerners had embargoed their own cotton back in 1861, when the Union blockade was so porous it would have been relatively easy to ship large amounts overseas to establish foreign credits. By the time southern lawmakers realized their error, the blockade had become more efficient and the opportunity was lost. Fat bales of cotton, with the "white gold" spilling out of their brown jute wrapping, piled up on the wharves of Charleston, Galveston, and Mobile. Confederate government officials urged planters to forgo another cotton crop and instead plant corn, sweet potatoes, and other staples that could feed the embattled rebel armies. Cotton production dropped from four and a half million bales in 1861 to half a million bales in 1863, but even this reduced amount could not find a ready market because of the blockade. Fox waxed biblical in telling John Hay that the rebellion was sustained "not by what entereth into their ports but by what proceedeth out." If the navy could prevent cotton exports, he insisted, the Confederate economy would collapse.[1]

The glut of cotton in the South frustrated not only the southern planters, who couldn't sell, but also the New England mill owners, who couldn't buy, for without southern cotton their spindles and looms fell silent. By the second summer of the war, only a quarter of the three and a half million spindles in New England were still operating. This naturally brought political pressure on Lincoln to act. Massachusetts governor John Andrew wrote Fox that his constituents were eager for the navy to make a lodgment on the coast of Texas to "open a way out for cotton." Andrew's goal was ideological as well as economic. He hoped to populate the coast of Texas with New England immigrants who would prove "that cotton can be raised without slaves." Naturally sympathetic, and always politically sensitive, Lincoln authorized the Massachusetts politician-turned-general Nathaniel P. Banks to lead an expedition to the Texas coast in the fall of 1862.* By the time Banks got ready to move, however, the political pressures had shifted. In the November elections that year, Democrats made large gains in the Midwest, including Lincoln's home state of Illinois. Politically, the opening of the Mississippi became more urgent than the possession of coastal Texas, and Lincoln redirected Banks to New Orleans to supersede Benjamin Butler and cooperate with Grant in the conquest of the Mississippi. The pressure from New England mill owners for access to cotton never faded, however, and while Grant besieged Vicksburg, a second and completely unrelated event brought even more pressure on Lincoln to push an expedition into Texas.[2]

On June 7, 1863, a French army marched into Mexico City. Ostensibly, the French were there to collect unpaid debts, but it was evident that Napoleon III hoped to use the circumstances to annex Mexico as part of a revived French empire. This move alarmed Lincoln less because it violated the Monroe Doctrine than because it had the potential to draw the United States into a foreign conflict. The French presence in Mexico might even lead to a Franco-Confederate rapprochement, with disastrous consequences. Three weeks after the fall of Vicksburg, therefore, Lincoln wrote Stanton to suggest a renewal of the effort "to organize a force to go into Western Texas." Hay noted in his diary that "the tycoon" was "very anxious that Texas should be occupied and firmly held in view of French possibilities." With the French in mind, Lincoln wrote again to Banks urging him to reprise his Texas plans. "Recent events in Mexico," he wrote, "render early action in Texas more important than ever," and based on that, Seward sent Banks new instructions. Once established on the Rio Grande, he was to maintain a scrupulous

---

*The historian Ludwell Johnson has plausibly speculated that Lincoln conceived of Banks' expedition to Texas much as he did McClernand's expedition to Vicksburg. Just as he appointed a Democratic general from Illinois to open the Mississippi in order to quiet complaints from that state, he appointed a Democratic general from Massachusetts to quiet complaints from that quarter about the scarcity of cotton. It provided employment for two influential War Democrats and showed the constituents of each area that he listened to their concerns.

neutrality and prevent supplies from being sent to either side, but above all he was to take no part in the conflict. "These directions," Seward told him, "result from the fixed determination of the President to avoid any departure from lawful neutrality, and any unnecessary and unlawful enlargement of the present field of war." As ever, Lincoln was determined to fight only one war at a time. Soon thereafter, Banks successfully occupied Brownsville, thus not only blunting a possible French incursion but also closing the Rio Grande to blockade runners.[3]

A third factor that influenced Lincoln's thinking about a campaign on the Red River was his eagerness to establish a functioning Union government in Louisiana. Almost from the first day of the war, Lincoln had considered how to bring the rebellious states back into a satisfactory relationship with the national government. Since Louisiana would be the first rebel state to be reconstructed, Lincoln was anxious to ensure that both the process and the product met the scrutiny of rebels and Unionists alike. On one hand, Lincoln did not want to dictate the specific terms of Louisiana's transformation—any legitimate government, he believed, had to spring from the people themselves. On the other hand, he did have certain goals for the state. The Emancipation Proclamation he had issued a year before affected only those parts of Louisiana not occupied by Union troops as of January 1, 1863, and it was essential, in his mind, that the new government "place the remainder of the state upon the same footing." His great fear was that "a few professedly loyal men" might set up a state government that—however loyal—repudiated emancipation. If that happened, he felt, he would be unable to "recognize or sustain" it. He therefore counted on the politically astute Banks to assemble "a tangible nucleus which the remainder of the State may rally around," and produce a government "which I can at once recognize and sustain." He wanted Banks to be the "master" of the reconstruction process in Louisiana as well as the military commander. Banks responded that he was confident he could restore the state government "upon the basis of an absolute extinction of slavery at the start," and Lincoln told him to "proceed with all possible despatch."[4]

Lincoln was reluctant to sacrifice military progress to either economic or political objectives, but he did believe that the acquisition of southern cotton and the organization of a Union government in Louisiana were of great importance. In explaining his goals in

Louisiana, he noted that while it was important, even essential, to continue the blockade, it was also "immensely important to us to get the cotton," and to do that, some compromises might be necessary. Likewise, it was "a worthy object to again get Louisiana into proper practical relations with the nation," and very likely compromises would be needed there, too. "I do not wish either cotton or the new State Government to take precedence of the military," he wrote, "but there is a strong public reason for treating each with . . . favor."[5]

All these factors—the North's thirst for cotton, the need to secure Texas in the face of a potential threat from France, and the desire to legitimize a Union government in Louisiana—led Lincoln to support a military thrust into east Texas via the Red River. Halleck also strongly supported the idea. He argued that occupation of the trans-Mississippi West would cut off the flow of supplies and starve rebel armies in the east. Not everyone agreed. Grant, who was soon to be elevated to general in chief, believed that Mobile was a far more important military objective than Shreveport, but Grant was a good subordinate, and if the president and Halleck favored a move to Shreveport, he would not complain.

The campaign would necessarily be another army-navy collaboration like Vicksburg or Charleston, and like those campaigns, the army and navy commanders (in this case Banks and Porter) would be equal partners with no unified commander. This time, however, the awkward command structure would be exacerbated by bickering over the spoils of war, and in particular all that stockpiled cotton waiting along the banks of the river. Cotton prices, which had hovered between 10 and 15 cents a pound through the 1850s, had soared to 65 cents a pound after the war began, and by 1863 cotton commanded as much as a dollar a pound in New England, where a single thousand-pound bale could fetch a sum nearly equal to a year's pay for a navy lieutenant. Even before the campaign was under way, concern over French imperialism, the size and character of the new Louisiana government, and even the war itself often gave way before the furious competition over the South's "white gold," and inevitably Lincoln himself was drawn into the squabbling.

FROM THE MOMENT Union forces occupied the lower Mississippi River, the War, Treasury, and Navy Departments had attempted to assert their authority over captured or abandoned rebel cotton. Legislation passed in 1862 and modified in March 1863 allowed U.S. Treasury Department agents to seize the cotton of disloyal persons and collect a reward—a kind of finders' fee—based on its market value. But as a practical matter, Treasury agents necessarily followed in the wake of the armies, and they were soon complaining to Secretary Chase that the army "seizes all cotton & all sugar found as the army advances," and once seized, it tended to remain in the jurisdiction of the War Department.[6]

When the army didn't get there first, the navy did. Back in December 1862, Porter had issued a general order directing all his captains to refuse to permit "any commerce to be carried on at any points not occupied by United States troops, no matter what permits they may have, unless they are mine." When in March of 1863 Welles ordered squadron commanders to turn over seized property to Treasury agents, Porter dutifully issued a revised general order. Porter's directive did not cover all contingencies. What, for example, was a ship commander to do if he encountered abandoned cotton bales piled up on the river bank? Welles' directive was pretty clear: All "abandoned, captured, or seized" property "shall be delivered to the said agents of the Treasury Department." When Lieutenant Joseph P. Couthouy, commanding the gunboat *Chillicothe*, came upon five unmarked bales of cotton lying abandoned on the riverbank, he asked his immediate superior a loaded question: "Shall I take the five bales of cotton on board as abandoned property—or leave them to be shipped by speculators or burned, as they may be any dark night."[7]

To answer such questions, Porter issued a third general order in October 1863 that essentially applied the prize laws used by the navy on the high seas to the Mississippi Valley: all enemy property—including cotton—was to be seized as a prize of war and sent to the prize court at Cairo for adjudication.[8] This was inconsistent with Welles' directive to "turn over all such property to the agent appointed by the Secretary of the Treasury," but to a navy man, it was a straightforward and even obvious solution. Prize law had ruled captures at sea for centuries; the possibility of prize money was the principal incentive held out by the government to encourage navy enlistments. Under that law, half of the value of all goods captured by U.S. Navy vessels and condemned by the prize courts went into a special fund for the support of disabled seamen. The other half was divided among the captors, with larger shares going to the officers and smaller shares to the enlisted men. Captains on the block-ade could, and did, make considerable fortunes seizing blockade run-ners, and even crewmen on a particularly lucky ship could emerge from the war with substantial nest eggs. There was nothing revolutionary about applying those same laws to captures made on the western rivers. Porter's order, however, became the subject of criticism not only be-cause Porter himself stood to benefit personally but also because, un-like captures on the high seas, the navy was now competing with the War Department and the Treasury Department.

In addition to the competition among government agencies, there were also legions of opportunists and entrepreneurs, both northern and southern, many of them politically connected, who hoped to make their fortunes in the cotton trade. They sought and often received li-censes from Chase's Treasury Department that allowed them to enter enemy territory and trade for cotton. The licenses required army and navy officials not only to allow these entrepreneurs free passage, but to protect and aid them in their work. Unsurprisingly, Welles expressed his "unequivocal opposition to the whole system of trade permits." As far as he was concerned, "if there is to be trade with the Rebels, let all participate." Despite his general disdain for Welles, Porter agreed. He could not understand how licensing trade with the enemy contributed to the war effort, and he was openly dismissive of the motives of Trea-sury agents, most of whom he considered mere charlatans. When Thomas Yeatman, the Treasury agent at Memphis, complained to him that his gunboats were interfering with the cotton trade, Porter shot back that he planned to seize "every vessel that attempts to trade except under the guard of a gunboat." This business of trading with the en-emy, he declared, was incomprehensible. "I know of but one way to carry on war, and that is to deprive these people of every hope of com-fort and means of living until they go down on their knees and beg for mercy. As to the cotton, I would like to see it all burned, for it has led to nothing but dishonesty." For all his outraged sensibilities, however, Porter was not so fastidious as to discourage his captains from seizing cotton wherever they found it.[9]

When Banks assumed command in New Orleans, he found that illicit trade with the enemy—with or without permits—was not only com-monplace but had a quasi-official character, since it had been condoned and even supported by Butler. Indeed, Butler's brother Andrew was one of the most notorious practitioners. After Banks assumed command, Andrew Butler coolly offered him $100,000 if he would simply allow the trade to continue. Banks rejected that offer and instead instituted a new program inviting local planters who professed loyalty to the Union government to bring their cotton to any one of several depots under U.S. military control. Half the crop would go to the Treasury agents "for the benefit of the Government," while the planters would be paid for the other half in greenbacks and U.S. government bonds. Banks reasoned that even if the planters who participated were less than fully loyal, his system would strengthen their loyalty, for without an eventual Union victory their greenbacks and bonds would be worthless. The cotton that went to the Treasury Department would be sold to New England mill owners, or to Europeans for gold, which would help alleviate the nation's gold drain.[10]

Chase agreed that gaining access to southern cotton might be a partial solution to the fluctuation of gold prices,* but he was unhappy with what he called "the Banks policy," because it took control of the cotton trade out of the hands of his Treasury Department agents. Stanton disliked it because it cut out the War Department, for he, too, had taken to issuing trade permits. Welles, of course, insisted that neither Chase nor Stanton should be in the business of authorizing trade with the enemy in the first place. He reminded his colleagues that the navy's goal was to *stop* trade by enforcing the blockade, and he did not see how allowing southern planters to sell their cotton contributed to that goal. Given his tendency to view most issues in terms of absolute right and wrong, he bluntly reminded Chase that this was war, after all.[11]

As usual, Lincoln adopted a wait-and-see attitude, encouraging programs that promised to work, then backing off when it appeared they

---

*The gold drain was mainly a product of having to pay for many imports in specie while taxes were generally paid with paper money—the so-called greenbacks. The greenbacks held their value so long as the public was confident that the government could meet its obligations. By 1864, the fluctuation in the price of gold had become an index of Union battlefield success. When Union armies won victories, confidence in the greenbacks rose and the price of gold fell; when Union armies suffered a setback, confidence plummeted and the price of gold rose. Lincoln could get a quick snapshot of public opinion simply by checking the daily price of gold in the New York markets.

had the potential to create more problems than solutions. As with so many things, he did not delineate a proactive policy regarding enemy cotton; instead he weighed and measured on a case-by-case basis the proposals that came to him. He was not averse to issuing trade permits—especially when the requests came from well-connected citizens. Nicolay and Hay recalled, "The pressure upon him to grant these permits was almost incredible, and he sometimes . . . gave way to it."[12]

The most infamous of Lincoln's personal interventions in the cotton trade, later seized on by his political enemies to discredit him, was the license he granted to Samuel Casey in December 1863. Casey was a former congressman from Kentucky who privately arranged to buy twenty thousand bales of Confederate cotton from Edmund Kirby Smith, the senior Confederate officer in the trans-Mississippi West. Apparently part of the arrangement was a secret understanding that Kirby Smith would not burn the stockpiled cotton along the Red River if Casey agreed to pay him for it in hard cash at a bargain price of $100 per bale. In his own hand, Lincoln wrote out an order directing "all Military and Naval commanders" to give Casey "protection and safe-conduct" while he brought cotton shipments out of the Red River Valley. Without question, this was trading with the enemy. The rebels would get $2 million in much-needed specie, but on the other hand New England mill owners would get fifteen times that value in cotton, and the government would get as much in new bond sales. Whatever benefit it provided the enemy, Lincoln concluded that it was "a worthy object" and that "it would be a public injury to have the cotton destroyed." Aware, no doubt, that such an arrangement would draw criticism, Lincoln sought to shield himself by requiring Casey to sign an agreement pledging to carry out the exchange at his own expense, to make no claim on Lincoln or the U.S. government for "any contingency whatever," and promising that he would "take absolutely nothing into the insurgent lines, which could be of value to them." Besides money, of course.[13]

A few days later, in January of the new year, Lincoln received a proposal from three well-connected entrepreneurs who claimed that there was a large number of secret loyalists in Louisiana who were hiding their cotton from rebel authorities. The petitioners declared themselves willing to go get the cotton, bring it out, and invest the proceeds in

U.S. government bonds. On the surface this looked promising. It would benefit the secret Unionists that Lincoln had always believed existed in the South, and it would shore up the Union economy. But Lincoln was wary. He wanted to know if these sellers of cotton (which Lincoln spelled "cotten") would be required to take the loyalty oath. He wondered, too, why having private individuals get the cotton was better than simply sending the military to get it. Still, Lincoln leaned toward giving them the go-ahead until Chase expressed his strong opposition. Almost certainly, Chase simply wanted to keep the management of southern cotton in the hands of the Treasury Department, though a few suspected that Chase also hoped to use his control of that trade as a pawn in the forthcoming presidential campaign.[14]

Though by now full cabinet meetings had become a rarity, Lincoln turned to his cabinet for a solution to the cotton trade issue, hoping that some consensus would emerge. Chase defended his reliance on trade permits issued to selected individuals, but Welles wanted to know why, if they were going to trade with the enemy at all, did they not open the whole region to trade? In effect that is what Lincoln did. Though he left Chase's Treasury Department in charge of it, he issued a new regulation "Concerning Commercial Intercourse with and in States Declared in Insurrection," the heart of which simply ordered that "property brought in for sale in good faith . . . shall be exempt from confiscation."[15]

Lincoln also stopped writing trade permits. When the governor of Ohio, William Dennison, wrote him in March to request consideration for a friend who was "anxious to improve his fortunes by purchasing of Cotton in Mississippi & adjoining states," Lincoln told Nicolay to reply that the "President thinks he cannot safely write that class of letters," though he might have added "anymore."[16]

When Casey learned of the pending expedition up the Red River by Banks and Porter, he became alarmed. Not without reason, he feared that Porter's gunboat captains would gobble up all the cotton they found as they moved upriver, which would surely cause Kirby Smith to burn the rest of the stockpiled cotton in Porter's path. The whole arrangement would come undone. Casey wrote to Lincoln in a panic, telling him, "Do not let Admiral Porter send an expedition up the Red River until you hear from me again," and two days later he followed this up with another plea to "have it [the expedition] delayed if you can."[17]

As it happened, the expedition was delayed, but not because Lincoln ordered it. Indeed, it almost didn't get started at all. Major General Frederick Steele in Arkansas, whose force was to cooperate with Banks, declared himself unwilling to make the march southward into Louisiana unless he was assured that a supply depot would be waiting for him when he arrived. Sherman, who had initially expected to command the expedition himself, now agreed to send Andrew Jackson Smith's veteran corps, but only if Banks pledged to return the men no later than the middle of April so that they could participate in the spring campaign in Georgia. All this negotiating was necessary because no one was in overall command. Banks, Steele, Sherman, and Porter were all independent of one another, and instead of giving them specific orders, Halleck merely told them to communicate "in regard to some general co-operation, and agree upon what is the best plan," which was hardly a blueprint for success.[18]

For his part, Porter professed to be ready to move as soon as the winter rains raised the Red River enough to float his gunboats, but all three of the generals involved found reasons to delay. Steele insisted that the circumstances in his theater were so precarious he could not leave just yet; Sherman was engaged in an extended raid into central Mississippi; and Banks was busy overseeing the election and subsequent inauguration of Louisiana's first reconstruction governor, Michael Hahn, an event in which Lincoln had a special interest. Indeed, for the president, the political organization of Louisiana's government was at least as important as the military expedition up the Red River. Lincoln was pleased to hear from Banks that eleven thousand citizens had participated in the election and that Hahn and his allies were "earnest, faithful, and efficient friends of your administration." The best news was that "the convention for Revision of the constitution will confirm the absolute extinction of slavery." Lincoln wrote to congratulate Hahn and to suggest privately that perhaps his new government could allow "some of the colored people" to vote, particularly the veterans. He would not order it—that would be inappropriate—but he hoped that Hahn would consider it.

Lincoln was pleased with Banks' political work, but he expressed some concern about his evident overconfidence about the forthcoming military campaign. Banks assured Lincoln that despite the delays, when the Red River campaign started, it would be both "decisive and successful." Lincoln was used to such promises. After reading this one, he remarked, "I am sorry to see this tone of confidence; the next news we hear from there will be of a defeat."[19]

THE SAME WEEK that Porter's gunboats entered the mouth of the Red River, Ulysses S. Grant arrived in Washington, D.C., and checked into Willard's Hotel. The desk clerk at the Willard did not recognize the travel-weary officer in front of him and was ready to assign him to one of the hotel's smaller rooms until he read the signature on the register: "U.S. Grant & son—Galena, Illinois." News of the western hero's arrival soon spread through the capital, and Lincoln sent a message inviting Grant to come over to the White House that night, which, as it happened, was the night of the president's weekly receptions. Lincoln was socializing with his guests when the stolid and taciturn general came into the room. Lincoln greeted him simply and without pretension ("I'm glad to see you, General") before Seward took Grant in tow and squired him about the room to introduce him to various dignitaries.[20]

Grant's arrival in Washington was the product of another shake-up in the Union command structure. Lincoln had long since concluded that for all his theoretical knowledge, Halleck simply lacked the temperament to give orders. Halleck offered innumerable suggestions but almost never issued an unequivocal order; he simply did not want to *command.* Meanwhile, Grant had demonstrated at Fort Donelson, at Vicksburg, at Chattanooga, and elsewhere that command was second nature to him. To honor this new hero of the war, Congress revived the rank of lieutenant general, and Lincoln ordered Grant east to become the new general in chief, making room for him by sliding Halleck into a new position as chief of staff, essentially a glorified clerk who would transmit the orders from Grant to the various field commanders.[21]

Lincoln had never met Grant, and once they were alone together the two men took stock of each other. Lincoln told Grant that he "never professed to be a military man or to know how campaigns should be conducted, and never wanted to interfere in them," but that the procrastination of some of his generals and the expectations of the public had forced him into making a series of military decisions. He conceded that some of these decisions—perhaps all of them—may have been "all wrong." What he wanted, he told his new general in chief, was "some one who would take the responsibility and act." Grant assured the president he would do the best he could. Lincoln did not ask Grant for a plan of operations, nor did Grant offer one. Though the new campaign would not begin until the spring, when the roads dried and there was grass for the horses and mules to eat, Lincoln hoped that he had at last found his general.[22]

While Grant wielded the sword, Lincoln sought to extend the olive branch. He was "very anxious" to spread the news of his amnesty proclamation across the South. In pursuit of that, on February 12 (his own fifty-fifth birthday) he sent for Brigadier General Judson Kilpatrick, a flamboyant and cocky young cavalry leader, to ask him about conducting an extended cavalry raid into Virginia in order to distribute information about his amnesty program. Kilpatrick was enthusiastic, and at Lincoln's suggestion he took the idea to Stanton, proposing to lead a raid by four thousand cavalry to destroy railroads, cut the telegraph, and "make an attempt to release our prisoners" in Richmond while all the time they worked to "scatter the proclamation along the line of march." Kilpatrick's boss, Major General Alfred Pleasanton, was cool to the idea, though he promised to "undertake to have [Lincoln's proclamation] freely circulated in any section of Virginia that may be desired." Meade was more enthusiastic and ordered Kilpatrick to "effect an entrance" into Richmond and "liberate our prisoners." In the process, the original idea of spreading word of Lincoln's amnesty proclamation was overwhelmed by other objects.[23]

Worse, the whole expedition turned into a nightmare of disasters. Richmond was not penetrated, no prisoners were released, and part of Kilpatrick's command, led by Admiral Dahlgren's son Ulric, was ambushed. The admiral was in Washington at the time, and whether he asked the president to do it or Lincoln acted on his own, Lincoln wired Butler at Fort Monroe to find out what he could about Ulric's fate. Initially, Butler wired back that "nothing had been heard." Then two days later he sent another wire: Colonel Dahlgren had been wounded but was "alive and well." Lincoln, "much affected," rushed over to share the news with Admiral Dahlgren and the two men had an emotional meeting.

A few days later, however, Butler wired that the *Richmond Sentinel* was now reporting that young Dahlgren had been killed. Since those same papers also declared that Dahlgren was carrying orders to capture and kill Jefferson Davis—reports that Admiral Dahlgren discounted—both the admiral and the president clung to hope that the report was false.* It was not. Confirmation of the young colonel's death reached Washington on March 10, and if that were not sufficiently devastating, the papers also reported that his body had been mutilated.[24]

Admiral Dahlgren was shattered, and all of Lincoln's natural sympathies were aroused by his friend's grief. Back in June 1862, Lincoln had gratified Dahlgren by asking Stanton to make young Ulric a lieutenant in the army. Stanton had gone one better and made him a captain. The young captain had been severely wounded during the Gettysburg campaign, losing a leg, yet by 1864 he was one of the youngest colonels in the army. Now, a month short of his twenty-second birthday, he was dead. Lincoln did not hold himself responsible for Ulric's death any more than he could shoulder responsibility for the tens of thousands of other deaths the war had caused. His natural sympathy as a friend—and as a father who had lost a son—led him to grieve, as much in sympathy for the father as for the son. But just as he had been compelled to wrench himself out of his personal grief after Willie's death to resume his duties, he could not give in to his sadness now. He had a war to fight.

Dahlgren, however, did surrender to his grief, and a month later he was still virtually immobilized by his loss. Welles called on him to tell him to get out of the house, to "mingle with the world," and try to overcome his despair. Instead, the death of his son, combined with his poor health and the lack of progress at Charleston, led Dahlgren to consider giving up his command. Fox thought that in addition to his grief, his service off Charleston had simply worn him out. "Poor fellow," Fox wrote to Porter, "hard work, forty-two courageous and

---

*Rebel newspapers reported that Dahlgren had on his person an address that he had read to his troopers calling upon them "to destroy and burn the hateful city [of Richmond] and kill the traitor Davis and his cabinet." Kilpatrick admitted that Dahlgren had shown him a speech he intended to give to his soldiers but that it had not contained the language reported in the southern papers.

persistent attacks, poor health, and the papers discussing and cussing him. The square flag is not the pleasant place the Washington Navy Yard was." The problem was that if Dahlgren returned to the Ordnance Bureau, it would displace Henry Wise, who had served as acting chief since Dahlgren's departure and who yearned to be confirmed as permanent Chief. Not only did Wise have Fox in his corner, but the Blair family was backing him, too. Fox concluded that Dahlgren could not be allowed to come home just yet.[25]

Meanwhile, news dribbled in from Louisiana. Lincoln continued his regular visits to the War Department telegraph office, often several times a day. By now he had his own desk there between the telegraph room and Stanton's office, and when he arrived he often gathered up the messages that had come in since his last visit and read through them. On rare occasions, he actually watched over the telegraph operator's shoulder to read the messages as they arrived. There were few telegraphic messages from Louisiana, however, since the closest telegraph office to that front was in Cairo, Illinois, nearly a thousand miles upriver. Porter's first report had to be sent upriver on the ram *Avenger* to Cairo before it could be telegraphed to Washington.[26]

That first dispatch announced the capture of Fort DeRussy, the principal rebel defensive position on the Red River, by A. J. Smith's corps assisted by Porter's gunboats. Porter betrayed his penchant for hyperbole by claiming that Smith's capture of Fort DeRussy was "one of the best military moves made this war." The next day, Porter's gunboats had thrust aside the ineffective barriers the rebels had placed in the river, and arrived safely at Alexandria, well ahead of the army, to find that the enemy had fled. These easy victories led Porter to conclude that the rebels in this part of the country were all bluster and no fight. He boasted: "The efforts of these people to keep up this war remind one very much of the antics of Chinamen, who build canvas forts, paint hideous dragons on their shields, turn somersets, and yell in the faces of their enemies to frighten them, and then run away at the first sign of an engagement." If Welles shared this report with the president, Lincoln might have reprised his thought about too much confidence leading to disappointment.[27]

A week later, Porter reported that "we have captured 2,021 bales of rebel cotton since we came into the river." That simple statement obscured the mad scramble for cotton that was taking place at Alexandria, and indeed all along the Red River Valley. The extent to which Porter instigated this scramble was then, and remains today, a subject of controversy. Certainly Porter was aware of the fortunes that could be made seizing contraband cotton. That first shipment of two thousand bales he forwarded to the prize court in Cairo had a potential market value of as much as $2 million, and according to the prize law, Porter's personal share of that would be $60,000. Unlike Goldsborough, Du Pont, Dahlgren, Lee, and the other commanders of coastal blockading squadrons whose ships made regular, even routine, seizures of valuable blockade runners, Porter had not won a lot of prize money in the war. The previous fall he had bemoaned his strained financial circumstances in a letter to his mother. "My position is one that subjects me to a great expense," he wrote plaintively. "My family is a large one, and the children [are] at that age when they cost me a great deal"—their school bills alone amounted to $684 a year. "When my salary is all whittled down," he noted bitterly, "I have . . . 70 dollars a month [left] to clothe myself in the expensive uniforms the government have foolishly got up." He worried what would happen to his family if an unlucky shot took his life. "I am nearly 50 years of age without a house of my own, and if I was to die tomorrow [my family] would be thrown helpless in[to] the world." A man with such thoughts was not insensitive to what a windfall of $60,000 could mean.[28]

Of course, even if Porter had been as rich as Cornelius Vanderbilt, he still would have encouraged the seizure of southern cotton, for not only was it one of the objects of the campaign, but also he believed it was the navy's job to intercept rebel commerce. Like every other sailor in the squadron, Porter saw no meaningful distinction between capturing a blockade runner loaded with cotton on the high seas and seizing enemy cotton that was piled up along the riverbank. Porter suspected that if he tried to prevent his captains and their crews from taking the cotton as a legitimate prize of war, he might have faced a mutiny. Much later, long after the war was over, he somewhat disingenuously described himself as a passive, even reluctant participant in the acquisition of cotton. "Naval officers complained to me that they were losing a chance to making prize-money," he wrote in 1885, "and they thought they were at least entitled to the cotton along the banks of the river.

I unwisely consented to that." In fact, he didn't have to "consent" because the question simply never came up. Of course the navy would take the cotton.[29]

If cotton along the riverbank was a legitimate prize, what about cotton stored on the farms and in the gin houses a few miles or more away from the river? Where was the line—if there was a line—between taking a lawful prize and simple looting? After taking on board all the cotton stored near the river, bands of sailors and marines headed by petty officers, and sometimes by officers, began to range as far as eight miles from the river to search out cotton, as well as hogs, cattle, and other "contraband." When Frank Howe, one of Chase's Treasury agents, arrived in Alexandria a few days after Porter, he was horrified by the scene of rampant pillaging that met his eye. Howe wrote disapprovingly to Chase that Porter's men were gathering up cotton as fast as they could. The gunboats were stuffed with it, and most of the navy ships towed barges that were filled to overflowing. On shore it was a scene "ludicrous and sad": Marines drove wagon loads of cotton and herded droves of cattle down to the river bank. Naturally this led Kirby Smith, the rebel commander, to burn the stockpiles of cotton upriver from Alexandria. Howe estimated that the enemy had burned fifty thousand bales so far, which not only frustrated Samuel Casey's plan to buy up all that cotton at $100 a bale but also frustrated Howe's ambition to take it into custody on behalf of the Treasury Department. It is not clear whether Howe was more appalled by the pillaging, by the loss of those fifty thousand bales, or by the fact that the navy had beaten him to the cotton. The most condemnatory thing he could think to say about the behavior of Porter's men was that it "was worthy of a New York Mob."[30]

Porter looked upon it all with a benign paternalism. Occasionally local planters complained that his sailors had taken ("stolen") the cotton of loyal citizens. When one woman claiming to be a loyal Unionist complained to Porter that his men had taken seven bales of cotton from her, Porter allowed her to choose any seven bales she pleased from what had been collected. Some officers did try to make a distinction between "enemy" cotton and "loyalist" cotton. When James Greer in the USS *Benton* arrived at a plantation just above Fort DeRussy, the owner, a Mr. Brochard, earnestly professed his loyalty to Lincoln's government, though when Greer questioned Brochard's slaves, they told him that the man was a committed rebel. His wife, they said, was the widow of a Confederate officer and Brochard had married her to get her property. Greer decided to take the cotton. A few days later, Greer encountered another planter who forthrightly confessed that he had been a Confederate up to now but was willing to take the loyalty oath if it meant he could keep his cotton. Greer took his cotton, too.[31]

Most navy foraging parties didn't bother with making distinctions between Confederate cotton and cotton belonging to self-professed Unionists. Hoping to validate their seizures as legitimate prizes of war, they took to stenciling "CSA" on all the cotton they found. On at least one occasion, they seized a barn full of raw cotton, ginned it and baled it, then marked the bales "CSA" before taking them into custody. The foraging parties then marked the seized bales "USN" to make sure that Treasury or War Department officials did not claim it. The number of bales marked with both "CSA" and "USN" labels led to jests that the initials stood for "Cotton Stealing Association of the United States Navy."[32]

When Banks and his army arrived in Alexandria, a number of businessmen bearing trade licenses arrived in his wake. They were even more disappointed than Chase's Treasury agents to find that most of the cotton had been swept up by the efficient foraging parties of Porter's squadron. Though Porter believed that Banks sponsored these speculators, the general refused to give them permission to trade, and at least one of them complained to Porter that even though he possessed "Treasury permits to buy cotton," Banks refused to honor them, and he asked Porter for permission "to buy at points below here on the Red River, also on the Black and Ouachita rivers." It also annoyed Porter that Banks seemed to be more interested in holding elections than he was in getting on with the campaign. Porter thought Banks ought to push on upriver at once. Instead, Banks rounded up all the male inhabitants of Alexandria and urged them to vote, promising amnesty for those who did and (in Porter's words) "threatening . . . his displeasure" if they declined. Despite Porter's annoyance, Banks knew that as far as Lincoln was concerned, holding elections in support of Louisiana's new government was one of the principal goals of the campaign. He was not alone in so thinking. The lead story in the *New York*

Tribune the next week was "Louisiana to be a Free State." Only further down in the column did the paper announce "Our Army and Navy Off to Shreveport."[33]

IN WASHINGTON, MEANWHILE, plans continued apace for the big spring offensive in Virginia. Grant had decided to keep Meade in command of the Army of the Potomac, but Grant himself would travel with it, like an admiral embarked on a flagship, to direct overall operations. Ambrose Burnside's Ninth Corps would move separately but cooperatively, and out in the West, Sherman would advance against the rebel army in north Georgia under Joseph E. Johnston. Smaller Union armies under Franz Sigel and Benjamin Butler would operate in the Shenandoah Valley and on the Virginia peninsula. Just as Lincoln had often urged, Union forces would move against the enemy at several places simultaneously.[34]

On April 25, Burnside's command of forty thousand men marched through the capital en route to the front. It was a magnificent sight as regiment after regiment snaked down Fourteenth Street and across the Long Bridge into Virginia. It took several hours for the column of soldiers in blue to pass, and John Hay thought it "the finest looking & best appointed force I have ever yet seen," though it reminded him a little of "the early regiments who went shining down to Bull Run." Nevertheless, it was both a stirring symbol of Union strength and a reminder of how much the world had changed since that other spring day three years before when Lincoln had gone out to the street to watch the arrival of the New York 7th regiment.[35]

The day after that stirring parade, there was another report from Louisiana. Banks had finally agreed to advance from Alexandria to Shreveport, and Porter had steamed upriver in advance of the army. He was halted briefly by a vessel the enemy had sunk across the river below Shreveport, but just as Porter had cleared that barrier and was approaching the town, he received a message from Banks announcing that the army had met a "reverse" and was falling back. "Here was a pretty kettle of fish for us," Porter wrote afterward to a newspaper correspondent, "with fifty vessels in a narrow river, and a victorious rebel army . . . between us and 'snug harbor.'" Porter had no choice but to retreat as well, subjecting his vessels to a series of ambushes from the riverbank.

During that retreat, the small stern-wheel *Cricket*, which Porter was using as a flagship, came under what Porter called "the heaviest fire I ever witnessed." In one five-minute period, it was struck thirty-eight times from batteries along the river bank and suffered twenty-five casualties—virtually half its crew.[36]

Though Porter made light of this harrowing retreat in his postwar writings, at the time he was pushed to the edge of panic, and his anxiety was evident in his confidential report to Welles. He began by telling Welles, "The whole affair has been seriously mismanaged." Just as he had earlier claimed that A. J. Smith's capture of Fort DeRussy was "one of the best military moves made this war," so he now asserted that Banks' campaign was "the worst managed affair that I ever heard of." What concerned him most was his fear that the army's need for naval support might keep the bulk of the Mississippi Squadron trapped in the river until the water became too shallow for his gunboats to escape. Porter wrote that he could save the squadron if he left at once, but that would mean abandoning the army, which he knew would be "a stain upon the Navy for all time to come." At the same time, Porter could easily—perhaps too easily—imagine a scenario in which the army might run away and abandon *him*, and he was annoyed by the mere thought of it. "I do not see why a fleet should not have the protection of an army as well as an army have the protection of a fleet." Though later he affected an attitude of unconcern ("I was quite indifferent whether they [the army] went away or not."), at the time he felt trapped in a conundrum and uncertain what to do about it. Should he stay by the army and risk his fleet, or save the fleet and leave Banks to get himself out of his own scrape? Perhaps the most telling indication of Porter's state of mind was that despite his previous derogation of Welles as a foolish and incompetent bureaucrat, he now appealed to him for guidance. "I wish the department would give me its views," he wrote. "I feel a little uncertain how to act."[37]

In receipt of these panicky messages, Welles blamed Banks. "Banks is no general," he wrote in his diary the night after Porter's message arrived. "I regret the President should adhere to him." As usual, he suspected that Seward was somehow behind it. He wondered if Seward had talked Lincoln into sending Banks to Louisiana for political reasons. "The President thinks he [Banks] has presidential pretensions and friends to back him, but it is a great mistake. Banks is not only no general, he is no statesman." Welles thought "the President should . . . dismiss Banks, or deprive him of military command." Lincoln's opinion of Banks was more positive than that of his navy secretary, and in any case the president would not remove a general from his command in the middle of a campaign merely on the say-so of another officer—maybe especially on the say-so of an officer such as Porter, whom Lincoln knew to be prone to both exaggeration and self-promotion. However the campaign unfolded, it would not do to try to micromanage it from Washington at this point. Banks and Porter would somehow have to work it out.[38]

Nor did Lincoln plan to interfere in the management of the campaign getting under way that same week in Virginia. Lincoln wrote Grant, "The particulars of your plans I neither know, or seek to know. . . . I wish not to obtrude any constraints or restraints upon you." As Lincoln understood his role, it was to keep his field commanders supplied with what they needed. "If there is anything wanting which is within my power to give," he told Grant, "do not fail to let me know it."[39]

GRANT'S ARMY CROSSED THE RAPIDAN on May 4, and almost at once it was assailed by Lee's army. For two days the battle raged, though only "fragmentary intelligence" of the fighting reached Washington. "Neither the President nor anyone else could get a word," Welles wrote his wife. Lincoln all but camped out in the telegraph office. His family was in New York, staying at the Metropolitan Hotel, and he consequently spent not only most of his days in the War Department but many of his nights as well.* He slept so little that when he visited Welles in the Navy Department, he lay down on Welles' sofa to discuss the unfolding events in Virginia.[40]

Finally on May 9 there was some news: good news from Virginia, and bad news from Louisiana. The reports from Virginia suggested, or at least implied, that Grant had won a victory. All that was known for sure was that the armies had met in a terrible battle in the Virginia Wilderness, and that afterward Grant had pushed past the enemy and

*Writing from New York, Mary Lincoln asked her husband for a $50 draft and added that Tad wanted to know how his pet goats were doing. Bemused, Lincoln replied: "Tell Tad goats and father are very well—especially the goats."

marched southward toward Spotsylvania Court House. This certainly looked like victory, and Lincoln allowed himself to celebrate a little.

The bad news came in the form of a visit by George H. Heap, whom Porter had sent to Washington as a special emissary. Heap brought with him a confidential letter from Porter, but Welles already had a notion of what was in it, for Heap had sent a wire from Cairo while en route to warn him that ten of Porter's warships were still trapped above the shallows at Alexandria. The army, he reported in the telegram, "threatens to evacuate Alexandria, in which case the loss of these vessels becomes inevitable." He declared that the troops had lost all confidence in Banks, and that it was imperative to replace him at once or all would be lost. Porter's report also blamed everything on "a too blind carelessness on the part of our military leader." Banks "holds no communication with anyone," had lost the confidence of the soldiers, and had no idea what to do next. "General Banks," Porter wrote, "has got himself into a bad scrape and involved me in it."[41]

Welles brought Heap in to see the president and make his report in person. The whole fiasco, Heap told Lincoln, was due to the "imbecility" of Banks, who spent all his time equivocating, electioneering, and speculating in cotton. This was more than a little unfair. Banks was unquestionably guilty of equivocating and poor judgment, but his electioneering had been conducted mainly at Lincoln's behest, and of all the major players in this drama, he was relatively innocent of cotton speculation.* To be sure, Banks had made blunders. His first was abandoning the winding river road from Alexandria to Shreveport to take the more direct inland road. Worried about Sherman's insistence that Smith's corps must be returned to him by mid-April, Banks sought to save some time by taking the shorter route, though in doing so he lost the protection of Porter's gunboats. His second error was sending his army forward in one long column with his best fighting troops (Smith's corps) at the rear, where they could not easily come up to the front when fighting broke out. Finally, he ordered a precipitous and unnecessary retreat from the battlefield

---

*The charge of cotton speculation was especially unfair. Indeed, of all the major players in this campaign, Banks seems to have been the only one who did not profit from it or even engage in it. As Nicolay and Hay pointed out, the best evidence of his innocence in this regard is that he spent his postwar life in what they called "honorable poverty."

at Pleasant Hill back to Grand Encore, near Alexandria. It was by no means a campaign to be proud of, but Porter seized on Banks' failures in order to explain his own predicament. The falling level of the river led Porter to fear that he might lose his command entirely. Of course, the river would have fallen whether Banks had continued on to Shreveport or not, and if he had—and if Porter had stayed there—his vessels would have been trapped even further upriver. There is irony in the fact that, as Porter's biographer has noted, "Banks's hasty retreat may have saved his [Porter's] squadron." But Porter didn't see it that way and blamed all his problems on the army general.[42]

Now Heap sat in Lincoln's office and, like Porter, pointed the finger of responsibility directly at Banks. It was hard for Lincoln to hear. He had never believed Banks to be a military genius, but he knew him to be a sage politician, and he had conceived of the Red River campaign as partly political in character. Now, with some regret, Lincoln acknowledged to Welles that "he had rather cousined up to Banks, but for some time past had begun to think he was erring in so doing." Then, exposing the depth of his disappointment, he quoted the children's poet Thomas Moore: "Oh, ever thus, from childhood's hour, / I've seen my fondest hopes decay."[43] *

That night a large crowd, led by the band of the 27th Michigan regiment, marched to the White House to serenade Lincoln in celebration of Grant's presumed victory in the Wilderness. Lincoln went out to thank them, but also to remind them that "there is a great deal still to be done," and he asked them to "be grateful to Almighty God, who gives us victory."[44]

BANKS DID NOT ABANDON THE NAVY, nor did Porter lose his squadron, though these facts were not known in Washington for another two weeks. While Grant hammered away at Spotsylvania, at one point telling Lincoln he would fight it out on that line if it took all summer,

---

*It may or may not be suggestive of his inner mood that Lincoln knew this poem, the full text of which reads: "Oh, ever thus, from childhood's hour, / I've seen my fondest hopes decay. / I never loved a tree or flower, / But 'twas first to fade away. / I never nurs'd a dear gazelle, / To glad me with its soft black eye, / But when it came to know me well, / And love me, it was sure to die."

an otherwise obscure lieutenant colonel of engineers named Joseph Bailey built a dam across the Red River in order to raise the water level and allow the gunboats to slip downriver. Ironically, to aid in the construction of the dam, Bailey appropriated the few score cotton bales that the disappointed entrepreneur Samuel Casey had managed to accumulate. Porter described the escape of the squadron in dramatic terms in his subsequent report. When a section of the dam broke prematurely, he wrote, "I jumped on a horse and rode to where the upper vessels were anchored" to order them to run the gap. In breathless prose he described what happened next:

> Thousands of beating hearts looked on anxious for the result; the silence was so great as the *Lexington* approached the dam that a pin might almost be heard to fall. She entered the gap with a full head of steam on, pitched down the roaring torrent, made two or three spasmodic rolls, hung for a moment on the rocks below, was then swept into deep water by the current and rounded to, safely into the bank.[45]

Other vessels followed, and eventually, after the dam was repaired, the rest of the fleet managed to get over the shallows and into deeper water downriver. Porter again resorted to hyperbole to report that Bailey's dam was "without doubt the best engineering feat ever performed." Now that his squadron was secure, he offered a public tribute to Banks that was at odds with his earlier confidential reports.

> To General Banks personally I am much indebted for the happy manner in which he has forwarded this enterprise, giving it his whole attention night and day, scarcely sleeping while the work was going on, tending personally to see that all the requirements of Colonel Bailey were complied with on the instant.[46]

Welles, and presumably Lincoln, learned of the escape of the squadron on May 23, but whatever relief the president felt was overwhelmed by his anxiety about the outcome of the fighting in Virginia. There was "a craving, uneasy feeling" in Washington as news of the nonstop fighting around Spotsylvania trickled in. On Friday, May 13, things had looked better, but a "painful suspense" returned the next week, an "intense anxiety" that "almost unfits the mind for mental activity." Finally, after pounding away at Lee's defensive lines around Spotsylvania without significant success, Grant moved around Lee's right flank and again headed south. Lincoln put the best face on it that he could. As Welles noted, "Grant has not obtained a victory but performed another remarkably successful flank movement."[47]

While great events unfolded in Virginia, the squabbling about cotton continued, both in Louisiana and in Washington. One of Chase's agents complained angrily to Welles that after hauling several bales of cotton to the riverbank and arranging to have the navy guard it while he went to Memphis for the appropriate paperwork, he came back to find that the navy had stolen it. The agent wanted Welles to order the gunboat's captain to return it. Welles asked Porter about it, and Porter replied that the cotton in question belonged to a Mr. Elgee, "a rebel in arms against the Government, and has two sons in the rebel army." Porter added that Chase's agents continuously conspired to get their hands on illicit cotton and that, indeed, "a good deal of it has been hauled away under cover of the night . . . by Treasury agents." At any rate, he concluded, this particular cotton had been sent to the prize court at Cairo, and its fate was now in the hands of the courts. "All cotton taken by the fleet," he declared, "has been reported and turned over to the judge of the district."[48]

Chase was unsatisfied with this response, and indeed with the behavior of the navy generally. His view was that cotton collected by Treasury agents was for the good of the country, whereas cotton seized by the navy was simply booty. During a party at his home, he cornered Welles and criticized the "great abuses in cotton speculation" out in Louisiana. Welles was puzzled that he should bring it up, assuming that he was referring to the horde of speculators, some of whom were Chase's own agents, but he agreed that it was "demoralizing." "Yes," Chase shot back, "your whole fleet out west is infected." He used the opportunity to abuse Porter in particular. Just as Porter had complained that Banks had showed up at Alexandria "in a steamer loaded with champagne and ice, cotton speculators, and brandy," Chase now declared that Porter lived aboard a grandly appointed flagship with a piano on board and that he lounged about on this floating pleasure palace while his minions conducted vast cotton raids. Welles was angry and defensive, but he merely pointed out that the navy could get nothing that was not legally accorded them by a prize court.[49]

Soon after this exchange, and perhaps as a result of it, Fox wrote Porter to warn him that Chase was attempting to throw all the blame for any indiscretions on him and cautioned him to "be prepared." By now the successful escape of his squadron from the Red River had allowed Porter to recover his customary equanimity, and Porter mentally snapped his fingers at the threats from the Treasury Department, whose minions, he declared, were engaged in "supplying the enemy." "Treasury agents have been the best friends the rebels have had," he insisted. "Almost every Treasury man . . . has been engaged in traffic instead of attending to the interests of the Government." Porter also scoffed at the criticism of the eastern newspapers, some of which had begun to publish vivid examples of his command's recent cotton-gathering work. To John Hay, he declared that "he could stand the criticism as long as he had his pockets full of prize money."[50]

This bickering among the War, Navy, and Treasury Departments concerned Lincoln enough that he decided to send a personal emissary out west to find out how bad it was. The man he sent was Major General Dan Sickles, a political general with a checkered past who was a self-proclaimed hero of the Battle of Gettysburg. It was a curious choice since Sickles was hardly a model of probity, but Lincoln had to do something with him and arguably, at least, he would cause fewer problems as a presidential emissary than as a battlefield commander. Lincoln told Sickles to report to him confidentially about the impact the squabble over cotton was having on the war, and Sickles wrote back from Memphis that "all trade with persons beyond our lines [should] be interdicted." He acknowledged that "some loyal people beyond our lines will suffer," if the trade were halted, but he insisted that it benefited "a hundred rebels where it relieves one Union man."[51]

Sickles' report, along with others, led Lincoln to reverse himself on the issue of cotton trading. He became convinced that the wartime inflation in cotton prices allowed the South to gain almost as much profit from its reduced cotton crop as it had before the war. Moreover, it was evident that paying the cotton planters in gold propped up the South's collapsing economy. Lincoln still believed that "it might be well to take measures to secure the cotton," but he was now opposed "to letting the Rebels have gold." In six months he had shifted from granting trade licenses (to allow entrepreneurs to pay rebel generals in gold for their cotton) to banning all such traffic. One fallout from this shift was a new law that removed cotton from the jurisdiction of the prize courts and made it the property of the government. Welles protested that this deprived sailors of their rightful prize, but no one in the cabinet supported him.[52]

By now, the Red River expedition had come to its inglorious end, and other issues were commanding the national attention. Grant was moving toward Richmond, and the presidential election was in full gallop. In effect, the dispute over cotton in the Mississippi Valley, and who had jurisdiction over it, simply died out. Banks absorbed the collective disappointment for the failure of the campaign and was relegated to a desk job in New Orleans by the new general in chief, Ulysses S. Grant. Fox wrote to Porter that he was sorry for Banks, for the expedition had "utterly extinguished him." As for the boisterous Porter, he emerged unscathed. He subsequently downplayed his role, claiming in a letter to a newspaper reporter that "the trip to Shreveport was intended merely as a little pastime to keep the troops from getting rusty." Casting himself as a victim of Banks' incompetence allowed him to emerge from the campaign with his reputation intact, even enhanced, and he was about to be tapped for even greater responsibilities. Fox suggested to him that "after you get your feathers smoothed and oiled, I don't see why you should not come East" to assume an even greater command.[53]

11

"A Vote of Thanks"
Lincoln and the Politics of Promotion

BY MIDSUMMER OF 1864, the U.S. Navy had more than six hundred warships in commission, and more on the way. A handful of older sailing vessels maintained a minimal American presence overseas in those parts of the world where Union merchant ships still carried on a global trade. They were augmented by several newer and faster steam frigates that hunted the elusive rebel commerce raiders, such as the *Alabama* and *Florida*, which threatened that trade. But most of those six hundred ships, including all of the ironclads, fought the war at home and were assigned to one of the various squadrons: on the western rivers, along the Gulf coast, and in the Atlantic. The largest of these squadrons was the North Atlantic Blockading Squadron under Acting Rear Admiral Samuel Phillips Lee, a career U. S. Navy officer who was a third cousin of Robert E. Lee and who bore more than a passing resemblance to his more famous kinsman. From his flagship, the stately steam frigate *Minnesota* in Hampton Roads, Lee supervised a large and widely dispersed force that included as many as 114 ships.* In the

---

*Volume 10 of the *Official Records of the Union and Confederate Navies in the War of the Rebellion* (Washington, DC: Government Printing Office, 1894–1922) lists a total of 166 ships that served in the North Atlantic Blockading Squadron from May 6 to October 27, 1864, but not all of these served simultaneously. The largest force under Lee's direction at any one time was 114 ships.

spring of 1864, thirty-one of those ships operated in Hampton Roads or on the James River; twenty-five more blockaded the several inlets to the Cape Fear River, which led to Wilmington, North Carolina, the last major port in rebel hands with direct rail connections to Richmond; and twenty others patrolled the Albemarle and Pamlico Sounds of North Carolina.

It was a lucrative assignment for Lee since, as the senior officer, he was entitled to a share of all the money generated by the scores of prizes captured by vessels within his far-flung command. He even hired an attorney to represent his interests at the prize court, paying him 2½ percent "of whatever part of the proceeds may fall to me," to ensure that he received his fair share. Still, Lee was not entirely satisfied with his circumstances. When, as a newly promoted captain, he had first replaced Goldsborough in command back in 1862, he had been delighted to be made an acting rear admiral, but since then other senior officers, including Goldsborough, had become statutory admirals while Lee remained an *acting* rear admiral. By 1864, he was the only squadron commander in the navy who had not been promoted to flag rank.[1]

Lee believed himself to be a victim of the policy that only those officers who won some dramatic victory and were consequently voted the formal thanks of Congress could be promoted. Du Pont had won his at Port Royal, Farragut at New Orleans, and Porter at Vicksburg. Even Goldsborough had earned a vote of thanks for presiding over the capture of Roanoke Island. But even though he commanded the largest naval force ever assembled by the United States, Lee had not yet managed to secure the kind of headline-grabbing success that would earn a congressional vote and a promotion to admiral. Lee's flag lieutenant described him in a letter home as "a very pleasant gentleman, and a very kind man," as well as "a hard worker." Lee's admiring biographers describe him as "a model of professional dedication, painstaking attention to detail, stern discipline, unbending integrity, and steadfast devotion to duty." Nevertheless, lacking a signal victory in combat, these virtues were not enough to win him an admiral's flag.[2]

Dahlgren's promotion to admiral in February 1863 had been particularly galling to Lee since Dahlgren had won neither a victory nor a congressional vote. That infuriated Lee's ambitious wife, Elizabeth Blair Lee (Lizzie), who wrote her husband that Dahlgren's elevation "defeats the object of making the Admirals & makes it too cheap." She was not averse, however, to taking the same route, for she, too, had powerful friends at court. One of her two brothers, Francis P. (Frank) Blair Jr., was both a former congressman and a major general in Sherman's army, and the other, Montgomery Blair, was Lincoln's postmaster general. Her father, the elder Frank Blair, still had great influence in Washington and was willing to exercise it. After the fall of New Orleans back in 1862, the senior Blair had prevailed upon William Dennison, the governor of Ohio and a close friend, to lobby Fox, Welles, and Lincoln to ensure that then-Commander Lee was included in the list of those who received the thanks of Congress. Lincoln did ask Congress for "a vote of thanks" for all of those (including Lee) who had commanded vessels in that operation. But there were thirty names on the list, and in the end Congress offered formal thanks only to Farragut. Nevertheless, Blair's influence did help Lee rise from commander to captain, a fact that did not sit well with several other officers. Farragut wrote his wife, "Nothing I think has occurred that has so disgusted the officers of this squadron as the promotion of Lee."[3]

Two years later, however, Lee was still a captain, and the elder Blair went again to see Lincoln and Welles to ask that he be "not overslaughed as Admiral." Lizzie went so far as to copy out a paragraph from one of her husband's frequent letters home for her father to show to the president. "If I have commanded this Squadron well," Lee wrote his wife, "my appointment should be made good." He expressed concern that the recent promotions of both John Rodgers and Stephen C. Rowan to the rank of commodore had all but destroyed his own prospects since both of them were junior to him as captains. Such action, he wrote, "ignores my services & position if I am not promoted also." Armed with this letter, Lizzie's father asked Lincoln bluntly why his son-in-law had not yet been promoted. Lincoln responded that he would be happy to promote Captain Lee whenever the secretary of the navy requested it. But when Blair went to see Welles, the secretary told him that Lee would have to accomplish "some marked event" to justify the thanks of Congress. "Higher appointments," Welles told him, "must be kept open to induce and stimulate our heroes."[4]

Throughout the war, Lincoln had been compelled by circumstances to deal with "political generals"—men such as Frémont, Banks, Butler, and McClernand—who ascended to their military rank because of their political influence or position. Lee was certainly no political admiral—he had served loyally and effectively in uniform since 1827—but Blair's visit was a reminder that political rivalries could still influence the selection of navy flag officers. Moreover, Lincoln had to keep in mind not only that Lee was connected to the Blairs but also that the Blairs were political rivals of Secretary Chase, and favors granted to one family might well be resented by the other. In spite of that—or perhaps because of it—Lincoln did not insert himself into the issue of Lee's promotion as he had done with Dahlgren. He told Welles that "he should be governed entirely" by the secretary's views.[5]

FOR HIS PART, Acting Rear Admiral Lee was perfectly willing to win his promotion by some heroic act, but so far fate had failed to grant him an opportunity. Indeed, since taking control of the squadron, he had come to Lincoln's attention mainly because of his central role in a long and often contentious dispute concerning the same kind of trade permits that sullied the Red River expedition, a dispute that once again put the Blairs and Chase on opposite sides.

During Goldsborough's tenure in command, army supply vessels bringing food and ammunition to McClellan's army on the Peninsula had routinely loaded up with shingles, tar, and other products of the region for the return trip to northern ports. When he took over from Goldsborough, the fastidious Lee checked with Welles to make sure that this kind of trade was approved by the department. It was not. "You will allow no vessel to import or export merchandise into Norfolk, Elizabeth River, or any port of the country blockaded," Welles informed him. Lincoln had declared Port Royal, New Orleans, and Beaufort, North Carolina, open to trade, but Norfolk, because of its easy communication with Richmond and other cities in the Virginia and North Carolina tidewater, remained under blockade even though it was occupied by Union forces. This made no sense to Major General John A. Dix, who had replaced John Wool in command of the Union garrison at Fort Monroe. Dix argued that the blockade of Union-occupied Norfolk was causing hardship for the twenty thousand residents of the city who were now "more destitute than when they came under our jurisdiction." He saw no reason why army transports, or even merchant ships, should not be allowed to touch there to deliver supplies and buy up the products of the region. Convinced that he was acting in accordance with Treasury Department guidelines, he began to issue trade permits to merchants to do exactly that.[6]

Welles would have none of it. He ordered Lee to ignore all permits except those issued by "the Secretary of the Treasury, War, or Navy." He insisted, "There must be no favoritism or license for trade given to any one or more of our own countrymen to traffic within the blockaded region." In a deliberate slap at Dix, he told Lee, "No officer of the Army or Navy is authorized to grant permits." Dix and Lee engaged in a lengthy and occasionally sharp correspondence about the trade in and out of Norfolk. Dix did not see how he could properly refuse to grant a permit requested by the authority of the secretary of the Treasury, and Lee felt compelled to obey the positive orders of the secretary of the Navy that "Vessels must not be permitted to pass the blockade for trading purposes." After the general and the admiral exchanged several lengthy missives trying to square these contradictory orders, Dix summarized their mutual dilemma: "It is a conflict between the two Departments of the Government, for which neither of us is responsible."[7]

The resolution to this dispute, if there was one, lay in the cabinet. Dix's argument that civilians were suffering needlessly in an area occupied by Union forces touched both Lincoln's humanitarian impulses and his political instincts. Lincoln was receptive to the idea that easing the burden of the war on wavering southerners might constitute a first step in their return to the Union. Welles, however, dug his heels in and said he wouldn't do it without a direct written order from the president. "To strictly maintain the blockade caused suffering," he acknowledged, but after all, "that was the chief object of the blockade." "The case was not one of sympathy but of duty," he insisted. Chase suggested that a suitable compromise might allow trade only for certain kinds of goods that the Union needed: shingles, barrel staves, tar, and other raw materials, many of which were useful to the navy. Sarcastically, Welles asked him why they did not simply "raise the blockade."[8]

Lincoln was the only person who could resolve the dispute, and while he was loath to overrule Welles on a naval issue, in the end that is what he did, issuing instructions that allowed "vessels or merchandise" to enter or leave Norfolk if the ships had a clearance from the Treasury

Department. When Dix noted that "the Nansemond river was not included" in his order, Lincoln issued another extending trade privileges to that river as well as to Suffolk.[9]

Lincoln's proclamation did not resolve the issue. Lee shared his frustration with his wife, who told her father about it, and Frank Blair rushed over to the White House again to tell Lincoln that it was "an unpardonable crime" to allow Secretary Chase to issue trade licenses that "defeated" the blockade. Moreover, even after Lincoln's new instructions, merchants continued to present passes written not only by Treasury Department officials but also by army officers and even civil functionaries. Ever punctilious, Lee enquired of Welles if "permits of this character are to be respected," and an unchastened Welles told him no. Even so, merchants who had acquired passes from one authority or another often assumed that their possession of a permit allowed them to ignore the navy. Frustrated when merchant ships refused to heave to in response to navy orders, Lee's captains wanted to know if they could fire on them. Welles told them to go ahead. If a captain "has used every means in his power to prevent vessels from running the blockade without success," Welles wrote, "he is justified in firing into such vessels." Though no shots were ever fired, tension between army officials who sought to encourage trade and navy captains who sought to prevent it was a constant battle.[10]

For Lincoln, the bickering over trade within Lee's command area was not a high priority. In February 1864 when Welles came into his office to complain—again—about the trade permits from the Treasury Department, one of which was found aboard a blockade runner loaded with contraband, Lincoln told him to go see Chase about it. Welles necessarily accepted this reply, but he was distressed that Lincoln was delegating the issue instead of dealing with it himself. Like Bates, Welles believed that Lincoln should take the reins of government more firmly into his own hands. Moreover, as far as Welles was concerned, Chase was one of the principal instigators of the problem. In this frame of mind, Welles wrote a blistering letter to Chase in which he asserted that the Treasury Department policy of allowing "parties clothed with permits to collect property not their own" led to "distrust, alienation, and enmity," and he equated granting trade permits with "robbing for the private benefit of speculating favorites who have contrived to get a permit to commit waste."[11]

Not surprisingly, Chase took offense at Welles' blunt language, writing to Welles that his letter "reads much like a lecture, and is as unacceptable as it is needless. I am sure that you neither read it nor dictated it." Welles declined this opportunity to back down gracefully, acknowledging that he had indeed written the letter; he justified its harsh language by adding that while he did not mean to give offense, he felt very strongly about the issue.[12]

Lincoln did not need any more squabbles in the cabinet, especially squabbles involving Chase, for Lincoln already had his hands full in dealing with the Treasury secretary. That same month, Kansas senator Samuel Clarke Pomeroy circulated a public letter that sharply criticized Lincoln and openly advocated a Chase presidency. Though Chase denied any complicity in—or even knowledge of—the letter, Lincoln knew that Pomeroy scarcely could have acted without Chase's approval. Lincoln dealt with the attack by ignoring it. He suspected, as Welles later put it, that the "recoil" would be more destructive than the "projectile," and time proved him correct. The Pomeroy circular, as it came to be called, marked the beginning of the collapse of the Chase candidacy.[13]

Chase, however, was also at the center of another mini-crisis, this one involving Admiral Lee's brother-in-law Frank Blair. At Lincoln's suggestion, Lizzie's brother had taken temporary leave from his command in Sherman's army to resume his seat in Congress. Lincoln had hoped at the time that Blair might be elected Speaker, but Blair spent most of his time in the House exonerating himself of a trumped-up charge that he had swindled the government of $8,000 while serving in the field. A formal congressional enquiry found not only that the charge was false but also that it had been manufactured by agents in the Treasury Department who had forged the incriminating documents. This caused a flare-up in the long political rivalry between Chase and the Blairs, and although Chase himself was very likely innocent of this clumsy hatchet job, Frank declared on the floor of the House, "These dogs have been set on me by their master, and since I have whipped them back into their kennel, I mean to hold their master responsible." Chase was infuriated, and concluded, with no evidence beyond his own disappointed presidential ambitions, that Blair had been encouraged in his tirade by Lincoln. Through intermediaries, Chase insisted that the president must repudiate Blair's remarks. In particular, Chase's friends informed the president that if Lincoln allowed Blair to resume his army command, it would effectively condone Blair's intemperate remarks, in which case, they insisted, Chase would be forced to resign.[14]

It was a delicate moment. When Lincoln had initially invited Blair to come to Washington to resume his congressional seat, he had asked him to "put his military commission in my hands," with the apparent understanding that Blair could return to the field at a moment of his choosing. Chase's allies found that disturbing, maybe even unconstitutional, and they wanted Lincoln to rescind Blair's orders. If he did so, not only would Sherman be denied an effective division commander, but it would give Chase the whip hand in the cabinet, if not the administration. On the other hand, if Lincoln refused the demand and Chase resigned, the radical wing of the Republican Party might openly rebel just before the national election. Lincoln managed this dilemma with his usual sensitivity. He thanked Chase's emissaries for coming, told them that he had been "mortified" by Blair's speech, and said that while he had considered revoking Blair's orders back to the field, General Sherman claimed to need him and, as always, the interests of the country must come first. Once again Lincoln managed to hold the middle ground without having to choose sides, but the middle ground was becoming narrower.[15]

Meanwhile, the interdepartmental bickering over trade and trade permits continued. Months before, a French company had petitioned to ship a cargo of seven thousand hogsheads of tobacco from Virginia to France to honor a previous contract. Eager to placate the French, Seward had convinced Lincoln to give his approval. Welles, of course, objected. If the French could secure previously purchased tobacco, why couldn't the British claim the right to previously purchased cotton? The whole concept of the blockade would collapse. Seward backed down. But then he learned that the French had sequestered the ordnance intended for two rebel warships being built in Bordeaux and Nantes, and to reward them, Seward reactivated the tobacco deal. Once again he secured Lincoln's approval. Now the French ships were in Hampton Roads, escorted by French warships, and before allowing them to proceed, Lee checked with Welles to ensure that Washington approved. Lincoln was in the telegraph office when Lee's query arrived, and he decided to talk to Seward and

Stanton about it. Welles was annoyed. It was bad enough that Lincoln regularly turned to Seward for advice on matters of state without consulting the full cabinet, but Welles considered this a naval matter. Lincoln, in turn, became annoyed when Welles brought up the issue in the cabinet. Welles attributed Lincoln's bad temper to his realization that he had made a mistake in agreeing to the scheme in the first place. Or perhaps he was simply growing tired of Welles' querulous harping. In the end, the tobacco remained unshipped.[16]

Another trade dispute grew out of Lincoln's decision to sanction a request from Benjamin Butler, who by now had replaced Dix in command at Fort Monroe. Butler sought a trade permit for businessman George W. Lane to go into the sounds and rivers of North Carolina "with cargoes of plows, harrows, trace chains, ropes, twine, and such supplies" and return with "cargoes of cotton, tobacco, and other products of the country." Welles was convinced that this was merely another "little, dirty, speculating intrigue," but Butler promoted it as a humanitarian enterprise "to send in ploughs, harrows and farming utensils to loyal farmers in North Carolina in exchange for cotton." The humanitarian argument convinced Lincoln to approve the request, and he endorsed it at the bottom: "I approve the object of the within."[17]

When Lane showed up in Pamlico Sound in June on board the steamer *Philadelphia* and presented his permit to Melancton Smith, the senior naval officer there, Smith was unsure of what to do. He was not concerned that the permit might have been falsified, nor did he question the president's decision, but he noted that the permit was dated March 19, almost three months before, and much had happened in the North Carolina sounds since then. The rebels had launched an ironclad, the *Albemarle*, built with great effort in a cornfield on the upper reaches of the Roanoke River, and its presence had dramatically shifted the balance of power on the river, allowing the rebels to reclaim the town of Plymouth, one of the places where Lane proposed to trade. In addition, Smith was concerned because the cargo manifest of the *Philadelphia* included many items beyond the "plows, harrows, and trace chains" listed in the permit, items that Smith believed "would afford comfort to the enemy," including fifteen barrels of whiskey. Given that, Smith detained the *Philadelphia* and sent an enquiry to his superior, who was, of course, Acting Rear Admiral Samuel Phillips Lee.[18]

Lee was not about to refuse a permit endorsed by the president. "The President's permit to Mr. Lane must be respected," he wrote to Smith. But just in case, he also forwarded the pertinent correspondence to Welles. By now, Welles was thoroughly disgusted by the whole issue of trade permits, and he was disappointed with Lee's decision, writing in his diary that Lee had "failed." Welles explained the circumstances to Lincoln and got his permission to rescind the original permit. In spite of that, Welles continued to believe that Lincoln was simply too credulous when confronted with such schemes, whether they came from the trickster Seward or the charlatan Butler. The president, Welles decided, had granted his consent out of kindness without sufficient consideration of the consequences.[19]

In fact, Lincoln's support for trade in the North Carolina sounds was neither accidental nor ill-considered. Not only was he sympathetic to the predicament of tidewater farmers, he believed that any trade that did not contribute directly to the South's military capability could prove salutary to eventual reunification, and of course the acquisition of southern cotton would relieve both New England mills and the gold-starved Treasury. Welles wanted a hard-and-fast rule, but Lincoln was more comfortable with ambiguity and was willing to authorize exceptions in exceptional circumstances. As a result, while Lee's far-flung squadron attempted to maintain a strict blockade of southern ports, merchants who bore trade permits from Chase, his agents, Butler, or others passed regularly through the blockade to land at Norfolk, Suffolk, and elsewhere.

These circumstances did not aid Lee's quest for recognition and promotion. Welles eventually became annoyed not only with Chase, Stanton, and Dix but also with Acting Rear Admiral Lee. Not only did Lee continue to ask the department for more men and more ships, but he sent altogether too many queries to Washington asking what he should allow and what he should prevent. Welles began to categorize Lee as one of those commanders who needed constant oversight.

Perhaps aware of that, Lee renewed his request for permission to undertake an attack on Wilmington, North Carolina, the largest rebel-held port within his command area. Surely the capture of Wilmington would win him a vote of thanks in Congress and allow him to hoist the square flag of a rear admiral. As early as December 1862, Lee wrote to

Fox proposing that the department send him a few ironclads to allow him to "make short work of Wilmington." His plan was to send one or two ironclads into New Inlet, move up the Cape Fear River, and shell the rebel batteries from the rear. He assumed that this would compel the rebels to abandon their largest work, called Fort Fisher, which in turn would allow Lee to take his squadron upriver to Wilmington. Welles and Fox were pleased by Lee's initiative, but at that time the department was sending all of its ironclads to Du Pont at Charleston.[20]

Lee's next proposal was to outflank the Wilmington forts by landing a few army brigades on the beach north of Fort Fisher in order to conduct a joint attack. But Halleck refused to release any troops for such a mission, and neither Welles nor Fox was eager to sign on for another combined operation. Just as Fox had told Du Pont to make the capture of Charleston purely a navy affair, he wrote Lee to tell him, "You must lay out your work for Wilmington if possible without much of an army operation." Lacking support from any quarter for an attack on Wilmington, Lee settled down to maintain the blockade, keep his careful records, and hope that fate would eventually provide him an opportunity to win congressional notice and promotion.[21]

THAT OPPORTUNITY SEEMED TO ARRIVE in the first week in May 1864. Grant called for a movement by Butler's Army of the James up its namesake river to Petersburg in order to cut Richmond off from the south. Since Grant planned to initiate his own campaign on May 4, he wanted Butler to begin his move that same night and "be as far up the James river as you can get by daylight" on May 5. The idea was that the rebels would be overmatched in attempting to deal simultaneously with Grant's advance from the north and Butler's from the south. As Lincoln explained it to John Hay: "Those not skinning can hold a leg." Butler's move, of course, would have to be made in conjunction with the navy. Though Fox worried that Butler would "bulge ahead and get badly handled," the news energized Lee. An advance up the James could result in the capture of Richmond, or at least a confrontation with the rebel ironclad fleet above Drury's Bluff, and provide Lee with the kind of signature victory that he needed to earn recognition. Butler came aboard Lee's *Minnesota* late on the afternoon of May 3 to finalize the plans for their joint operation, but despite a genuine determination by both men to work together, the absence of a unified command again led to misunderstanding, confusion, and disappointment.[22]

It began well enough. Butler had said that he had "positive orders" from Grant to start on schedule, and Lee told his captains, "No excuse will be received for not being ready to move at the appointed time." Lee's five ironclads led the advance, each of them under tow, followed by nearly two hundred other vessels of every size and shape: tugs, double-enders, fat supply ships, packed army transports, squat river steamers, and tall oceangoing ships. The armada virtually filled the river. In the end, the movement took place without incident, and Lee was pleased to report to Welles "the successful landing of the army at City Point and Bermuda Hundred."[23]

That was nearly the last piece of good news to come from Butler's theater of operations. After a few tentative probes west, south, and even north toward Richmond, Butler soon retreated to his beachhead within a broad curve of the James River, an area known as Bermuda Hundred, where he fortified. It became clear almost at once that Butler was more concerned with maintaining the security of his campsite than he was in assaulting the enemy. In effect, by landing in Bermuda Hundred, Butler had thrust his army into a cul-de-sac where he was pinned down as effectively as if his men had been interred in a POW camp, or as Grant put it, "in a bottle strongly corked."[24]

Just as bad, the essential cooperation between army and navy began to break down almost at once. Butler wanted Lee to use his gunboats to cover his flanks; Lee wanted Butler to clear the riverbank of enemy artillery so he could sweep for torpedoes. Each looked to the other for support, but lacking a unified command, they perforce couched their requests deferentially. "Would it not be possible for you to bring up the gunboats, monitors, opposite Dr. Howlett's so as to cover my flank?" Butler asked Lee on May 13. Not really, Lee replied. The rebel position at Howlett's was "over high hills and woods," and his gunboats could reach them only if they could advance further upriver, which was impossible unless they could somehow clear the torpedoes. Lee put his "Torpedo Division" to work clearing the mines, but it was tedious work that required "dragging the river with grapnels & searching the banks for torpedo lines and wires." Moreover, it was likely to be interrupted at any time when rebel masked batteries opened fire from the riverbank. Lee's concerns were punctuated by the loss of the *Commodore Jones*, "torn into splinters" by a two-thousand-pound torpedo on May 6, and the *Shawsheen*, which was ambushed from shore and captured the next day. Eager as he was to move upriver, Lee insisted that he could not help Butler with the rebel batteries at Howlett's unless Butler helped clear the riverbank of enemy batteries. "In this way the two services will support each other," Lee wrote.[25]

It didn't happen. Instead, interservice relations worsened. Lee suggested that "it will promote the public service if you can conveniently keep up communication with me and apprise me of your movements." But when Butler decided to make a concerted thrust northward toward Fort Darling, he did not bother to ask Lee for his cooperation or even to inform him of the move. After Butler's northward thrust was badly mauled and he returned to his entrenchments at Bermuda Hundred, Lee asked him about it and Butler declared that his move had been only "a feint." Meanwhile the rebels continued to improve their entrenchments at Howlett's, and Lee's queries to Butler about cooperation took on a sharper edge. All through the afternoon of May 18, while Robert E. Lee fended off Grant's furious attacks at Spotsylvania, Samuel Phillips Lee bombarded Butler with a series of telegrams urging him to do something about those rebel guns at Howlett's. At three-thirty he wired: "Enemy vigorously entrenching . . . only a land attack can dislodge them." A half hour later, he reminded Butler, "The enemy are working on entrenchments near Howlett's house. . . . They will mount guns to-night." An hour later he wrote: "The rebel artillery is getting in position there." And a half hour after that: "Can not the enemy be prevented from mounting guns at Howlett's to-night by a land attack?" Butler was immune to such prodding, however, and it was soon evident that for all the hopes associated with this assault on Richmond's back door, Butler had simply moved his command from Fort Monroe to Bermuda Hundred.[26]

Lee still hoped that he might achieve something worthy of notice if the rebel ironclad squadron came downriver to challenge him. On May 28 he learned that the rebel warships—three ironclads and six more lightly armored gunboats—had dropped down the river to Drewry's Bluff. A rebel deserter informed him that the enemy planned to send down fire ships followed by an attack with their armored vessels. Butler urged Lee to protect himself from such an attack by sinking obstructions in the river in much the same way that Butler had protected himself by building entrenchments across the neck of Bermuda Hundred. Lee was dismissive of such timidity. "The Navy is not accustomed to putting down obstructions before it," he declared haughtily.[27]

But the rebel ironclads did not come downriver, and a few days later a staff officer from Grant's headquarters came on board the *Malvern* to tell him that Grant was seeking "a good location for a pontoon bridge." It was evident that if Grant bridged the James, the Appomattox, or both for an attack on Petersburg, it would be prudent to ensure the security of those bridges by blocking the river channel. Both Butler and Gillmore urged him to do it. Lee feared that if he did, others would assume he was afraid to fight the rebel squadron. Anxious about what to do, he characteristically decided to "lay the subject before the Department." He asked Welles whether it was more important to block the river to ensure its security or to keep it open to invite an engagement with the rebel ironclads.[28]

By now Welles had grown weary of Lee's constant queries. He endorsed Lee's letter: "Left to discretion of admiral in command, in whom the Department has confidence," though, in fact, that confidence was beginning to wane.* When Lee got that response, he next sought to place the onus of the decision on Butler. Obstructing the river, he wrote to Butler, "must be your operation, not mine." Not surprisingly, Butler refused to take responsibility. "The vessels are wholly at your service," the general replied, "upon your good judgment, and not mine, must rest their use." Lee's penchant for careful record keeping compelled him to insist that Butler assure him, in writing, that the navy would not incur any "pecuniary liability" for the ships if he did use them to block the river. Butler did so, but Lee still did not act. He

---

*That same week, Lee wrote to Welles to ask that he be allowed to retain the new ironclad *Tecumseh*, which was slated to join Farragut's squadron in the Gulf. Welles was never happy to receive requests for reinforcements from nervous commanders, and he responded to Lee's request with a little lecture: "You have the six best ironclads in the Navy, and Admiral Farragut, threatened by a larger force than is opposed to you, has not a single one. Let the Tecumseh and her consort go, as ordered." In August 1864, the *Tecumseh* sank with most of its crew as Farragut fought his way into Mobile Bay.

held the schooners in readiness in case of need, but he left the channel open.[29]

In the end, Lee did not have to make the decision after all. When Grant decided to move once again around the right flank of the rebel army, bypassing the old battlefields of the Seven Days, to land behind Butler at City Point, he ordered Butler to block the river to protect the pontoon bridges. Lee may have felt some relief in not having to make the decision himself, but he was also a little defensive about it, assuring himself in his private journal that "the sinking of obstructions is an army measure from first to last." He also made sure to notify Welles that the sinking of the block ships to obstruct the river had been done by the army, under the orders of the army commander, and not by him.[30]

It did not get him off the hook. James Gordon Bennett's *New York Herald* announced that "Admiral Lee has just performed an act that, we doubt not, has called an honorable blush to the cheek of every officer in his fleet. He has sunk boats in the river—obstructed the channel—to prevent the rebel fleet from getting out at his ships. He has iron-clad vessels enough to blow every ram in the confederacy to atoms; but he is afraid of the trial." The *Herald* subsequently admitted that the obstructions had been sunk by Grant's order, but it also insisted that Grant had ordered it because he doubted the ability of the navy to make his communications "absolutely safe." That order, the *Herald* concluded, was a "distinct declaration on the part of General Grant that he has no confidence in Admiral Lee."[31]

Lee was furious. Like Du Pont and Wilkes, he had a thin skin when it came to slurs on his character. Someone, he suspected, had bribed Bennett to attack him. "Who pays it?" he asked rhetorically in his journal. "Is it the trading interest? . . . the jealousy in the navy of my persistent prize money, political feeling against the Blairs . . . ?" In fact, Bennett's real target was not Lee but Gideon Welles and, beyond him, Lincoln himself. Bennett noted in a subsequent editorial that Lee's explanation for not attacking the rebel ironclads was that the river was too shallow to bear his own ironclads. Lee's defense, Bennett wrote sarcastically, was that "God Almighty did not make that river to fit our gunboats." A better question, he suggested, was why Welles had not made the gunboats to fit the river. That, Bennett remarked triumphantly, "throws the blame where we might naturally have supposed it ought to be thrown—on the Navy Department." And he called yet again for Lincoln, whom he called a "blundering trifler," to replace Welles with someone competent. None of this contributed to Lee's chances for promotion.[32]

LINCOLN FOLLOWED GRANT'S MOVEMENT to the James River with his usual interest from the War Department telegraph office, but much of his attention was focused on Baltimore, where the Republican National Convention was meeting to nominate a candidate for the 1864 election. A week after learning that Grant had landed at City Point, Lincoln received official notice that the convention had nominated him for another term as president, and with that resolved, he determined to assuage his "intense anxiety" about Grant's progress by visiting the army himself. Welles opposed the visit, believing that it would do no good and possibly could do harm: it put the president in physical jeopardy and removed his hand from the helm of government in Washington. But Fox encouraged it and even accompanied the president, who also took along young Tad. They boarded the steamer *Baltimore* at the Navy Yard on June 20 and steamed out into the Chesapeake, where Lincoln was again miserably seasick during the voyage down to Hampton Roads. The *Baltimore* headed up the James River past Harrison's Landing, where Lincoln had met McClellan two years before, to City Point. Once there, a helpful army officer suggested to him that champagne was "a certain cure for seasickness." Mustering up a wry smile, Lincoln replied, "No, my friend; I have seen too many fellows seasick ashore from drinking that very stuff."[33]

Grant was waiting for Lincoln at the wharf. Lincoln enthusiastically grasped the general's proffered hand and held on to it as he told Grant how grateful he was for all that he had accomplished. After lunch at Grant's headquarters tent, where Lincoln bent over campaign maps and discussed impending operations, Grant invited the president to accompany him on an inspection tour. They rode through the campsite, stopping to observe enemy works across the river, and then returned to headquarters. Word of Lincoln's visit spread through the camp, and soldiers gathered along their route to call out greetings as the president rode past. Grant then suggested that they go see the black troops, who were encamped separately, and Lincoln eagerly agreed. During the ride, Lincoln confessed that he had initially been "opposed on nearly every side" to the notion of black regiments, but he acknowledged that "they have proved their efficiency." As was often the case, it reminded him of a story. A westerner who was a newcomer to Shakespeare and therefore unfamiliar with the tradition of using a white actor in black-face to play the role of Othello watched that play with great interest, and afterward remarked, "Waal, layin' aside all sectional prejudices and any partiality I may have for the race, derned ef I don't think the nig-ger held his own with any on 'em." Just so, Lincoln thought the black regiments had more than held their own in the campaign so far.[34]

Lincoln's arrival produced a frenzy of excitement among the black soldiers. The men were "perfectly wild with excitement and delight," and they crowded around him cheering, laughing, and crying, some reaching out to touch his hands or his clothes, tears running down their faces. Lincoln was deeply moved and bowed his head in response, his voice breaking as he thanked them for their service and for their reception.[35]

Lincoln slept aboard the *Baltimore* that night, and the next morning he went upriver to meet Admiral Lee at Deep Bottom. Since this was within range of the rebel artillery, there was no gun salute or other for-mal demonstration to call attention to the president's arrival on board Lee's flagship, the *Malvern*. Butler was on board, too, and together the admiral and the general took Lincoln on a short tour of the battlefront, pointing out strategically important sites. Lincoln conversed easily on a wide variety of subjects. According to one witness, "His face would light up for a time while telling an anecdote illustrating a subject under discussion, and afterward his features would relax and show the deep lines which had been graven upon them." Afterward, Lincoln thanked Lee for his hospitality and returned to Grant's headquarters. Lee was pleased the visit had gone so well, and more pleased when Fox told him to ignore the sniping from the press about the river obstructions; he, for one, had been "in favor of obstructions from the beginning," and he planned to send a dozen more canal boats to make the obstruction complete.[36]

Lincoln returned to Washington "sunburnt and fagged but refreshed and cheered." Welles conceded that "the journey has done him good, physically, and strengthened him mentally." The next day the president rode out to the Navy Yard to watch the firing of some new rockets and other experimental ordnance, staying until ten that night. But, as ever, there were problems waiting for him in Washington. Chief among them was Salmon P. Chase. By now, Lincoln had begun to appreciate that for all his many skills, Chase had become the source of as many problems as solutions, even without his active competition for the presidency. The price of gold had shot up so fast that Congress suspended trading. On a more immediate level, Welles was complaining that the pay for sailors was often delayed, sometimes by several months. The judgmental Welles thought Chase lacked "the sagacity, knowledge, taste, or ability of a financier," and concluded that "we are hurrying onward into a financial abyss." He rued the fact that Lincoln had "surrendered the finances to [Chase's] management entirely," though he conveniently ignored the fact that Lincoln had done pretty much the same thing in "surrendering" management of the navy to Welles.[37]

Admiring as he was of Chase's abilities, and sensitive as always to Chase's political importance, Lincoln still saw that something would have to give. In the end, the crisis came over a relatively inconsequential issue when John Cisco, the veteran assistant treasurer of New York, announced his retirement. Chase backed his own candidate for the post and stuck by that choice even when most of the New York establishment objected. Lincoln told him, "I can not, without much embarrassment, make this appointment." Chase managed to get Cisco to withdraw his resignation, but in a gambit that was designed to make the president back down as well, he also offered his own resignation. It was the third time Chase had tried this gambit, and, as Lincoln explained to John Hay, Chase was telling him, "Unless you say you are sorry, & ask me to stay & agree that I shall be absolute and that you shall have nothing, no matter how long you beg for it, I will go." Rather than concede, Lincoln stunned Chase, and much of the country, by accepting the proffered resignation. "Of all I have said in commendation of your ability," Lincoln wrote him, "I have nothing to unsay, and yet you and I have reached a point of mutual embarrassment in our official relations which it seems can not be overcome, or longer sustained."[38]

It caused fewer problems than many feared, though some members of the more progressive wing of the party worried that by firing Chase,

Lincoln had effectively sided with the Blairs. After all, Lincoln had sent Frank Blair back to his command in Georgia, and he continued to keep Montgomery Blair at his post in the cabinet. Appreciating the awkwardness of Lincoln's position in this respect, Monty Blair offered to resign anytime the president thought it would be politically helpful. Lincoln thanked him but told him, in effect, not yet.

The good news that week was the intelligence that the USS *Kearsarge* had sunk the "pirate" ship *Alabama* off the coast of France near Cherbourg. Welles took great satisfaction in bringing the information to the cabinet meeting on July 5, and there were congratulations all around. Indeed, the news triggered celebrations across the North, and Welles found himself in the unusual position of being popular. He took pride in the fact that British "perfidy" and rebel "treason" had been whipped by "a Yankee ship with a Yankee commander and a Yankee crew," though he also grumbled privately in his diary about all the criticism that had been heaped on him and on the Navy Department for not catching the *Alabama* sooner.[39]

THE WAR CAME TO WASHINGTON that month. Seeking to loosen Grant's tightening grip around Richmond and Petersburg, Robert E. Lee dispatched Jubal Early's corps on an extended raid down the Shenandoah Valley and across the Potomac into Maryland. News of Early's advance raced ahead of him like an evil rumor. After Early's raiders swept aside a scratch force cobbled together by Major General Lew Wallace at the crossing of the Monocacy River only thirty miles northwest of Washington, it was evident that the target of this raid was the capital itself. On July 10, rebel pickets appeared in front of the forts north and west of the city. Though some were greatly alarmed, Lincoln was more concerned with cutting off the raiders' escape, and he suggested to Grant that he come personally to Washington to coordinate it. Grant did not come himself, instead sending Horatio Wright's Sixth Corps, the first elements of which arrived on July 11 after a swift voyage from the James River. That effectively ended any chance that the rebel thrust might actually seize the capital. Nevertheless, there remained a muted sense of alarm in the city, though not in the White House, where Lincoln remained "in very good feather" according to John Hay, who wrote in his diary that the president "seems not in the least concerned."[40]

Lincoln twice went to the front to see as much of the fighting as he could for himself. On July 11, as the first elements of Wright's reinforcements marched up the Seventh Street Pike, he rode with them out to Fort Stevens, where he borrowed a field glass from a signal officer to study the gray-and-butternut-clad soldiers in the near distance. He made "a very conspicuous figure" there on the rampart in his frock coat and top hat. Years later, the jurist Oliver Wendell Holmes claimed that, without recognizing whom he was addressing, he told Lincoln, "Get down, you fool" (sometimes rendered as "Get down, you *damn* fool"). Whether or not Holmes actually so addressed the president, Lincoln soon descended from the ramparts and returned to the White House. The next day, the rest of Wright's Sixth Corps veterans marched out Seventh Street to take up positions in front of Fort Stevens, and Lincoln cancelled the cabinet meeting that morning to ride out to the fort once again, this time with Mary as company. At Fort Stevens, Wright invited the president to have a look, and once again the president ascended the parapet. Rebel sharpshooters had occupied a "fine mansion" only about three hundred yards away and were looking for targets of opportunity. When a surgeon standing near Lincoln was shot in the thigh, Wright asked the president to take cover. Lincoln demurred and continued to study the panorama before him until Wright declared that if he did not step down, he would have the president forcibly removed. A bemused Lincoln then sat in the shade of the rampart leaning back against the fort's exterior wall, though he occasionally stood up to peer over it to see what was happening. Welles, who had also come out to see the fighting, found him there, "his back against the parapet towards the enemy." A nearby battery soon opened on the house being used by the rebel sharpshooters, sending three or four shells into it, after which two regiments of Union troops charged it, and the rebel pickets fled. Welles, and presumably Lincoln, could see them "running across the fields, seeking the woods."[41]

Like Lincoln, Welles privately disparaged the alarmism of some Washingtonians, but before going out to Fort Stevens, he had taken the precaution of ordering Admiral Lee to send "three or four of your gunboats" from Hampton Roads to Washington, including the ironclad *Atlanta*. When he did not get an immediate acknowledgment, Welles sent another telegram asking why. Lee replied that the telegraph line from Fort Monroe had been out of order, and he assured Welles that he had already issued orders for the designated warships to head for the Potomac at once.* But he did more than that, for on that same day, Lee also received a wire from Fox informing him that the rebel raiders were in Silver Spring, where Lizzie's father and brother lived. Fox may have intended to offer comfort by reporting that their homes were "not burned yet," though very likely this image only elevated Lee's concern. The next day, Lee learned that communications between Washington and Annapolis had been cut, and he telegraphed Welles that he was leaving Hampton Roads in the *Malvern* "to look after [the] Potomac Division of my squadron." At least part of his concern was personal. Though Lizzie and their son, Blair, had fled the capital for Cape May, New Jersey, Lee was worried about their personal possessions, noting in his diary, "We shall lose everything if the rascals get into the city."[42]

By the time Lee wrote that line, the rebels were gone. Welles affected to be unsurprised, claiming that he had known all along that it had been only a feint and that there had never been any real danger. Consequently, he was extremely annoyed to learn that Admiral Lee was steaming up the Potomac in the *Malvern*. It didn't help that the *New York Herald* that day reported that ships "in Rear Admiral Lee's inactive flotilla . . . have been ordered up to Washington to protect the scared imbeciles of the capital." Marking his reply "Immediate," Welles fired off an order to Lee to "return to Hampton Roads. There is no necessity of your presence in the Potomac," punctuating it with the terse order "Answer." When he got no answer, he tried again: "The Department disapproves your leaving your station without orders in an emergency like the present. Return to Hampton Roads without anchoring your vessel."[43]

Too late. Before he got either telegram, Lee had docked at the Navy Yard and made his way to the Navy Department. There he met with Fox and Welles, both of whom told him he should return at once to his post. He headed back to the *Malvern*, sending out calls for the officers who had gone ashore to return to the ship at once. When they were all

---

*Circumstantial evidence suggests that despite his declarations of confidence, Welles wanted at least one of these gunboats to stand by in order to evacuate the president from Washington if it came to that. Lincoln was upset when he learned of this since it implied that he would be willing to abandon the capital.

on board, he got under way again for Hampton Roads. Nevertheless, he was frustrated and angered by his cold reception. He was especially angry at Fox, who, he decided, had written the two terse telegrams from Welles telling him that the department disapproved of his actions. Though Fox was family (his wife was the sister of Montgomery Blair's wife), Lee suspected that Fox was also an enemy. Lee had risen to his position in part, at least, because of his relationship with the Blairs and Fox, but now Lee and Monty Blair were no longer speaking, and Lee decided that Fox, too, had turned on him. He recalled that Fox had disapproved, back when the war first started, of his decision to return at once from Africa when he had learned of the attack on Fort Sumter. "He disapproved my return then!!!" Lee wrote in his private journal during the passage down the Potomac, the three exclamation points reflecting his anger. Writing in the black darkness of the middle of the night as the *Malvern* cruised back down the Potomac River, Lee decided that Fox had become "swollen" with his sense of position, and he ended his journal entry with a sarcastic gibe: "Big man!"[44]

Later, having calmed down in the light of a new day, Lee penned an explanatory letter to Welles. "I am deeply concerned at this censure of the Department," he wrote. He justified his action by emphasizing how dire and dangerous the rebel raid on Washington had been. Of course, this was exactly the wrong tack to take since Welles had already decided there never had been any real danger. Lee considered making a formal protest of his treatment, and he sent copies of his correspondence "with applicatory notes" to his father-in-law so that Frank Blair could defend his interests. Wisely, Lizzie advised him to "drop the discussion." She wrote that her father "recommends silence & forbearance," and Lee did not pursue it. Nevertheless, the episode did not enhance his professional standing with the Navy Department. For all his earnestness and commitment, Lee's constant queries about trade permits, his association with Butler's failed thrust upriver, his dithering over placing obstructions in the James River, his perceived overreaction to Jubal Early's raid, and his apparent willingness to play politics all undermined his dimming prospects for promotion.[45]

OF COURSE, THERE WAS ALWAYS WILMINGTON. The capture of that crucial port would go a long way toward erasing all the negatives that

Welles had been tallying against Lee's name, and certainly Welles was eager to assail Wilmington. In August, Welles pressed Lincoln again on the idea of capturing Wilmington and cutting off the rebel supply line to Richmond and Petersburg; in September he sent Fox to convince Grant that "closing Wilmington" was "paramount to all other questions— more important, practically, than the capture of Richmond." Once it was evident that the president had signed on, Grant, too, became a supporter. But Grant also told Fox that he wanted someone other than Phillips Lee to command the attack. The *New York Herald* had not been entirely incorrect in claiming that Grant had lost confidence in Acting Admiral Lee. Whether it was a matter of personality or the fact that Lee was associated in Grant's mind with Butler's failed move to the Bermuda Hundred, Grant made it clear that "he would not be satisfied with Lee . . . in regard to operations at Wilmington." Welles agreed. "He is true and loyal," Welles wrote of Lee in his diary, but also "prudent and cautious," and in this context, "prudent and cautious" were not words of praise. As for the attack on Wilmington, Welles concluded: "Lee is not the man for that." Consequently, only a week after he had returned to Hampton Roads, Lee received a telegram from Welles informing him that his squadron was to be broken into two "divisions," one at Hampton Roads under Captain Melancton Smith, and the other under himself at Beaufort, North Carolina. Lee remained the putative commander of the North Atlantic Blockading Squadron, but he understood at once. "It is evident that I am sent away to make room for some one here. Who is the man?"[46]

Farragut was the man. Even before news arrived in Washington of Farragut's victory at Mobile Bay, Welles had decided that Farragut should be brought from the Gulf to command the North Atlantic Blockading Squadron and lead the attack on Wilmington. The news from Mobile, which arrived on August 9, only confirmed it. Farragut had accomplished at Mobile what neither Du Pont nor Dahlgren had been able to do at Charleston: run past the forts protecting the harbor to take command of the bay. Although the new large monitor *Tecumseh* had struck a torpedo and gone down with all but a few of her crew, the rest of Farragut's fleet had not only survived the run into the bay but engaged and defeated the rebel squadron, including the ironclad *Tennessee,* and captured the Confederate admiral Franklin Buchanan.

Farragut noted that his flagship, the *Hartford*, had "poured her whole port broadside" into the rebel ironclad "at a distance of no more than twelve feet." It was precisely the kind of victory Lee had yearned for, and it provoked the formal thanks of Congress and a proclamation from the president, who offered "the applause and thanks of the nation" for the "brilliant success."[47]

To his credit, Lee expressed genuine joy at the news from Mobile. Publicly, he ordered an artillery salute and three cheers around the fleet; privately, he noted in his journal that Farragut was a "true patriot." Even so, Lee saw that his tenure of command in the North Atlantic was coming to an end, and along with it any chance of achieving the kind of victory he needed to secure promotion. "I am banished to Beaufort and forbid[den] to return to H[ampton] R[oads] without an emergency," he wrote in his journal. It was, he thought, a deliberate and calculated bit of "cool impudence" to shove him aside and make room for Farragut. His father-in-law, Frank Blair Sr., thought that there was a political motive to Farragut's pending appointment. By bringing the Union's greatest naval hero to the principal theater of war, the administration would highlight recent military and naval successes and stoke pro-war sentiment, which might translate into Republican votes. In Blair's words: "Farragut's success has given him a prestige which makes him a strong card to play for the election."[48]

Whatever was behind it, it completely deflated Lee's enthusiasm and optimism. He suspected that his effective banishment was a product of the "trader's interest," and he was both saddened and disgusted that his former friends apparently had turned on him. Like Du Pont, he concluded that Fox was one of these traitors. "I think Fox is implicated," he wrote, "Fox is in with them [the traders] & means to defeat my promotion."[49]

Welles' plans to bring Farragut to the North Atlantic, however, were overturned when Farragut wrote to Lincoln that he didn't want the job. He was tired, he said, and needed a leave of absence, after which he preferred to stay with his command in the Gulf. Lincoln went to see Welles to ensure that this fit in with department plans, and Welles told the president that Farragut "could remain as long as he pleased in the Gulf." This put Welles in a quandary, however, for he had already moved Lee aside to make room for Farragut. "I am exceedingly embarrassed how to proceed," he confided to his diary. He solved it by giving the North Atlantic command to Porter and sending Lee out to the Mississippi, essentially swapping squadron commanders. Porter was "to hurry up his business" out west and then "return and organize the expedition" to Wilmington. Welles knew that Lee would be offended by this turn of events. He might have tolerated being superseded by Farragut, the nation's hero, but Porter, to whom he had been senior for all of his naval career, was another matter. Still, whatever Lee's reaction, Welles consoled himself, as he usually did, with the thought that "personal considerations must yield to the public necessities." Lizzie blamed it all on Fox, the family traitor, who in her view had removed her husband simply because "Fox likes Porter best."[50]

There was more. That same week, Lincoln notified Montgomery Blair that he was now ready to accept his earlier offer to resign whenever it would be helpful. Chase's friends had made it clear to Lincoln that by letting Chase go and keeping Blair, Lincoln was in danger of alienating the progressive wing of the party. More immediately, Zachariah Chandler told Lincoln that if he dismissed Blair from the cabinet, Frémont would agree to drop his third-party run for the presidency. It is not clear that there was a quid pro quo on this issue, but Frémont did withdraw, and the next day Lincoln notified Blair that he was now ready to accept his resignation. There were other factors, too. Blair had so angered Stanton that the secretary of war refused to attend cabinet meetings if he knew Blair was going to be there. And finally, the perception was growing that the Blairs collectively had altogether too much influence in the administration and particularly in the Navy Department. As Bennett put it in the *Herald*: "Old Blair, and young Blair, Postmaster Blair and General Blair, all the small Blairs and all the little Blairs, all the sons-in-law [Lee] and all the brothers-in-law [Fox] of the Blairs have their broad hands and broad feet upon the Navy Department."[51]

Sacrificing Blair to these demands also had repercussions. The twin blows of Lee's reassignment and Montgomery Blair's resignation led old Frank Blair to go once more to see Welles. The navy secretary consoled the senior Blair on the resignation of his son, which Welles thought a genuine loss. As for his son-in-law, Welles told Blair that "Lee was not degraded in being assigned to another command," though Welles also told Blair candidly that while Lee was "cautious and vigilant," he was "not, perhaps, the man for an immediate demonstration, an assault requiring prompt action." Blair left unsatisfied. Later, writing in his diary, Welles went further. Lee, Welles wrote, had "discharged his duties intelligently and firmly. But he can never be a great commander."[52]

So Porter came east, as Fox had promised that he would, and for all his tired disillusionment, Lee went west to take over the Mississippi squadron. He was not happy. "I am already sick and dispirited," he wrote in early August, even before his reassignment. "My health is failing from long confinement & overwork on shipboard. I shall quit this fall & seek repose from active service." But he did not quit. Professional that he was, he assumed command of the Mississippi River Squadron and supervised its activities for the rest of the war, though by then the Mississippi had become something of a strategic backwater. He never won his great victory or obtained the formal thanks of Congress, and remained an acting rear admiral until the end of the war. A year later he was promoted to commodore, and on April 22, 1870, five years and two weeks after Appomattox, he finally received his long-coveted promotion to rear admiral.[53]

12

"I Must Refer You to General Grant"
Lincoln Relinquishes the Conn

THE HIGH HOPES OF SPRING evaporated amidst the apparent military stalemate of late summer. The casualty lists printed in northern papers were horrifying, and the price of gold continued to climb as speculators lost confidence in the ability of the national government to satisfy its creditors. Lincoln's call for five hundred thousand more troops in July, only five months after calling for five hundred thousand in February, produced cries that the meat grinder of war was insatiable. Halleck was so concerned about the public reaction to this latest call for troops he suggested to Lincoln that some units should be withdrawn from Grant's army to police cities in the North to prevent the kind of civil violence that had roiled New York in 1863. Lincoln rejected this advice, telling Grant to hold on where he was and "chew & choke as much as possible."[1]

Nevertheless, Lincoln was aware that the disappointed mood of the country could jeopardize his chances for reelection. On August 12, Seward's political guru, Thurlow Weed, reported that he had carefully canvassed public opinion in New York, and it was now evident that Lincoln's reelection had become "an impossibility." There was, Weed insisted, not "the slightest hope of success." Henry Raymond, editor of the *New York Times* and chairman of the Republican National Committee, agreed. "Unless some prompt and bold step be now taken,"

Raymond concluded, "all is lost." Lincoln took these dire predictions to heart. "You think I don't know I am going to be beaten," he wrote, "*but I do* and unless some great change takes place *badly beaten.*" Rumors spread that Lincoln had admitted he was "a beaten man." John Nicolay sent out letters to concerned supporters denying it, but the outlook was certainly bleak.[2]

These political circumstances provided the context for a letter that Lincoln received from Horace Greeley, the meddlesome but influential editor of the *New York Tribune*. Greeley wrote that a Confederate delegation had arrived in Canada to discuss peace terms and urged Lincoln to engage with them. Lincoln hardly needed Greeley to remind him that "our bleeding, bankrupt, almost dying country . . . longs for peace," and he knew he could not appear to refuse an opportunity to end the war. But neither could he be seen as willing to abandon the cause for which a quarter of a million men had died. He therefore designated Greeley as his emissary to meet with these delegates, and sent along John Hay with a letter addressed "To Whom It May Concern" specifying that "any proposition which embraces the restoration of peace, the integrity of the whole Union, and the abandonment of slavery" would be seriously considered. Of course, Lincoln knew that Jefferson Davis's government would never accept such terms, and as he foresaw, the "negotiations" collapsed before they got started.[3]

In spite of that, Lincoln's electoral prospects remained grim. Democrats complained that by setting such strict conditions, the president foreclosed any possible negotiations that might end the bloodshed. If only the president were willing to sacrifice the Negro, the Democrats argued, peace could be had at once. This Lincoln was unwilling to do. The promise of freedom had been made, and, as he had written the year before, "the promise being made, must be kept." Lincoln was aware, however, that this stance was losing him support among War Democrats, and in consequence he signaled that he might be willing to bend on the question. When one War Democrat complained that Lincoln was prolonging the war by insisting that "no steps can be taken towards peace . . . unless accompanied with an abandonment of slavery," Lincoln chose his words carefully in drafting a reply. "Saying reunion and abandonment of slavery would be considered, if offered," he wrote, "is not saying that nothing *else* or *less* would be considered." "If Jefferson

Davis wishes, for himself, or for the benefit of his friends at the North, to know what I would do if he were to offer peace and re-union, saying nothing about slavery, let him try me." A few modern critics of Lincoln have read into this letter evidence that Lincoln was willing to backslide on the slavery issue. Lincoln himself was confident that Davis would reject even these terms, and he very likely saw it as a safe way to defuse the public criticism without any real consequences. But even as a ploy, he worried about making such a public offer, and before sending the letter, he met at length with Frederick Douglass to assay how that spokesman for black America would react to the publication of such an offer. In effect, Lincoln asked Douglass if he should send the letter. Douglass advised against it. "It would be taken as a complete surrender of your anti-slavery policy," Douglass told him, "and do you serious damage." Lincoln agreed, and in the end he did not send it.[4]

Lincoln, however, may have envisioned the possibility that he might have to take a step back under certain circumstances. He was politically sensitive enough to know that Weed might well be correct about his chances for reelection, and in light of that, he wrote a short memorandum that he took to a meeting of the cabinet and, without disclosing its contents, asked each man present to sign the back. The note read that "for some days past" it had become evident to him that he would not be reelected. In such case, he asserted, "it will be my duty to cooperate with the President elect, as to save the Union between the election and the inauguration; as he [Lincoln's opponent] will have secured his election on such ground that he cannot possibly save it afterwards." Lincoln subsequently sealed the note in an envelope and put it in his desk. Why did Lincoln write such a note, and what compelled him to have it witnessed so dramatically? It may have been no more than a fit of self-indulgence, the product of a depressed mood. But even in his bouts of depression, Lincoln was not given to such indulgences. It is more likely that he believed he might lose the election, and in order to end the war quickly, before a Democrat took office, he would have to make some unpalatable compromises—compromises that included the survival of slavery. The sealed letter would be his explanation of why such a retreat had become necessary.[5]

What Lincoln needed most was some manifest evidence of progress in the war. The news of Farragut's success at Mobile helped some, but Lin-

coln knew that a naval victory, however important or dramatic, was neither strategically nor politically decisive in the public mind. It was good
news, to be sure, but Lincoln was more concerned about how Farragut's
success at Mobile might affect Sherman's prospects in Georgia. Like the
rest of the nation, Lincoln had his eye fixed on the two great Union
armies: Grant's outside Petersburg, and Sherman's outside Atlanta.

Then on September 3, a wire from Sherman reported that "Atlanta
is ours and fairly won." Welles doubted that "the zealous partisans"
who had already decided "the war was a failure" would be any more
impressed with Sherman's victory than they had been with Farragut's.
Lincoln, however, saw at once that the fall of Atlanta would greatly affect the political calculus. To showcase the good news, he ordered two
massive public salutes of a hundred guns each: one on September 5 to
celebrate Farragut's victory at Mobile, and another two days later in
honor of Sherman's capture of Atlanta. In a separate proclamation,
Lincoln ordered a day of thanksgiving, asking citizens to pray "for the
Divine protection to our brave soldiers" and to express public gratitude
for "His mercy in preserving our national existence against the insurgent rebels."[6]

As Lincoln had foreseen, the news from Atlanta had an electrifying
effect on the citizenry. One supporter wrote, "I have never seen such a
sudden lighting up of the public mind since the late victory at Atlanta."
In addition, Lincoln's refusal to abandon the Negro undercut a plot by
radical Republicans to nominate a more progressive alternative, and after Atlanta even Thurlow Weed changed his mind, writing to Seward
that he now thought it likely that Lincoln could win reelection after all.[7]

WITH TANGIBLE MILITARY PROGRESS in the war and the revival of his political hopes, Lincoln turned his attention to the consideration of postwar questions. He spent less time in the telegraph office and more at
his desk. He had never sought to be a hands-on commander in chief,
and he had assumed the burden of directing armies and naval
squadrons out of perceived necessity rather than inherent interest. Now
that he had generals—and admirals—whom he trusted, he interfered
less, in effect turning the management and conduct of the war over to
Grant, especially as it was evident that Grant had absorbed Lincoln's
strategic vision about how the war should be fought. Lincoln remained

captain of the ship, but it was now Grant's watch and, insofar as military strategy was concerned, his hand on the tiller.

Lincoln also began to ease the strictures on trade with the South. In August, the provisional governor of Texas, Andrew Jackson Hamilton, concocted a scheme by which wavering cotton planters in Texas would agree to switch sides in exchange for being allowed to ship their cotton out through the blockade. Seward, though skeptical, thought it worth a try, and Lincoln, looking to the end of the war, thought it might ease the transition toward eventual reunion. Lincoln told Seward to draft suitable orders, and without telling Welles, Seward composed a letter for the president to sign ordering Farragut to let Hamilton or his agents take cotton out through the blockade and send it to Treasury agents in New Orleans.[8]

Lincoln should have known that this was sure to annoy Welles. After all, cutting off the cotton trade was the navy's primary task. Now Lincoln was asking squadron commanders to stand by and watch as ships filled with cotton passed out through the blockade unmolested. This was frustrating not only because these commanders had spent months—in some cases years—trying to interdict this very trade, but also because it was like watching a potential fortune in prize money sail away uncollected. Farragut first heard of the new arrangement when General E. R. Canby sent him a copy of Lincoln's letter and asked him to forward appropriate orders to officers on the blockade. Farragut did so, though at the same time he also wrote to Welles suggesting that "the whole matter will prove another swindle."[9]

Eventually Lincoln came to the same conclusion. After Welles convinced him that this arrangement virtually nullified the blockade, Lincoln fired off a telegram to Farragut: "Do not, on any account, or on any showing of authority whatever, from whomsoever purporting to come, allow the blockade to be violated." That order implicitly contradicted his earlier order, and a few days later Lincoln made it explicit, specifically revoking his order to allow Hamilton's agents to take cotton out of Texas.[10]

Still looking for a workable trade policy in anticipation of eventual reunion, Lincoln signed off on a new set of rules proposed by William P. Fessenden, Chase's replacement as secretary of the Treasury. Fessenden's protocol abolished Chase's permit system and simply opened trade to northern merchants or government officials, who would now be allowed to purchase products from the states in insurrection without permits. Lincoln believed that "extensive regions lay open where neither army was in possession, where there was an abundance of cotton." But every time the planters sought to bring that cotton to market, it was seized by the Union army or navy as "plunder," which naturally encouraged the planters to hoard it. The new rules protected both the buyers and the sellers of cotton from interference by federal authorities. They required "officers commanding fleets, flotillas, and gunboats" to give "safe conduct" to any persons engaged in this trade and to the products traded. The only prohibition was that the officers themselves could not participate in this traffic. Welles continued to object, but he was less offended by a system that allowed everyone to trade than he had been by the "mischievous machinery" of Chase's system, which had granted favors to particular individuals.[11]

Despite that, Lincoln began once again to issue trade permits himself. In December, he granted one James Harrison permission to take three steamers, and as many barges as they could tow, up the Red River "beyond our Military lines," returning "with any cargoes he may bring." A few days later, at the request of Vice President Hamlin, he wrote another permit for Fergus Peniston, the reputed owner of "large amounts of cotton and naval stores in Louisiana and Southern Mississippi," authorizing him to bring out 23,640 bales of cotton under the protection of the navy. This was, in Lincoln's words, "not merely a concession to private interest and pecuniary greed" but rather a deliberate policy decision to ease up on the isolation of the South. Having constricted, the anaconda would now begin to uncoil.[12]

IT WAS IMPOSSIBLE to keep politics and strategy completely separate. Soldiers in camp and sailors at sea openly discussed the forthcoming national election, and though there was some sentiment that the Democratic candidate, George B. McClellan, might be able to bring the war to an end more swiftly, the clear majority wanted to finish the job and favored the reelection of Old Abe. Even the prisoners at Andersonville, who more than anyone stood to benefit from an early peace, favored Lincoln's reelection, voting overwhelmingly for him in a mock election. Officers and men alike looked upon McClellan's supporters as defeatists and saw Lincoln's reelection as an integral part of the war effort.

Knowing that, Weed and Seward were eager to find some way to ensure that the soldiers and sailors had an opportunity to vote. Lincoln met with Seward, Stanton, and Welles to discuss various ways to achieve this. While most states allowed their men to vote in the field, Indiana, Illinois, and New Jersey required their presence at the polls. Warned by Indiana's governor that the vote there was likely to be very close, Lincoln asked Sherman if could see his way to "let her soldiers, or any part of them, go home and vote in the State election" in October. He emphasized that "this is, in no sense, an order," and made it clear that this was not for his personal benefit, telling Sherman that the men could be recalled before the presidential canvass in November, but he also noted that the loss of Indiana in the October elections "would go far towards losing the whole Union cause." Sherman responded by granting furloughs en masse to Indiana regiments.[13]

Sending sailors home to vote was more problematical, and Lincoln and Seward decided that they should be encouraged to vote aboard ship. They deputized Charles Jones of the New York election commission to collect the ballots, and bearing a note from Lincoln, Jones went to see Welles about it. Welles was cool to the idea. It seemed indelicate to him to go out and collect votes in this way, though he acknowledged "it seemed ungracious to oppose it." In the end, he placed the iron-hulled steamer *Circassian* at Jones' disposal and ordered all squadron commanders to cooperate. In addition, Fessenden sent a revenue cutter along the coast to collect additional ballots. Weed was prepared to go further. He wanted to poll the workers in the Brooklyn Navy Yard, dismiss those who were not politically loyal, and levy financial contributions on the rest. Though this had been common practice in previous administrations, Welles found the idea offensive, and despite a visit from party chairman Henry Raymond, he refused to allow it.[14]

Three key states held local elections in October that everyone presumed would be a bellwether for the national vote in November. Lincoln went to the War Department telegraph office on October 10 to keep track of the returns as they came in. By now, he had grown more confident of the outcome, and his confidence was soon vindicated. Whether or not Sherman's veterans made the difference, Indiana came in strongly for the government, and both Ohio and Pennsylvania showed good results. Republican officials in Philadelphia predicted a twenty-thousand-vote majority, though later returns made it closer than that. Between telegrams, Lincoln read aloud from a collection of the humorous letters of Petroleum V. Nasby, the pseudonym of humorist David Ross Locke, whose bombastic missives satirized southern pretensions. As always, Lincoln chuckled aloud as he shared Locke's pointed gibes. The election news improved through the night, and soon it was clear that the Republicans not only had held their own but had gained seats. The returns from the soldiers' hospitals showed that the wounded favored the administration ten to one. Lincoln was pleased to learn that Company K of the 150th Pennsylvania Volunteers, the personal escort that rode with him daily to and from the White House, had voted 63 to 11 for the Union ticket, though he might have wondered about the eleven naysayers.[15]

A month later, on national election night (November 8), Lincoln again went over to the telegraph office.* It was raining and already dark at seven o'clock as Lincoln made his way to the War Department, slipping on the wet cobblestones and nearly falling. As he entered the side door, someone handed him a telegram bearing the news that he had won a ten-thousand-vote majority in Philadelphia. Then another: he had a majority of fifteen thousand in Baltimore, five thousand in Boston. The good news cascaded in and elevated Lincoln's mood. Lincoln asked an orderly to take the news to his wife. "She is more anxious than I," he explained. Not only was Lincoln comfortably ahead, his foes were foundering. John P. Hale and Henry Winter Davis, who had proved such thorns in the side to Welles and the navy, both went down to defeat. Fox, who was present, exulted over the news, but Lincoln was more philosophical. "You have more of that feeling of personal resentment than I," he said to Fox. "Perhaps I may have too little of it, but I never thought it paid." At half past two in the morning, a military band showed up to serenade the president. For a while it

---

*Lincoln had been invited to attend the National Sailors' Fair in Boston that week but declined in order to monitor the election returns. In extending his regrets, he wrote the organizer: "To all, from Rear Admiral, to honest Jack I tender the Nation's admiration and gratitude."

seemed possible that Lincoln would get the electoral votes of not only all the free states but also the border states. And in the end he nearly did, winning all but New Jersey among the free states and carrying two of the four border states, Maryland and Missouri.[16]

At the cabinet meeting two days later, Lincoln asked John Hay to open the letter, the back of which he had asked each of them to sign in August. It was securely sealed and Hay had a bit of trouble trying to wrestle it open without tearing it. Lincoln then took the letter and read it aloud, sharing his resolve, if he had not been reelected, to work with his successor to try to end the war before his term expired, but he offered no details about what that might have meant. In the satisfaction of the moment, no one on the cabinet thought to ask him, though Seward made a few remarks at McClellan's expense about how McClellan likely would have been as uncooperative as president-elect as he had been as a general.[17]

Across most of the North, and throughout the fleet, the news of Lincoln's reelection was received with the same celebrations of joy as news of a great military victory. Just as Lincoln had ordered the firing of a national salute in recognition of victories by Farragut and Sherman, Thomas T. Craven, commodore of the European Squadron, whose flagship was anchored in Antwerp, ordered a salute of twenty-one guns in honor of Lincoln's election victory. He confessed to Welles that he knew this was an unusual, maybe even inappropriate, demonstration, but in his view the election had been "the greatest and most important contest of the war," and he "could not resist the impulse to thus manifest my joy."[18]

THE SAME DAY that Lincoln learned of his reelection, he also learned of the capture of the notorious rebel raider *Florida*. The telegram arrived in Washington early on Election Day, and Lincoln passed the welcome news on to Seward, adding, "The information is certain." Most likely Lincoln did not stop to consider the ramifications of the news until after the election was resolved. For his part, Welles was delighted to learn that USS *Wachusett* had rammed and seized the *Florida*, but he might have experienced a sense of foreboding to read that the *Wachusett* (ironically, Charles Wilkes' former flagship) had made its attack clandestinely, at night, in a neutral harbor.[19]

The captain of the *Wachusett* was Commander Napoleon Collins, the same officer who had captured a suspected blockade runner off Sand Key in the Caribbean two years before, provoking a protest from the British and triggering a rebuke from Lincoln. Apparently unchastened by that experience, Collins had outdone himself this time. His preliminary report indicated that he had rammed and taken possession of the *Florida* at three o'clock in the morning on October 7 "in the Bay of San Salvador, Brazil." Collins did not offer a justification, saying merely that his ship had struck the *Florida* "on her starboard quarter, cutting down her bulwarks and carrying away her mizzenmast and main yard." Satisfying as it was to learn that the notorious rebel "pirate" had been taken, Welles knew there was no getting around the fact that Collins had blatantly violated Brazilian neutrality.[20]

For most of two years, the U.S. Navy's inability to end the rampage of a handful of rebel commerce raiders had been the single most frustrating and challenging aspect of Welles' job. Newspapers—even friendly newspapers—wondered publicly why the navy with its hundreds of vessels could neither find nor capture a handful of pirates. Sensitive to this pressure, Welles' letters to his squadron commanders hinted that they should use any means at hand to bring these piratical cruisers to bay. Captain John Winslow of the *Kearsarge*, who had sunk the *Alabama* off Cherbourg in June, had found the *Florida* in port at Brest the year before and had sought direction from Welles about what he should do about it. Welles wouldn't say. Though Winslow sent Welles a score of detailed reports, Welles sent back no orders beyond telling him, "The Department enjoins vigilance on the part of yourself and other commanders of our vessels." The silence from Washington was frustrating. "The Department will not answer one [question]," Winslow wrote a friend, "but goes on the rule—give no orders, take no responsibility." Given these circumstances, it was entirely possible for officers to conclude, as one modern student of the war has put it, that "aggressive actions on their part would be supported by their seniors as long as they were successful in their mission." Indeed, Winslow concluded that Welles' message was: "If the commander of a vessel succeeds, all is well; if not, make him responsible."[21]

Unlike Winslow, Collins was not one to agonize. Finding himself in a neutral harbor with the *Florida*, Collins did not ask Welles or anyone else for orders. Indeed, learning that the American consul, Thomas F. Wilson, had promised local authorities that the *Wachusett* would do nothing to violate Brazilian neutrality, Collins told Wilson he would "not be bound by anything he said," and declared that he planned "to act on my own discretion." Bold words but unnecessary, since Wilson's promise was worthless. The consul's complicity in Collins' plans (and his duplicity to the Brazilians) was evident in the fact that he was on board the *Wachusett* when Collins rammed the rebel warship. Although Collins had ordered his men not to fire except in self-defense, gunners on the *Wachusett* also fired two shots into the *Florida.* Collins subsequently filed charges against Lieutenant Commander L. A. Beardslee for opening fire, though the distinction between ramming a ship and firing into her was meaningless. About half the crew of the *Florida* was ashore at the time, including her captain, and the skeleton crew on board had little choice but to surrender the ship. Confederate Lieutenant Thomas K. Porter came aboard the *Wachusett* to protest this illegal attack in vigorous terms, but Collins ignored him. Collins had expected that his assault would sink the *Florida*, but seeing that she was not going to sink after all, he ordered up a hawser and towed her out to sea, making his way to Danish St. Thomas in the Caribbean, from which place he sent in his report.[22]

There was no hint of apology in that report. Collins admitted that he had made a deliberate calculation that "the Brazilian authorities would forbear to interfere" and was surprised when "they fired three shotted guns at us while we were towing the Florida out." Not only that, but a Brazilian sloop-of-war set out in pursuit, though even with the *Florida* in tow, the *Wachusett* managed to outdistance it. Collins was more concerned about the health and safety of his own crew in a crowded ship, and he worried that the fifty-eight men and twelve officers whom he held as prisoners might try to retake the *Florida.* As a result, Collins made another calculated decision: he allowed eighteen of the prisoners—Italians, Spaniards, and Dutchmen—to escape ashore in St. Thomas. Afterward, when it became evident that some of these men had been exposed to smallpox, his decision to allow them to go ashore triggered a protest by the Danish government, and Collins had to make a contrite apology. He was not at all contrite, however, about his decision to attack the *Florida* in the first place.[23]

As had been the case three years before during the *Trent* affair, American newspapers cheered Collins' feat, declaring that even if he had violated the "nice legal distinctions" of international law, the Brazilians deserved little sympathy, for they also had erred in providing sanctuary for a robber and pirate. Collins got a congratulatory letter from Charles Wilkes, to whom Collins replied, "In taking the Florida in port I felt that I was only doing what you would have done." Perhaps so, but Wilkes was hardly a role model for diplomatic behavior. Even when the reactions were less supportive, Collins remained unrepentant. "If I have made mistakes," he wrote, "I am sure greater men have made greater ones during this war."[24]

Lincoln remained silent, waiting to learn what the reaction of the Brazilian government would be. Willing as ever to wait until the consequences became evident, he was less concerned by Collins' flagrant violation of the law than he was by what it might cost the government in terms of international goodwill. For his part, Seward acknowledged that the United States "owed a respectful apology to Brazil," but he did not want to have to return the *Florida*. Welles assured him that it would not be necessary. Collins had been "guilty of discourtesy," he admitted, but after all, Brazil had "given refuge and aid to the robbers whom she does not recognize as a government." The belligerent Welles wanted to put Brazil on the defensive and even suggested putting the *Florida*'s crew on trial as pirates. Having already tried that gambit with regard to rebel privateers, Seward vetoed the idea. Any policy response, however, would await the reaction of the Brazilians.[25]

The initial protest was signed by the president of the Brazilian province of Bahia, Antônio Joaquim da Silva Gomes, and was directed not to the U.S. government but to Thomas Wilson, the U.S. consul who had pledged his word of honor that the *Wachusett* would not interfere with the *Florida* while it was in Bahia Harbor (San Salvador). Gomes protested the dishonesty and disrespect evident in Wilson's false promises, and he cut off "all official relations" with Wilson, but, significantly, not with the United States. Moreover, while Gomes declared that henceforth the *Wachusett* would be banned from all Brazilian ports, he did not extend the ban to other Union ships. When the USS *Iroquois*, under C. R. P. Rodgers, entered the harbor at Rio de Janeiro a month later, he reported that his reception was "not only civil but cordial."

Rodgers concluded, "So far as I am able to judge there is a manifest desire here to show good feeling toward the United States."[26]

There was some passing concern that the British might intervene. The London *Times* called Collins' ramming of the *Florida* "an act of simple piracy," and Lord Palmerston hinted that it might be necessary for "the maritime Powers" to "interfere" in order to restore the principle of neutral harbors. The American press bristled at such a notion and insisted that the *Florida* had forfeited the right to sanctuary by capturing American ships within the three-mile limit of the Brazilian coast. Moreover, the British were hardly in a position to take umbrage, since during the War of 1812 British warships had cut out and destroyed the American frigate *Essex*, commanded by David Dixon Porter's father, while it was in Chilean waters. Finally, Britain could hardly come to the aid of Brazil unless Brazil herself protested more vehemently, and the Brazilians signaled from the outset that their protest was more perfunctory than peremptory.[27]

Once the damaged and still-leaking *Florida* arrived in Hampton Roads, Welles assigned David Dixon Porter, now commanding the North Atlantic Blockading Squadron, to take charge of the prisoners and the ship's papers, including those in the *Florida*'s safe. Welles' first inclination was to deliver the prisoners to the POW camp at Point Lookout, Maryland, and Collins actually took them there, but, perhaps advised by Seward, Welles changed his mind and ordered them to Boston, where Wilkes had taken Mason and Slidell back in 1861. Welles then ordered Porter to anchor the *Florida* where she would be safe from both seasonal gales and rebel saboteurs; Fox ordered her guns removed and sent to the Ordnance Bureau. John Hay saw the stripped-down *Florida* anchored in Hampton Roads and described her as "a dirty looking beast: the worst kept craft I ever saw."[28]

Collins' violation of Brazil's neutrality was so flagrant it was impossible not to convene a court-martial, but since the Brazilians were less insistent than the British had been over the *Trent* affair in 1861, there seemed to be no particular hurry, and the court did not assemble until March 1865, five months later. Called upon to respond to the charges, Collins boldly declared himself "guilty," but at the same time insisted that his actions were not unlawful. Asked to provide testimony in support of his plea, Collins submitted, in writing, a single sentence: "I respectfully request that it may be entered on the records of the court as my defense that the capture of the Florida was for the public good." The court handed down its ruling on April 7, while the armies of Grant and Lee converged on Appomattox Court House. It had little option but to find Collins guilty of the charges, and sentenced him to be dismissed from the navy of the United States.[29]

Lincoln made no public or private statement about the event, nor did he send a letter of either praise or criticism to Collins. In his annual message the previous December, with Collins' court-martial still pending, he noted merely that "unforeseen political difficulties have arisen, especially in Brazilian and British ports," and these difficulties required "a just and conciliatory spirit on the part of the United States." While he clearly recognized the need to assuage the Brazilians, Lincoln's silence suggests that, unlike his anger at Collins' actions at Sand Key two years before, this time Collins had not earned "the displeasure of the president." After the court-martial, Lincoln remained mute on the issue, but by then he was preoccupied by the fact that the war was reaching a crescendo in Virginia. Consequently, Collins remained in a kind of administrative limbo: found guilty by a court, but unpunished by the administration. Not until September 17, 1866, almost two years after the event, and a year and half after Lincoln's death, did Welles send Collins a letter informing him that "the sentence of the court is not approved" and restoring him to service.[30]

Well before that, the *Florida* itself had come to an end. Porter had placed a prize crew on board her under Acting Master Jonathan Baker, but the day after Baker took charge, the army transport *Alliance* collided with the *Florida*, carrying away part of her forward rigging and rail. Although the *Florida* had been leaking steadily from the initial collision with the *Wachusett*, it had managed to stay afloat even after being towed more than a thousand miles to Hampton Roads. Now, however, the leaking increased to five inches an hour, and soon to eight inches an hour. Porter ordered her to be anchored near the *Atlanta* so that her crew could assist the prize crew in case of emergency, and he ordered Baker to keep the pumps going. Despite that, the water continued to rise, and at one o'clock in the morning on November 28, Baker showed the prearranged distress signal of a blue light. The *Atlanta* sent two boat crews to assist, and they joined the prize crew in working the hand pumps "until the water came over the berth deck." In spite of their efforts, the *Florida* slowly settled to the bottom in nine fathoms of water.[31]

Though the modern mind leaps to the question of whether the *Florida* might have been sunk deliberately by U.S. Navy agents to prevent its possible return to Brazilian—and perhaps eventually Confederate—authorities, Porter suspected that the sinking was due to rebel sabotage, and ordered an inquiry. After interviewing everyone involved, the court concluded, "There is nothing to show that the collision was designed, or that it was anything more than one of the common accidents which occur in a crowded roadstead," and that remains the most likely explanation.[32]

On the diplomatic front, Seward acknowledged to the Brazilians that "the capture of the *Florida* was unauthorized, unlawful, and indefensible," that Collins was being court-martialed, and that Wilson, the U.S. consul, would be dismissed. As for the sinking of the *Florida*, Seward wrote that it was an "unforeseen accident" for which the United States bore no responsibility. The crew of the *Florida*, Seward wrote, would be set at liberty "to seek a refuge wheresoever they may find it." They were given $20 each (which Welles made sure to charge to the State Department) and released under orders to leave the country within ten days.[33]

Once again in response to this mini-crisis, Lincoln allowed his cabinet members to make pragmatic and ad hoc decisions based less on policy, law, or even principle than on what the circumstances would support. It had been his policy since the war began to adjust to events as they unfolded. On this occasion, his administration offered up to the Brazilians what was asked so long as it did not jeopardize the continuing war effort. As part of the settlement, Seward agreed that a U.S. warship would fire a twenty-one-gun salute to the Brazilian flag to compensate for the insult to its sovereignty. It was a small enough price to pay, but naval officers were touchy about making concessions on matters of honor and protocol. When Sylvanus Godon arrived in Rio de Janeiro in early September 1865 in the USS *Susquehanna* and learned of this arrangement from the U.S. consul there, he positively refused to offer a twenty-one-gun salute unless he received written orders from Secretary Welles. Those orders did not arrive until June 1866, and as a result, the salute was rendered in July, nearly two years after the event and more than a year after the war had ended. Soon afterward, Collins was restored to active duty. Nevertheless, the Brazilians announced themselves fully satisfied. The sequence of events suggests that Brazil's protest had been largely pro forma, that the United States knew that it was, and that both sides had carried out a kind of pantomime of conciliation. In effect, the U.S. government, and its president, accepted Collins' argument that his illegal act had been "for the public good."[34]

ON CHRISTMAS EVE, 1864, Lincoln learned that Sherman had captured the city of Savannah. An agent from the Treasury Department suggested to Sherman that he should present Savannah as a "Christmas-gift" to the president, and, believing that Lincoln "particularly enjoyed such pleasantry," Sherman did so, noting that the gift came "with 150 heavy guns & plenty of ammunition & also about 25000 bales of cotton." However it was presented, Lincoln was delighted and more than a little relieved by the news. Though he had approved Grant's proposal that Sherman be allowed to carry out his march from Atlanta to the sea, Lincoln had been concerned when Sherman virtually disappeared into Georgia after leaving Atlanta on November 16. For more than a month, he had heard nothing from the red-haired general or his army except what could be gleaned from rebel newspapers. On December 6 he remarked to a crowd of well-wishers: "We all know where he went in at, but I can't tell where he will come out at." Now, finally, Sherman had arrived safely at the coast, and characteristically, Lincoln gave him all the credit. "I was anxious, if not fearful," he admitted in a note to Sherman, "but feeling that you were the better judge, and remembering that 'nothing risked, nothing gained,' I did not interfere. Now, the undertaking being a success, the honor is all yours." Sherman's ability to march an army through the heart of the Confederacy was further evidence that, as Welles put it, "the Rebellion is drawing to a close."[35]

On the other hand, the news from Wilmington, North Carolina, reminded Lincoln that the war was not over yet. On the day after Christmas, Porter wrote that he, too, had hoped "to present the nation Fort Fisher and surrounding works as a Christmas offering," but instead he had to report that the attack had been badly bungled and that the fort "has not been taken yet." Like his predecessor, Samuel Phillips Lee, Porter had been partnered for the expedition with the politically savvy but so far spectacularly unsuccessful Benjamin Butler, who had suggested that Fort Fisher could be wiped off the face of the earth by exploding a powder-filled hulk next to it. The experts disagreed about whether such an explosion would, in fact, destroy the fort, but Fox was supportive and Porter thought it was at least worth a try. Six months before, in July, the Union army had tried to blow up rebel entrenchments around Petersburg by digging a tunnel under the rebel lines, packing it with powder, and setting it off. It had ended in disaster, as Union troops had rushed into the resulting crater only to be picked off by rebel reinforcements. Now the navy prepared to try the maritime equivalent of that gambit. Lincoln was dubious, but since so many of his generals and admirals said it was worth a try, he gave his approval. On December 27, Lincoln was grimly bemused to read in a Richmond newspaper that one of the Union Navy's gunboats had "got aground and was blown up." He was pretty sure that this was the much-ballyhooed powder vessel, and if so, it had apparently made no impression on the enemy at all.[36]

And so it was. The next day Lincoln learned from Grant that "the Wilmington expedition has proved a gross and culpable failure." The explosion of the powder vessel had been, in Welles' words, "a puff of smoke, doing no damage." Porter moved in to bombard the fort with his warships nonetheless, shelling it for several hours until, according to Porter's subsequent testimony, the fort was "nearly demolished." At one point, Porter maneuvered his flagship alongside Butler's command vessel and called over to him, "There is not a rebel within five miles of the fort. You have nothing to do but march in and take it." Porter was wrong about the strength of the fort, for there were quite a few rebels in it, and the murky weather and heavy surf prevented Butler from getting all of his own force on the beach. More important, perhaps, Butler did not go ashore personally, and since he had counted heavily on the powder vessel to destroy the fort, he was mentally unprepared to launch a conventional attack. Instead, in Porter's condemning words, "the army landed and reembarked, considering it impracticable to assault the place."[37]

Grant's anger at this turn of events was palpable. "Who is to blame I hope will be known," he wrote to Lincoln, though he had already decided that both Butler and Porter were at fault, and he was even angrier when he learned that the Union plan of attack had been printed in the Richmond newspapers beforehand. Someone, clearly, could not keep his mouth shut.[38]

The next day, Welles and Fox arrived at the White House with a copy of Porter's lengthy report. John Rodgers, who had commanded the new ironclad *Dictator* in the assault, also came along. Lincoln silently read Porter's dispatch while the others waited. In that report, Porter admitted that "there were some mistakes made" by several of the navy vessels, which took incorrect positions for the bombardment, but on the whole, he made it clear the blame for this failure rested entirely on Butler and the army. Just as he had held Banks at fault for the collapse of the Red River campaign, so now he held Butler at fault for the failure to take Fort Fisher. Porter noted that a few brave soldiers had gone forward and actually entered the fort, one of them taking away a rebel flag that had been shot away by the naval bombardment, but the army did not make a concerted effort. Porter enclosed a copy of a letter he had sent to Butler suggesting that if his soldiers had only made the attempt, "they would have found it an easier conquest than is supposed."[39]

When Lincoln looked up after reading Porter's missive, Welles asked him, what now? Lincoln replied by saying that all military questions should be referred to General Grant, and as for the navy, "he did not know that we wanted any advice on naval matters." Welles took Lincoln's point but replied that he could not keep Porter's enormous squadron of more than a hundred ships off Fort Fisher indefinitely unless something important was to be attempted. Should there be a second attempt? Lincoln refused to be drawn in. Now that he had Grant in charge, the president was unwilling to participate in a discussion of military plans. In his congratulatory note to Sherman following the capture of Savannah, Lincoln had conversationally remarked, "What next?" Then, catching himself, he concluded: "I suppose it will be safer if I leave Gen. Grant and yourself to decide." Now in response to Welles' question about what to do next at Wilmington, his answer was much the same. He told Welles: "I must refer you to General Grant."[40]

Grant was willing to give it another try. His new enthusiasm for a campaign against Wilmington derived at least in part from Sherman's request that he be allowed to march northward from Savannah through the Carolinas. If he did so, it would be helpful to have a friendly base from which he could draw supplies if necessary. Charleston, Sherman thought, was "wrecked," and New Bern, North Carolina, which the federals had occupied for more than a year, was too distant from his line of march. Wilmington was just the ticket. But while Grant was now an active supporter of a renewed attack on the Wilmington forts, he was determined that the expedition must have a new command team. Just as he had effectively blackballed Samuel Phillips Lee a few months earlier, he now insisted that Butler be replaced.[41]

Porter agreed. Indeed, the admiral was scathing in his criticism of Butler, writing, "There never was a fort that invited soldiers to walk in and take possession more plainly than Fort Fisher." The fort would be in Union hands now, Porter insisted, if the army had had any kind of leader. "I feel ashamed that men calling themselves soldiers should have left this place so ingloriously," but it was no more than he expected, he wrote, when he learned that Butler was "mixed . . . up in this expedition." Such candor was more than blunt, it was unprofessional. Porter didn't care. "I am not very particular, I am well aware, how I express myself in these cases. I have always said what I thought since the first day I took up arms to fight this rebellion, and I intend to do so (impolitic though it may be) until the war is over."[42]

Ironically, however, Grant was almost as unhappy with Porter as he was with Butler. Despite their partnership at Vicksburg, Grant now wondered if Porter should be replaced, too. He communicated these views to Stanton, and at the cabinet meeting the next day, Stanton declared that in addition to replacing Butler, he wondered "whether Porter is any better." He insisted that Porter was "blatant, boisterous, bragging, etc.," all of which was certainly true, but of course Stanton lacked the authority to dismiss or replace a naval officer. That power rested with Welles, and Welles came to Porter's defense. The navy secretary agreed that Porter had his flaws, but insisted that he was also energetic and conscientious. Porter would no doubt have been astonished to learn that the man he counted as an "imbecile" had to defend him to Stanton and the president, both of whom he considered special allies. Porter believed that Lincoln had supported him against Welles on at least two previous occasions when, in fact, it had been quite the reverse. He counted Stanton, too, as a friend. In his memoirs, Porter described a visit by Stanton to his flagship when the secretary of war jumped up, embraced him, kissed him, and declared: "I love you . . . , the President loves you, the people love you." Porter contrasted this effusion of thanks to Welles' more pro forma congratulations, which Porter categorized as "rude." Nevertheless, it was thanks largely to Welles that Porter kept his job.[43]

Porter's new partner was to be Major General Alfred H. Terry. In addition to installing a new commander, Grant also was determined to keep the expedition secret this time to prevent a repetition of the intelligence leak that had preceded the last attack. Officially, Grant let it be known that Terry's force of ten thousand men was being sent to Sherman at Savannah. Even Terry did not know the object of his mission until the day he left. Meanwhile Butler arrived in Washington, summoned by the congressional Committee for the Conduct of the War. Even as he prepared to testify that with the failure of the powder vessel Fort Fisher now could not be taken except by a lengthy siege, news arrived that Fort Fisher had been taken by assault.[44]

The news arrived in the army transport *Atlantic*. Just as Stanton had been annoyed that Welles had the privilege of reporting the fall of Vicksburg the year before, so now Welles was annoyed that Stanton got to announce to Lincoln the fall of Fort Fisher. He was so annoyed, in fact, that he asked Porter how he could have let such a thing happen. Porter explained that he had arranged to have the swift *Vanderbilt* standing by to bring news of the victory, but the captain of *Vanderbilt* had waited to recover his landing party before proceeding. Consequently, it was several hours behind the *Atlantic* in the race to bring Lincoln the good news. Whoever brought the news, Welles noted in his diary, "The President was happy." And why not? With Grant closing in on Petersburg and Richmond, with Sherman moving northward through the Carolinas, and now with the last rebel port closed to trade, Lincoln could reasonably anticipate an imminent end to the war. Seward went so far as to suggest that with the capture of the *Florida* and the fall of Fort Fisher there was now nothing left for the navy to do.[45]

On January 24, Lincoln sent a resolution to Congress proposing the thanks of the nation to Porter for his role in the capture of Fort Fisher. Here was the token of national gratitude that had escaped

Phillips Lee throughout his command tenure. Porter may not have been Lincoln's favorite admiral, but luck and pluck once again had put him in the right place at the right time. Congress approved the resolution the same day, and Lincoln was able to tender Porter "the thanks of Congress to yourself, the officers and men under your command, for. . . . their 'brilliant and decisive victory.'"[46]

1865

FINAL HARBOR

———⊃◦○◦⊂———

EPILOGUE

"Thank God That I Have Lived to See This"
Lincoln and the End of the War

STANTON WAS WRONG about the navy having no more work to do. To be sure, the *Alabama* had been sunk and the *Florida* taken, but the *Shenandoah* was still at sea, burning its destructive way through America's Pacific whaling fleet. In fact, the *Shenandoah* never would be caught, and turned up eventually in Liverpool seven months after the war ended. As for the blockade, with the fall of the Wilmington forts, all the major rebel ports were now closed, but a score or more of enemy gunboats remained in commission, none of them more important than the eleven ships—including three ironclads—of the James River Squadron near Richmond. Only a few days after Lincoln congratulated Porter on his victory at Fort Fisher, this rebel squadron made a bid to unhinge Grant's siege of Petersburg. Winter rains had washed away some of the river obstructions above Trent's Reach, and on January 24, 1865, the rebel warships took up advanced positions at Howlett's, near Butler's old defensive lines. If the rebels succeeded in removing the rest of the obstructions, they would be able to continue downriver to destroy Grant's crucial supply depot at City Point. Equally disturbing was the news that Union naval forces on the river had fled as soon as the rebel squadron appeared.[1]

The senior U.S. Navy officer on the James River was Commander William A. Parker, whom Porter had selected for the job because he believed he was likely to be more aggressive than Melancton Smith. Porter described Parker as "a sturdy old chap who looked as if he had been cut out of a big timber-head," but Porter should have known by now that looks could be misleading. Despite thirty-three years of active service, Parker remained a commander mainly because he was more comfortable following orders than exercising initiative. Given that, it was perhaps unfortunate that when Porter left with the bulk of the squadron to subdue Fort Fisher, he told Parker to "run no risks at present or while I am away."[2] Parker had only one ironclad in his diminished command, though that ironclad was the powerful double-turreted *Onondaga*, which boasted two 15-inch guns and two 150-pound Parrott rifles. Nevertheless, when the Confederate James River Squadron appeared at Trent's Reach, instead of challenging the rebel thrust, Parker took Porter's cautionary words to heart and retired downriver, claiming later that his purpose was to gain "more room to maneuver."*

Lincoln heard about the rebel sortie from Stanton, who appeared bearing a telegram from Grant. From the start, Grant had feared that the navy would be unable or unwilling to protect his pontoon bridges or his supply depot. Now he was disgusted that at the first appearance of the rebel squadron the Union navy had turned tail and run. Grant wanted Parker to send everything he had to reestablish control of the river. "It would be better to obstruct the channel of the river with sunken gunboats than that a rebel ram should reach City Point," he wired Parker. He followed this up with an even more urgent telegram: "It is your duty, in view of the large amount of stores here, to attack with all the vessels you have." None of this seemed to have any effect.

---

*Several weeks later, Porter wrote to Parker from off Fort Fisher to express a hope that the James River Squadron would sortie, in which case, he wrote, "I should expect a report that they had all been destroyed." Porter ended his letter by declaring: "I should be very much disappointed if any vessel of your division budges an inch downstream owing to any rebel ram" (*Official Records of the Union and Confederate Navies in the War of the Rebellion* [Washington, DC: Government Printing Office, 1894–1922], 11:644). This letter was dated January 26, two days after Parker fled downriver. While it is possible that Porter had not yet heard the news of Parker's action, it is also possible that he had, and that he wrote the letter, possibly even backdating it, to protect himself from criticism that he had not directed Parker to be sufficiently aggressive.

Grant reported to Fox that he "expected little from the navy under Captain Parker," who seemed "helpless."[3]

These complaints provoked Lincoln to send for Welles, who, after discussing the situation with Lincoln and Stanton, agreed that Parker must be replaced. Welles ordered Commodore William Radford to go upriver and relieve Parker of his command, but he also mentioned to Lincoln that Admiral Farragut was in the city, staying at Willard's Hotel after bringing the *Hartford* back from the Gulf. At once, Lincoln decided to send for him, too. Farragut hastened over from the Willard, and once he was apprised of the command problem on the James, he agreed to go there himself. Welles notified Grant that Farragut was on his way, but neither he nor Radford could arrive in less than twenty-four hours, and until then there seemed to be no choice but to leave Parker in command, though Welles told Grant that "Captain Parker will be removed to-night if you desire it."[4]

Unwilling to wait for Radford or Farragut, Grant took matters into his own hands. He acted very much like a joint commander by issuing orders directly to the gunboat captains: "All gunboats now in the James River," he ordered, "will immediately proceed to the front above the pontoon bridge. . . . This order is imperative, *the orders of any naval commanders to the contrary notwithstanding.*" And perhaps because of the seriousness of the moment or simply because of the momentum of war, the naval officers obeyed. When one of Grant's aides, a mere lieutenant, came on board the USS *Minnesota* to inform Commodore Joseph Lanman that "General Grant desired the *Atlanta* to proceed to Dutch Gap," Lanman immediately ordered that ship "to report to Lieutenant-General Grant."[5]

In the end, the rebel threat sputtered out when two of their three ironclads ran aground. The next morning, Parker returned upriver and opened fire on the grounded rebel ships. The *Onondaga*'s fifteen-inch bolts easily punched through their armor, and after the Confederates managed to refloat them, the whole rebel squadron retired upriver. By the time Farragut arrived, he was able to report to Washington, "All appears to be right. Radford is at his post with ample force." But he also added: "Things do not look well for Parker."[6]

He was right. Parker's belated return to action with the *Onondaga* was not enough to save either his reputation or his career. He seemed to be genuinely perplexed that Grant wanted him to be relieved. "I was not aware that General Grant was dissatisfied with me," he wrote plaintively to Welles, and to Porter he begged for "one more chance to retrieve my reputation and your good opinion." Porter was unforgiving. He had been furious when he had first heard of Parker's timidity ("I don't care if they hang him," he wrote to Fox). He was less draconian in his personal response to Parker's plea for another chance, writing that he regretted Parker's circumstances, but he regretted even more the fact that Parker had fumbled his opportunity. "No man ever had a better chance than you had," he wrote, and it was painful "to see such an opportunity lost." Eventually, Parker was found guilty by a court-martial for failing to do his utmost, though the court urged clemency in consideration of Parker's three decades of active service. In the end, Welles simply placed him on the retired list.[7]

The most important consequence of this mini-crisis, however, was not Parker's dismissal, or even the threat to Grant's supply depot. It was the extent to which the navy proved willing to subordinate itself to Grant's command direction. Gone was the haughty insistence by naval officers that all orders must come through the Navy Department. Gone, too, was resentment in the Navy Department over the army's meddling in its affairs. Instead of taking exception to Grant's assertion of authority, Welles, Fox, and particularly Lincoln sustained him. It was a far cry from the instructions that Welles and Fox had issued throughout the war to Du Pont, Dahlgren, Lee, Porter, and others to avoid involvement with the army whenever possible. One difference was that on those other occasions, Welles had been worried that the army might horn in on what he considered a navy operation. This time it was an army operation that was at risk. Indeed, this was the first time since the *Merrimack* had jeopardized McClellan's Peninsular Campaign in the spring of 1862 that a Confederate naval force seriously imperiled a major army campaign. On both occasions, Lincoln was willing to blur the lines of separation between the services to ensure success. In 1862, he had allowed Stanton to orchestrate the blocking of the Potomac River and to acquire the *Vanderbilt*, both done over the objections of the Navy Department. Now in 1865, he approved Grant's determination to exercise the authority of a joint commander. From the beginning of the war, Lincoln had sought someone who could manage the war for him. Now that he had such a man, he made sure he had all the authority he needed to succeed.

PEACE TALK WAS IN THE AIR that winter. In January, Frank Blair Sr. went south to Richmond to assay Confederate willingness to discuss peace, and in February, Lincoln himself went again to Hampton Roads, this time to meet with a trio of southern peace commissioners that included Confederate Vice President Alexander Stephens. As Lincoln fully expected, nothing came of it. In a curious reprise of a suggestion that Seward had made almost exactly four years earlier, and which Blair had raised in his visit to Richmond, the Confederate emissaries suggested that the two sides declare an armistice and join together to drive the French from Mexico. Lincoln would not accept the premise that there *were* two sides. All that was necessary to end the war, he asserted, was for those in arms against the government to cease fighting and accept the national authority. When the Confederate representatives pressed Lincoln on the status of slavery in a reunified nation, Lincoln was vague, even disingenuous, but he did mention that Congress had just approved the Thirteenth Amendment to the Constitution, abolishing slavery. This news was decisive. Though Lincoln talked vaguely about time limits for wartime proclamations and possible compensation for the owners of emancipated slaves, it was clear now that slavery was dying and that the momentum of events had made it impossible to turn back.[8]

A month later, Lincoln stood in front of the Capitol and took the oath for a second term as president. Unlike his first inauguration, when he had tried to reason with the seceded states to prevent both war and disunion, this time he mused almost speculatively about the fates that had brought the nation to this moment. Slavery, it was clear, had been at the root of it. "All knew," he noted, "that this interest was, somehow, the cause of the war." Even so, no one at the time, least of all him, had anticipated that this "cause" would end with, or even before, the war itself. Nor had anyone anticipated the horrible cost of the war—"this mighty scourge," as Lincoln called it. Almost as if the conflict were an unstoppable force of history, Lincoln noted that regardless of expectations, "the war came." It continued still, and, Lincoln reflected a bit mournfully that "if God wills that it continue, until all the wealth piled by the bond-man's two hundred and fifty years of unrequited toil shall be sunk, and until every drop of blood drawn with the lash, shall be paid by another drawn by the sword, as was said three thousand years ago, so still it must be said, 'the judgments of the Lord are true and righteous altogether.'"[9]

Two weeks later, Lincoln accepted an invitation from Grant to visit the front. He went in part to escape the horde of office seekers who were hoping to find a position in the second Lincoln administration. He took Mary and Tad along with him, making it a kind of family adventure. They left on March 23 on board the steamer *River Queen* in the midst of another storm, which roiled the bay and occasioned another bout of presidential seasickness. That, combined with a recent illness and the press of business, wore Lincoln down so much that when he arrived in Hampton Roads, Porter thought "the enormous expense of the war seemed to weigh upon him like an incubus." Despite his exhaustion, Lincoln was eager, almost frantic, for Grant to move forward and bring the conflict to a final end. Porter noted that the president carried a campaign map in his pocket wherever he went, and often stopped to pick out various terrain landmarks. In the middle of an inspection tour, he would stop, take out his map, spread it on his knee, and enquire about possible military movements. But eager as he was, he did not order Grant to move. The general was in command, and Lincoln accepted his own status as an observer.[10]

On the twenty-seventh, Grant came on board the *River Queen* with Sherman in tow. The redheaded general had come up from North Carolina by sea, leaving his army under the temporary command of John Schofield. Mary remained in her stateroom with Tad and sent her apologies, but Lincoln was happy to see Sherman and pumped him for information about the great march across Georgia and into South Carolina, asking in particular about the famous "bummers" and their adventures. He also expressed concern that the army might be in peril without its commander there. Sherman assured him that the army was safe and in good hands. The next day, Grant and Sherman returned. This time Porter joined the group, and the talk was more purposeful. Indeed, it was as close as Lincoln ever got to meeting with his full command team. Grant told the president that he had set in motion another coordinated advance on Lee's lines and that "matters were drawing to a crisis." Sherman assured Lincoln that his own army was powerful enough to beat those of both Lee and Johnston. There might be one more bloody battle, they said, but "it would be *the last*." For his part, Lincoln expressed the hope that another battle could be avoided. There had been too many bloody battles as it was.[11]

After this conference, Lincoln left Mary and Tad on the *River Queen* and transferred himself to Porter's *Malvern* for a trip upriver to the front. The *Malvern* was the former blockade runner *Ella and Annie*, which had been captured back in 1862 and refitted in Boston as a blockader. Built for speed rather than comfort, it had the characteristic low-slung hull and oversize side paddlewheels of blockade runners. There was a generous central cabin that served as a wardroom, but only two small private cabins, one used by Porter and the other by his secretary. Porter offered the president his own cabin, but Lincoln "positively declined" and accepted instead the secretary's smaller compartment, which was only six feet by four feet. In order to sleep, Lincoln had to draw up his knees or angle his long frame from corner to corner. The room was so small that when Lincoln prepared for bed, he put his shoes and socks outside the door. Porter noted that the president's socks had holes in the toes and ordered a sailor to mend the socks and shine the shoes.[12]

The next morning, when Lincoln came to breakfast, he announced that "a miracle" had happened during the night. "When I went to bed I had two large holes in my socks," he said, "and this morning there are no holes in them." When Porter asked him how he had slept, Lincoln told him well enough, "but you can't put a long blade in a short scabbard." After breakfast, Lincoln, still accompanied by Porter, went ashore and spent most of March 29 in the telegraph office of Grant's headquarters in City Point. Grant maintained a telegraph wire from the front lines back to City Point, and as he had in Washington, Lincoln sat at the end of the wire to follow the military movements in near real time. He knew that Grant was planning to try to get around Lee's extended right flank south of Petersburg, and Grant was considerate enough to keep him informed of how it was going, sending him several telegrams a day. When one of these arrived, Lincoln would bend over his map and trace the movements with his finger. "Here," he would say, pointing to a spot on the map, "they are at this point, and Sheridan is just starting off up this road. That will bring about a crisis."[13]

At first there was little to report, then late in the afternoon, Grant wrote that the rebels had counterattacked near Gravelly Run and had been repulsed. After checking his map, Lincoln wired back: "Despatches received. . . . How do things look now?"[14] While he waited for more news, Lincoln noticed three small kittens on the floor of the telegraph office. He scooped them up and placed them on top of his map. "What brought you into this camp of warriors?" he asked them. "Where is your mother?"

"Their mother is dead," said the colonel who was in charge of the telegraph office.

"Then she can't grieve for them as many a poor mother is grieving for her sons," Lincoln replied. "Ah, kitties, thank God you are cats, and can't understand this terrible strife." He put them back on the floor and asked the colonel if he would see to it that they got some milk. "There is too much starvation going on in this land," he mused aloud, and they should "mitigate it when we can."[15]

That night he was back on board the *Malvern*. In his absence, the ship's carpenters had remodeled his small cabin, knocking out the bulkhead and extending its length to over eight feet and widening it as well. Lincoln did not mention it when he turned in, but at breakfast the next morning he announced that "a greater miracle" had happened in the night: "I shrank six inches in length and about a foot sideways."[16]

By April 2 it was clear that the end was near. Grant had broken through the rebel lines south of Petersburg and was closing in on the city. On board the *Malvern* that night, Lincoln asked Porter: "Can't the navy do something at this particular moment to make history?"

"Not much," Porter replied, explaining that the navy's role was to ensure the security of Grant's base at City Point.

"But can't we make a noise?" Lincoln asked.

"Yes," Porter told him. "We can make a noise, and if you desire it, I will commence."

"Well, make a noise."

Porter ordered the ships of the squadron to open fire on the enemy forts above Trent's Reach. Lincoln seemed pleased with the effect, and after an hour or so, a particularly loud explosion caused him to jump up and exclaim, "I hope to heaven one of them has not blown up." It was instead the death rattle of the rebel navy. Unknown to Lincoln or

Porter, Confederate Rear Admiral Raphael Semmes (of *Alabama* fame) had received orders that night from Stephen Mallory, the rebel navy chief, to destroy the ships of the James River Squadron and attach his men to Lee's army. From the deck of the *Malvern*, muffled explosions could be heard throughout the night, and the flames from burning buildings could be seen in the distance.[17]

"Thank God that I have lived to see this!" Lincoln declared to Porter. "It seems to me that I have been dreaming a horrid dream for four years, and now the nightmare is gone. I want to see Richmond."[18]

Lincoln returned to the *River Queen* for the trip up to the rebel capital. Escorted by Porter's *Malvern*, the vessel steamed slowly up the winding course of the river past the obstructions at Trent's Reach and the Confederate navy yard at Rocketts. The procession was quite grand, with the escorting warships flying their largest national flags from the mast peaks, but as the river narrowed and shoaled, one by one the ships had to anchor or risk running aground. Still eager to see the city that had eluded his armies for four years, Lincoln asked Porter to take him up to the wharf in his barge. And so instead of a triumphal procession of great warships, it was a small rowboat that took Lincoln to Richmond. Unsurprisingly, it reminded Lincoln of a story.

"Admiral," he said to Porter, "this brings to mind a fellow who once came to me to ask for an appointment as a minister abroad. Finding he could not get that, he came down to some more modest position. Finally he asked to be made a tide-waiter. When he saw he couldn't get that, he asked for a pair of old trousers. But it is well to be humble."[19]

It was just as well that Lincoln reminded himself of that, for almost from the moment he landed, he was besieged by throngs of grateful blacks who fell to their knees and greeted him as the Messiah. "That is not right," Lincoln told them. "You must kneel to God only." Throughout that magical day as he toured the captured city, he was cheered by Richmond's black residents and its occupying Union troops and viewed suspiciously from behind closed blinds by the few white residents who remained. Finally he made his way to the Confederate White House, where he sat at Jefferson Davis's desk and, as few others could, imagined what it must have been like to occupy that chair.[20]

On April 9, five days after visiting Petersburg, Lincoln arrived back in Washington just after sunset to the news that Lee had surrendered his army to Grant at Appomattox Court House. The city was filled with happy crowds, and bonfires were being lit at several locations. Before he joined in the general celebration, however, he first went to visit Seward, who had been injured in a carriage accident while Lincoln had been away.

WITH LEE'S SURRENDER, Lincoln knew that the end of the war was at hand. His entire presidency had been dominated by that war, and now it was over, or very nearly over. It had been mainly an army war, but the navy, too, had played its part. Lincoln had begun knowing "but little about ships," as he had confessed to Welles at the time, and throughout its course he had been a reluctant commander who preferred to let others manage the conflict. Nevertheless, circumstances had compelled his involvement in the naval war. The blockade, the *Trent* affair, the French invasion of Mexico, and the overeagerness of several of his navy captains had forced him to intervene diplomatically. The uncertain and confusing command relationship between the army and the navy had forced him to play an active role on the western rivers, where he coordinated the manufacture and distribution of mortar schooners. The reluctance of some of his officers to seize the moment, such as Goldsborough in Hampton Roads and Du Pont at Charleston, had compelled him to become involved in the planning and execution of particular campaigns, even directing an amphibious landing on the Virginia coast to capture Norfolk. His distrust of some of those officers and his admiration for others had led him to make suggestions about the promotion of particular individuals. Farragut, Porter, and especially Dahlgren had all benefited from those suggestions; Du Pont, Samuel Phillips Lee, and Charles Wilkes had not. For the most part, however, Lincoln remained a reluctant commander in chief, and once he had a command team in place that he trusted, he backed away.

Most important, perhaps, was the fact that throughout the war Lincoln had proved a remarkably patient navigator. Though he knew his destination—or at least he clearly envisioned his destination—he frequently waited for events to clarify themselves before charting a course. It was not false modesty that led him to confess that "events have controlled me." Time and again he deliberately waited to assess the momentum of events before making a decision: about the relief of Fort Sumter, about the central and crucial issues of emancipation and colonization, and about Reconstruction. He pushed a little here, resisted a little there; he tried out ideas on various constituencies until it became clear where the thrust of history was taking him. But all that time as he shepherded history along, nudging gently or prodding forcefully, he believed he was guiding the country in the direction that history, or fate, or Providence, would choose for itself. He was history's instrument, not its prime mover.

On Good Friday, April 14, Lincoln met with his cabinet in the morning, and after lunch he invited his wife to join him for a carriage ride through the city. Buoyed by the prospect of peace, he was in an ebullient mood. He made some lighthearted remarks about the need to be "more cheerful" in the future, and Mary's mood rose to match her husband's. She thought she had never seen him so happy. They drove down Pennsylvania Avenue, past the new Capitol dome, now in the final stages of completion, to the Navy Yard, where Lincoln had frequently gone to escape the pressure of his office or to chat with Dahlgren in the days before he had made Dahlgren an admiral and sent him off to the interminable campaign off Charleston.

The ranking officers at the yard came out to greet the president and First Lady. As it happened, several of the monitors that had participated in Porter's attack on Fort Fisher were in the yard for repair, and one of them, the *Passaic*-class monitor *Montauk*, was tied up at the wharf. Lincoln expressed a desire to go on board, and eager to accommodate the president, the officers escorted the First Couple down to the gangplank, where they were piped aboard "with all the appropriate ceremonies." The president and First Lady had a complete tour of the vessel, with the gaggle of officers trailing behind them. Afterward, they were presented formally to the ship's officers and crew, and Lincoln responded with a short speech of thanks and congratulations in which he expressed his gratification that "this war was over, or *so near* its end." One of the officers present recalled that the president "seemed *very* happy," and his mood spread through the ship's company. Feeling expansive, Lincoln told the officers that he and his wife were going to Ford's Theater that evening to see the play *Our American Cousin*, and he spontaneously invited "as many of the officers and crew as could be spared" from their duties, to join him as his guests. Many of them accepted at once. It promised to be a festive evening.[21]

ABBREVIATIONS USED IN NOTES

———◦◦◦———

AHR   *American Historical Review*

AL   Abraham Lincoln

Bates Diary   Edward Bates, *The Diary of Edward Bates, 1859–1866*. Edited by Howard K. Beale. Washington, DC: Government Printing Office, 1933.

Browning Diary   Orville Browning, *The Diary of Orville Hickman Browning*. Edited by Theodore Calvin Pease and James G. Randall. Springfield: Illinois State Historical Library, 1925.

Chase Diary   Salmon P. Chase, *Inside Lincoln's Cabinet: The Civil War Diaries of Salmon P. Chase*. Edited by David Donald. New York: Longmans, Green, 1954.

CW   *Collected Works of Abraham Lincoln*. Edited by Roy P. Basler. 8 vols. plus index. New Brunswick, NJ: Rutgers University Press, 1953–55.

Dahlgren Diary   John A. Dahlgren, *Memoir of John A. Dahlgren, Rear-Admiral United States Navy, by His Widow, Madeleine Vinton Dahlgren*. New York: Charles L. Webster, 1891.

DGW   Gideon Welles, *Diary of Gideon Welles: Secretary of the Navy Under Lincoln and Johnson*. Edited by Howard K. Beale. 3 vols. New York: W. W. Norton, 1960.

FoxCC   *Confidential Correspondence of Gustavus Vasa Fox, Assistant Secretary of the Navy, 1861–1865*. Edited by Robert Means Thompson and Richard Wainwright. 2 vols. Freeport, NY: Books for Libraries, 1920.

Hay Diary   John Hay, *Lincoln and the Civil War in the Diaries and Letters of John Hay.* Edited by Tyler Dennett. New York: Dodd, Mead, 1939.

HEHL   Henry E. Huntington Library, San Marino, California

LC   Library of Congress, Washington, DC

MHSP   *Massachusetts Historical Society Proceedings*

NA   National Archives of the United States, Washington, DC

N&H   John G. Nicolay and John Hay, *Abraham Lincoln: A History.* 10 vols. New York: Century, 1890.

NYHS   New-York Historical Society, New York, New York

OR   *Rebellion Records. Official Records of the Union and Confederate Armies in the War of the Rebellion.* Washington, DC: Government Printing Office, 1880–1901. All references are to Series I unless otherwise indicated.

ORN   *Official Records of the Union and Confederate Navies in the War of the Rebellion.* Washington, DC: Government Printing Office, 1894–1922. All references are to Series I unless otherwise indicated.

SFDPL   *Samuel Francis Du Pont: A Selection from His Civil War Letters.* Edited by John D. Hayes. 3 vols. Ithaca, NY: Cornell University Press, 1969.

NOTES

Introduction

1. T. Harry Williams, *Lincoln and His Generals* (New York: Dorset Press, 1952), vii. Geoffrey Perret has also authored a book on Lincoln as commander in chief entitled *Lincoln's War: The Untold Story of America's Greatest President as Commander in Chief* (New York: Random House, 2004), which has two entries in the index under "Navy Department." A new book by William Lee Miller which appeared just as this book went to press and which is entitled *Abraham Lincoln: Duty of a Statesman* (New York: Knopf, 2008) deals more with Lincoln and the navy than most Lincoln books. The latest, and best, work on Lincoln as commander in chief of the army is James M. McPherson's *Tried by War: Abraham Lincoln as Commander-in-Chief* (New York: Penguin, 2008).
2. AL to Albert G. Hodges, April 4, 1864, CW, 7:282.
3. AL to Welles, May 14, 1861, CW, 4:370.
4. Charles Hamlin, *The Life and Times of Hannibal Hamlin* (Cambridge, MA: Riverside Press, 1899), 394.
5. Ibid.

Chapter 1

1. Anderson's February 28 letter is missing from the OR, which contain his letters numbered 56 (February 26) and 59 (March 1), but not 57 or 58. However, sections of the February 28 letter are included in the correspondence of others, including, for example, Cameron to Lincoln, March 15, 1861, printed in Samuel W. Crawford, *The Genesis of the Civil*

War: The Story of Fort Sumter, 1860–61 (New York: Charles L. Webster, 1887), 355. The quotations are from Anderson to Cooper, March 6, 1861, and Cooper to Anderson, February 28, 1861, both in OR, 1:191, 187. For the impact of Anderson's report see Holt to AL, March 5, 1861, *The Works of James Buchanan*, edited by John Bassett Moore (New York: Antiquarian Press, 1960), 11:158.

2. CW, 4:264, 266, 271.

3. DGW (undated entry), 1:4.

4. AL to Hamlin, December 24, 1860, CW, 4:161. Lincoln asked Hamlin which of three men—Welles, Nathaniel Banks, or Amos Tuck—should represent New England in the cabinet. Hamlin responded that "Mr. Wells [*sic*] is the better man." Hamlin to AL, September 29, 1860, Lincoln Papers, LC, Series I. See also Howard to Welles, February 25, 1861, Papers of Gideon Welles, AL Library and Museum, Springfield, IL.

5. John Niven, *Gideon Welles, Lincoln's Secretary of the Navy* (New York: Oxford University Press, 1973); Thurlow Weed, *The Life of Thurlow Weed*, Vol. I: *The Autobiography of Thurlow Weed* (Boston: Houghton-Mifflin, 1883), 611. For evidence of Weed's early support of Welles' nomination, see Allyn to Welles, January 1861, Papers of Gideon Welles, AL Library and Museum, Springfield, IL.

6. Gideon Welles, *Lincoln and Seward* (New York: Sheldon, 1874), 8, 11.

7. The quotations are paraphrases by Welles in an article he wrote for *Galaxy* magazine in 1874: "Facts in Relation to the Expedition Ordered by the Administration of Abraham Lincoln for the Relief of the Garrison in Fort Sumter," available in Gideon Welles, *Civil War and Reconstruction: Selected Essays by Gideon Welles*, edited by Albert Mordell (New York: Twayne Publishers, 1959), 44.

8. Seward's policy goals are in Lord Lyons to Lord John Russell, March 26, 1861, in Charles F. Adams, "The British Proclamation of May 1861," MHSP 48 (October 1914–June 1915): 220–21. Conversation in the cabinet is reflected in Welles, "Facts in Relation to . . . Fort Sumter," 44; and Hay Diary (September 26, 1864), 219. AL's message to Congress, July 4, 1861, is in CW, 4:424. Italics in original.

9. Gideon Welles, "Facts in Relation to the Reinforcement of Fort Pickens in the Spring of 1861," *Galaxy* (January 1871), in Welles, *Civil War and Reconstruction*, 89.

10. "Can Fort Sumter Be Taken?" *New York Tribune*, reprinted in *Washington Constitution*, January 24, 1861; Bates Diary (addendum [March 15?] to entry of March 9, 1861), 177.

11. DGW (undated entry), 1:4; Welles, "Mr. Welles in Answer to Mr. Weed," *Galaxy* (July 1870), in Welles, *Civil War and Reconstruction*, 22; Scott to Adams, March 11, 1861, OR, 1:360.

12. Crawford, *Genesis of War*, 364. Frank Blair wrote his son "I may have said things that were impertinent & I am sorry I ventured on the errand. . . .

You must contrive some apology for me." Francis P. Blair to Montgomery
Blair, March 12, 1861, AL Papers, LC, Series I. Welles was convinced this
was the moment that Lincoln decided to hold Sumter, but while it no
doubt had an impact, Lincoln did not make his decision until March 28.
DGW, 1:13–14.

13. See *Wartime Washington: The Civil War Letters of Elizabeth Blair Lee*,
edited by Virginia Jeans Laas (Urbana: University of Illinois Press, 1991).

14. Fox's original memorandum, presented in January, is in FoxCC, 1:8–9.

15. CW, 4:271.

16. Henry Smith to Welles, March 30, 1861, Welles Papers, LC, reel 19.

17. Seward to AL, March 15, 1861, in Crawford, *Genesis of the Civil War*,
348–53.

18. Seward to R. M. T. Hunter, March 8, 1861, according to a Hunter
memorandum quoted in Crawford, *Genesis of the Civil War*, 322; the
Campbell manuscript is also quoted in Crawford, 328n. The affidavit is
on p. 330.

19. Fox memo of February 24, 1865, ORN, 4:247; Crawford, *Genesis of the
Civil War*, 370.

20. Hurlbut to AL, March 27, 1861, Lincoln Papers, LC, Series I. The report
was printed as Stephen A. Hurlbut, *Between Peace and War: A Report to
Lincoln from Charleston* (New York, 1953); Ward Hill Lamon, *Recollections
of Abraham Lincoln* (1895; repr., Lincoln: University of Nebraska Press,
1984), 75. See also Welles, "Facts in Relation to . . . Fort Sumter," 47.

21. Scott's undated memorandum is printed in Crawford, *Genesis of the Civil
War*, 363.

22. The "cold shock" quotation is from the diary of Montgomery Meigs
(March 31, 1861) in Meigs, "General M. C. Meigs on the Conduct of the
Civil War," AHR 26 (January 1921): 300. Meigs also wrote that Seward
had told him that the president "had not slept the night before he saw
me," which was Thursday night, March 28. The precise moment that
Lincoln decided to reinforce Anderson is impossible to pinpoint with
certainty. Scott's memo is undated, though Blair, in a letter to Crawford
in 1882, dates it as March 15, the day of the cabinet meeting when Lincoln
asked for written responses (Blair to Crawford, May 6, 1882, in Crawford,
Genesis of War, 365). Welles claimed that Lincoln "finally decided on the
30th of March" (Welles, "Mr. Welles in Answer to Mr. Weed," *Galaxy*
[July 1870], in Welles, *The Civil War and Reconstruction*, 25). Ari
Hoogenboom argues that Lincoln decided to reinforce Sumter even
before he received Scott's unsolicited letter (Hoogenboom, "Gustavus
Vasa Fox and the Relief of Fort Sumter," *Civil War History* [December
1963], 9:387). The date offered here (March 28) is based partly on
Seward's testimony that Lincoln did not sleep at all that night, but
mainly on the assumption that Lincoln would not have made a firm
decision without acting upon it, and he acted on March 29.

23. The notes by Bates, Chase, Welles, Blair, and Seward to AL, all dated March 29, 1861, are in the Lincoln Papers, LC, Series I.

24. Seward to AL, March 29, 1861, Lincoln Papers, LC, Series I; Meigs' diary (March 31, 1861), in Meigs, "General M. C. Meigs on the Conduct of the Civil War," AHR 26 (January 1921): 300. The reference to Wolfe is in the entry of March 29.

25. Cameron to Fox, April 4, 1861, and Scott to H. L. Scott, April 4, 1861, both in ORN, 4:232–33.

26. Welles to Breese, Buchanan, and McCauley, all dated March 30, 1861, and Welles to Commandant Navy Yard (Foote), April 1, 1861, all in ORN, 4:228–29; Fox to Blair, March 31, 1861, FoxCC, 1:12. See also the correspondence between Welles and Foote on pp. 230–32.

27. The text of Seward's memo is in CW, 4:317–18n; his declaration to Lord Lyons is in Lord Lyons to Lord John Russell, January 7, 1861, in Charles Francis Adams, "The British Proclamation of 1861," MHSP 48 (October 1914–June 1915): 214–15.

28. AL to Seward, April 1, 1861, CW, 4:316–17; Benjamin P. Thomas, *Abraham Lincoln: A Biography* (New York: Alfred A. Knopf, 1952), 254.

29. Chester Hearn, *Admiral David Dixon Porter: The Civil War Years* (Annapolis: Naval Institute Press, 1996), 1–35; Hay Diary (November 16, 1864), 240; DGW, 1:19–20.

30. Scott to AL, April 1, 1861, Lincoln Papers, LC, Series I. Seward's afternoon visit was likely triggered by a note from Meigs in which he wrote: "I think that Porter should be ordered to take the Powhatan and sail from New York into Pensacola Harbor at once." Meigs to Seward, April 1, 1861, Lincoln Papers, LC, Series I. See also David Dixon Porter, *Incidents and Anecdotes of the Civil War* (New York: Appleton, 1885), 13–15.

31. AL to Porter, AL to Mercer, AL to Commandant Navy Yard, and Scott to Brown (approved by AL), all dated April 1, 1861, ORN, 4:108–9.

32. The letter concerning Barron appears in DGW, 1:16–17, but not in the ORN since it was subsequently withdrawn; Porter, *Incidents and Anecdotes*, 16. See also Niven, *Gideon Welles*, 324–25.

33. DGW (undated entry), 1:17.

34. Ibid., 1:17–18.

35. Ibid., 1:21.

36. Welles to Foote, April 1, 1861, and Foote to Welles (two letters both dated April 2, 1861), all in ORN, 4:229, 230–31; AL to Foote, April 1, 1861, ORN, 4:109.

37. Fox to Blair, March 31, 1861, FoxCC, 1:12–13; Fox memo of February 24, 1865, in ORN, 4:247; N&H, 4:28.

38. Craig L. Symonds, *Confederate Admiral: The Life and Wars of Franklin Buchanan* (Annapolis: Naval Institute Press, 1999), 136.

39. Anderson to Thomas, April 1, 1861, OR, 1:230; Cameron to Anderson, April 4, 1861, OR, 1:235. Cameron's order to "hold out" did not reach Anderson before the first shots were fired.

40. Welles, "Facts in Relation to . . . Fort Sumter," 50; N&H, 4:35; CW, 4:323; DGW, 1:62.

41. AL to Foote, April 1, 1861, and Foote to Welles, April 4, 1861, both in ORN, 4:109, 234.

42. Welles to Mercer, Rowan, and Gillis, April 5, 1861, ORN, 4:235–36.

43. DGW (undated entry), 1:24.

44. Ibid, 24.

45. Porter to Foote [April 5?], 8:00, ORN, 4:111–12; Meigs' diary (April 5, 1861), in Meigs, "General M. C. Meigs on the Conduct of the Civil War," AHR 26 (January 1921): 27:301.

46. New York Times, April 6, 1861; Seward to Porter, April 6, 1861, ORN, 4:112.

47. Porter to Seward, dated "At Sea," April 6, 1861, ORN, 4:112.

48. DGW (undated entry), 1:29; Adams to Welles, April 1, 1861, ORN, 4:110. The orders concerning the truce are Holt and Toucey to James Glynn et al., January 29, 1861, ORN, 4:74. The orders to Captain Vodges from the Asst. Adjutant General, dated March 12, 1861, are in ORN, 4:90.

49. DGW (undated entry), 1:30; Welles to Adams, April 6, 1861, Welles Papers, LC, reel 19.

50. Fox to M. Blair, April 8, 1861, Lincoln Papers, LC, Series I; Fox to Mrs. Fox, April 6, 1861, FoxCC, 1:26.

51. Fox to Welles, February 24, 1865, and Welles to Gillis and Faunce, both dated April 5, 1861, all in ORN, 4:249, 236; Fox to Blair, April 17, 1861, FoxCC, 1:31–35.

52. Fox memo dated February 24, 1865, ORN, 4:249. See also Fox to Blair, April 8, 1861, Lincoln Papers, LC, Series I.

53. Gillis to Welles, April 16, 1861, and Rowan to Welles, April 19, 1861, both in ORN, 4:251–52, 253–54.

54. David Detzer, Allegiance: Fort Sumter, Charleston, and the Beginning of the Civil War (San Diego: Harcourt, 2001), 308.

55. Worden to Welles, April 15, 1861, ORN, 4:118; abstract log of USS Sabine in ORN, 4:208–9; undated handwritten "Sketch of My Trip to Pensacola" in the John L. Worden Papers, Lincoln Memorial University, Harrowgate, TN; Welles, "Facts in Relation to the Reinforcement of Fort Pickens," from Galaxy (January 1871), in Welles, Civil War and Reconstruction, 98.

56. Porter to Seward, April 21, 1861, Brown to Meigs and Meigs to Porter, both dated April 17, 1861, and Adams to Porter, April 27, 1861, all in ORN, 4:122–23, 131; Porter, Incidents and Anecdotes, 25; D. D. Porter Journal, Porter Papers, 1:108, LC, box 22.

57. Porter, Incidents and Anecdotes, 24; Lamon, Recollections of Abraham Lincoln, 69.

58. Fox to Cameron, April 19, 1861, ORN, 4:245; Fox to Blair, April 17, 1861, and Fox to Mrs. Fox, May 2, 1861, both in FoxCC, 1:33, 43. The missing word, "traitor," is barely perceptible in the original copy of Fox's May 2 letter in the New-York Historical Society.

59. Seward to AL, March 15, 1861, in Crawford, *Genesis of the Civil War*, 352; Hay Diary (June 24, 1864), 211–12.

60. DGW (undated entry), 1:36; Porter to Seward, April 21, 1861, ORN, 4:122.

61. Porter, *Incidents and Anecdotes*, 22. Porter was not alone in this view. Welles' biographer John Niven concluded, "Circumstantial evidence indicates that Lincoln was fully aware of Seward's plan and approved of it." Niven, *Gideon Welles*, 613n.

62. AL to Welles, May 11, 1861, CW, 4:366–67.

63. Fox to Mrs. Fox, March 19, 1861, FoxCC, 1:9–10; AL to Fox, May 1, 1861, CW, 4:350–51 and ORN, 4:251; Fox to Mrs. Fox, May 4, 1861, FoxCC, 1:45; AL to Welles, May 8, 1861, CW, 4:363.

64. Welles to "My dear son" [Tom?], undated letter, Welles Papers, LC, reel 20.

65. Charles E. Hamlin, *The Life and Times of Hannibal Hamlin* (Cambridge, MA: Riverside Press, 1899), 394.

Chapter 2

1. Abstract log of the USS *Niagara*, ORN, 4:206.

2. The term "naval sieve" is from William N. Still, "A Naval Sieve: The Union Blockade in the Civil War," *U.S. Naval War College Review* 36 (May–June 1983): 38–45. Another expert who disputes the importance or effectiveness of the Union blockade is Stephen R. Wise in *Lifeline of the Confederacy: Blockade Running During the Civil War* (Columbia: University of South Carolina Press, 1988).

3. Even before his inauguration, Lincoln had asked Seward to take charge of foreign policy. See Frederick W. Seward, *Reminiscences of a War-Time Statesman and Diplomat* (New York: G. P. Putnam's Sons, 1916), 147.

4. *New York Herald*, July 8, 1867.

5. Lord Lyons to Lord John Russell, March 26 and April 9, 1861, both in Charles F. Adams, "The British Proclamation of May 1861," MHSP 48 (October 1914–June 1915): 222, 224.

6. CW, 5:429, 429n.

7. Lyons to Russell, April 27, 1861, in Adams, "The British Proclamation," 225.

8. The text of the 1856 Declaration of Paris is available in *Conventions and Declarations Between the Powers Concerning War, Arbitration and Neutrality* (The Hague: Martinus Nijhoff, 1915).

9. Letter from the Boston Board of Trade (Lorenzo Sabine) to AL, April 18, 1861, and letter from "Citizens of New York," April 18, 1861, both in Lincoln Papers, LC, Series I; CW, 4:338; Welles to McKean, May 2, 1861, ORN, 4:367.

10. Lyons to Russell, April 27, 1861, in Adams, "The British Proclamation," 226; Jay Monaghan, *Diplomat in Carpet Slippers: Abraham Lincoln Deals with Foreign Affairs* (Indianapolis: Bobbs-Merrill, 1945), 82; Henry Adams, *Historical Essays* (Boston: Charles Scribner's Sons, 1891), 264.

11. Blockade Proclamation, April 19, 1861, CW, 4:339.
12. Parrott to Stringham, June 5, 1861, and Stringham to Welles, June 6, 1861, both in ORN, 1:28–29; excerpts from logbook of the *Perry*, ORN, 1:42.
13. Davis to AL, July 6, 1861, *The Papers of Jefferson Davis*, edited by Lynda Lasswell Crist and Mary Seaton Dix (Baton Rouge: Louisiana State University Press, 1992), 7:221–22.
14. Mark A. Weitz, *The Confederacy on Trial: The Piracy and Sequestration Cases of 1861* (Lawrence: University of Kansas Press, 2005), 78. Algernon Sullivan survived Seward's displeasure and went on to found one of the most powerful corporate law firms in America, Sullivan and Cromwell, which later helped secure the Panama Canal and included such luminaries as John Foster Dulles.
15. Ibid.
16. Welles to AL, August 5, 1861, ORN, 6:53–56.
17. *Congressional Globe*, 37th Congress, 1st session, 137; Lincoln's proclamation is in ORN, 6:91. His instructions to C. F. Adams are in CW, 4:378. See also Stuart Bernath, *Squall Across the Atlantic: American Civil War Prize Cases and Diplomacy* (Berkeley: University of California Press, 1970), 20.
18. Dana to C. F. Adams, March 9, 1863, Charles F. Adams, *Richard Henry Dana, A Biography* (Boston: Houghton Mifflin, 1891), 2:267; David M. Silver, *Lincoln's Supreme Court* (Urbana: University of Illinois Press, 1956), 105.
19. Ibid., 115; Weitz, *The Confederacy on Trial*, 198.
20. CW, 5:109–10, 162, 520.
21. Welles to Squadron Commanders, January 1862, Letters to Officers Commanding Squadrons, NA, RG 45.
22. CW, 4:338–39.
23. Charles O. Paullin, *Paullin's History of Naval Administration, 1755–1911* (Annapolis: U.S. Naval Institute Press, 1968), 269.
24. AL to Welles, March 18, 1861, and Welles to AL, March 20, 1861, both in Lincoln Papers, LC, Series I.
25. Welles to Mary Welles, April 21, 1861, Welles Papers, LC, reel 19.
26. Thurlow Weed, *The Life of Thurlow Weed*, Vol. 1: *Autobiography* (Boston: Houghton-Mifflin, 1883), 603; N&H, 4:152; AL to Welles, April 23, 1861, CW, 4:342.
27. The report that prompted Welles to send the *Pawnee* is Isherwood to Welles, April 18, 1861, ORN, 4:280–81. Welles' orders to Paulding of the same date are on p. 282. Welles also ordered the *Keystone State* at Philadelphia and the *Anacostia* at Washington to proceed immediately to Norfolk. Neither arrived in time. The "stupefied" quotation is from DGW (undated entry), 1:45.
28. McCauley's report dated April 25, 1861, is in ORN, 4:288–89.
29. N&H, 4:148, 151.

30. *New York Times*, May 1, 1861; Seward, *Reminiscences*, 167; Welles to Mary Welles, May 5, 1861, Welles Papers, LC, reel 19; Hay Diary (May 7, 1861), 19.

31. Browning Diary, 1:489 (entry of July 28, 1861). Lincoln's supplementary blockade declaration is in CW, 4:346–47.

32. Welles to Mary Welles, April 21, 1861, Welles Papers, LC, reel 19; DGW (August 12, 1863), 1:401.

33. Examples of Lincoln's deferring to Welles are AL to Welles, June 18 and August 19, 1861, CW, 4:412, 494. His letter concerning Lawrence is AL to Welles, May 14, 1861, CW, 4:370.

34. Welles to Mary Welles, May 5, 1861, Welles Papers, LC, reel 19; AL to Welles, July 11, 1861, CW, 4:447; Welles Letter, May 13, 1861, ORN, 4:391; Welles to Edgar Welles, May 19, 1861, Welles Papers, LC, reel 19; William Dudley, *Going South: U.S. Navy Officer Resignations and Dismissals on the Eve of the Civil War* (Washington, DC: Naval Historical Foundation, 1981), 13.

35. AL to Welles, May 7, 1861, CW, 4:361; Dudley, *Going South*.

36. AL to Welles, May 11, 1861, CW, 4:366; Welles to AL, May 16, 1861, Lincoln Papers, LC, Series I.

37. AL to Morgan, May 20, 1861, CW, 4:375.

38. Welles to Du Pont, April 21, 1861, SFDPL, 1:56; Morgan to Welles, May 2, 1861, Welles Papers, LC, reel 19. Lincoln's statement that he "directed" the Navy Yard commandants to purchase or charter five steamships each is in his letter to Congress, May 26, 1862, CW, 5:241.

39. The quotation is from Oliver S. Halsted to AL, August 27, 1861, Lincoln Papers, LC, Series II. Hale introduced a bill on the first day of the special session (July 4) that required Welles to report "all contracts made" along with "the price paid for purchase." *Congressional Globe*, 37th Congress, 1st session, 1. See also Hale to Welles, April 24, 1861 (marked "Private"), and May 29, 1861, both in Welles Papers, LC, reel 19.

40. William H. Roberts, *Now for the Contest: Coastal and Oceanic Naval Operations in the Civil War* (Lincoln: University of Nebraska Press, 2004), 18. Morgan's apology to Welles is Morgan to Welles, September 7, 1861, Welles Papers, HEHL, box 2. Welles' defense of Morgan is in Senate Exec. Doc. No. 15 (37th Congress, 2nd session), 1–16. Significantly, perhaps, a copy of this document is included in the Lincoln Papers, LC, Series I.

41. Morgan to Welles, December 27, 1861, and January 10, 1862, Welles Papers, HEHL, box 2.

42. Seward, *Reminiscences*, 160. Lincoln's defense of Welles and Cameron is in his letter to Congress, May 26, 1862, CW, 5:243; Welles' comments are in DGW, 1:25, 54, 69. A copy of Morgan's letter to Montgomery Blair, in which he defended himself against Hale's "unjust censures," is in Lincoln's papers: Morgan to Blair, December 30, 1861, Lincoln Papers, LC, Series I.

43. DGW (undated entry), 1:54.
44. T. Harry Williams, *Lincoln and His Generals* (New York: Dorset Press, 1952), 20.
45. Quoted in Du Pont to Sophie Du Pont, July 24, 1861, SFDPL, 1:109.
46. "Memoranda of Military Policy," July 23, 1861, CW, 4:457–58.
47. Browning Diary (July 28, 1861), 1:489; AL to Heads of Bureaus, June 22, 1861, CW, 4:415.
48. Du Pont to Sophie Du Pont, July 26, 1861, SFDPL, 1:113–14.
49. Craig L. Symonds, *Confederate Admiral: The Life and Wars of Franklin Buchanan* (Annapolis: Naval Institute Press, 1999), 118–19; Kevin Weddle, *Lincoln's Tragic Admiral: The Life of Samuel Francis Du Pont* (Charlottesville: University of Virginia Press, 2005), 76–77.
50. Du Pont to Sophie Du Pont, April 23, 1861, Du Pont to Matthew Maury (cousin of Matthew Fontaine Maury), August 30, 1861, and Du Pont to Henry Winter Davis, September 4, 1861, all in SFDPL, 1:160, 138, 142.
51. McClellan to Ellen McClellan, July 27, 1861, quoted in Stephen W. Sears, *George B. McClellan, The Young Napoleon* (New York: Ticknor and Fields, 1988), 95; Du Pont to Sophie Du Pont, August 4, 1861, SFDPL, 1:124.
52. Du Pont to Sophie Du Pont, July 4, 1861; Du Pont to William Whetten, March 1 and 26, 1861; Du Pont to Henry Winter Davis, April 14, 1861; and Du Pont to Samuel Mercer, March 13, 1861, all in SFDPL, 1:38–39, 46, 94, 51, and 42–43. Italics in original.
53. Hay Diary (April 25, 1861), 11.
54. Du Pont to Henry Winter Davis, September 29, 1861, SFDPL, 1:160.
55. AL to Scott, September 18, 1861, CW, 4:528.
56. The account of the meeting in Seward's house in this and following paragraphs is from Du Pont to Henry Winter Davis, October 8, 1861, SFDPL, 1:162–64.
57. General order, October 4, 1861, CW, 4:548; Welles to Du Pont, October 12, 1861, and Scott to Sherman, October 14, 1861, both in ORN, 12:215, 220.
58. Du Pont to Sophie Du Pont, October 23 and 26, 1861, SFDPL, 1:181, 185.
59. Williams, *Lincoln and His Generals*, 44.
60. *New York Herald*, November 4 and 9, 1861.
61. Welles' order, November 13, 1861, and Lincoln's recommendation, dated February 4, 1862, are in ORN, 12:290–91. Welles' letter of "heartfelt congratulations" is dated November 16 and is in ORN, 12:294.

Chapter 3

1. Du Pont to Fox, November 9, 1861, FoxCC, 1:65; also in SFDPL, 1:230.
2. Charles Wilkes, *The Autobiography of Rear Admiral Charles Wilkes, U.S. Navy, 1798–1877*, edited by W. J. Morgan et al. (Washington, DC: Naval History Division, 1978), 769; D. MacNeil Fairfax, "Captain Wilkes's Seizure of Mason and Slidell," *Battles and Leaders of the Civil War*, edited

by Robert U. Johnson and Clarence C. Buel (New York: The Century Co., 1888). 2:139.

3. William Stanton, *The Great United States Exploring Expedition of 1838–1842* (Berkeley: University of California Press, 1975).

4. Wilkes, *Autobiography*, 530–31.

5. Fairfax, "Captain Wilkes's Seizure," 2:136.

6. Wilkes to Welles, November 15, 1861, ORN, 1:129–31.

7. Fairfax, "Captain Wilkes's Seizure," 1:136.

8. Ibid.

9. Wilkes to Fairfax, November 8, 1861, ORN, 4:132; Fairfax, "Captain Wilkes's Seizure," 1:136.

10. W. H. Russell in a letter to the *Times*, December 10, 1861, quoted in Charles Francis Adams Jr., *The Trent Affair: An Historical Retrospect* (Boston, 1912), 8n; Fairfax, "Captain Wilkes's Seizure," 2:138.

11. Fairfax, "Captain Wilkes's Seizure," 2:138; Greer to Wilkes, November 12, 1861, ORN, 4:136.

12. Houston to Wilkes, Greer to Wilkes (PS), and Hall to Wilkes, all dated November 13, 1861, all in ORN, 4:136–37.

13. Fairfax to Wilkes, and Greer to Wilkes, both dated November 12, 1861, ORN, 4:133–34, 135; Slidell, Mason, et al. to Wilkes, November 9, 1861, ORN, 1:139–41.

14. Fairfax, "Captain Wilkes's Seizure," 2:140.

15. Seward to C. F. Adams, May 21, 1861, CW, 4:378–79.

16. Frederick Seward, *Reminiscences of a War-Time Statesman and Diplomat* (New York: G. P. Putnam's Sons, 1916), 147; Seward to A. F. Adams, May 21, 1861, CW, 4:378–79. Seward's original memo, and Lincoln's changes to it, are in N&H, 4:270–75.

17. Henry Adams to C. F. Adams Jr., July 2, 1861, and C. F. Adams to C. F. Adams Jr., June 21, 1861, both in *A Cycle of Adams Letters, 1861–1865*, edited by Worthington Chauncey Ford (Boston: Houghton Mifflin, 1920), 17, 14; C. F. Adams, "The British Proclamation of 1861," in MHSP 48 (October 1914–June 1915): 214–15.

18. Henry Adams to C. F. Adams, September 28, 1861, *A Cycle of Adams Letters*, 48.

19. The telegram is Goldsborough to Welles, November 15, 1861, ORN, 1:142; the claim of Lincoln's prescience is from N&H, 5:25–26; *New York Herald*, November 18, 1861. See the summary of newspaper views in Norman B. Ferris, *The Trent Affair: A Diplomatic Crisis* (Knoxville: University of Tennessee Press, 1977), 32–33.

20. Seward is quoted in Thornton K. Lothrop, *William Henry Seward* (Boston, 1896), 325; Welles to Tom Welles, November 17, 1861, Welles Papers, LC, reel 20.

21. Parsons is quoted in C. F. Adams, *The Trent Affair*, 18; Cushing's public letter to Fernando Wood was dated December 6, 1861, and appeared in

the *New York Times* on December 18, 1861. C. F. Adams Jr. to C. F. Adams, November 19, 1861, *A Cycle of Adams Letters*, 71.

22. *New York Herald,* November 19, 1861.

23. Lincoln's statements are from Titian J. Coffey in Allen T. Rice, ed., *Reminiscences of Abraham Lincoln by Distinguished Men of His Time* (New York: North American Review, 1888), 245. The date of Lincoln's visit to Bates is unknown. Coffey said it was "a few days" after Wilkes' act, but the context suggests it was later. Bates' comments here are from his diary (November 16, 1861), 202.

24. DGW (August 10, 1862), 1:73; Gideon Welles, "The Capture and Release of Mason and Slidell," *Galaxy* (May, 1873), reprinted in *Civil War and Reconstruction: Selected Essays by Gideon Welles*, edited by Albert Mordell (New York: Twayne Publishers, 1959), 273. It is in this essay (p. 275) that Welles asserts that Lincoln "personally expressed his cordial approval of my letter." The letter itself is Welles to Wilkes, November 30, 1861, ORN, 1:148. See also John Niven, *Gideon Welles: Lincoln's Secretary of the Navy* (New York: Oxford University Press, 1973), 446–47.

25. Wilkes, *Autobiography*, 841, 777, and 779.

26. C. F. Adams, *The* Trent *Affair*, 18; OR, II, 2:1113; CW, 5:38, 40–41.

27. Wilkes, *Autobiography*, 776.

28. David Donald, *Charles Sumner and the Coming of the Civil War* (New York: Knopf, 1967), 383; C. F. Adams, *The* Trent *Affair*, 18. Sumner reported his conversation to his friend Emerson, who recorded it in his journal: Ralph Waldo Emerson, *Journals of Ralph Waldo Emerson*, edited by Edward Waldo Emerson and Waldo Emerson Forbes (Boston: Houghton Mifflin, 1913), 9:380. See also David Donald, *Charles Sumner and the Rights of Man* (New York: Knopf, 1970), 36.

29. Ferris, *The* Trent *Affair*, 50.

30. Earl Russell to Lord Lyons, November 30, 1861, in N&H, 5:29–30; Ferris, *The* Trent *Affair*, 53.

31. C. F. Adams, "The British Proclamation," 48:214–15; Ferris, *The* Trent *Affair*, 125. The passage from the London *Times* was reprinted in the *New York Times*, January 1, 1862.

32. *New York Times*, December 8, 1861.

33. Ferris, *The* Trent *Affair*, 170; Wilkes, *Autobiography*, 741, 776, 846.

34. Ibid., 847.

35. *Congressional Globe*, 37th Congress, 2nd session, 101.

36. Ibid.

37. Fillmore to AL, December 16, 1861, Lincoln Papers, LC, Series I.

38. Lord John Russell to Lord Lyons, November 30, 1861, Lincoln Papers, LC, Series I. See also Ferris, *The* Trent *Affair*, 134.

39. Lincoln's memo is in CW, 5:63. The original is in the Lincoln Papers, LC, Series I. In the upper right corner of the first page someone (Nicolay?) made the pencil notation "December 10?" In their biography, Nicolay

and Hay also used that date for the memo, and Basler followed suit in compiling the *Collected Works*. But since Lincoln's memo mentions "the despatch of Her Majesty's Secretary for Foreign Affairs dated November 30," a memo that did not arrive in Washington until December 18, it could not have been written before that date. Moreover, it had to have been written before December 21, on which date Lincoln read a draft of it to Orville Browning. The most likely date, therefore, is December 20.

40. Chase Diary (December 25, 1861), 53–55; Browning Diary (December 25, 1861), 1:519.
41. Bates Diary (December 25, 1861), 216, italics in original; Chase Diary (December 25, 1861), 53–54.
42. Seward, *Reminiscences*, 189.
43. Seward to Lyons, December 26, 1861, ORN, 1:177–87.
44. Seward, *Reminiscences*, 190.
45. *Congressional Globe*, 37th Congress, 2nd session, 176–77, 208–9.
46. Drayton to Dahlgren, January 10, 1862, Dahlgren Papers, LC, box 5.
47. Bates Diary (December 25, 1861), 216.
48. C. F. Adams to C. F. Adams Jr., February 21, 1862, *A Cycle of Adams Letters*, 114.
49. DGW (August 10, 1862), 1:73.
50. Chase Diary (January 1, 1862), 56.
51. Bates Diary (January 10, 1862), 223–24; (February 3, 1862), 228; and (December 31, 1861), 220.

Chapter 4

1. Hay Diary (April 25, 1861), 11.
2. AL to Buell, January 13, 1862, CW, 5:98. Italics in original. Lincoln sent a nearly identical copy of this letter to Halleck the same day. Lincoln also expressed his strategic views in a private conversation with Orville Browning the night before: Browning Diary (January 12, 1862), 1:523.
3. AL to Cameron, January 11, 1862, CW, 5:97.
4. The "despair" in East Tennessee is in AL to Buell, January 6, 1861, CW, 5:91. Halleck's unhelpful letter, also dated January 6, is in the Lincoln Papers, Series I, LC (Lincoln's endorsement, but not the letter, is in CW, 5:92, 95); AL to Cameron, January 11, 1862, CW, 5:97; Chase Diary (January 6, 1862), 57; Meigs' diary (January 10, 1862), in Meigs, "General M. C. Meigs on the Conduct of the Civil War," AHR 26 (January 1921): 302.
5. Bates Diary (December 31, 1861, and January 10, 1862), 218, 223; Browning Diary (January 12, 1862), 1:523; Meigs' diary (January 10, 1862), in Meigs, "General M. C. Meigs on the Conduct of the Civil War," AHR 26 (January 1921): 292, 302.
6. McDowell's notes on the meeting are in Henry J. Raymond, *The Life and Public Services of Abraham Lincoln* (New York: Derby and Miller, 1865),

772–77; Franklin's notes are in W. B. Franklin, "First Great Crime," *Annals of the War* (Philadelphia: Times, 1879), 76–77. See also Mark Snell, *From First to Last: The Life of Major General William B. Franklin* (New York: Fordham University Press, 2002), 77–78.

7. T. Harry Williams, *Lincoln and His Generals* (New York: Dorset Press, 1952), 56–57; George B. McClellan, *McClellan's Own Story* (New York: C. L. Webster, 1887), 155–59; Snell, *From First to Last*, 80–81.

8. CW, 5:111–12.

9. AL to McClellan, February 3, 1862, CW, 5:118–19. See also the lengthy "Memorandum" (pp. 119–25) in which Lincoln enlarged on these questions. The president may have sent the longer memorandum to McClellan as well, but it does not appear in the McClellan Papers and it is more likely that the president wrote it for his own benefit and kept it in a drawer.

10. Welles to Rodgers, May 16, 1861, and Rodgers to Welles, June 8 and September 7, 1861, all in ORN, 22:280, 288, 318–20.

11. Welles to Rodgers, June 11 (telegram) and June 12 (letter), 1861. ORN, 22:286, 284–85.

12. Welles to Rodgers, June 17, 1861, Rodgers to Welles, August 9, 1861, and Welles to Joseph Davis, August 12, 1861, all in ORN, 22:287, 297–98, 299.

13. The authority is Benjamin Franklin Cooling, *Forts Henry and Donelson: The Key to the Confederate Heartland* (Knoxville: University of Tennessee Press, 1987), 23; DGW, 1:345. Welles gave Rodgers the option of staying on at Cincinnati to assist Foote, and Rodgers might have done so but for the fact that Welles also ordered Commander Henry Walke to the western flotilla. Since Walke was senior to Rodgers, that would have been a further humiliation. Instead, therefore, Rodgers accepted Welles' offer of an unspecified assignment at sea. Foote, who may have been embarrassed by these circumstances, sent a private note to Fox praising Rodgers' work in preparing the flotilla, and Fox saw to it that Rodgers got a good assignment. He joined Du Pont's squadron in time to take part in the expedition to Port Royal, where he personally raised the American flag over Fort Walker.

14. Foote's General Orders Nos. 3 and 6, ORN, 22:465–67. See also Spencer C. Tucker, *Andrew Foote: Civil War Admiral on Western Waters* (Annapolis: Naval Institute Press, 2000).

15. Welles to Foote, August 30, 1861, Foote to Welles, September 30, 1861, Foote to Meigs, September 30, 1861, and Foote to Cameron, October 2, 1861, all in ORN, 22:307, 355, 356. Foote's letter to Dahlgren is dated September 10, 1861, which was before he took command. It is in the Dahlgren Papers, LC, box 5. Bates' comment is from his diary (January 10, 1862), 223. Italics in original.

16. Foote to Fox, November 2, 1861, and Foote to Welles, November 9, 1861, both in ORN, 22:390–92, 399.

17. AL to Frémont, September 22, 1861, and Foote to Welles, September 25, 1861, both in ORN, 22:344, 347.

18. David Dixon Porter, *Incidents and Anecdotes of the Civil War* (New York: D. Appleton, 1885), 64; Chester G. Hearn, *Admiral David Dixon Porter: The Civil War Years* (Annapolis: Naval Institute Press, 1996), 70–71.

19. Gideon Welles, "Admiral Farragut and New Orleans," *Galaxy* (November 1871), reprinted in *Selected Essays by Gideon Welles*, edited by Albert Mordell (New York: Twayne, 1959), 130; Porter, *Incidents and Anecdotes*, 64.

20. Fox to Foote, January 10, 1862, ORN, 22:491. See Eugene Canfield, "A Postscript on Mortar Boats," *Civil War Times Illustrated* 6 (October 1967): 36.

21. The passage about AL's conversation with Jessie Frémont is in Hay Diary (December 19, 1863), 133. Meigs to Foote, November 15, 1861, ORN, 22:495; Foote to Meigs, November 20, 1861 (marked "Private"), Foote Letter Book, NA.

22. Foote to Fox, January 11, 1862, Foote Letter Book, NA.

23. Ibid.; Porter to Wise, July 7, 1862, Wise to Porter, undated drawing, and Porter to Wise, December 30, 1862, all in Henry A. Wise Papers, NYHS, box 1; AL to Foote, January 23, 1862, CW, 5:108, 108n.

24. Wise to Foote, January 23, 1862, ORN, 22:518; AL to Stanton, January 24, 1862, CW, 5:110; D. D. Porter Journal, 1:194–95, D. D. Porter Papers, LC, box 22.

25. Foote to Symington, January 29, 1862, ORN, 22:525.

26. Foote to AL, January 27, 1862, Lincoln Papers, LC, Series I; Wise to Ripley, February 8, 1862, Wise Letter Book, NA, vol. I; Wise to Foote, January 27, January 31, March 1, and March 5, 1862, all in ORN, 22:523, 526–27, 650, and 657.

27. Wise to Foote, January 28, 1862, and Fox to Foote, January 27, 1862, both in ORN, 22:522–23. Italics in original.

28. Wise to Foote, January 31, 1862, Fox to Foote, January 27, 1862, and Wise to Foote, March 1, 1862, all in ORN, 22:527, 522, 650.

29. Foote to Welles, February 6, 1862 [received February 7], ORN, 22:537.

30. Wise to Foote, February 10, 1862, and A. S. Johnston to J. P. Benjamin, February 8, 1862, both in ORN, 22:549, 563.

31. Foote to Welles, February 11, 1862, and Welles to Foote, February 13, 1862, both in ORN, 22:570, 547.

32. Scott (Ass't Sec'y of War) to Foote, February 8, 1862, and Halleck to Foote, February 9, 1862, both in ORN, 22:576, 547.

33. Halleck to Foote, February 11, 1862, Grant to Foote, February 10, 1862, and Foote to Halleck, February 11, 1862, all in OR, 7:603–4, 600, 604.

34. Halleck to Buell, February 12, 1862, OR, 7:608. There is no indication in the OR that Halleck sent this information on to Washington, but it would have been irresponsible for him not to have done so. See also Halleck to McClellan, February 15, 1862, OR, 7:616. Halleck's telegrams

to McClellan, dated February 15, 1862 (3:00 P.M. and 8:00 P.M.), are in OR, 7:616, 617. Foote to Welles, February 15, 1862, ORN, 22:584.

35. AL to Halleck, February 16, 1862, CW 5:135 (also in OR, 7:624); Cullum to McClellan, February 17, 1862, Lincoln Papers, LC, Series, I.

36. David Donald, *Lincoln* (New York: Simon and Schuster, 1995), 336.

37. Welles to Edgar Welles, February 25, 1862, Welles Papers, LC, reel 20; Foote to Mrs. Foote, February 23, 1862, and Foote to Welles, February 24, 1862, both in ORN, 22:626, 632.

38. Wise to Halleck, February 28, 1862 (midnight), ORN, 22:641; AL to Welles, March 11, 1862, CW, 5:156; Bates Diary (January 10, 1862), 223–24.

39. Foote to Wise, February 24, 1862, Foote Letter Book, NA; Wise to Foote, February 25, 1862, ORN, 22:636.

40. Lincoln's memo reorganizing the departments, titled President's War Order No. 3 and dated March 11, 1862, is in CW, 5:155.

41. Bates' comments are in his diary (March 15, 1862), 242.

42. All these telegrams are in ORN, 22:691–95. Wise's cover letters indicating that he took them directly to Lincoln for a reply are in the Henry A. Wise Letter Book, NA, vol. I.

43. Foote to Welles, April 5, 1862 [received April 6], ORN, 22:711; Bates Diary (April 8, 1862), 246–47; Foote to Welles, April 7, 1862 [received April 8], ORN, 22:720; Bates Diary (April 9, 1862), 247; Stager to Stanton, April 8, 1862 [received 6:30 P.M.], Lincoln Papers, LC, Series I.

44. Browning Diary (April 10, 1862), 1:540; AL to McClellan, April 9, 1862, and his "Proclamation of Thanksgiving," April 10, 1862, both in CW, 5:185.

45. Pennock to Chief of Bureau of Ordnance, April 16, 1862 [received April 17], ORN, 23:6.

46. Fox to Porter, February 24, 1862, David Dixon Porter Papers, LC, box 17; Porter to Fox, March 28, 1862, and April 8, 1862, both in FoxCC, 2:91, 98.

47. Fox to Welles, April 29, 1862, Lincoln Papers, LC, Series I; Charles L. Dufour, *The Night the War Was Lost* (Garden City, NY: Doubleday, 1960), 265–85; Chester G. Hearn, *The Capture of New Orleans, 1862* (Baton Rouge: Louisiana State University Press, 1995), 209–36.

48. Dufour, *The Night the War Was Lost*, 287–98; Hearn, *The Capture of New Orleans*, 237–48.

49. Fox to Farragut, May 17, 1862, ORN, 18:498–99; Welles to Farragut, May 19, 1862, David Farragut Papers, HEHL, box 1. Welles sent a follow-up order by the *Dacotah*, ORN, 8:502.

50. Foote to Welles, April 19, 1862, ORN, 23:9.

Chapter 5

1. C. S. Bushnell, "Negotiations for the Building of the 'Monitor,' " *Battles and Leaders of the Civil War*, 1:748.

2. Wayne C. Temple, *Lincoln's Connections with the Illinois & Michigan Canal: His Return from Congress in '48 and His Invention* (Springfield,

IL: Illinois Bell, 1986), 35. I am grateful to Budge Weidman for sending me a copy of Lincoln's original patent.

3. Hay Diary (May 9, 1861), 185.
4. Bushnell, "Negotiations," 748.
5. Gideon Welles, "The First Iron-Clad Monitor," *Annals of the War* (Philadelphia: Philadelphia Weekly Times, 1879), 20.
6. Bushnell, "Negotiations," 748.
7. Ibid.
8. Ibid., 749.
9. Ibid.
10. Welles, "The First Iron-Clad," 23; Bushnell, "Negotiations," 749.
11. Welles, "The First Iron-Clad," 20.
12. Ibid.; Wool to Stanton, March 8, 1862, ORN, 7:4–5.
13. Welles, "The First Iron-Clad," 24.
14. DGW (undated entry), 1:62–63; John G. Nicolay, *With Lincoln in the White House: Letters, Memoranda, and Other Writings of John G. Nicolay* (journal entry of March 9, 1862), edited by Michael Burlingame (Carbondale: Southern Illinois University Press, 2000), 74; Welles, "The First Iron-Clad," 24–25.
15. Welles, "The First Iron-Clad," 25.
16. Ibid.; Stanton to the governors of New York, Massachusetts, and Maine, March 9, 1862, ORN, 7:80.
17. The description of Dahlgren is from a clipping in the Dahlgren Papers, LC, box 4; Dahlgren to AL, March 9, 1862 (3:00 P.M.), Dahlgren Papers, LC, box 5; Browning Diary (March 9, 1862), 1:533; Dahlgren Diary (March 9, 1862), 358.
18. Van Vliet to Dahlgren, March 9, 1862, Dahlgren Papers, LC, box 5; Charles Wilkes, *Autobiography of Rear Admiral Charles Wilkes, U.S. Navy, 1798–1877* (Washington, DC: Naval History Division, 1978), 766–67.
19. Wilkes, *Autobiography*, 767; Welles, "The First Iron-Clad," 26.
20. Dahlgren to AL, March 9, 1862 (9:00 P.M.), ORN, 7:78; Sanford to Dahlgren, March 9, 1862, Dahlgren Papers, LC, box 5.
21. Fox to Welles, March 9, 1862, and Welles to Dahlgren, March 10, 1862 (1:00 A.M.), both in ORN, 7:6, 80.
22. Welles, "The First Iron-Clad," 27.
23. Ibid., 27–28.
24. OR, 7:129, 144–49; Browning Diary (March 19, 1862), 1:535.
25. Welles to Fox, March 19, 1862 (10:27 A.M.), and Fox to Welles, March 10, 1862, both in ORN, 7:83, 85.
26. Dahlgren Diary (March 10, 1862), 360; John L. Worden, undated memo in the John L. Worden Papers at Lincoln Memorial University. That Lincoln personally ordered that Worden be promoted to commander is in Welles to Worden, August 5, 1862, John L. Worden Papers.
27. Ericsson to AL, August 2, 1862, Lincoln Papers, LC (Series I).

28. Tucker to Stanton, April 5, 1862, OR, 5:46.
29. McClellan to Goldsborough, April 5, 1862, ORN, 7:205; Lincoln's order to McClellan to "leave Washington secure" is in CW, 5:157.
30. AL to McClellan, April 6 and April 9, 1862, both in CW, 5:182, 184–85.
31. Henry C. Baird, "Narrative of Rear Admiral Goldsborough, U.S. Navy," *U.S. Naval Institute Proceedings* 59 (July 1933), 1025; see also McClellan to Goldsborough, April 3, 1862, 7:195–96, and Goldsborough to Missroon, April 4, 1862, ORN, 7:199.
32. "Quietness of the Capital," *New York Herald*, April 27, 1862; Frederick W. Seward, *Reminiscences of a War-Time Statesman and Diplomat* (New York: G. P. Putnam's Sons, 1916), 173.
33. Seward, *Reminiscences*, 173–74; *New York Herald*, April 27, 1862.
34. Seward, *Reminiscences*, 174.
35. Chase to "My darling Nettie," May 7, 1862, in Chase Diary, 75; Egbert Viele, "A Trip with Lincoln, Chase, and Stanton," *Scribner's Monthly* 16, October 1878, 813.
36. Viele, "A Trip with Lincoln," 813.
37. Welles, "The First Iron-Clad," 29.
38. Ibid., 29–30.
39. Chase to "My darling Nettie," May 7, 1862, in Chase Diary, 75–76.
40. Viele, "A Trip with Lincoln," 818. See also Chester D. Bradley, "President Lincoln's Campaign Against the *Merrimac*," *Journal of the Illinois State Historical Society* 51 (1958), 51:59–85.
41. Chase to "My darling Nettie," May 7, 1862, in Chase Diary, 76.
42. Ibid., 77.
43. Frederick Keeler to "Dear Anna," May 7, 1862, in *Aboard the USS Monitor*, edited by Robert W. Daly (Annapolis: U.S. Naval Institute Press, 1964), 107.
44. Chase to "My darling Nettie," May 8, 1862, in Chase Diary, 78; Gillis to Goldsborough, May 8, 1862, Constable to Chase, May 9, 1862, both in ORN, 22:332–33.
45. Ibid., 79.
46. AL to Goldsborough, May 7, 1862, CW, 5:207. Stanton to McClellan, May 9, 1862, and Jeffers to Goldsborough, May 9, 1862, both in ORN, 22:338–39, 340.
47. Chase to "My darling Nettie," May 11, 1862, in Chase Diary, 82. Sixteen years later, Viele claimed that "by the light of the moon [Lincoln] landed on the beach and walked up and down a considerable distance to assure himself there could be no mistake" of the suitability of the landing site. No other contemporary source confirms this landing, however, and it is difficult to believe that Lincoln would have taken such a chance or, if he had, that it would have gone unnoticed by others.
48. Ibid., 85; McClellan to Stanton, May 7, 1862, OR, 11 (pt. 3), 146.
49. Baird, "Narrative of Rear Admiral Goldsborough," 1026–8; Stanton to McClellan, May 7, 1862 (midnight), OR, 11 (pt. 3): 147.

50. Viele, "A Trip with Lincoln," 821; the soldier witness is Harry Williams, who is quoted in Stephen W. Sears, *To the Gates of Richmond* (New York: Ticknor and Fields, 1992), 90.

51. Stanton to Watson, May 10, 1862, OR, 11 (pt. 3): 162; Chase to "My darling Nettie," May 11, 1862, in Chase Diary, 85.

52. Chase to "My darling Nettie," May 11, 1862, in Chase Diary, 85.

53. Ibid.; *Washington Star*, May 12, 1862. See also Tattnall to Mallory, May 14, 1862, ORN, 22:335–38.

54. Goldsborough to AL, May 9, 1862, ORN, 7:331; AL to Goldsborough, May 10, 1862, CW, 5:209.

Chapter 6

1. *New York Times*, May 13, 1862; Hunter's Proclamation (May 9, 1862) is included in Lincoln's response (May 19, 1862) in CW, 5:222.

2. Du Pont to Welles, April 23, 1862, ORN, 12:773; Fulton to Welles, November 13, 1861, ORN, 12:293.

3. The various reports concerning the *Planter* and Robert Smalls are in ORN, 12:820–25.

4. John B. Marchand, *Charleston Blockade: The Journals of John B. Marchand, U.S. Navy, 1861–1862* (entry of May 21, 1862), edited by Craig L. Symonds (Newport: Naval War College Press, 1976), 176–77.

5. Ibid. (entries of May 22 and May 29, 1862), 181, 192.

6. Ammen to Du Pont, December 29, 1861, and January 21, 1862, both in ORN, 12:431, 516–17.

7. Charles F. Adams Jr. to Charles F. Adams, March 11, 1862, in *A Cycle of Adams Letters*, edited by Worthington Chauncey Ford (Boston: Houghton Mifflin, 1920), 117.

8. Welles to Du Pont, September 25, 1861, ORN, 12:210.

9. DGW (January 10, 1863), 1:218.

10. Benjamin Quarles, *Lincoln and the Negro* (New York: Oxford University Press, 1962), 75. AL's note to Chase, dated February 15, 1862, is in CW, 5:132.

11. Lincoln's recall order, dated May 19, 1862, is in CW, 5:222; Chase's dissatisfaction with it is in Chase to Greeley, May 21, 1862, *The Salmon P. Chase Papers*, edited by John Niven (Kent, OH: Kent State University Press, 1996), 3:202.

12. AL to Albert Hodges, April 4, 1864, CW, 7:281; speech at Peoria, October 16, 1854, CW, 2:256. See also LaWanda Cox, *Lincoln and Black Freedom: A Study in Presidential Leadership* (Columbia: University of South Carolina Press, 1981); and Quarles, *Lincoln and the Negro*.

13. *New York Herald*, March 9, 1862.

14. Speech at Peoria, October 16, 1854, CW, 2:256; debate at Ottawa, Illinois, August 21, 1858, CW, 3:16.

15. Diary of George Templeton Strong (January 29, 1862), 3:204–5; Lincoln's State of the Union Message is in CW, 5:337.

16. Michael J. Bennett, *Union Jacks: Yankee Sailors in the Civil War* (Chapel Hill: University of North Carolina Press, 2004), 163; Drayton to Hoyt, January 18, 1862, *Naval Letters from Captain Percival Drayton, 1861–1865* (New York, 1906), 11.

17. Du Pont to Charles Du Pont, February 20, 1862, SFDPL, 1:336–37. Italics in original.

18. Mitchel to Chase, September 22, 1862, *Salmon P. Chase Papers*, 3:281.

19. Thompson to Welles, August 8, 1861, Lincoln Papers, LC, Series I.

20. Edwards to AL, August 9 and 10, 1861, both in Lincoln Papers, LC, Series I; AL to Smith, October 23, 1861, ibid. (also printed in CW, 4:561); Blair to AL, November 16, 1861, Lincoln Papers, LC, Series I.

21. The extent to which Lincoln was committed to black equality has become grist for historians. George Fredrickson has argued that Lincoln was skeptical about the possibilities of racial equality in America until the day he died and that he genuinely hoped that a colonization program could remove blacks from the country altogether. Don Fehrenbacher concluded that Lincoln's involvement with colonization was principally to create a social safety valve, partly for the freed slaves, but also to assuage the fears of northern whites. The most extreme view, that Lincoln was a representative nineteenth-century racist who wanted to ban all African Americans from the country, has been forwarded by Larone Bennett in a much-discussed book. For examples of these views see: Fredrickson, "A Man but Not a Brother," *Journal of Southern History* 41 (February 1975): 39–58; Fehrenbacher, "Only His Stepchildren," *Civil War History* 20 (December 1974): 293–310; and Bennett, *Forced into Glory: Abraham Lincoln's White Dream* (Chicago: Johnson, 2000). See also Quarles, *Lincoln and the Negro*, 93–123, and Allen Guelzo's thoughtful account: *Lincoln's Emancipation Proclamation* (New York: Simon and Schuster, 2004).

22. See AL to Greeley, March 24, 1862, CW, 5:169. Lincoln's calculation of the costs of buying up the slaves in the border states is in AL to James McDougall, March 14, 1862, CW, 5:160; his Message to Congress, March 6, 1862, is in CW, 5:144–46.

23. Stevens is quoted in Guelzo, *Lincoln's Emancipation Proclamation*, 96; *New York Times*, March 15, 1862, and *New York Herald*, March 8 and 9, 1862.

24. Guelzo, *Lincoln's Emancipation Proclamation*, 87.

25. Bates Diary (April 14, 1862), 250.

26. Schurz to AL, June 12, 1862, Lincoln Papers, LC, Series I.

27. McClellan to AL, June 25, 1862, OR, 11 (pt. 1): 51; AL to McClellan, June 28, 1862, CW, 5:289. Lincoln repeated the phrase "save the army" three more times in letters dated July 1, 2, and 4, CW, 5:298, 301, 305; AL to Goldsborough, June 28, 1862 (2:45 P.M.), ORN, 7:521; AL to Seward, June 28, 1862, CW, 5:292.

28. McClellan to Stanton, June 28, 1862, OR, 11 (pt. 1): 61; AL to McClellan, July 3, 1862, CW, 5:303.

29. McClellan to AL, July 7, 1862, OR, 11 (pt. 1): 73.

30. Henry C. Baird, "Narrative of Rear Admiral Goldsborough, U.S. Navy," *U.S. Naval Institute Proceedings* (July, 1933), 59:1025. The administration's dissatisfaction with Goldsborough is in C. R. P. Rodgers to Du Pont, July 18, 1862, SFDPL, 2:163; Welles' orders to Wilkes are in ORN, 7:548.

31. Goldsborough to Welles, July 15, 1862, and Welles to Goldsborough, July 21, 1862, both in ORN, 7:573–74; notification of the vote by Congress is in ORN, 7:612; the order relieving Goldsborough is in ORN, 7:695. Goldsborough's letter to his wife, dated August 18, 1862, is in the Goldsborough Papers, New York Public Library, New York, New York.

32. Wilkes, *Autobiography*, 877–81.

33. AL's order making Halleck general in chief is in CW, 5:312–13; Wilkes to Welles, August 5, 1862, ORN, 7:629–31.

34. Charles E. Hamlin, *The Life and Times of Hannibal Hamlin* (Cambridge, MA: Riverside Press, 1899), 429; DGW, 1:70–71.

35. Thompson's utopian vision is quoted in Usher to AL, August 2, 1862, Lincoln Papers, LC, Series I; Mitchell to AL, July 1, 1862, Lincoln Papers, LC, Series I. Italics in original.

36. A transcript of AL's remarks is in CW, 5:370–75. Versions appeared in the *New York Tribune* and *Washington Star* on August 15.

37. Davis to AL, October 14, 1862, and Robert Smith to Richard Yates, October 13, 1862, both in Lincoln Papers, LC, Series I.

38. Guelzo, *Lincoln's Emancipation Proclamation*, 123.

39. *New York Tribune*, August 20, 1862; AL to Greeley, August 22, 1862, CW, 5:388.

40. CW, 5:404.

41. Lincoln's three telegrams to McClellan are dated September 8, 10, and 12, and are in CW, 5:410, 412, 418. Thompson's letter to AL, September 11, 1862, and the "Articles of Agreement" of the same date are in Lincoln Papers, LC, Series I.

42. DGW, 1:142–45; Chase Diary, 150. Both entries dated September 22, 1862.

43. DGW (September 26 and October 1, 1862), 1:152, 158; Bates Diary (September 25, 1862), 262–64; Van Vliet to AL, October 4, 1862, Lincoln Papers, LC, Series I.

44. CW, 5:520–21.

45. John F. Witt, *Patriots and Cosmopolitans: Hidden Histories of American Law* (Cambridge, MA: Harvard University Press, 2007), 137; CW, 7:30.

46. Browning Diary (December 26, 1862, 1:604; CW, 6:13.

47. CW, 5:145.

48. CW, 5:433–36.

49. Frederick W. Seward, *Reminiscences of a War-Time Statesman and Diplomat* (New York: G. P. Putnam's Sons, 1916), 227. See also Guelzo, *Emancipation Proclamation*, 153–56.

Chapter 7

1. Porter to Fox, June 7, 1863, FoxCC, 2:117; David Dixon Porter, *Incidents and Anecdotes of the Civil War* (New York: D. Appleton, 1885), 120–21.
2. Charles O. Paullin, *Paullin's History of Naval Administration, 1775–1911* (Annapolis: U.S. Naval Institute Press, 1968), 261; Davis to Welles, August 8, 1862, ORN, 23:288–89; Porter to Fox, July 26, 1862, FoxCC, 2:125.
3. DGW (October 1 and 10, 1862), 1:157–58, 167; AL to Hooker, January 26, 1863, CW, 6:78–79.
4. Dudley Taylor Cornish and Virginia Jeans Laas, *Lincoln's Lee: The Life of Samuel Phillips Lee, United States Navy, 1812–1897* (Lawrence: University Press of Kansas, 1986).
5. Paullin, *Naval Administration*, 237–38.
6. Dahlgren Diary (August 4, 1862), 341; Robert J. Schneller Jr., *A Quest for Glory: A Biography of Rear Admiral John A. Dahlgren* (Annapolis: Naval Institute Press, 1996), 176–89.
7. Schneller, *Quest for Glory*, 231–34; Dahlgren to AL, October 1, 1862, Dahlgren Papers, box 5, LC.
8. DGW (October 1 and 2, 1862), 1:158–60.
9. Du Pont to Fox, October 8, 1862, SFDPL, 2:243.
10. DGW (October 9, 1862), 1:164.
11. The quotation is from Clement Vallandigham, quoted in David Donald, *Lincoln* (New York: Simon and Schuster, 1995), 416.
12. Porter, *Incidents and Anecdotes*, 125; DGW (October 10, 1862), 1:167; Chase Diary (September 27, 1862), 161.
13. Welles' undated memo covering the period October 1862 to May 1963 is in ORN, 23:397. Fox to Porter, October 24, 1862, all in ORN, 23:443. Lincoln's comment about Vicksburg being "the key" is in Porter, *Incidents and Anecdotes*, 95.
14. Porter to Fox, December 5, 1862, and Welles memo, December 18, 1862, both in ORN, 23:535, 638.
15. Porter to Fox, undated letter in the Lincoln Papers, Series I, LC; Porter to Fox, January 3, 1863, ORN, 23:603.
16. Welles to Stanton, and Ellet to Porter, both October 21, 1862, both in ORN, 23:429–30. See also Chester Hearn, *Ellet's Brigade: The Strangest Outfit of All* (Baton Rouge: Louisiana State University Press, 2000).
17. DGW (November 4, 1862), 1:180; Fox to Porter, November 8, 1862, and Porter to Welles, December 12, 1862, both in ORN, 23:469, 543.
18. Porter to Fox, November 12, 1862, FoxCC, 2:150; Sherman to Porter, November 8, 1862, and Porter to Sherman, November 12, 1862, both in ORN, 23:473, 479.

19. Porter to Sherman, November 24, and Porter to Welles, December 13, 1862, both in ORN, 23:500–2, 542–44.
20. Porter to Welles, December 12 and 27, 1862, both in ORN, 23:542–44, 572–74.
21. The best coverage of Lincoln's Cabinet crisis is in Doris Kearns Goodwin, *Team of Rivals: The Political Genius of Abraham Lincoln* (New York: Simon and Schuster, 2005); McClernand to AL, January 7, 1863, and AL to McClernand, January 22, 1863, both in CW, 6:70–71, 71n.
22. That the expedition to Fort Hindman was Sherman's notion is in Porter to Sherman, February 3, 1863, ORN, 24:227.
23. Porter to Welles, January 28, 1863; Grant to Halleck, January 11, 1863; and Porter to Welles, January 16, 1863, all in ORN, 24:127, 106, 154.
24. McClernand to AL, February 14, 1863, Lincoln Papers, Series I, LC; Porter to Welles, January 18, 1863, ORN, 24:180.
25. Welles to Porter, January 19, 1863, and Fox to Porter, February 6, 1863, both in ORN, 24:181, 242.
26. AL to Grant, July 13, 1863, CW, 6:326.
27. DGW (May 26, 1863), 1:314; Fox to Du Pont, June 3, 1863, FoxCC, 1:126.
28. E. Milby Burton, *The Siege of Charleston, 1861–1865* (Columbia: University of South Carolina Press, 1970). See also Stephen R. Wise, *Gate of Hell: Campaign for Charleston Harbor, 1863* (Columbia: University of South Carolina Press, 1994).
29. Fox to Du Pont, June 3, 1862, FoxCC, 1:126.
30. Kevin Weddle, *Lincoln's Tragic Admiral: The Life of Samuel Francis Du Pont* (Charlottesville: University of Virginia Press, 2005), 158.
31. Chase Diary (September 13, 1862), 138.
32. Weddle, *Lincoln's Tragic Admiral*, 166–67, 201; Du Pont to Henry Winter Davis, October 25, 1862, and Du Pont to Sophie Du Pont, October 21, 1862, both in SFDPL, 2:253, and 253n.
33. Du Pont to Sophie Du Pont, October 22, 1862, SFDPL, 2:353n; Welles to Du Pont, January 6, 1863, and Du Pont to Welles, January 24, 1863, both in ORN, 13:503, 535.
34. Du Pont to Welles, February 8 and February 9, 1863, ORN, 13:651, 655; Du Pont to Fox, March 2, 1863, ORN, 13:712; Fox to Du Pont, March 3, 1863, FoxCC, 1:188. See also Andrew A. Castiglione, "Politics of Command During the Civil War: Du Pont, the Navy Department, and the Charleston Campaign," honors thesis, U.S. Naval Academy, 1998.
35. Fox to AL, February 1863, Lincoln Papers, Series I, LC; AL to Dix, January 30, 1863, CW, 6:84; Du Pont to Sophie Du Pont, February 1, 1863, SFDPL, 2:407.
36. Fox to Du Pont, February 16, 1863, SFDPL, 2:443–44.
37. DGW (February 16, 1863), 1:236. The shaving scene is described in Virginia Fox to "Ma and Frank," February 28, 1863, Fox Papers, NYHS, box 19. Fox to Du Pont, February 16, 1863, SFDPL, 2:443–45; and Fox to Du Pont, February 20 and 26, 1863, in FoxCC, 1:181, 185.

38. DGW (February 16, 1863), 1:236–37; Dahlgren Diary (February 14, 1863), 388.

39. Elizabeth Blair Lee to S. P. Lee, January 25 [1863], in *Wartime Washington: The Civil War Letters of Elizabeth Blair Lee*, edited by Virginia Jeans Laas (Urbana: University of Illinois Press, 1991), 235; DGW (February 22, 1863), 1:239.

40. Report of Captain Drayton, March 3, 1863, Dahlgren Papers, LC, box 5. A note on the original reads: "Forwarded to the President for information requested." Lincoln returned the reports to Dahlgren on April 4. "Uncle Abe came to see you yesterday and returned the Iron Clad papers." Wise to Dahlgren, April 4, 1863, Dahlgren Papers, LC, box 5. Also DGW (March 17, 1863), 1:248; Castiglione, "Politics of Command," 16–17.

41. Du Pont to Sophie Du Pont, March 27, 1863, and Du Pont to Henry Winter Davis, April 1 and May 11, 1863, all in SFDPL, 2:250, 533, and 3:102. Also Du Pont to Welles, June 3, 1863, ORN, 14:70.

42. Du Pont to Welles, March 7, 1863, and Stimers to Welles, March 11, 1863, both in ORN, 13:728, 729.

43. DGW (March 12 and April 2, 1863), 1:247, 259; Du Pont to Sophie Du Pont, March 27, 1863, SFDPL, 2:519. Italics in original. Fox to Du Pont, April 2, 1863, SFDPL, 2:538; DGW (April 9, 1863), 1:264; Elizabeth Blair Lee to Samuel Phillips Lee, April 6, 1863, in *Wartime Washington*, 256.

44. *New York Herald*, April 3, 1863; Dahlgren Diary (February 6 and March 29, 1863), 387, 389.

45. Bates Diary (April 4, 1963), 287; DGW (April 8, 1863), 1:263; AL to Welles, April 9, 1863, ORN, 14:37.

46. DGW (April 11 and 12, 1863), 1:266–67; Du Pont to Welles, April 8, 1863, ORN, 14:3–4.

47. Elizabeth Blair Lee to Samuel Phillips Lee, April 15, 1863, in *Wartime Washington*, 258; DGW (April 12, 1863), 1:268; AL to Du Pont, April 13, 1863, and AL to Hunter and Du Pont, April 14, 1863, both in ORN, 14:132, 132–33.

48. Du Pont to Sophie Du Pont, April 13, 1863, and Du Pont to Welles, June 3, 1863, both in SFDPL, 3:21, 153; Du Pont to Welles, April 16, 1863, ORN, 14:139.

49. Fox to Porter, April 6, 1863, ORN, 24:533. Lincoln's observation about the importance of the Red River is from Porter, *Incidents and Anecdotes*, 95.

50. DGW (April 17, 1863), 1:274; Welles to Porter, April 15, 1863, ORN, 24:552.

51. Welles to Porter, May 5, 1863, ORN, 24:565; Porter to Welles, February 7, 1863, ORN, 24:320 and 322.

52. DGW (April 20 and 21, and May 27, 1863), 1:276–77, 314; Fox to Porter, July 16, 1863, G. V. Fox Papers, NYHS, box 5.

53. Dahlgren Diary (April 21, 1863), 390.

54. *Baltimore American*, April 15, 1863; the article is also printed in ORN, 14:57–59.

55. Du Pont to Welles, April 22, 1863, ORN, 14:51–56; DGW (April 30, 1863), 1:288.

56. This and the ensuing paragraphs are all from Davis to Du Pont, listed as May 2 but probably May 3, 1863, SFDPL, 3:80–83.

57. Ibid.; Henry Winter Davis to AL, May 4, 1863, Lincoln Papers, Series I, LC.

58. AL to Hooker, May 6, 1863, CW, 6:198–99.

59. Elizabeth Blair Lee, *Wartime Washington*, 61; AL to Hooker, May 7, 8, and 14, all in CW, 6:201, 202–3, 217.

Chapter 8

1. Dahlgren Diary (May 17, 1863), 391; AL to Isaac Arnold, May 26, 1863, CW, 6:230.

2. Welles' complaints are in DGW (September 16, 1862), 1:134–35; AL's "story" about taking to the woods is in DGW (February 2, 1864), 1:519–20.

3. DGW (April 2, 1863), 1:257; *New York Herald*, April 6, 1863.

4. David Donald, *Charles Sumner and the Rights of Man* (New York: Alfred A. Knopf, 1970), 109–11.

5. Welles to Seward, March 31, 1863, DGW, 1:253. See also John Niven, *Gideon Welles: Lincoln's Secretary of the Navy* (New York: Oxford University Press, 1973), 448–51.

6. DGW (April 4, 1863), 1:261.

7. Welles to Wilkes, September 8, 1862, ORN, 1:470–71; DGW (September 5, 1863), 1:110.

8. Welles to Wilkes, September 20, 1862, and Wilkes to Welles, September 29, 1862, both in ORN, 1:476, 483.

9. Stevens to Wilkes, October 1, 1862, ORN, 1:488–89.

10. Ord to Wilkes, October 1, 1863, ORN, 1:495–96.

11. Ord to Wilkes, and Wilkes to Ord, both October 1, 1862, both in ORN, 1:496, 499.

12. Wilkes to Welles, October 12, 1862, ORN, 1:503–4; Charles Wilkes, *Autobiography of Rear Admiral Charles Wilkes, U.S. Navy, 1798–1877* (Washington, DC: Naval History Division, 1978), 783.

13. Whiting to Wilkes, November 23, 1862, ORN, 1:555.

14. Wilkes to Welles, December 4, 1862, ORN, 1:571.

15. Welles to Wilkes, December 2, 1863, ORN, 1:569–70. See also Lyons to Seward, December 29, 1862, ORN, 2:13.

16. Wilkes to Welles, January 23, 1863, ORN, 2:55–56.

17. *New York Herald*, April 3, 1863; Baldwin to Welles, and Wilkes to Welles, both February 25, 1863, and both in ORN, 2:97–98.

18. Welles to Seward, April 13, 1863, DGW, 1:271; Navy Dept. Instructions, August 18, 1862, ORN, 1:417–18; John Niven, *Gideon Welles*, 455–56.

19. DGW (April 11, 1863), 1:266–67.

20. See, for example, excerpts from British and French papers in the *New York Herald*, April 15 and May 5, 1863; DGW (April 18, 1863), 1:275.

21. Welles to Seward, April 13, 1863, DGW, 1:270–71.

22. DGW (April 18, 1863), 1:275–76; Seward to Welles, April 20, 1862, ibid., 1:282–83.

23. DGW (April 21, 1863), 1:278.

24. AL to Seward and Welles, April 21, 1863, CW, 6:183–84.

25. *Peterhoff* case memorandum, probably by Welles [April 1863], in Lincoln Papers, Series I, LC; DGW (April 28 and 30, 1863), 1:287, 289.

26. DGW (May 15, 1863), 1:302–3.

27. See, for example, Coffey to Welles, May 30, 1863, marked "Private and Confidential," in Welles Papers, LC, reel 22.

28. Bates Diary (May 16, 1863), 293; DGW (April 22, 1863), 1:285.

29. DGW (April 2 and 28, 1863), 1:258, 287.

30. Lyons to Russell, July 17, 1863, quoted in Glyndon Van Deusen. *William Henry Seward* (New York: Oxford University Press, 1967), 255; AL to Welles, July 21 and July 25, 1863, CW, 6:343, 348–49 (also in ORN, 2:410–11); DGW (the entry is dated August 12, but covers the period late July to early August), 1:398. Welles' new instructions are in ORN, 10:61.

31. Welles to Seward, May 14, 1863, Welles Papers, LC, reel 22; Collins to Welles, July 5, 1863, ORN, 1:599. Welles was annoyed that Lincoln acted so precipitously and blamed it on Seward, who, in Welles' view, had panicked. Collins, he insisted, had "probable cause" to seize the *Mont Blanc* since Sand Key was an unoccupied island. The prize court agreed. See DGW, 1:416–27.

32. Welles to Wilkes, March 6, 1863, and Wilkes to Welles, March 23, 1863, both in ORN, 2:113, 134.

33. "Commodore Charles Wilkes' Court Martial," House Exec. Doc. 102, 38th Cong., 1st sess., p. 22; DGW (May 29, 1863), 1:316.

34. DGW (May 12 and June 4, 1863), 1:298–99, 322.

35. DGW (May 23, 1863), 1:309; Fox to Gillmore, July 16, 1863, G. V. Fox Papers, NYHS, box 5.

36. See Welles to Edgar Welles, June 7, 1863, Welles Papers, LC, reel 22.

37. Hunter to AL, May 22, 1863, ORN, 14:33–34.

38. DGW (May 25, 1863), 1:312.

39. DGW (May 29, 1863), 1:317; Dahlgren Diary (May 29 and June 2, 1863), 392, 393.

40. Dahlgren Diary (June 2, 1863), 393; Welles to Foote and Du Pont, June 6, 1863, ORN, 14:241.

41. Dahlgren Diary (June 2, 1863), 395; Welles to "My dear son" (Edgar?), June 21, 1863, Welles Papers, LC, reel 22. See Robert J. Schneller, *A Quest for Glory: A Biography of Rear Admiral John A. Dahlgren* (Annapolis: Naval Institute Press, 1996), 245.

42. DGW (June 21, 1863), 1:337–38.

43. AL's victory announcement is in CW, 6:314.
44. Meade's general order is in OR, 27:567. Lincoln's reaction is recorded in Allan T. Rice, ed., *Reminiscences of Abraham Lincoln by Distinguished Men* (New York: North American Review, 1888), 402.
45. DGW (July 7, 1863), 1:364.
46. DGW (July 14, 1863), 1:371.
47. AL to Meade, July 14, 1863, CW, 6:328.
48. AL to Grant, July 13, 1863, CW, 6:326.
49. DGW (July 13, 1863), 1:369.
50. Stephen R. Wise, *Gate of Hell: Campaign for Charleston Harbor, 1863* (Columbia: University of South Carolina Press, 1994), 33–62.
51. Dahlgren Diary (July 10, 1863), 399. Also printed in ORN, 14:326.
52. Dahlgren Diary (July 18, 1863), 403.
53. Gillmore to Dahlgren, July 20, 1863; Dahlgren to Gillmore, July 21, 1863; and Gillmore to Halleck, July 21, 1863, all in OR, 28 (pt. 2): 22–24; DGW (July 26, 1863), 1:382.
54. DGW (July 26, 1863), 1:383.
55. Halleck to Gillmore, July 28, 1863, OR, 28 (pt. 2): 29.
56. Dahlgren to Welles, August 18, 1863, ORN, 14:452–54; DGW (August 24, 1863), 1:415.
57. The telegraphic messages between Gillmore and Dahlgren, all dated August 17, 1863, are in ORN, 14:450–51, and OR, 28 (pt. 2): 44.
58. Dahlgren Diary (September 5, 1863), 413.
59. Welles to Dahlgren, October 9, 1863, ORN, 15:26–27.
60. Hay Diary (January 21, 1864), 156; Dahlgren to Wise, October 18, 1863, Henry A. Wise Papers, NYHS, box 1; Dahlgren Diary (August 28 and September 2, 1863), 410, 412.
61. Dahlgren Diary (September 27, 1863), 416.
62. Hay Diary (October 24 and 25, 1863), 107; DGW (October 24, 1863), 1:474–75.
63. Hay Diary (October 20 and 24, 1863), 103–4.
64. Dahlgren to AL, January 23, 1864, ORN, 15:252.

Chapter 9

1. AL to James C. Conkling, August 26, 1863, CW, 6:409, 410.
2. The summary of a "typical" day in Lincoln's presidency is from the *New York Herald*, October 2, 1863. His breakfast menu is from Benjamin Thomas, *Abraham Lincoln: A Biography* (New York: Alfred A. Knopf, 1952), 456. His intense interest in newspapers is from Herbert Mitgang, *Abraham Lincoln: A Press Portrait* (New York: Fordham University Press, 2000), xiii. The "story" is from Francis F. Browne, *The Every-day Life of Abraham Lincoln: A Narrative and Descriptive Biography with Pen-Pictures and Personal Recollections by Those Who Knew Him* (Chicago: Browne and Howell, 1913), 429. See also Welles' assessment of the "national" papers in

DGW (August 13, 1864), 2:103–4. I am grateful to Frank Williams for his insight concerning Lincoln's newspaper-reading habits.

3. For examples of Lincoln's notes supporting job applicants, see CW, 6:126, 128, 137, 150, and 157, and elsewhere.

4. Tom Wheeler, *Mr. Lincoln's T-Mails: The Untold Story of How Abraham Lincoln Used the Telegraph to Win the Civil War* (New York: Harper/Collins, 2006), 13.

5. Meade to Halleck, September 18, 1863, CW, 6:467–68n.

6. AL to Halleck, September 19, 1863, CW, 6:466–67.

7. DGW (September 21, 1863), 1:439–40.

8. Hay Diary (November 1, 1863), 115; T. Harry Williams, *Lincoln and His Generals* (New York: Dorset Press, 1952), 280–81.

9. Jane Renwick Wilkes to Welles, June 4, 1863, Welles Papers, LC, reel 22; Charles Wilkes, *Autobiography of Rear Admiral Charles Wilkes, U.S. Navy, 1798–1877*, edited by William Morgan et al. (Washington, DC: Naval History Division, 1978), 891–92.

10. Du Pont to Sophie Du Pont, June 5, 1863, SFDPL, 3:161.

11. DGW (May 20, 1863), 1:307.

12. Du Pont to Sophie Du Pont, June 4, 1863, SFDPL, 3:164; Hay Diary (March 30, 1864), 169.

13. Stimers' testimony was printed in the *New York Herald*, November 7, 1863; the court's verdict is Gregory to Sleeper, October 20, 1863, ORN, 14:65.

14. Du Pont to Welles, October 22, 1863, SFDPL, 3:253–57.

15. Welles' letter of "congratulations" (July 15, 1863) is in ORN, 14:343. His five-thousand-word diatribe (November 4, 1863) is in SFDPL, 3:257–71. The quotations are from pp. 258 and 268.

16. David Davis to Henry Winter Davis, undated note in Du Pont to Percival Drayton, December 9, 1863, SFDPL, 3:289; C. R. P. Rodgers to Du Pont, November 16, 1863, and Du Pont to Drayton, December 9, 1863, both in SFDPL, 3:283, 290.

17. *New York Herald*, November 18 and October 9, 1863.

18. Preble to Farragut, September 4, 1862, and October 10, 1862, ORN, 1:432, 436–38.

19. J. Thomas Scharf, *The Confederate States Navy* (New York: Rogers and Sherwood, 1887), 2:790.

20. Preble to Farragut, September 4, 1862, and Farragut to Welles, September 8, 1862, both in ORN, 1:432, 431.

21. DGW (September 20, 1862), 1:141; Welles to Preble, September 20, 1862, ORN, 1:434.

22. Farragut to Welles, October 18, 1862, Preble to AL, October 10, 1862, and AL to the U.S. Senate, February 12, 1863, all in ORN, 1:455–56, 441, and 459.

23. Emmons to Farragut, January 21, 1863, ORN, 2:28–30.

24. DGW (August 29, 1863), 1:429.

25. *New York Herald*, August 9, 1863; DGW (December 26, 1863), 1:497–97.
26. Lincoln's Annual Message, CW, 7:36–53. The quotations are from pp. 43, 45n.
27. DGW (December 1863), 1:479; Welles' "Report of the Secretary of the Navy," dated December 7, 1863, is in House Exec. Doc. No. 1, 38th Cong., 1st sess., v–vi, xxiv.
28. *New York Times*, December 18, 1863, 4.
29. DGW (December 19, 1863), 1:490; Wilkes to Welles, December 11, 1863, and Welles to Wilkes, December 15, 1863, both in ORN, 2: 267–68, 570; *New York Times*, December 18, 1863, 4.
30. Wilkes' court-martial, House Exec. Doc. 102, 38th Cong., 1st sess., 2, 9.
31. Browning Diary (April 30, May 5 and 10, and June 18, 1864), 668, 669, 673; AL to Browning, and AL to Ewing, both May 16, 1864, CW, 7:342, 343, and 343n. Smith Pyne to AL, May 5, 1864, Lincoln Papers, Series I, LC; AL to Welles, December 26, 1864, CW, 8:182; DGW (December 20, 1864), 2:203.
32. AL to McClellan, October 24, 1862, CW, 5:474.
33. AL to Curtis, June 8, 1863, CW, 6:253.
34. AL to Meade, July 27, 1863, CW, 6:350.
35. DGW (July 31, 1863), 1:387; Grant to Lorenzo Thomas, June 23, 1863, OR, 24 (pt. 1): 158–59; McClernand to AL, August 3, 1863, CW, 6:380n.
36. AL to McClernand, August 12, 1863, and McClernand to AL, August 24, 1863, both in CW, 6:383–84.
37. Welles to George Morgan, March 18, 1864, and Welles to "My dear son" (Edgar?), December 13, 1863, both in Welles Papers, LC, reel 22.
38. Sophie Du Pont to Henry Winter Davis, November 10, 1863, SFDPL, 3:281n. It is entirely possible that the officer to whom Sophie refers in this passage was Wilkes himself.
39. Chase to AL, Coffey to AL, McVeigh to AL, and *Cincinnati Gazette* to AL, all dated October 13, 1863, Lincoln Papers, Series I, LC.
40. Lincoln's "story" is in DGW (February 2, 1864), 1:519–20. He told it in reference to quite a different crisis—the role of Spain in Dominica—but it is equally pertinent here.
41. *New York Herald*, November 9 and 19 and December 18, 1863.
42. Ibid., October 1, 1863.
43. Ibid., November 28, 1863.
44. AL to Grant, November 25, 1863, CW, 7:30.
45. Thomas to AL, October 24, 1863, OR, series 3, 3:916–17; Fowler to AL, October 27, 1863, Lincoln Papers, Series I, LC; William C. Harris, *With Charity for All: Lincoln and the Reconstruction of the Union* (Lexington: University of Kentucky Press, 1997), 125–27.
46. Proclamation of Amnesty and Reconstruction, December 8, 1863, CW, 7:53–56.
47. Ibid.

48. Hay Diary (December 9, 1863), 131; AL to Alpheus Lewis, January 23, 1864, and AL to James Wadsworth, January 1864 [?], both in CW, 7:102, 145.

49. Hay Diary (January 13–March 1, 1864), 154–65, quotation from entry of March 1, p. 165; AL to Andrew Johnston, January 25, 1864, CW, 7:149–50.

50. CW, 7:43, 43n, 44.

Chapter 10

1. The quotation is from the Hay Diary (September 25, 1864), 219. For background and analysis of the Red River campaign, see the several works by Gary D. Joiner, especially *One Damn Blunder from Beginning to End: The Red River Campaign of 1864* (Wilmington, DE: Scholarly Resources, 2003), and *Through the Howling Wilderness: The 1864 Red River Campaign and Union Failure in the West* (Knoxville: University of Tennessee Press, 2006). Though older, Ludwell Johnson's *Red River Campaign: Politics and Cotton in the Civil War* (Baltimore: Johns Hopkins University Press, 1958), remains an excellent source.

2. Johnson, *Red River Campaign*, 13; Andrew to Fox, November 27, 1861, OR, 15:412.

3. AL to Stanton, July 29, 1863, OR, 26 (1): 659; AL to Banks, August 5, 1863, CW, 6:364; Seward to Banks, November 23, 1863, OR, 26 (1): 815.

4. AL to Banks, November 5, 1863, AL to Thomas Cottman, December 15, 1863, Banks to AL, December 27 and 30, 1863, and AL to Banks, January 13, 1864, all in CW, 7:1, 66, 102, 123–25. Also Hay Diary (December 23 and 24, 1863), 139–42.

5. AL to R. S. Canby, December 12, 1864, CW, 8:163–64.

6. George S. Denison to Chase, May 9, 1863, *The Salmon P. Chase Papers*, edited by John Niven (Kent, OH: Kent State University Press, 1997), 4:25.

7. Porter's General Order No. 21 (December 2, 1862) and No. 47 (April 15, 1863) are both in ORN, 26:344. Welles' directive, dated March 31, 1863, is in ORN, 8:647–49. Couthouy's letter to Frank Ramsay, February 1, 1864, is in the David Dixon Porter Papers, HEHL, box 7. Ramsey answered Couthouy's query by telling him to "seize the five bales of cotton." Subsequently, the owner of cotton protested to Porter that Couthouy had promised to "protect it" while Miller obtained a trade permit. When he got back from Natchez with his permit, he found the cotton missing and demanded that Porter return it. Porter responded that the matter was now in the hands of the prize courts. See Ramsey to Couthouy, February 3, 1864, and Miller to Porter, March 5, 1864, both in David Dixon Porter Papers, HEHL, boxes 7 and 8.

8. General Order No. 109 (October 14, 1863), ORN, 26:345–46.

9. DGW (December 28, 1863), 1:498; Porter to Yeatman, November 11, 1863, ORN, 26:349–50.

10. Johnson, *Red River Campaign*, 52 (see also pp. 64–65); Denison to Chase, August 12, 1863, *Salmon P. Chase Papers*, 4:100–1; Banks to AL, December 18, 1863, Lincoln Papers, Series I, LC.

11. Chase to Bullitt, April 14, 1863, and Chase to Stanton, June 5, 1863, both in *Salmon P. Chase Papers*, 4:12, 55; Banks to AL, December 18, 1863, Lincoln Papers, Series I, LC.

12. N&H, *Lincoln*, 8:307.

13. AL to Casey, December 14, 1863, and unsigned letter written by Casey for AL's signature, February 29, 1864, both in CW, 7:63, 214. The agreement was dated December 14, 1863, and is in CW, 7:62. Lincoln's protective young secretaries distrusted Casey and suspected that his real motive was political: "to elect Banks or Yates to the Presidency with the money they were to coin out of their cotton." N&H, *Lincoln*, 8:308n.

14. AL to Wright et al., January 7, 1864, CW, 7:114; Johnson, *Red River Campaign*, 69–71.

15. DGW (January 12 and 19, 1864), 1:510–11. Lincoln's proclamation was dated January 26, 1864, and is in CW, 7:151.

16. William Dennison to AL, March 28, 1864, and Nicolay to Dennison, April 7, 1864, both in Lincoln Papers, Series I, LC.

17. Casey to AL, December 19 and 21, 1863, both in Lincoln Papers, Series I, LC.

18. Halleck to Banks, January 4, 1864, OR, 34 (2): 15–16.

19. Banks to AL, February 25, 1864, Lincoln Papers, Series I, LC; N&H, *Lincoln*, 8:291.

20. The encounter is described with particular flair by Shelby Foote in *The Civil War: A Narrative* (New York: Random House, 1974), 3:3–5.

21. John Marszalek, *Commander of All Lincoln's Armies: A Life of General Henry W. Halleck* (Cambridge, MA: Belknap Press of Harvard University Press, 2004).

22. Ulysses S. Grant, *Personal Memoirs of U. S. Grant* (Boston: Little, Brown, 1885), 2:122.

23. Kilpatrick to Parsons, February 16, 1864, Pleasanton to Humphries, February 17, 1864, and Meade to Townsend, April 8, 1864, all in OR, 33:170–76.

24. AL to Butler, March 4, 1864, CW, 7:222; DGW (March 7, 1864), 1:536; *New York Tribune*, March 10, 1864.

25. DGW (April 8, 1864), 2:7; Fox to Porter, May 25, 1864, ORN, 26:324–25.

26. DGW (April 22, 1864), 2:16; Tom Wheeler, *Mr. Lincoln's T-Mails: The Untold Story of How Abraham Lincoln Used the Telegraph to Win the Civil War* (New York: HarperCollins, 2006), 10–11. The arrival of the *Avenger* in Cairo was reported in the *New York Tribune*, March 25, 1864.

27. Porter to Welles, March 15 and 16, 1864, ORN, 26:24–25, 29.

28. Porter to Welles, March 24, 1864, ORN, 26:35; Porter to his mother, November 13, 1863, David Dixon Porter Papers, LC, box 6.

29. David Dixon Porter, *Incidents and Anecdotes of the Civil War* (New York: D. Appleton, 1885), 229.

30. Howe to Chase, April 1, 1864, *Papers of Salmon P. Chase*, 4:361–63.

31. Greer to Porter, May 17, 1864, ORN, 26:306–7.

32. Howe to Chase, April 1, 1864, Chase Papers, 4:362; Porter, *Incidents and Anecdotes*, 229.

33. Halliday to Porter, April 14, 1864, David Dixon Porter Papers, HEHL, box 9; Porter, *Incidents and Anecdotes*, 228; Porter to Headley, October 16, 1866, Porter's Journal, Porter Papers, LC, box 22; *New York Tribune*, April 8, 1864.

34. Hay Diary (April 30, 1864), 179.

35. Bates Diary (April 25, 1864), 360; Hay Diary (April 28, 1864), 173.

36. Porter to Welles, April 14, 1864, ORN, 26:45; Porter to Headley, October 16, 1866, Porter Journal, Porter Papers, LC, box 22, 1:13.

37. Porter to Welles, April 14, 1864, ORN, 26:45, 47; Porter to Headley, October 16, 1866, Porter Journal, Porter Papers, LC, box 22, 1:20–21.

38. DGW (April 26, 1864), 2:18.

39. AL to Grant, April 30, 1864, CW, 7:324.

40. Welles to Mrs. Welles, May 8, 1864, Welles Papers, LC, reel 22; DGW (May 7, 1864), 2:25.

41. Porter to Welles, April 28, 1864 (marked "Confidential"), ORN, 26:93.

42. See Porter to Welles, April 23 and 28, 1864, ORN, 26:68–70, 92–95. Chester Hearn, *Admiral David Dixon Porter: The Civil War Years* (Annapolis: Naval Institute Press, 1996), 251. Despite this comment, Hearn offers a very favorable view of Porter's conduct of the campaign.

43. DGW (May 9, 1864), 2:26.

44. Lincoln's remarks are in CW, 7:334.

45. Porter to Welles, May 16, 1864, ORN, 26:131.

46. Ibid., 132.

47. Welles notes the receipt of Porter's report in his diary (May 23, 1864), 2:37. The quotations are from DGW (May 11, 13, and 30, 1864), 2:28, 33 39.

48. The captain was John V. Johnston of the *Forest Rose*. See Burnet to Johnston, March 22, 1864, ORN, 26:193–94; Porter to Welles, May 18, 1864, ORN, 26:308–9; Porter to Welles, June 6, 1864, ORN, 26:363.

49. DGW (May 21, 1864), 2:36–37; Porter to Headley, October 16, 1866, Porter Journal, Porter Papers, LC, box 22, 1:10.

50. Fox to Porter, May 25, 1864, and Porter to Welles, May 31, 1864, both in ORN, 26:324–25, 340–43; Hay Diary (November 16, 1864), 241.

51. Sickles to AL, May 31, 1864, ORN, 26:351–52.

52. DGW (July 5, 1864), 2:66.

53. Porter to Headley, October 16, 1866, Porter Journal, LC, box 22; Fox to Porter, May 25, 1864, ORN, 26:325.

Chapter 11

1. A list of captured blockade runners is in ORN, 10:157–58; Lee to Eames, April 2, 1864, Misc. Letter Book, S. P. Lee Papers, LC, box 4. Lee's biographers estimate that he netted between $110,000 and $150,000 during the war—a huge sum at the time and more than double what Porter earned during the Red River campaign. Dudley T. Cornish and Virginia Jeans Laas, *Lincoln's Lee: The Life of Samuel Phillips Lee, United States Navy, 1812–1897* (Lawrence: University Press of Kansas, 1986), 123.

2. Lamson to "Flora," July 18, 1864, in Roswell H. Lamson, *Lamson of the Gettysburg*, edited by J. M. McPherson and P. R. McPherson (New York: Oxford University Press, 1997), 122; Cornish and Laas, *Lincoln's Lee*, xii.

3. E. B. Lee to S. P. Lee, January 25 [1863], in Virginia Jean Laas, ed., *Wartime Washington: The Civil War Letters of Elizabeth Blair Lee* (Urbana: University of Illinois Press, 1991), 235; Dennison to F. P. Blair, May 16, 1862, Blair-Lee Family Papers, Princeton University, box 72, folder 2; AL's request for a vote of thanks is in CW, 5:214–15. Farragut to "My dearest wife," October 10, 1862, Farragut Papers, HEHL, box 2; E. B. Lee to S. P. Lee, March 7, 1863, *Wartime Washington*, 250.

4. The undated excerpt is accompanied by a note in the hand of Elizabeth Blair Lee that reads: "Extracts from P's letter for father." (Lizzie called her husband Phil, so "P" is a reference to him.) The excerpt is in the Welles Papers, LC, reel 22. It is not clear whether Phillips Lee knew his wife had used his private letter in a back-door effort to secure his promotion, but he may well have. DGW (March 1, 1864), 1:533; E. B. Lee to S. P. Lee, March 3, 1863, *Wartime Washington*, 247–48.

5. DGW (March 3, 1864), 1:535.

6. Lincoln's order opening Beaufort, Port Royal, and New Orleans to trade is in ORN, 8:21; Dix to Stanton, September 4, 1862, ORN, 8:24.

7. Welles to S. P. Lee, September 18 and October 16, 1864, both in ORN, 8:20, 45; Dix to S. P. Lee, October 18, 1864, ORN, 8:51.

8. DGW (October 10, 1862), 1:165; Welles to S. P. Lee, October 11, 1862, ORN, 8:31.

9. Lincoln's order was dated November 11, 1862, ORN, 8:66; Dix to AL, December 26, 1862, and AL's endorsement, both in ORN, 8:320.

10. E. B. Lee to S. P. Lee, January 25 [1863], *Wartime Washington*, 235; S. P. Lee to Welles, February 11, 1863, and Welles' endorsement, both in ORN, 8:521; S. P. Lee to Welles, January 24 and January 27, 1863, both in ORN, 8:475, 480.

11. Chase to Welles, February 17, 1864, *The Salmon P. Chase Papers*, edited by John Niven (Kent, Ohio: Kent State University Press, 1997), 4:296. See also John Niven, *Gideon Welles, Lincoln's Secretary of the Navy* (New York: Oxford University Press, 1973), 463–66.

12. Chase to Welles, February 17, 1864, *Chase Papers*, 4:296–97; DGW (February 18, 1864), 1:527.

13. Doris Kearns Goodwin, *Team of Rivals: The Political Genius of Abraham Lincoln* (New York: Simon and Schuster, 2005), 606–7; DGW (February 22, 1864), 1:529.

14. *Cong. Globe*, 38th Cong., 1st sess., 1829; Goodwin, *Team of Rivals*, 621–22.

15. *Goodwin, Team of Rivals*, 623; David Donald, *Lincoln* (New York: Simon and Shuster, 1995), 468–69.

16. S. P. Lee to Welles, April 11, 1864, ORN, 9:606–7. In the end, the tobacco stayed in the Richmond warehouses, where it still was when Richmond fell. See Lynn Case and Warren F. Spencer, *The United States and France: Civil War Diplomacy* (Philadelphia: University of Pennsylvania Press, 1970), 525–44.

17. DGW (June 23, 1864), 2:56; Butler's permit is dated March 19, 1864, and is in ORN, 10:13–14.

18. Melancton Smith to S. P. Lee, June 15, 1864, ORN, 10:163.

19. Lee to Welles, June 20, 1864, ORN, 10:163; DGW (June 23, 1864), 2:65–67; and Welles to Gansevoort, June 24, 1864, ORN, 10:207. The evidence here is circumstantial. Welles wrote in his diary on June 23 that he would wait until the president returned before responding to Lee. Lincoln returned to Washington the next day, and on that same day Welles sent his letter to Gansevoort. Presumably, then, Lincoln agreed to rescind permission.

20. S. P. Lee to Fox, December 14, 1862, FoxCC, 2:242.

21. Fox to S. P. Lee, February 12, 1863, FoxCC, 2:246.

22. Hay Diary (April 28 and 30, 1864), 175, 179; Grant to Butler, April 28, 1864, and Butler to S. P. Lee, May 1, 1864, both in ORN, 9:713. Butler sent Lee a copy of Grant's order.

23. Lee's instructions are dated May 4, 1864, and are in ORN, 9:725; his letter to Welles is dated May 6, 1864, and is in ORN, 10:3.

24. Grant's comment is in OR, 36 (pt. 2): 840.

25. Butler to S. P. Lee, May 13, 1864, (9:00 P.M.), ORN, 10:51; Lamson to "Kate," May 14, 1864, *Lamson of the Gettysburg*, 162; S. P. Lee to Butler, May 17, 1864, ORN, 10:65.

26. S. P. Lee to Butler, May 17, 1864, and Lee to Welles, May 21, 1864, ORN, 10:65, 76. The several telegrams from Lee to Butler are in ORN, 10:68–69.

27. S. P. Lee to Welles, May 28 and 30, and June 7, 1864, all in ORN, 10:101, 105, 129.

28. S. P. Lee Journal, May 26 and June 6, 1864, Blair-Lee Family Papers, Princeton University, box 52, folder 4; Butler to S. P. Lee, May 30, 1864, ORN, 10:106; S. P. Lee to Welles, June 7, 1864, ORN, 10:129.

29. Welles' endorsement is in ORN, 10:130. The notes between S. P. Lee and Butler about responsibility are dated June 2, 1864, in ORN, 10:131; the second set of notes, about "pecuniary liability," is dated June 3 and is in ORN, 10:132–33.

30. S. P. Lee Journal, June 15, 1864, Blair-Lee Family Papers, Princeton University, box 52, folder 4; S. P. Lee to Welles, June 15, 1864, ORN, 10:149.

31. *New York Herald*, June 23, 25, and 29, 1864.

32. *New York Herald*, June 29, 1864; S. P. Lee Journal, July 1, 1864, Blair-Lee Family Papers, Princeton University, box 52, folder 4.

33. DGW (June 30, 1864), 2:55; Horace Porter, *Campaigning with Grant* (New York: Century, 1897), 217.

34. *New York Herald*, June 25, 1864; Porter, *Campaigning with Grant*, 217, 219. It was at this meeting with Grant that the general told Lincoln, "You will never hear of me being farther from Richmond than now, till I have taken it."

35. Porter, *Campaigning with Grant*, 220; *New York Herald*, June 25, 1864.

36. S. P. Lee Journal, June 22, 1864, Blair-Lee Family Papers, Princeton University, box 52, folder 4.

37. Hay Diary (June 23, 1864), 195; DGW (June 24, 1864), 2:58; Browning Diary (June 25, 1864), 1:673; DGW (June 25 and 28, 1864), 2:58–59, 61.

38. Hay Diary (June 30, 1864), 198, 199; AL to Chase, June 30, 1864, CW, 7:419.

39. DGW (July 5 and 9, 1864), 2:65–71. The quotation is from the July 9 entry, p. 71.

40. AL to Grant, July 10, 1864 (2:00 P.M.), CW, 7:437; Hay Diary (July 11, 1864), 209.

41. DGW (July 12, 1864), 2:75; John Henry Cramer, *Lincoln Under Enemy Fire: The Complete Account of His Experiences During Early's Attack on Washington* (Baton Rouge: Louisiana State University Press, 1948), 30; Frederick C. Hicks, "Lincoln, Wright, and Holmes at Fort Stevens," *Journal of the Illinois States Historical Society*, September 1946, 323–32.

42. Welles to S. P. Lee, July 10 and 11, 1864, and S. P. Lee to Welles, July 11 and 12, 1864, all in ORN, 10:252–53, 260–61; Fox to S. P. Lee, July 12, 1864, and S. P. Lee to Welles, July 13, 1864, both in ORN, 10:261, 265. S. P. Lee Journal, July 14, 1864 (2:00 A.M.), Blair-Lee Family Papers, Princeton University, box 52, folder 4. See also Cornish and Laas, *Lincoln's Lee*, 134–35.

43. DGW (July 14, 1864), 2:77; *New York Herald*, June 12, 1864; Welles to S. P. Lee, July 14, 1864, ORN, 10:271, 272. Lee believed that Fox had written both telegrams and signed Welles' name.

44. S. P. Lee Journal, July 14, 1864 (2:00 A.M.), Blair-Lee Family Papers, Princeton University, box 52, folder 4.

45. S. P. Lee to Welles, July 14, 1864, ORN, 10:272–73; S. P. Lee Journal, July 24, 1864, Blair-Lee Family Papers, Princeton University, box 52, folder 3. See also Cornish and Laas, *Lincoln's Lee*, 134–35.

46. Chris E. Fonvielle Jr., *Last Rays of Departing Hope: The Wilmington Campaign* (Campbell, CA: Savas, 1997), 59; DGW (September 15, 1864), 2:146; Welles to S. P. Lee, July 26, 1864, ORN, 10:307; S. P. Lee Journal, July 26, 1864, Blair-Lee Family Papers, Princeton University, box 52, folder 3.

47. DGW (August 15, 1864), 2:105; Farragut to Welles, August 5, 1864, ORN, 21:405. The orders specifically detailing Farragut to the NABS did not arrive until September (ORN, 10:467), though Lee was aware of Farragut's selection for the job as early as mid-July. Lincoln's proclamation of thanks, dated September 3, 1864, is in ORN, 21:543.

48. F. P. Blair to S. P. Lee, September 27, 1864, in Cornish and Laas, *Lincoln's Lee*, 138; S. P. Lee Journal, July 28, 1864, Blair-Lee Family Papers, box 52, folder 3.

49. S. P. Lee Journal, July 28, 1864, Blair-Lee Family Papers, Princeton University, box 52, folder 3.

50. DGW (September 15, 1864), 146; Hay Diary (September 25, 1864), 219; DGW (October 1, 1864), 165. Welles' orders to Porter, dated September 22, 1864, are in ORN, 21:657; E. B. Lee to S. P. Lee, November 9, 1864, *Wartime Washington*, 439.

51. AL to M. Blair, September 23, 1864, CW, 8:18; *New York Herald*, June 30, 1864. The "arrangement" concerning Blair and Frémont is discussed in Benjamin Thomas, *Abraham Lincoln: A Biography* (New York: Knopf, 1952), 449. See also Goodwin, *Team of Rivals*, 658–59.

52. DGW (September 27, 1864), 2:161.

53. S. P. Lee Journal, August 7, 1864, Blair-Lee Family Papers, Princeton University, box 52, folder 3.

Chapter 12

1. Grant to Halleck, August 15, 1864, OR, 41 (pt. 2): 193–94; AL to Grant, August 17, 1864, CW, 7:499.

2. Weed to Seward, August 22, 1864, Lincoln Papers, Series I, LC; Lincoln's note that he would be "badly beaten" is quoted in David Donald, *Lincoln* (New York: Simon and Schuster, 1995), 529; and Nicolay to Tilton, September 6, 1864, Lincoln Papers, Series I, LC. See also Benjamin Thomas, *Abraham Lincoln: A Biography* (New York: Knopf, 1952), 441–44.

3. Greeley to AL, July 7, 1864, and Greeley to AL, July 9, 1864, both in CW, 7:435. See also David Donald, *Lincoln* (New York: Simon and Schuster, 1995), 522–23.

4. AL to Conkling, August 26, 1863, CW, 6:409; AL to Charles Robinson, August 17, 1864, CW, 7:499–501. For Lincoln's meeting with Douglass, see Douglass to Tilton, October 15, 1864, *The Life and Writings of Frederick Douglass*, edited by Philip S. Foner (New York: International Publishers, 1952), 422–24.

5. The sealed letter is in CW, 7:514.

6. DGW (September 3, 1864), 2:135–36; AL's order is in ORN, 21:543; his proclamations are in CW, 7:532–33.

7. Tilton to Nicolay, September 6, 1864, and Weed to Seward, September 10, 1864, both in Lincoln Papers, Series I, LC. See also David Long, *The*

Jewel of Liberty: Abraham Lincoln's Re-election and the End of Slavery (New York: Da Capo, 1997), 235–48.

8. Lincoln's letter is dated August 9, 1864, CW, 7:488–89. See also Glyndon Van Deusen, *William Henry Seward* (New York: Oxford University Press, 1967), 377–78.

9. Farragut to Welles, September 15, 1864, ORN, 21:644. See the extensive correspondence on this issue in ORN, 21:707–29.

10. AL to Farragut, November 6 and November 11, 1864, CW, 8:93, 103.

11. DGW (September 9, 1864), 2:139. Lincoln's proclamation is dated September 24, 1864, and is in CW, 8:21. "Mischievous machinery" is from DGW (July 5, 1864), 2:67.

12. AL's order is dated December 23, 1864, and is in CW, 8:178; AL to Peniston, January 4, 1865, CW, 8:196–97; AL to Canby, December 12, 1864, CW, 8:163. Lincoln's reference to "pecuniary greed" concerned Canby's expedition and not Peniston's, but the spirit of the comment reflects Lincoln's concern over balancing these issues. See Chapter 10.

13. Hay Diary (October 11, 1864), 226; AL to Sherman, September 19, 1864, CW, 8:11.

14. Hay Diary (October 11 and 12, 1864, 226, 230; AL to Welles, October 10, 1864, CW, 8:43; DGW (August 8 and October 11, 1864), 2:97–98, 175.

15. Hay Diary (October 10, 1864), 226–28; *New York Herald*, October 13, 1864.

16. Hay Diary (November 8, 1864), 234. Lincoln won 2,206,938 votes (55%) to McClellan's 1,803,787 votes (45%).

17. Hay Diary (November 11, 1864), 237–38.

18. Craven to Welles, November 22, 1864, ORN, 3:378.

19. AL to Seward, November 8, 1864, CW, 8:97; Collins to Welles, October 31, 1864, ORN, 3:255–56. Collins' preliminary report was sent by sea from St. Thomas to Boston, from where it was telegraphed to Washington, arriving in the early morning hours of November 8.

20. Collins to Welles, October 31, 1864, ORN, 3:254–55.

21. Winslow to De Gueydon, October 25, 1863, in J. M. Ellicott, *The Life of John Ancrim Winslow, USN* (New York: G. P. Putnam's Sons, 1902), 122. The "modern student" was one of my students at the Naval Academy: Llewellyn D. Lewis, " 'For the Public Good': A Study of International Law and Naval Operations During the American Civil War," honors thesis, U.S. Naval Academy, 1990, 23.

22. Collins to Welles, October 31, 1864, ORN, 3:254.

23. Ibid.; Collins to Porter, November 20, 1864, and Collins to Welles, December 25, 1864, both in ORN, 3:263, 267.

24. *New York Herald*, November 9, 1864; Collins to Wilkes, December 1, 1864, ORN, 3:264.

25. DGW (November 26, 1864, and December 16, 1864), 2:185–86, 196.

26. Gomes to Thomas Wilson, October 7, 1864, Rodgers to Welles, November 11, 1864, both in ORN, 3:270, 369.

27. *New York Herald*, November 15, 21, and 23, 1864.
28. Welles to Porter, November 15, 1864, ORN, 3:271; Hay Diary (November 16, 1864), 242.
29. Excerpt from trial transcript, ORN, 3:268–69.
30. Welles to Collins, September 17, 1866, ORN, 3:269.
31. Baker's report is in ORN, 3:277; Porter's orders are on 273–75; Woodward to Porter, November 28, 1864, ORN, 3:277–78.
32. The finding of the court of inquiry is in ORN, 3:280.
33. Seward to Gomes, December 26, 1864, ORN, 3:285–86.
34. Godon to Welles, September 7, 1864, and Welles to Godon, October 28, 1864, both in ORN, 3:288–89. Also Lewis, "For the Public Good."
35. William T. Sherman, *Memoirs* (New York: Da Capo, 1875, 1984), 231; Sherman to AL, December 22, 1864, CW, 8:182n; AL to Sherman, December 26, 1864, CW, 8:181; DGW (December 25, 1864), 2:208. Lincoln's "Response to a Serenade," December 6, 1864, is in CW, 8:154.
36. DGW (December 25 and 27, 1864), 2:209, 210.
37. Benson J. Lossing, "The First Attack on Fort Fisher," *Annals of the War* (Philadelphia: Philadelphia Weekly Times, 1879), 238; Grant to AL, December 28, 1864, CW, 8:187n; DGW (December 28, 1864), 213; Porter to Welles, December 26, 1864, ORN, 11:253.
38. Grant to AL, December 28, 1864, OR, 42 (pt. 3): 1087; Fox to Rodgers, December 25, 1864, ORN, 11:205.
39. Porter to Butler, December 26, 1864, Porter to Welles, December 26, 1864, both in ORN, 11:252, 254–60. The quotation is from 256. Subsequently, several army officers labeled Porter's report as "misleading." See Lossing, "The First Attack," *Annals of the War*, 239.
40. DGW (December 29, 1864), 2:214; AL to Sherman, December 26, 1864, CW, 8:181–82.
41. Chris E. Fonvielle, *Last Rays of Departing Hope: The Wilmington Campaign* (Campbell, CA: Savas, 1997), 192.
42. Porter to Welles, December 27, 29, and 31, 1864, all in ORN, 11:261, 263–64, 266. In his subsequent reminiscences, Porter described Butler as "all feathers and jingles." Porter's Journal, Porter Papers, LC, box 22.
43. DGW (December 30, 1864), 2:215; David Dixon Porter, *Incidents and Anecdotes of the Civil War* (New York: D. Appleton, 1885), 279–80.
44. Fonvielle, *Last Rays of Departing Hope*, 197.
45. See Porter to Pickering, January 15, 1865, Porter to Welles, January 21, 1865, and Pickering to Welles, January 31, 1865, all in ORN, 11:520–22.
46. AL to Porter, February 10, 1865, CW, 8:285.

Epilogue

1. See Robert Browning, *From Cape Charles to Cape Fear: The North Atlantic Blockading Squadron During the Civil War* (Tuscaloosa: University of Alabama Press, 1993), and John Coski, *Capital Navy: The Men, Ships and*

Operations of the James River Squadron (Campbell, CA: Savas Woodbury, 1996).

2. Porter to Fox, October 11, 1864, Fox Papers, NYHS; Porter to Parker, December 8, 1864, ORN, 11:155–56; Parker to Porter, January 31, 1864, ORN, 11:656.

3. Grant to Parker, January 24, 1865, ORN, 11:636; Grant to Fox, several telegrams all dated January 24, 1865, ORN, 11:635–36. Only one of these is marked with a time of day (6:00 P.M.).

4. Grant to Fox, January 24, 1865 (two telegrams), ORN, 11:635; DGW (January 24, 1865), 2:230. Fox to Grant (two telegrams), January 24, 1865, ORN, 11:637. Though both of these were signed by Fox, the orders were issued by Welles. Fox joined the group in Lincoln's office late in the discussion, and Welles assigned him to take the orders to the telegraph office. Fox did so but signed his own name to the telegrams. Afterward both Welles and Farragut expressed irritation that Fox had done so.

5. Fox to Grant, January 24, 1865, and Grant to Gunboat Commanders, January 24, 1865, both in ORN, 11:637, 635 (italics added); Lanman to Porter, January 25, 1865, ORN, 11:643.

6. Farragut to Welles, January 26, 1865, ORN, 11:646.

7. Parker to Welles, January 26, 1865, and Parker to Porter, January 31, 1865, both in ORN, 11:644–45, 656; Porter to Parker, February 14, 1865, ORN, 11:658.

8. David Donald, *Lincoln* (New York: Simon and Schuster, 1995), 559–60.

9. Lincoln's Second Inaugural Address is in CW, 8:332–33.

10. David Dixon Porter, *Incidents and Anecdotes of the Civil War* (New York: D. Appleton, 1885), 81.

11. William T. Sherman, *Memoirs of General William T. Sherman* (New York: Da Capo Press, 1875, 1984), 324–26. See also Porter's account included in Sherman's *Memoirs*, pp. 328–31.

12. Porter, *Incidents and Anecdotes*, 284.

13. Ibid., 286.

14. Grant's telegrams, plus Lincoln's reply, are in CW, 8:376–77. See also Tom Wheeler, *Mr. Lincoln's T-Mails* (New York: HarperCollins, 2006), 173.

15. Porter, *Incidents and Anecdotes*, 286–87.

16. Ibid., 285.

17. Ibid., 293.

18. Ibid., 294.

19. Ibid., 294–95.

20. Ibid., 295.

21. George B. Todd to "Dear Bro," April 15, 1865 (9:00 P.M.), Abraham Lincoln Papers, Chicago History Museum, folio 263. See also Michael W. Kaufman, *American Brutus: John Wilkes Booth and the Lincoln Conspirators* (New York: Random House, 2004), 220.

BIBLIOGRAPHY

Manuscript Sources

Abraham Lincoln Library and Museum, Springfield, Illinois
    Abraham Lincoln Papers
    Gideon Welles Papers

Chicago History Museum, Chicago, Illinois
    Abraham Lincoln Papers

Firestone Library, Princeton University, Princeton, New Jersey
    Blair-Lee Family Papers

Hagley Museum and Library, Wilmington, Delaware
    Samuel Francis Du Pont Papers

Henry E. Huntington Library, San Marino, California
    David Glasgow Farragut Papers
    David Dixon Porter Papers
    Gideon Welles Papers

Library of Congress, Washington, D.C.
    John A. Dahlgren Papers
    Louis M. Goldsborough Papers
    Samuel P. Lee Papers

Abraham Lincoln Papers
George B. McClellan Papers
David Dixon Porter Papers
Gideon Welles Papers

Lincoln Memorial University, Harrowgate, Tennessee
John Lorimer Worden Papers

National Archives of the United States, Washington, D.C. (Record Group 45)
"Confidential" Letters and Telegrams Sent, 1861–1876
Letters Received by the Secretary of the Navy from Commanding Officers of
Squadrons (Squadron Letters), 1841–1886 (microfilm)
Letters Received from the President and Executive Agencies
Personal Letter Books of U.S. Naval Officers (Entry 603)
Letters Sent by Capt. Andrew H. Foote (Foote Letter Book)
Correspondence of Rear Adm. David G. Farragut
General Orders Issued by Rear Adm. Samuel F. Du Pont
Letters Sent by Flag Officer William W. McKean
Letters Sent by Rear Adm. Charles H. Davis (Davis Letter Books)
Letters Sent by Capt. Henry A. Wise (Wise Letter Books)
Correspondence of Rear Adm. David D. Porter
a. Commanding Mississippi Squadron, 1862–64
b. Commanding the North Atlantic Blockading Squadron, 1864–65

New-York Historical Society, New York, New York
Blair Family Papers
Gustavus Vasa Fox Papers
John Ericsson Papers
Henry A. Wise Papers
Gideon Welles Papers

New York Public Library, New York, New York
Louis M. Goldsborough Papers
Naval Letters from Captain Percival Drayton, 1861–1865

Public Documents

"Commodore Charles Wilkes's Court Martial," House Executive Document 102,
38th Congress, 1st session

Congressional Globe

Letter of the Secretary of the Navy, January 14, 1862, Senate Executive Document
No. 15, 37th Congress, 2nd session
"Report on Corruption in the War Department," Reports of Committees, No. 2,
37th Congress, 2nd session, vols. 1 and 2

"Report of the Secretary of the Navy," July 5, 1861, Senate Document No. 1, 37th Congress, 1st session

"Report of the Secretary of the Navy," December 3, 1861, Senate Document No. 1, Vol. 3, 37th Congress, 2nd session

"Report of the Secretary of the Navy," December 1, 1862, House Executive Document No. 1, Vol. 3, 37th Congress, 3rd session

"Report of the Secretary of the Navy," December 5, 1863, House Executive Document No. 1, Vol. 5, 39th Congress, 1st session

"Report of the Secretary of the Navy," December 5, 1864, House Executive Document No. 1, Part 6, Vol. 6, 38th Congress, 2nd session

"Report of the Secretary of the Navy," December 4, 1865, House Executive Document No. 1, Vol. 5, 39th Congress, 1st session

Newspapers

National Intelligencer
New York Herald
New York Times
New York Tribune
Washington Constitution
Washington Star
Washington *Tribune*
London *Times*

Published Primary Sources

A Cycle of Adams Letters, 1861–1865. Edited by Worthington Chauncey Ford. Boston: Houghton Mifflin, 1920.

Adams, Charles F. "The British Proclamation of May 1861." *Massachusetts Historical Society Proceedings* 48 (October 1914–June 1915): 190–242.

Baird, Henry C. "Narrative of Rear Admiral Goldsborough, U.S. Navy." *U.S. Naval Institute Proceedings* 59 (July 1933): 1023–31.

Bates, David Homer. *Lincoln in the Telegraph Office*. New York: Century, 1907.

Bates, Edward. *The Diary of Edward Bates, 1859–1866*. Edited by Howard K. Beale. Washington, DC: Government Printing Office, 1933.

Brooks, Noah. *Lincoln Observed: Civil War Dispatches of Noah Brooks*. Edited by Michael Burlingame. Baltimore: Johns Hopkins University Press, 1998.

Browning, Orville Hickman. *The Diary of Orville Hickman Browning*. 2 vols. Edited by Theodore Calvin Pease and James G. Randall. Springfield: Illinois State Historical Library, 1925.

Chase, Salmon P. *Inside Lincoln's Cabinet: The Civil War Diaries of Salmon P. Chase*. Edited by David Donald. New York: Longmans, Green, 1954.

———. *The Salmon P. Chase Papers*. 5 vols. Edited by John Niven. Kent, OH: Kent State University Press, 1993–1998.

Clark, Charles. *The Trent and San Jacinto*. London: Butterworths, 1862.

Crawford, Samuel Wylie. *The Genesis of the Civil War: The Story of Fort Sumter, 1860–61.* New York: Charles L. Webster, 1887.

Dahlgren, John A. *Memoir of John A. Dahlgren, Rear-Admiral United States Navy, by His Widow, Madeleine Vinton Dahlgren.* New York: Charles L. Webster, 1891.

Davis, Charles Henry. *Life of Charles Henry Davis, Rear Admiral, 1807–1877.* Boston: Houghton Mifflin, 1899.

Davis, Jefferson. *The Papers of Jefferson Davis.* Edited by Lynda Lasswell Crist and Mary Seaton Dix. 8 vols. to date. Baton Rouge: Louisiana State University Press, 1992.

Douglass, Frederick. *The Life and Writings of Frederick Douglass.* Edited by Philip S. Foner. New York International Publishers, 1952.

Du Pont, Samuel Francis. *Samuel Francis Du Pont: A Selection from His Civil War Letters.* Edited by John D. Hayes. 3 vols. Ithaca, NY: Cornell University Press, 1969.

Emerson, Ralph Waldo. *Journals of Ralph Waldo Emerson.* Edited by Edward Waldo Emerson and Waldo Emerson Forbes. 11 vols. Boston: Houghton Mifflin, 1913.

Fox, Gustavus Vasa. *Confidential Correspondence of Gustavus Vasa Fox, Assistant Secretary of the Navy, 1861–1865.* Edited by Robert Means Thompson and Richard Wainwright. 2 vols. Freeport, NY: Books for Libraries, 1920, 1972.

Grant, Ulysses S. *Personal Memoirs of U.S. Grant.* 2 vols. Boston: Little, Brown, 1885.

Hay, John. *Inside Lincoln's White House: The Complete Civil War Diary of John Hay.* Edited by Michael Burlingame and John R. Turner Ettlinger. Carbondale: Southern Illinois University Press, 1997.

———. *Lincoln and the Civil War in the Diaries and Letters of John Hay.* Edited by Tyler Dennett. New York: Dodd, Mead, 1939.

———. *Lincoln's Journalist: John Hay's Anonymous Writings for the Press, 1860–1864.* Edited by Michael Burlingame. Carbondale: Southern Illinois University Press, 1998.

Keeler, William Frederick. *Aboard the USS Monitor: 1862.* Edited by Robert W. Daly. Annapolis: U.S. Naval Institute Press, 1964.

Lamon, Ward Hill. *Recollections of Abraham Lincoln.* 1895. Reprint, Lincoln: University of Nebraska Press, 1984.

Lamson, Roswell H. *Lamson of the Gettysburg: The Civil War Letters of Lieutenant Roswell H. Lamson, U.S. Navy.* Edited by James M. McPherson and Patricia R. McPherson. New York: Oxford University Press, 1997.

Lee, Elizabeth Blair. *Wartime Washington: The Civil War Letters of Elizabeth Blair Lee.* Edited by Virginia Jeans Laas. Urbana: University of Illinois Press, 1991.

Marchand, John B. *Charleston Blockade: The Journals of John B. Marchand, U.S. Navy, 1861–1862.* Edited by Craig L. Symonds. Newport: Naval War College Press, 1976. (Reprinted by University Press of the Pacific in 2005.)

Meigs, Montgomery. "General M. C. Meigs on the Conduct of the Civil War." *American Historical Review* 26 (January 1921): 285–305.

Moran, Benjamin. "Extracts from the Diary of Benjamin Moran." *Massachusetts Historical Society Proceedings* 48 (1908): 431–92.

Nicolay, John G. *With Lincoln in the White House: Letters, Memoranda, and Other Writings of John G. Nicolay.* Edited by Michael Burlingame. Carbondale: Southern Illinois University Press, 2000.

Nicolay, John G., and John Hay. *Abraham Lincoln, A History.* 10 vols. New York: Century, 1890.

Porter, David Dixon. *Incidents and Anecdotes of the Civil War.* New York: D. Appleton, 1885.

Porter, Horace. *Campaigning with Grant.* New York: Century, 1897, 1981.

Rice, Allen T., ed. *Reminiscences of Abraham Lincoln by Distinguished Men.* New York: North American Review, 1888.

Seward, Frederick W. *Reminiscences of a War-Time Statesman and Diplomat.* New York: G. P. Putnam's Sons, 1916.

[Viele, Egbert L.]. "A Trip with Lincoln, Chase, and Stanton." *Scribner's Monthly* 16 (October 1878): 813–22.

Weed, Thurlow. *The Life of Thurlow Weed.* Vol. I: *The Autobiography of Thurlow Weed.* Edited by Harriet A. Weed. Boston: Houghton-Mifflin, 1883.

Welles, Gideon. *Civil War and Reconstruction: Selected Essays by Gideon Welles.* Edited by Albert Mordell. New York: Twayne Publishers, 1959.

———. *Diary of Gideon Welles, Secretary of the Navy Under Lincoln and Johnson.* Edited by Howard K. Beale. 3 vols. New York: W. W. Norton, 1960.

———. *Lincoln and Seward.* New York: Sheldon, 1874.

Wilkes, Charles. *The Autobiography of Rear Admiral Charles Wilkes, U.S. Navy, 1798–1877.* Edited by William James Morgan, David D. Tyler, Joye L. Leonhart, and Mary F. Loughlin. Washington, DC: Naval History Division, 1978.

U.S. Congress. *War of the Rebellion. Official Records of the Union and Confederate Armies in the War of the Rebellion.* 128 vols. Washington, DC: Government Printing Office, 1894–1922.

U.S. Congress. *Official Records of the Union and Confederate Navies in the War of the Rebellion.* 30 vols. Washington DC: Government Printing Office, 1894–1922.

Books

Adams, Charles Francis. *Richard Henry Dana: A Biography.* 2 vols. Boston: Houghton Mifflin, 1891.

Bennett, Michael J. *Union Jacks: Yankee Sailors in the Civil War.* Chapel Hill: University of North Carolina Press, 2004.

Bernard, Mountague. *A Historical Account of the Neutrality of Great Britain during the American Civil War.* New York: Burt Franklin, 1870, 1971.

Bernath, Stuart L. *Squall Across the Atlantic: American Civil War Prize Cases and Diplomacy.* Berkeley: University of California Press, 1970.

Brooksher, William R. *War Along the Bayous: The 1864 Red River Campaign in Louisiana.* Washington: Brassey's, 1998.

Browning, Robert M., Jr. *From Cape Charles to Cape Fear: The North Atlantic Blockading Squadron During the Civil War.* Tuscaloosa: University of Alabama Press, 1993.

Bruce, Robert V. *Lincoln and the Tools of War.* Indianapolis: Bobbs-Merrill, 1956.

Burton, E. Milby. *The Siege of Charleston, 1861–1865.* Columbia: University of South Carolina Press, 1970.

Canny, Donald L. *Lincoln's Navy: The Ships, Men and Organization, 1861–1865.* Annapolis: Naval Institute Press, 1998.

Case, Lynn, and Warren F. Spencer. *The United States and France: Civil War Diplomacy.* Philadelphia: University of Pennsylvania Press, 1970.

Cooling, Benjamin Franklin. *Forts Henry and Donelson: The Key to the Confederate Heartland.* Knoxville: University of Tennessee Press, 1987.

Cornish, Dudley Taylor, and Virginia Jeans Laas. *Lincoln's Lee: The Life of Samuel Phillips Lee, United States Navy, 1812–1897.* Lawrence: University Press of Kansas, 1986.

Cramer, John Henry. *Lincoln Under Enemy Fire: The Complete Account of His Experiences During Early's Attack on Washington.* Baton Rouge: Louisiana State University Press, 1948.

Current, Richard Nelson. *Lincoln and the First Shot.* Philadelphia: J. B. Lippincott, 1963.

Davis, William C. *Duel Between the First Ironclads.* Baton Rouge: Louisiana State University Press, 1975.

Detzer, David. *Allegiance: Fort Sumter, Charleston, and the Beginning of the Civil War.* San Diego: Harcourt, 2001.

Donald, David. *Charles Sumner and the Coming of the Civil War.* New York: Alfred A. Knopf, 1967.

———. *Charles Sumner and the Rights of Man.* New York: Alfred A. Knopf, 1970.

———. *Lincoln.* New York: Simon and Schuster, 1995.

Duberman, Martin B. *Charles Francis Adams, 1807–1886.* Boston: Houghton Mifflin, 1960.

Dudley, William S. *Going South: U. S. Navy Officer Resignations and Dismissals on the Eve of the Civil War.* Washington, DC: Naval Historical Foundation, 1981.

Dufour, Charles. *The Night the War Was Lost.* Garden City, NY: Doubleday, 1960.

Ellicott, J. M. *The Life of John Ancrim Winslow, USN.* New York: G. P. Putnam's Sons, 1902.

Ferris, Norman B. *The* Trent *Affair: A Diplomatic Crisis.* Knoxville: University of Tennessee Press, 1977.

Fonvielle, Chris E., Jr. *Last Rays of Departing Hope: The Wilmington Campaign.* Campbell, CA: Savas, 1997.

Forsyth, Michael J. *The Red River Campaign of 1864 and the Loss by the Confederacy of the Civil War.* Jefferson, NC: McFarland, 2002.

Friend, Jack. *West Wind, Flood Tide: The Battle of Mobile Bay*. Annapolis: Naval Institute Press, 2004.

Goodwin, Doris Kearns. *Team of Rivals: The Political Genius of Abraham Lincoln*. New York: Simon and Schuster, 2005.

Guelzo, Allen C. *Lincoln's Emancipation Proclamation: The End of Slavery in America*. New York: Simon and Schuster, 2004.

Hamlin, Charles E. *The Life and Times of Hannibal Hamlin*. Cambridge, MA: Riverside Press, 1899.

Harris, Thomas L. *The Trent Affair*. Indianapolis: Bobbs-Merrill, 1896.

Harris, William C. *With Charity for All: Lincoln and the Reconstruction of the Union*. Lexington: University of Kentucky Press, 1997.

Hearn, Chester G. *Admiral David Dixon Porter: The Civil War Years*. Annapolis: Naval Institute Press, 1996.

———. *The Capture of New Orleans, 1862*. Baton Rouge: Louisiana State University Press, 1995.

———. *Ellet's Brigade: The Strangest Outfit of All*. Baton Rouge: Louisiana State University Press, 2000.

Johnson, Ludwell H. *Red River Campaign: Politics and Cotton in the Civil War*. Baltimore: Johns Hopkins University Press, 1958.

Joiner, Gary D. *One Damn Blunder from Beginning to End: The Red River Campaign of 1864*. Wilmington, DE: Scholarly Resources, 2003.

———. *Through the Howling Wilderness: The 1864 Red River Campaign and Union Failure in the West*. Knoxville: University of Tennessee Press, 2006.

Jones, Howard. *Union in Peril: The Crisis over British Intervention in the Civil War*. Chapel Hill: University of North Carolina Press, 1992.

Klein, Maury. *Days of Defiance: Sumter, Secession, and the Coming of the Civil War*. New York: Alfred A. Knopf, 1997.

Lewis, Charles Lee. *David Glasgow Farragut: Our First Admiral*. 2 vols. Annapolis: Naval Institute Press, 1943.

Litwack, Leon. *North of Slavery: The Negro in the Free States, 1790–1860*. Chicago: University of Chicago Press, 1961.

Long, David E. *The Jewel of Liberty: Abraham Lincoln's Re-election and the End of Slavery*. New York: Da Capo Press, 1997.

Mahin, Dean B. *One War at a Time: The International Dimensions of the American Civil War*. Washington, DC: Brassey's, 1999.

Marszalek, John F. *Commander of All Lincoln's Armies: A Life of General Henry W. Halleck*. Cambridge, MA: Belknap Press of Harvard University Press, 2004.

McPherson, James M. *Battle Cry of Freedom: The Civil War Era*. New York: Oxford University Press, 1988.

———. *Tried by War: Abraham Lincoln as Commander-in-Chief*. New York: Penguin, 2008.

Miers, Earl Schenck. *Lincoln Day by Day, 1809–1865*. Washington: Lincoln Sesquicentennial Commission, 1960.

Miller, William Lee. *President Lincoln: Duty of a Statesman*. New York: Knopf, 2008.

Mitgang, Herbert. *Abraham Lincoln: A Press Portrait.* New York: Fordham University Press, 2000.

Monaghan, Jay. *Diplomat in Carpet Slippers: Abraham Lincoln Deals with Foreign Affairs.* Indianapolis: Bobbs-Merrill, 1945.

Niven, John. *Gideon Welles, Lincoln's Secretary of the Navy.* New York: Oxford University Press, 1973.

Paullin, Charles O. *Paullin's History of Naval Administration, 1775–1911.* Annapolis: U.S. Naval Institute Press, 1968.

Perrett, Geoffrey. *Lincoln's War: The Untold Story of America's Greatest President as Commander in Chief.* New York: Random House, 2004.

Quarles, Benjamin. *Lincoln and the Negro.* New York: Oxford University Press, 1962.

Randall, James G. *Lincoln the President.* 4 vols. New York: Dodd, Mead, 1945–55.

———. *Constitutional Problems Under Lincoln.* New York: D. Appleton, 1926.

Schneller, Robert J., Jr. *A Quest for Glory: A Biography of Rear Admiral John A. Dahlgren.* Annapolis: Naval Institute Press, 1996.

Sears, Stephen W. *George B. McClellan: The Young Napoleon.* New York: Ticknor and Fields, 1988.

———. *To the Gates of Richmond: The Peninsula Campaign.* New York: Ticknor and Fields, 1992.

Silver, David M. *Lincoln's Supreme Court.* Urbana: University of Illinois Press, 1956.

Snell, Mark A. *From First to Last: The Life of Major General William B. Franklin.* New York: Fordham University Press, 2002.

Swanberg, W. A. *First Blood: The Story of Fort Sumter.* New York: Charles Scribner's Sons, 1957.

Symonds, Craig L. *Confederate Admiral: The Life and Wars of Franklin Buchanan.* Annapolis: Naval Institute Press, 1999.

Temple, Wayne C. *Lincoln's Connections with the Illinois & Michigan Canal: His Return from Congress in '48 and His Invention.* Springfield, IL: Illinois Bell, 1986.

Thomas, Benjamin. *Abraham Lincoln: A Biography.* New York: Alfred A. Knopf, 1952.

Tucker, Spencer C. *Andrew Foote: Civil War Admiral on Western Waters.* Annapolis: Naval Institute Press, 2000.

Valuska, David L. *The African American in the Union Navy: 1861–1865.* New York: Garland, 1993.

Weddle, Kevin. *Lincoln's Tragic Admiral: The Life of Samuel Francis Du Pont.* Charlottesville: University of Virginia Press, 2005.

Weitz, Mark A. *The Confederacy on Trial: The Piracy and Sequestration Cases of 1861.* Lawrence: University of Kansas Press, 2005.

West, Richard S., Jr. *Gideon Welles.* Indianapolis: Bobbs-Merrill, 1943.

———. *Mr. Lincoln's Navy.* Westport, CT: Greenwood Press, 1957.

Wise, Stephen R. *Gate of Hell: Campaign for Charleston Harbor, 1863.* Columbia: University of South Carolina Press, 1994.

————. *Lifeline of the Confederacy: Blockade Running During the Civil War.*
  Columbia: University of South Carolina Press, 1988.
Witt, John Fabian. *Patriots and Cosmopolitans: Hidden Histories of American Law.*
  Cambridge: Harvard University Press, 2007.

Articles

Beck, Warren A. "Lincoln and Negro Colonization in Central America."
  Abraham Lincoln Quarterly 6 (September 1950): 162–83.
"Beginning of the End: A Greeting for the New Year." *Atlantic Monthly*, January
  1864, 112–22.
Bradley, Chester D. "President Lincoln's Campaign Against the *Merrimac*."
  Journal of the Illinois State Historical Society 51 (1958): 59–85.
Canfield, Eugene. "A Postscript on Mortar Boats." *Civil War Times Illustrated* 6
  (October 1967):29–36.
Castiglione, Andrew A. "Politics of Command During the Civil War: Du Pont,
  the Navy Department, and the Charleston Campaign." Honors thesis, U.S.
  Naval Academy, 1998.
Edwards, Owen. "Inventive Abe." *Smithsonian* 37 (October 2006): 32.
Fehrenbacher, Don E. "Lincoln's Wartime Leadership: The First Hundred
  Days." *Journal of the Abraham Lincoln Association* 9 (1987): 1–19.
————. "Only His Stepchildren." *Civil War History* 20 (December 1974):
  293–310.
Fredrickson, George. "A Man but Not a Brother: Abraham Lincoln and Racial
  Equality." *Journal of Southern History* 41 (February 1975): 39–58.
Harris, William C. "The Hampton Roads Peace Conference: A Final Test of
  Lincoln's Presidential Leadership." *Journal of the Abraham Lincoln Association*
  21 (Winter 2000). 30 62.
Henig, Gerald. "Admiral Samuel F. Du Pont, the Navy Department, and the
  Attack on Charleston, April, 1863." *U.S. Naval War College Review*, February
  1979, 68–77.
Hoogenboom, Ari. "Gustavus Vasa Fox and the Relief of Fort Sumter." *Civil
  War History* 9 (December 1963): 383–98.
Johnson, Ludwell H., III. "Abraham Lincoln and the Development of
  Presidential War-Making Powers: Prize Cases (1863) Revisited." *Civil War
  History* 35 (1989): 208–24.
Lewis, Llewellyn D. " 'For the Public Good': A Study of International Law and
  Naval Operations During the American Civil War." Honors thesis, U.S.
  Naval Academy, 1990.
Paludan, Phillip Shaw. "Lincoln and Colonization: Policy or Propaganda?"
  Journal of the Abraham Lincoln Association 25 (Winter 2004): 22–38.
Paullin, Charles O. "President Lincoln and the Navy." *American Historical
  Review* 14 (January 1909): 284–303.
Roberts, A. Sellew. "The Federal Government and Confederate Cotton."
  American Historical Review 32 (1926–27): 262–75.

Scheips, Paul J. "Lincoln and the Chiriqui Colonization Project." *Journal of Negro History* 37 (October 1952): 418–53.

Stampp, Kenneth M. "Lincoln and the Strategy of Defense in the Crisis of 1861." *Journal of Southern History* 11 (August 1945): 297–323.

Still, William N. "A Naval Sieve: The Union Blockade in the Civil War." *U.S. Naval War College Review* 36 (May–June 1983): 38–45.

Vorenberg, Michael. "Abraham Lincoln and the Politics of Black Colonization." *Journal of the Abraham Lincoln Association* 14 (Summer 1993): 22–45.

West, Richard. "Lincoln's Hand in Naval Matters." *Civil War History*, June 1958, 175–83.

INDEX